Foundations of Primary Teaching

Fourth edition

Denis Hayes

Routledge
Taylor & Francis Group

LONDON AND NEW YORK

First edition published 1996 by David Fulton Publishers
Second edition published 1999
Third edition published 2004
Reprinted 2005, 2006

This edition published 2008
by Routledge
2 Park Square, Milton Park, Abingdon, Oxon OX14 4RN

Simultaneously published in the USA and Canada
by Routledge
270 Madison Ave, New York, NY 10016

Routledge is an imprint of the Taylor & Francis Group, an informa business

© 2008 Denis Hayes

Typeset in Bembo by
HWA Text and Data Management, Tunbridge Wells
Printed and bound in Great Britain by
MPG Books Ltd, Bodmin

British Library Cataloguing in Publication Data
A catalogue record for this book is available from the British Library

Library of Congress Cataloging-in-Publication Data
Hayes, Denis, 1949–
Foundations of primary education / Denis Hayes. – 4th ed. p. cm.
Includes bibliographical references and index.
1.   Elementary school teaching–Great Britain. 2. First year
teachers–Great Britain. 3. Classroom management–Great Britain. I. Title.
LB1555.H43 2008
372.1102–dc22   2007044181

ISBN10: 0–415–45232–5 (pbk)

ISBN13: 978–0–415–45232–8 (pbk)

Contents

Preface

The content of a book about education and classroom life depends on many sources, including the author's thoughts and ideas, the effect of countless experiences and the combined wisdom and influence of colleagues, past and present. The content of *Foundations of Primary Teaching* is no exception. While the responsibility for what is contained in the book is entirely my own, I want to acknowledge the help and assistance of teachers, students and tutors associated with the Faculty of Education (formerly known as Rolle), University of Plymouth, whose insights and practical advice have been of immense value. I have tried very hard to give credit to all the direct sources of information that I have used and quoted. If there are instances where this has not been explicit, I will do my best to ensure that it is remedied in any future edition. In particular, I want to thank my colleagues Jeff Lewis for writing about Inclusion issues, Peter Noon for contributing part of the section on ICT and Clare Dowdell and Peggy Woods for their assistance in revising the sections on literacy and mathematics, respectively. The expert contributions of all these experts in their field have been a major factor in enhancing the quality of the fourth edition of the book.

It is my earnest hope that *Foundations* will prove to be of some assistance to everyone who reads it. In this way, I shall feel that I am repaying in part something of the many benefits that I have accrued from the knowledge and guidance of others throughout my professional life.

I dedicate this edition to all aspiring teachers who, like me, have a passionate desire to help our children learn, grow and prosper.

Introduction

Schools are about people

People matter. They matter because regardless of the quality of the education system, the level of training, the height of test achievements and the accolades that follow academic success, prosperity in its richest sense ultimately depends upon the way that people relate, respond and use the knowledge they possess. People matter because education is not principally about helping governments to meet targets or fulfil their political aspirations or even about guaranteeing a job and an income or to satisfy parents and other stakeholders. These goals are worthy ones but they pale in comparison with the main aim of education, which is to create a civilised, moral and contented society, at ease with itself. Most teachers are in the job because they want to make the world a better place. Such sentiments may sit uneasily within the materialistic, statistics-driven and competitive emphasis that has dominated education thinking for many years, but they need to be reactivated if children are to fulfil their potential as grown-up people in the making.

Foundations of Primary Teaching is based on a belief that the role of the teacher is complex and complicated and that the job of teaching cannot be compressed into a set of standards or statements, however carefully presented or convincingly portrayed. Rather, issues associated with confidence, self-assurance, sensitivity and empathy are of fundamental significance if children are to receive a comprehensive education that equips them for life. The book deals with many practical and pragmatic elements with which every teacher needs to be familiar. However, it also seeks to promote a fuller understanding and appreciation of the ways in which concerns for the people involved, the strategies for planning and implementing a curriculum and the teaching approaches employed are mutually dependent. *Foundations* is posited on a belief that a successful education consists of considerably more than a set of grades and exam passes, however laudable these outcomes may be. Care, compassion, understanding, informed tolerance and a deep appreciation of the beauty that surrounds us are just as much part of the educative process as the formal curriculum. The barren philosophy of 'anything goes' and 'me first' has been exposed as a dangerous illusion. Sensitivity, creativity and liberation to fulfil our potential and help others to fulfil their own are back on the agenda as the hallmark of a truly educated person.

The content of this book will not surprise anyone associated with primary schools. Part One considers the role and significance of the many different persons associated with school: children, teachers, parents, support staff. Part Two examines the strategies necessary for successful teaching and learning: learning styles, teaching skills, classroom management, assessment, recording and reporting, behaviour management and inclusion issues. Part Three discusses the induction year and career development. The main themes for each chapter are summarised in an introduction and there are a number of 'Activate your thinking!' and 'Good practice' boxes to stimulate further consideration of key issues and their implementation. To assist with the task of monitoring progress through the Standards for qualified teacher status (QTS), the relevant standards are listed at the end of each chapter, together with a case study and suggestions for further reading. Details of specific curriculum subjects do not form a major part of *Foundations*. All names used are fictitious and some details in the quoted extracts have been altered to protect identity.

The book has been written in the belief that teaching and learning is only possible in a school climate where everyone's rights are respected, responsibility for oneself and others is encouraged, and the promotion of positive images of self-worth, potential and belonging are central to the process. Although it is important to develop systems and plans for the curriculum, present them in the classroom, monitor and assess them and use the results to improve achievement, the real world of teaching and learning is far messier, less linear and more unpredictable than a simple action plan implies. Structure in teaching and learning is preferable to chaos, of course, but account must also be taken of the school context, the personalities of those involved and the need for emotional safeguards, especially for vulnerable children and busy teachers (whose welfare is also important). No amount of policy, strategy or cleverly designed managerial system will be effective if emotional wellbeing is neglected. Frightened, insecure or disillusioned people, whether adults or children, have little hope of achieving their potential, fulfilling their goals or responding to the opportunities presented to them. Whether pupil, teacher, teaching assistant (TA), parent or head teacher, everyone needs encouragement, affirmation and the belief that they are valued. Learning resides as much in the heart as it does in the head. It is not uniform in character, but like the waves of the sea creeping up a beach, ebbs and flows in unexpected ways with times of calm and moments of unexpected and thrilling progress. And you are now a contributor to this exciting world.

Terminology used in the book

Trainee teacher: someone following a recognised route into teaching. In a one-year PCGE course in the UK, students spend 18 weeks in the classroom. In a four-year BEd course, they spend 32 weeks.

Newly qualified teacher (NQT): someone in the first year of qualified teaching.

Inexperienced teacher: someone with limited classroom experience.

Supervising teacher: an experienced teacher in whose classroom trainee teachers are based for their school placement.

Host teacher: a teacher who works in the placement school.

Tutor: someone with responsibility for guiding and evaluating the progress of trainees.

School-based mentor: the teacher with responsibility for a trainee teacher's school experience, including regular assessment of his or her teaching ability.

Teaching assistant (TA): a paid employee who supports the work of teachers.

Higher level teaching assistant (HLTA): they work alongside the teacher, providing support for teaching and learning activities. Some HLTAs work across the curriculum; others have a specialist role for a specific subject or help to plan lessons and develop support materials.

Advanced skills teacher: the role of Advanced Skills Teacher (AST) was devised to reward excellent teachers who wanted to remain in the classroom and spend the equivalent of one day a week supporting other teachers in developing their skills and experience by sharing best practice ideas and teaching approaches

What trainee teachers say about teaching

Trainee teachers come from different backgrounds and are motivated in different ways, but they all have a single ambition: to teach. The following quotations are typical of many:

> In truth, I never had any life long ambition about teaching (except in childhood games when I almost always played the part). My mum is a teacher and I would often go into school to help her out whenever I was at home from college. I got on really well with the children. They were so lively and enthusiastic, made me laugh and were a source of joy. I've never felt the kind of exhaustion I felt after coming back from a day spent with 5–7 year olds. It was quite alarming but also felt like a reward for a job well done. Then suddenly the penny dropped that I could be a teacher too if I wanted to be. And I did!
>
> Shima

> Initially I worked in advertising and worked my way up to the position of manager by opening up a lot of business with large organisations. However, I wasn't happy in the job and had to make the very hard decision of giving up this very well paid employment to pursue a career that would be more rewarding. At this point I started to think about the possibility of teaching. After talking the matter through with many teachers, including my mum, two aunts and many friends, I decided to do three weeks as a voluntary classroom assistant in two schools with very different catchment areas. Nothing could have reinforced my decision to leave the advertising industry more! I loved my time in the schools and decided that teaching was the only job for me.
>
> Archie

Studies of the dominant motivating factors that influence people to select primary teaching as a career point to the importance of altruistic and romantic notions of the job, but with a stern realism threaded between. People often choose to train as teachers because they like children and have enjoyed working with them in a voluntary capacity. Factors such as salary, holidays, job security and status in society are also attractions, but the principal motivator is the opportunity to exercise a positive influence over children's lives through contributing positively to their education, including social and moral development. When asked why they had selected teaching as a career, responses from trainee teachers have included:

> I needed to find a career that would give me the chance to make a positive difference to children's lives.

> You can make a real difference. It is a very challenging yet rewarding career.

> What other job is more important? Without teachers you would not have any other professions.

> I am motivated by knowing I can give the children opportunity, fun and success in the classroom and outside world.

Trainee primary teachers are also interested in the self-satisfaction that they extract from the job. They want a career that offers variety and fulfilment, opens up avenues for learning and is engrossing, not tedious. In a wide-ranging survey, Spear *et al.* (2000) found that those associated with job satisfaction were (in order of priority) the chance to work with children, relating to colleagues, and developing warm personal relationships with pupils. More recent studies include Smethern (2007) and Manuel and Hughes (2006) who confirm that altruism and a desire to care for children provide the most powerful incentives for the vast majority of trainees to pursue teaching as a career. The authors conclude that many prospective teachers enter teaching 'with a sense of mission to transform the lives of young people and open opportunities for growth through learning and connecting' (Manuel and Hughes 2006: 21). A second selection of students' comments listed below provides a reminder of how powerful these motivating factors are:

> I love the sense of achievement you get from working with the children and teaching them.

> I feel I just know this is what I want to do and my decision to teach was my own from the heart.

> Children offer enthusiasm that adults cannot!

> Being a teacher is one of the most rewarding and satisfying jobs that you can do, and I can't think of anything I want to do more than to teach.

People decide to train as teachers because they are passionate about doing the job (Day 2004). The publicity description offered by the Training and Development Agency (TDA) in England gives the same powerful message:

> Teaching is like no other job. It is as inspiring, challenging and unique as each child you teach. It's a career that genuinely does make a difference.

> No two children are the same. No two days are the same. You have the privilege of opening doors to learning, to turning children on to lifelong interests.

Your development as a teacher should start from day one and continue until the end of your career (Continuous Professional Development, CPD). The more that you can engage with education issues and think through their practical implications, the more likely that over time they will have a positive impact upon your working practice. The journey will not always be a smooth one. Some trainee teachers find that it is not until they have their own class that they can begin to exercise their preferences and implement their own ideas, and even then the situation is not always straightforward, for school policies may run counter to their aspirations. Nevertheless, the principle of interacting with teaching and learning issues rather than being a passive recipient of other people's wisdom (however helpful it may be) should characterise your approach. There are four principles for effective development as you train for teaching:

- To learn from every situation, whether good or disappointing
- To clarify your beliefs about teaching and regularly review them
- To ask probing questions about the things you are told and observe happening
- To monitor your own progress with reference to advice from others and your own reflections.

When they first go into school, it is a source of amazement for many trainee teachers that experienced teachers seem to cope with classroom life so effortlessly, to respond spontaneously to the constant demands upon their time and to always make the best use of learning opportunities with the children. Resources seem to be in the right place at the right time, children do as they are told (usually) and the working atmosphere is purposeful and calm. Inexperienced teachers find it hard to believe that they will eventually become like their experienced colleagues and fear that they face many years of trial-and-error, setbacks, hardship and emotional strain before they can achieve similar success. The belief that 'there's no gain without pain' can be a daunting thought for all but the most highly committed trainee teacher.

Although the route to success requires fortitude and courage, the path to fulfilment in teaching does not have to be tortuous. Whereas mistakes are part of the learning process and confidence levels may pitch from one extreme to another, it is important to acknowledge that there are proven strategies available to shorten the time needed for you to reach a place of competence and ease in the classroom. While it is true that there is no substitute for hard-earned experience, this book is written to help trainee and newly qualified teachers to enjoy success in the job as quickly and completely as possible, and to establish habits and attitudes that will ensure optimum future progress.

Activate your thinking!

Eaude (2006) wisely comments that: 'It is tempting to think of what happens in the classroom as being mainly about what you, as a teacher, do ... But, ultimately, education is about enabling children to learn' (2006: 7).

Further reading

Arthur, J., Davison, J. and Lewis, M. (2005) *Professional Values and Practice: Achieving the Standards for QTS*, London: RoutledgeFalmer.

The authors use the eight standards from the General Teaching Council as the basis for their book.

Kendall–Seatter, S. (2005) *Primary Professional Studies*, Exeter: Learning Matters.

Quotes at length from a range of influential texts to illustrate and analyse aspects of teaching, learning and professional behaviour.

Medwell, J. (2007) *Successful Teaching Placement*, Exeter: Learning Matters.

Contains a lot of advice and practical suggestions to assist trainee teachers in preparing for, enjoying and making fullest use of their time in school.

Sedgwick, F. (2007) *So you want to be a School Teacher?* London: Sage.

A comprehensive guide for people deciding whether or not to teach and what to expect in the job.

People in School

1

The Children

Introduction

This opening chapter is about the way in which children experience school and the child–child and adult–child relationships that constitute such an essential element of their lives and learning. The chapter also addresses the realities of school for children, especially the impact of friendships, behaviour and success on their emotional and educational wellbeing. Children have a unique status; they are not merely mini-adults.

A child's view of the world

> We find delight in the beauty and happiness of children that makes the heart too big for the body.
> Ralph Waldo Emerson, nineteenth century American poet, essayist and lecturer

School is an important element of children's lives and although they may not know or understand everything that happens there, they are aware of a great deal more than some adults give them credit for. Children may not express their views openly to teachers but they do have insights about school life that affect their attitude to work as they interpret and misinterpret situations and circumstances. Teachers who make a habit of inviting children to express their views are often surprised by the perceptiveness and certainty of their comments. One teacher asked the nine- and ten-year-old children in his class to comment on the most significant event that happened during the past term. Several children referred to the class outings, another to the sports' day, but Yvette, a bright girl with a mischievous smile was happy to share her most vivid memory:

> I remember when you came into the room carrying a pile of books and looking angry. You slammed the books down on the desk, went red in the face and told us that you were ashamed of what another teacher had told you about our behaviour in the playground.

Oh dear! Hopefully there were more positive events that Yvette stored in her memory, too. Nevertheless, teachers need to be sensitive to the varied experiences of being a pupil in school and the things that they remember and relish. There are many aspects of school that children enjoy. They like to have access to friends, to learn interesting things and to feel part of a community. They like to enjoy the work they do and have some fun. They love the sense of fulfilment gained

3

from successful task completion, the admiration of friends and adult praise. Children are very happy when they have opportunity to do something practical or go outside to study. All pupils get excited when adults share ideas with them, take an interest in their life beyond the school gate and celebrate their smallest achievements. Children like to get praise from adults they respect (but not from ones they resent) and receive external reward for their efforts (such as certificates and merit cards). Children like teachers who have a sense of humour but are not cynical, and are fascinated when they watch grown-ups behaving in a slightly frivolous way. Nearly all children enjoy games, competitions and puzzles. They love to draw, paint, create things from materials and work with others to produce models and murals. Children are happiest when they feel secure and are clear about what is permissible and what is unacceptable. They respond best when they feel that they are being treated like important individuals and not as 'articles' to be taught, tested and processed through the school system.

Activate your thinking!

Children seldom misquote. In fact, they usually repeat word for word what you should not have said!

Anon

There are also many things in school that children dislike intensely. They hate to be unfairly accused of something, especially when the adult concerned has jumped to an unwarranted conclusion or refused to give them time to offer their perspective. Children also get irritated if they ask the teacher a question and are scolded for doing so or told that they should have listened in the first place. Teachers who show favouritism are particularly disliked by children, who become resentful if they perceive that one child gets away with something that another child is punished for doing. This perception is difficult to avoid when the adult takes account of a child's past history and temperament when making a decision about appropriate action, and modifies the sanction as a result. Consequently, two children may be treated rather differently for a similar misdemeanour or one child may be given a privilege ahead of the other. If you find yourself in this situation it is important to explain (but not apologise; apologies should be reserved for when you make a mistake and not for when you make a decision). Unsurprisingly, children are not impressed when they are moaned at by a teacher for working slowly when they are doing their best to be conscientious. Children have little time for teachers who are always serious and those who use an artificial or unnatural voice, especially if it comes across as patronising. While schools do not exist for the sole purpose of keeping its pupils happy, it is a long established principle that children who have a positive view of their situation are more likely to learn effectively than those who have negative ones. Thankfully, studies show that the vast majority of children are contented with their experiences of primary school.

Salo (2002) carried out research into adult's memories of their time in school and discovered that they recalled incidents that probably seemed trivial to the teacher at the time, but burned deeply into the child's consciousness. Respondents remembered these critical moments in detail, including the teacher's clothes, the expression on their faces and even the teacher's scent. In particular, moments of humiliation and guilt were powerfully engraved into the mind, as were times of delight and shared pleasures. Teachers bear a heavy responsibility to ensure that pupils are provided with a secure learning climate and, in cases where children have to be disciplined or admonished, it is done so with forbearance and in moderation. Fisher (2005) argues that a positive learning climate evolves out of six conditions: loyalty; trust; support; dynamism; expectation and communication. Pupils must be willing to attentively listen to their peers, resist the temptation to put others down, reserve the right to remain silent and respect confidentiality.

> Never fear spoiling children by making them too happy. Happiness is the atmosphere in which all good affections grow.
>
> Thomas Bray, seventeenth century Christian minister

Children need to be allowed to behave like children and not like mini-adults. The opportunity to mix with their friends, have the occasional giggle and feel good about themselves is a means of promoting a purposeful learning environment, enhancing creativity and generating a sense of enjoyment (Jones and Wyse 2004). Adults working with children need to remember that young lives are directly affected by their experiences outside the school as well as in it. Children who arrive at school in an emotionally or physically distressed condition are very unlikely to make the most of their opportunities in school and require sensitive treatment, even when they are unco-operative. Similarly, a child who has a birthday or a special event is bound to be more excitable than usual and may behave out of character. Illness and disappointment can also take its toll, as children struggle to concentrate and apply themselves to their work. Sudden dips in performance may be due to children failing to work hard enough but can also be due to extrinsic factors over which they have little control. Wise teachers are alert to such possibilities.

The UK Government has recognised the significance of these social, physical and emotional factors and introduced the *Every Child Matters* (ECM) agenda into schools, whereby every child should be offered the support that they need to be healthy, stay safe, enjoy life and achieve, make a positive contribution and (rather oddly) achieve economic well-being. Issues arising from the ECM 'agenda' are explored in Chapter 9. In practice, this policy promotes the principle that all the child-service organisations should work co-operatively to share information and work together so as to protect children and young people from harm and support their aspirations. Of course, teachers have always tried hard to support children in the way that ECM dictates; however, having a national policy is a means of monitoring implementation and strengthening its impact. Unfortunately, as with every national initiative there is a danger of formal compliance at the expense of a sincere desire to help children.

Activate your thinking!

Don't just give the impression of caring by correctly following the ECM guidelines; care deeply and genuinely, because you are passionate about children and their welfare.

In a very small number of cases, children may be aware of a conflict between home and school over learning priorities, allocation to a particular ability group, amounts of homework, lost or damaged clothing, personal possessions, and so forth. Children can feel trapped between their loyalty for a parent and a teacher, especially if negative things are attributed to the school by the parent with which a child is uneasy. As a trainee teacher in the school it is important to refer to the class teacher any adverse comments that a parent might make to you about an aspect of school life but, as far as possible, not to take it personally. Similarly, it is important to pass on to colleagues any commending comments that parents make about them. Being told that their efforts are recognised and appreciated can uplift struggling and weary teachers.

It is worth remembering that all children have moments of anxiety about things that may appear trivial to adults, who have a much fuller grasp of what is going on. Factors such as friendship patterns, anxieties about rougher children, fear of humiliation in front of the rest of the class, embarrassment about getting changed for PE, dread of the water in swimming and being labelled as slow, can all disturb and worry a child. Older children are anxious not to lose face and desperately want to be included with the majority group. This desire to be included explains in part the 'gang' culture that pertains among those of junior age. Younger children nearly always want someone to play with, though occasionally an aloof child may be insistent about being left alone. Regardless of age, all children want to be valued, respected and treated fairly. Whether you are training to be a teacher or have a class of your own, the same principles apply:

- To avoid unfairly favouring one group of children over others on the basis of background, ethnicity or home circumstances
- To help children assimilate and understand school conventions by explaining and reminding, rather than by rebuking and getting exasperated
- To understand that one measure that parents use to judge a school's success is their child's happiness
- To make allowance for lively, assertive children as much as for passive, compliant ones
- To reassure parents that the school and the teachers are working in the children's interests
- To do everything in your power to ensure that children achieve their academic potential.

Many schools work hard to include the children in decision-making and give them a 'voice' through the use of school councils and the like. A *school council* is a group of children who are elected by their peers to represent their views with a view to improving the school. The school council usually meets with a teacher present to discuss and sort out problems that affect a majority of pupils, such as organising playground games during break time, school lunches, unwanted behaviour and bullying or ideas for fundraising events. Opportunities also exist each day for adults to ask children what they think, canvass their views and demonstrate an interest in their opinions and perspectives. The thinking behind this interactive approach is that if pupils are invited to contribute to the decision making process, then certain advantages accrue, namely that they will:

- have a sense of ownership about decisions that affect them
- behave more responsibly
- offer a fresh perspective on situations
- provide suggestions about improving the school that are of genuine value.

Children do not always understand what is happening to them at school or why it is necessary to do or not do something, which to adults is perfectly plain. They will not feel pleased or agree with every decision. Their opinions will sometimes be distorted because of their own prejudices or those of adults at home. Nevertheless, part of the great privilege of being a teacher is to delve into the 'secret world of the child' and discover its hidden treasures. And you are an integral part of this world.

Activate your thinking!

Consider the following questions that a child might be asking:

- Will I make friends?
- Is the teacher strict?
- Will the work be hard?
- Will I get bored?
- Can I sit where I want to?
- Will we do fun things?
- Will we go on trips?
- Can I bring toys to school?

All sorts of children

Effective teachers are professional observers of children (Sharman *et al.* 2000). See Monica, smartly dressed, climbing out of the family car. Her quality clothes and relaxed manner bear testimony to the secure and consistent life that she enjoys. Watch as she runs into school, confident that whatever the day holds for her, there is the safety of home and family awaiting her return. She skips about, calls to her friends, laughs excitedly and, eyes shining, looks expectantly towards the classroom door. Then see Charley as she wanders alone through the school gate shortly before eight o'clock to head for the breakfast club and companionship, still bewildered by the experiences of the previous night: the strange adult behaviour, the responsibility for younger brothers and sisters, the disturbed sleep, the early morning wakening and the temporary lodgings. How will Charley view school life today? As a haven, perhaps, and a chance to escape from the grimness of life she experiences daily in the outside world. Perhaps the harsh words that greeted her from irritable adults when she was scarcely awake will fade from her mind and heart as she now experiences kindness and patience from people like you. In school Charley will find sensitive and caring adults who will provide security through clearly explained rules, interesting and relevant work and the authority to protect her from the playground bully. Charley can relax now. Both Monica and Charley enter the school. Both remove their coats, chat to class mates, walk towards the classroom door. They notice teachers, assistants, parents, pictures on walls and familiar objects. Their noses tingle at the intoxicating mixed scents of floor polish, electronic equipment, damp clothing and toilets that greet them. A random set of sounds impinges on their consciousness: chattering voices, clatter and thud of feet, doors creaking and adults talking animatedly. Their eyes light up as they enter the classroom and glimpse the familiar, reassuring sights. They sit down on a carpet or line up at a door, answer to their names, respond to a request or command. The familiar sounds of teachers' voices issue instructions; the children are sensitive to tonal patterns and intonation. They recognise when teachers are cross, sad, bored or pretending, and modify their behaviour accordingly.

The day begins and the bum-numbing effects of registration and, perhaps, class assembly are replaced by work sessions and activities. Playtimes and mealtimes provide relief from their toil. The children disappear into the frantic world of games, chasing, arguments, intensive relationships, erratic behaviours and unpredictable weather. They wonder about the paradoxes of school life: why teachers insist that they wear a coat when it isn't cold or enthuse that going outside is good for them when it is obviously miserable and damp. They see the teachers disappearing into the warmth and security of the staffroom and catch the odd snippet of conversation, wave of laughter, smell of coffee.

As each playtime ends, a few children hanker for a turn to knock on the staffroom door, return a teacup and inform the disappointed teachers that Miss Jenkins says that it's in-time (an expression used only in primary schools). The day continues. A hall-time offers chance for some fun … if teacher allows. Laces are tied, buttons fumbled and socks tugged. The end-of-afternoon story or sharing draws children and teacher together, and soon home-time heralds the end of another school day. Coats are pulled off pegs or scrambled for on the floor; odd gloves mysteriously disappear and reappear; accusations over property and other disputes reverberate down the corridors. Mothers, fathers and grandparents are there to pick up the children, ask brightly about the day, exchange a word with the teacher, flash a smiling 'thank you' and head for home. Pushchairs and a stream of young mums line up across the front of the building. Parents check lunch boxes, stare at the latest school letter and herd their little flocks towards the exit. Monica skips off happily, keen to tell mother about her successes and show off her new reading book. Charley edges out of the room, casting a hopeful glance at the teacher, before moving away to pick up her younger brothers and sisters, and usher them along the pavements to the local shop to buy them a snack for tea. The teacher gives Charley a reassuring smile and wink: '*Take care, Charley. See you tomorrow.*' Charley can hardly wait for tomorrow to come: '*Goodbye Miss.*' She sighs inwardly and slopes off into the forbidding world that awaits her. Eaude (2006) writing from a child development perspective emphasises the role of adult language and gesture in encouraging and caring for children. Thus 'In comforting a child or sharing a moment of significance, unspoken messages, such as touch or a smile, are just as important as overt ones' (2006: 94).

A few minutes later the welter of bodies has subsided. Children melt into the privacy of their own lives, although a few linger, savouring the last moments of the school atmosphere, swinging their bags around their heads in joyful abandon before racing to the entrance with a whoop and a yell. In the distance, a few others are heard excitedly anticipating the after-school football or netball practice, impatiently waiting for the teacher. A few hardy souls find the teacher who is offering them additional support for their work to 'boost' their performance in national tests and settle to work with a will that is not always apparent under normal classroom circumstances.

Children leave but the teachers and some assistants remain, engaged in a variety of planning, administrative and organisational tasks that parents and pupils know little about, but which form the engine room of the school.

Classrooms are mainly about teaching and learning, but effectiveness depends upon pupils being in the right frame of mind to participate in their education, well motivated and convinced that the effort is worthwhile. Classroom activity can be a mirage. Busy children may or may not be engaged in learning; for no amount of coercion can match a child's genuine desire to succeed. Every adult associated with school has a vital role to play in the process of motivating and encouraging children to engage enthusiastically with the curriculum and, perhaps more importantly, to help them to learn how to learn. Schools, therefore, are about people, both small and large.

Induction into school life

It is difficult for adults to remember the excitement generated by a special school event, especially if parents are invited, the tingling associated with particular smells or the first cut of a birthday cake. As we grow older, the imaginings of childhood are replaced by more pragmatic considerations and vain efforts to cram too much into too little time. Yet if teachers want to create a purposeful classroom environment, it is worth recalling some of the emotions, ideals and uncertainties which characterise childhood. Jackson (1987) argues that, to make sense of school, children draw on past experiences and their own understandings. She reminds us that these perceptions 'may not necessarily match the perceptions of the teacher, for learning in school can be a very different thing from learning at home' (1987: 86). Furthermore, Smidt (2006) reminds us that 'it was only towards the end of the 20th century that the view of children as social beings—as players in their own life stories—began to be accepted as a principle' (2006: 12). She quotes from the UN Convention on the Rights of the Child, which states that children should be encouraged to express their views freely and given opportunity to be heard, especially in decisions that relate to life decisions. Yet common experience suggests that a collegial perspective of this kind cannot be taken for granted within each house and home, or even within each classroom. The edict that 'children should be seen and not heard' still has many supporters, notably in the case of very young children, who are not considered capable of offering a considered opinion owing to their inability to distinguish between fact and fantasy.

Regardless of background, all children are gradually inducted, both by peers and teachers, into patterns of behaviour and understanding that reflect and maintain school life. It is hard to come to a school for the very first time and have to learn unfamiliar and sometimes baffling procedures, routines and rituals. After all, where else but in school do you need to stick your arm up in the air before being allowed to speak or to sit still for half an hour on an uncomfortable wooden floor listening to a grown-up reading stories? Only in a classroom do you have to ask for permission to leave the room, get dressed and undressed with lots of other children before going to clamber over large apparatus in a hall or endure the windy conditions of an exposed tarmac playground. Contrast the freedom of a park, typified by laughter, yells and screams, with the controlled atmosphere of a gym lesson and the scolding from teachers if the noise level rises. Compare the expectations of school and playgroup, babysitter or home. Little wonder that children who are new to school take time to settle, sometimes become confused, make mistakes, and find the experience unsettling.

Thankfully, over the weeks and months, the unfamiliarity fades and is normally replaced by a healthy adjustment to the vagaries of school life (Brooker 2002). Indeed, a reluctance to conform sometimes evolves into a zealous eagerness to defend the *status quo*. Older infants and younger juniors often vie with one another to see who can most vigorously uphold justice. We all recognise these comments as typical:

'You're not allowed …'

'Miss says you can't …'

'A-ah, I'm *tellin'*

All are examples of crossly disputed versions of the truth, accusations and counteraccusations. Imagine, too, the plight of the insecure younger child, unable to trust herself to place confidence in the teacher, yet shyly longing to hold an adult's hand at playtimes. See her in the classroom, holding back when there's a scramble for the best equipment or place in the queue, passively accepting her lowly position in the pecking order and storing up a growing belief that she will never be able to compete with her stronger, more assertive peers. Such children need your attention, care and influence if they are ever to fulfil their potential.

As they witness classroom and school encounters, children gain a view of what is important and what is trivial, of adult status and tolerance (Charlton *et al.* 1996; Cullingford 2002). As they become more experienced in school, their intuition and familiarity with school routines and relationships alert them to the teacher's apprehension when certain significant adults (especially if they are wearing smart suits and carrying a clipboard) enter the room. In the playground they are keenly aware of who dominates and who submits; which children are most popular and which are the target of derisive comment; who are the rough and noisy ones and who always get told off. They make a mental note that such-and-such a child can usually be blamed for misdemeanours, regardless of the truth, and occasionally prey upon the fact to divert attention from their own naughty behaviour. Some children discover how to approach a teacher in such a way as to gain sympathy or favour. Some children are expert at handling adults; others don't care enough to try. A few take delight in finding every opportunity to take advantage of grown-ups and luxuriate in the excitement of undetected disobedience.

Children rarely comment at the time but they soon know if different teachers are at odds with one another or if there is tension in the air. Some teachers wonder why the standard of children's behaviour deteriorates when life is most stressful in school. In fact, it is easily explained. Children are extremely sensitive to mood and atmosphere, so as teachers become strained and less able to cope, the edginess is picked up by the children, who respond accordingly. Each adult working in school therefore contributes to the sense of ease or restlessness, to contentment or fractiousness. There are no neutral zones.

Every school has its own culture and traditions that children gradually absorb and make their own as they become familiar with them through regular immersion. School life passes through many phases in a year (Brandling 1982; Sedgwick 1989, Smith and Lynch 2005) such as the conker season, marbles, swapping the latest card collections, paper aeroplanes, skipping, dances, songs, hairstyles, humour, plus the quirkiness of the latest electronic gadget and the 'must have' fashions. Playtimes are characterised by waves of chasing games or children clutching the coat-tails of another as they imitate horses, charioteers or railway engines. Older children imitate their favourite pop stars or football hero. Many schools employ a variety of strategies to foster positive play: boxes of dressing-up clothes and toys freely available, brightly coloured motifs to stimulate children's imagination, the promotion of traditional co-operative games and quiet corners for those who simply want to relax and chat to their friends. It has also become popular to promote a policy of ensuring that no child is left out by creating cross-age groupings of children who 'look out' for one another, and the promotion of 'never say no' behaviour whereby it is not permitted to refuse a child entry to an existing playground game if requested. See Smith (2007) for an interesting pupil perspective on playgrounds.

School life falls into well-defined categories for children and they sometimes confuse them. The energetic playtime behaviour can be brought into the classroom; the anticipation of going home can result in premature excitement; the tedium of sitting still during a long school assembly can lead to lethargy when work commences. Teachers have to adjust their teaching and temperament to allow for these vagaries without losing the smooth flow of classroom routines or neglecting basic standards and attitudes by being unnecessarily strict or grumpy. The best teachers act decisively but refuse to be rattled by spontaneous behaviour that is typical of most children the world over. Some inexperienced teachers over-react to these unexpected situations and become nervy and edgy, cross and agitated. Wiser ones learn to take circumstances in their stride, to discriminate between sabotage and exuberance, between insolence and informality, between hostility and high spirits.

A minority of children take a long time to adjust to school life and to a new teacher. Bear this in mind if you take charge of a class. Ironically, the more comfortable and relaxed they feel in the classroom, the more likely the boundaries between home and school will become blurred. The teacher who admonishes a child, 'Don't do that, you're not at home now', may be failing to recognise that such behaviour is often a sign of a positive and relaxed attitude towards school. It pays to spend time studying and interpreting the way that children respond and react. You don't have to become a child to understand one.

It should encourage you to know that the vast majority of pupils love being at school. It gives them opportunity to meet their friends, experience challenges, handle stimulating equipment, contribute to collaborative ventures and work closely with a range of different adults, all of whom have a concern for them. Little wonder that one little boy commented:

I like school because the teachers care about us and help us to learn good things.

Wally, aged six years

Enough said!

Adults helping children

We noted earlier that most children have moments of anxiety about school. Some are concerned with their work and whether they can keep up with their peers; others worry about friendships or how to please the teacher. Even children who seem bold can harbour doubts about their ability to cope. The early days of a new school year can be a particularly troubling time for some children as they try to discover exactly what new teachers expect of them.

Part of a teacher's role is to provide reassurance for children, giving a clear message to them that everything is under control and that adults can be relied upon to be fair, supportive and firm. This positive picture may not be every child's experience of adults outside school and it may be a little time before some of them settle. Occasionally, older children seem to feel that certain adults, particularly those whom they perceive as powerless (notably mealtime assistants, cleaners and even trainee teachers) can be treated casually and mischievous youngsters find great pleasure in pushing their patience to the limit. Thankfully, the majority of primary-age children are willing to trust adults, enthusiastically enjoy school and do their best. For the adults concerned, this is a privilege and a joy.

It is important for children to know that their teachers and helpers want the best for them and will do all they can to assist them in achieving it. This is different from mollycoddling children or preventing them from gaining independence and the ability to make decisions for themselves. There is often a fine line between supporting children and smothering them with kindness. To assist a child at a moment in time has the ultimate purpose of fostering independence. Smothering makes the adult feel good but does not help children to become self-sufficient. The end result of making children over-reliant on adults is known as 'learned helplessness' (LH). Children 'learn' to be helpless and may gradually begin to lose the ability to make their own decisions. Such children are probably already anxious and constantly call for adult help. If you hear a child asking for your approval and advice about every tiny nuance of the work, you can be fairly certain that LH has struck. It will take time, lots of reassurance and a gradual severing of the reliance link before the child has been delivered from the effects of this suffocating condition.

The importance of enjoying a good working relationship with children is rightly stressed as being important for learning, though this should not be confused with over-familiarity. Nias (1997) argues that 'There are dangers in placing too much emphasis upon the help and support which teachers can give to one another or to children' (1997: 18). She suggests that although adults in school gain great personal satisfaction in helping children, it is possible to care *too* much and lose sight of the children's academic needs. Nevertheless, MacGrath (2000) reminds us of that from a child's perspective it is important to feel special:

> Remembering to make everyone feel special can make a difference. It may be simply a brief word, a warm look, but it can be powerful. It is often paying attention to things which may seem trivial to an adult but are very big in the life of a child, which help children feel you are on their side, you do notice and care. One of the most important things is to listen. (2000: 74)

Where all teachers actively demonstrate their commitment to children, a framework of mutual support and encouragement is constructed that results in a happy school. Clark (1995), in considering significant factors when studying children, refers to the humbling experience of working with 'flesh-and-blood children in their need and vulnerability, in their optimism and eagerness … For these children – all children – are subjects, not objects' (1995: 21). In similar mood, Killick (2006) reminds us of the sobering fact that 'children who receive persistent criticism will soon learn it is easier not to try than to risk failure' (2006: 46). Teachers need to remember that however frustrating or objectionable a pupil may be, he or she is somebody's precious child.

Against this, every adult has observed the strategies used by a minority of children to gain attention, cause disruption or avoid responsibility. After all, it is easier to fool about and gain the admiration of your peers than to acknowledge that you don't understand, cannot remember instructions, or are confused by the teacher's comments. Some of these circumstances are discussed later in the chapter. The teacher's position will be examined more fully in Chapter 2.

McNess *et al.* (2003) provide an important reminder that teachers should be deeply committed to the affective ('felt') dimension of teaching and learning. They argue that in the complex and difficult task that teachers undertake, there are many dimensions of their role to consider and negotiate. Thus, mastery of a curriculum area, organisational and pedagogic skills needed to plan and assess children's learning, and also social and emotional factors. In the UK there has been increasing emphasis on social and emotional aspects of learning (using the acronym SEAL). The purpose of this school curriculum resource is to develop the underpinning qualities and skills that help promote positive behaviour and effective learning. The materials focus on five social and emotional aspects of learning: self-awareness, managing feelings, motivation, empathy and social skills. The SEAL resources are organised into seven themes:

- New beginnings
- Getting on and falling out
- Say no to bullying
- Going for goals
- Good to be me
- Relationships
- Changes.

McNess *et al.* (2003) suggest that the emotional factor has great significance for teachers as the affective dimension of teaching 'relied heavily upon joint negotiation and a close personal relationship between the teacher and the learner' (2003: 248). In other words, part of the skill of good teaching is not only to possess subject knowledge, or even to be able to put things across systematically and clearly, but also to empathise with the learner and build effective working relationships with each pupil. Richards (2006) is more forthright when he claims that primary teaching is:

> an extremely complex activity … an amalgam of many elements: interpersonal, intellectual, physical, spiritual, even aesthetic … It involves notions such as respect, concern, care and intellectual integrity that are impossible to define but which are deeply influential in determining the nature of life in classrooms … *It is a moral enterprise as well as a practical activity.* (2006: 13, emphasis added)

To put it simply, consideration of the affective is necessary if you are to be effective.

Activate your thinking!

- Do you believe that every child has the potential to lead a purposeful and useful life, regardless of his or her academic qualities and background?
- Do you agree that every child is capable of being exceptional in some area of his or her life?
- How much and when do you trust children to make decisions for themselves?
- Do you agree that children flourish in a *risk-free* or a *risk-supported* environment? If so, what are the implications for the way that you approach teaching?
- What attitudes to learning do you want children to possess when they eventually leave your class?
- What do you want children to say to their friends and relatives about you as a teacher?
- How is a pupil in your class likely to answer if asked by a younger child what it is like being in your class?

In the hurly-burly of daily life in school it is possible to lose sight of the fact that influencing children is not only important for their sakes but for the welfare of the community and, ultimately, the nation and world as a whole. The seven-year-old with the paint-spattered shirt and flapping shoelaces today is the potential shop assistant, business executive, builder, social worker or dentist of tomorrow. Everyone in society benefits from a good academic and social education. Your job is to assist in providing it.

Good practice

Get into the habit of commending children as much for their kindness, thoughtfulness and the effort that they make to succeed as for the quality of their academic work.

Commitment to pupils

All teachers need to demonstrate that they are committed to ensuring that pupils are given the opportunity to achieve their potential and meet the high expectations set for them. This priority must also apply to trainee teachers when they enter school on teaching placement. From start to finish you must not only want to benefit children's learning but strongly demonstrate that this is so by your words and actions. When children meet a new teacher, they want to know whether she or he is going to be fair with them, keep control and provide interesting lessons. Part of your task is to convince them that you will do all of the above, but it will take time to overcome their understandable reluctance to entrust themselves wholeheartedly to someone before being certain that the person is fully reliable. A small number of trainee teachers have lots of commitment to the job but little understanding of the way that children learn and think. Others have an intellectual grasp of teaching but lack the personality to inspire children in the classroom, while others have understanding and enthusiasm but cannot provide the orderly framework for effective learning and therefore struggle with class order. The best teachers are characterised by exhibiting all of these attributes.

It is one thing to say that you are enthusiastic about teaching the children; it is quite another to demonstrate it. Commitment is a professional as well as a moral choice and involves ensuring that your planning is thorough, that you are clear about the teaching approach you intend to adopt (and why) and, in presenting lessons, take full account of children's learning needs and preferences. Important elements of the quality assurance process include the following:

- Stating clearly to children that you want to help them do well
- Insisting of them that they have a responsibility to do well
- Explaining how they can improve their standard of work by offering them strategies for doing so
- Showing children examples of good quality work and clarifying your expectations
- Offering constructive feedback about their progress and encouraging them to self-evaluate.

In providing this support, remember that enthusing about high standards, improvements, expectations, aiming high or any other superlative will have little impact upon your pupils unless you can succeed in convincing them that these outcomes are worthwhile. Your commitment needs to be transformed into pupil *self-commitment* as they catch your enthusiasm and zest for learning. It is quite common for the same set of children to underachieve with one teacher and excel with another. There is no secret attached to this anomaly. It is simply that the first teacher has engaged with the children and transmitted a 'can do' message, whereas the second teacher has not. The best teachers tend to:

- Take a keen interest in the standard of a pupil's work and make constructive comments about its quality and, where appropriate, how it can be improved
- Use discipline strategies that avoid humiliation or repression yet maintain consistent control, producing a healthy respect in the children for the teacher as leader
- Answer children's questions helpfully, in which case the child is more likely to venture other questions and see the teacher as an ally, and not as a detached assessor.

Whereas weaker teachers tend to:

- Tolerate sloppy standards of work, with the result that the child gains the impression that 'good enough' is all that is expected or required
- Use harsh control methods without taking account of the circumstances thereby, producing fear or resentment in the children

- Ignore or fail to explain and answer questions clearly, in which case the child is likely to feel that it isn't worth making the effort and avoids asking questions in future.

Children like teachers who are fair-minded, interested in them as people, transparent in their dealings, clear about their intentions, helpful in their explanations, non-judgemental in their words and unflinching in confronting situations when it is necessary. Fisher (2005) argues that there are occasions when all learners feel vulnerable and need to be reassured. Thus:

> Time spent on building a sense of inclusion and trust is time well spent. Learning is not easy to achieve at times of emotional disturbance or social disruption. If emotional needs are ignored, the energy of the learner is deflected away from his or her capacity to accomplish learning tasks (2005: 138).

Children are not looking for 'pals' but for approachable, dependable adults who can be relied upon to give and take, provide a relevant learning environment, give credit where it is due, act swiftly to combat unacceptable behaviour and show that they value each child. Furthermore, children are drawn towards teachers who are interesting and interested people. The more that you can use your talents, gifts, experience and knowledge of the wider world in your teaching, the more likely that the children will come to view you as an adult who deserves their loyalty and best effort. It is a mistake to think that maintaining a suitable 'distance' from the class necessitates becoming detached and mechanical; in fact, nothing could be further from the truth.

Good practice

Stand physically close and face to face with children (though not intimidatingly so) when you are holding a conversation with them

Non-conformist children

Regardless of the care with which teachers handle their day-to-day encounters, there will always be some children who find it difficult to conform or (more seriously) deliberately resist all attempts to help them do so. Some trainees become dispirited when their sincere attempts to support and encourage particular pupils is rebuffed or even scorned. It is important to bear a number of considerations in mind as we examine these important issues.

Misbehaviour

Classroom misbehaviour is many teachers' secret fear. Losing control of a class is a trainee teacher's worst nightmare. The prospect of indiscipline affects both teachers and children: teachers, because they want to avoid being humiliated; children, because they do not always possess the life-skills or strategies to avoid confrontation, steer clear of trouble or helpfully influence the behaviour of their peers. This last point is particularly important, for although a teacher may speak of a class of children as being 'difficult', it is often the case that the problems are confined to a very small number whose influence in the classroom gradually becomes pervasive. While it is true that a minority of children are reluctant to obey, won't listen to adults and prefer to antagonise other children rather than conform to the rhythm of classroom life, the vast majority of children are desperate for the security that comes through effective teacher control. Be careful not to be drawn into constant criticism of a class, even if the class teacher tends to do so.

We need to be realistic here. Some children are unpredictable and restless; others are born wanderers; some seem unable (perhaps, *are* unable) to sit and concentrate for long; a very small number will delight in making life difficult for the teacher, regarding it as a personal challenge to see what they can get away with. It is also true that despite a teacher's best efforts to make lessons relevant and interesting and to create a positive working environment, there may still be children who persist in inappropriate behaviour. For this troublesome minority, there are usually sanctions that can be applied, varying from school to school, but such procedures can be time-consuming and wearisome (though sometimes necessary). In truth, most teachers have no desire to impose a strict regime upon the class if it is possible to avoid it, and would prefer to coax, persuade, encourage and set targets for achievement as a means of keeping children on the straight and narrow. Such action nearly always pays dividends with most children and increases the likelihood that the environment will be relaxed and purposeful, though the rewards are not usually immediate and you will need to persevere.

> Ah, yes, but you haven't had to teach Harrison in my class. If you had, you wouldn't be so relaxed about discipline!

This is an understandable response from teachers when issues of control are discussed from the child's perspective and it is true that even one disruptive child can make life extremely tough for a teacher and the rest of the class (see Chapter 8). However, it is worth reflecting upon the fact that the child may be used to different codes of behaviour outside school – the degree of strictness employed, use of threats, loudness of verbal exchanges, imposition of sanctions. The accumulation of these emotions, experiences and expectations from home are brought into school and a child may find it genuinely difficult to adjust to different expectations and the need for conformity in school. Such tensions are common and teachers require time and perseverance as they attempt to explain the rules to confused children or to insist upon them with unco-operative ones. This is not to argue for a weak and passive approach to children's misdirected energies but rather to look behind the action and acknowledge the factors contributing to the behaviour before deciding upon appropriate steps. Despite the temptation to become gloomy about the attitude and behaviour of a minority, it is far better to stress positive aspects of children's actions whenever possible. In particular, it is worth remembering that as well as academic achievements, social successes and responsible behaviour are an important part of a child's full education. As James and Brownsword (1994) rightly remind us, not all children know how to behave; positive reinforcement of the appropriate behaviour of pupils by brief, sincere words of praise can spur other children to adjust and improve their own behaviour. Thus:

> If these acts or types of behaviour are recorded and praised, it will increase the likelihood that they will occur again and will inform the children what is expected of them. (1994: 10)

Behaviour management and discipline are dealt with more fully in Chapter 8.

Success and failure

> I like going to school because my teacher tells us to have a go and do our best, then she helps us when we are stuck.
>
> Clarissa, aged eight years

Success in learning is the ultimate goal for everyone involved in children's education, but defining success is difficult. In its simplest terms, children are successful when they achieve measurably good results in their academic work. Most children are willing to persevere with their work for three principal reasons: (a) to achieve something worthwhile for their own satisfaction; (b) to compete with their classmates; and (c) to please the teacher. Children will be motivated to a different extent by each of these three factors. Some children are strongly self-motivated and gain enormous pleasure at achieving something by their own efforts. They show a relentless determination to do well and relish the opportunity to demonstrate their competence publicly. Some children are highly competitive and view every task as a challenge to outperform everyone else. It is not possible to prevent children from being so single-minded and it can act as a spur to achievement, but if it becomes the dominating factor it can lead to an unhealthy situation in which individuals are vying with each other to complete work quickest or gain the best mark, with scant regard for those around them. The majority of children want to please their teachers; in the majority of cases this is because they like them, in a minority of cases because they fear them. While it is obviously desirable for children to want to seek a teacher's approval, it is more important for a child to seek *self-fulfilment* than to hanker after adult approval. You have an important role in encouraging children to feel proud of their achievements, however modest, to allow a degree of competitiveness without tolerating rancour and to acknowledge their successes warmly and wholeheartedly.

At its deepest level, judging success should lie *within* each child and relate not only to how well the individual has done with respect to fellow pupils or stated criteria but the degree of satisfaction that she or he feels after completing the task. Teachers have to exercise fine judgement when offering feedback to children about their work and effort. At one level there is a need to explain to the child how the work can be improved. At another level there is a pressing need, especially with children who have experienced limited academic success in the past, to encourage, praise and celebrate achievement. McNamara (1997) rightly reminds us that if academic attainment is influenced by self-worth, then 'it is possible that a focus on raising self-esteem … could provide an increase in academic achievement' (1997: 73). Katz (1995) suggests that parents and teachers can strengthen and support a healthy sense of self-esteem in children in at least seven ways:

- Help them to build healthy relationships with peers
- Clarify your own values to them and those of others that may differ
- Offer them reassurance that your support is unconditional
- Appreciate, rather than merely praise, their interests, and avoid flattery
- Offer them opportunities to face challenges as well as to have fun
- Treat them respectfully, take their views seriously and offer meaningful feedback

■ Help them to cope with setbacks and use the knowledge they gain to advantage in the future.

Robson (2006), referring to Dweck (2000) points out that children's sense of self-competence and self-efficacy begins to develop from an early age and can have a significant impact on their attitude to learning. Dweck suggests that when faced with difficulty or potential failure, children tend to react in one of two ways. The first way is when children display a 'mastery-orientated' attitude, characterised by increased effort; the second set of children display a 'helpless pattern' of behaviour. Mastery-orientated children do not blame themselves for not doing well, whereas helpless children feel personally responsible and are reluctant to persist with the task. According to Dweck, as well as not viewing themselves as failures, mastery-orientated children engage in self-motivating strategies, self-instruction and self-monitoring. They remain confident of success and learn from their failures rather than allowing them to undermine confidence in their own abilities. By contrast, the helpless type of children denigrate their abilities, quickly lose confidence, focus on failures rather than successes, soon lose heart and even abandon successful strategies (see Robson 2006: 52–3; Dweck 2000: 7–10).

While the dichotomy between 'mastery' and 'helpless' does not tell the whole story – such as the way that some children are masterful under one set of circumstances and helpless when faced with another – it alerts us to the different approaches adopted by pupils and helps to explain why some children inexplicably abandon their work and others appear almost arrogantly confident. One important role is for you to get alongside the unhappy child and provide careful advice and feedback, without seeming to 'mollycoddle', and to ensure that the self-confident children are set high standards, so that they don't sacrifice accuracy for the sake of speed.

Most primary children are optimistic about being part of a school that caters for their individual and friendship needs, with adults that spend time and effort in helping them to learn and giving them opportunities to do exciting things. However, we have already noted that not all children feel equally comfortable in school and this sometimes leads to problems in attention span and conforming to adult expectations. If pupils have come from home backgrounds in which schooling is not considered to be a priority, it is almost certain that their brothers and sisters will exhibit similar nonconformist tendencies and the whole family may (not always fairly) be referred to by staff as 'a difficult lot'. Many of these unsettled children, though enjoying the companionship and informal opportunities which school provides, are likely to fight shy of the formal learning process and may question the need to complete tasks that appear to have little relevance for them.

To understand one specific aspect of classroom life that often has a bearing on pupil behaviour, it is important to appreciate what is involved in a child's reaction to *failure*. It doesn't take too much imagination to grasp what it is like to be constantly near the bottom of the pile: often coming last, unable to compete with more able classmates, hearing little but criticism from exasperated adults, struggling to make an impression; taken off for 'booster' classes by well-meaning assistants, and over time wondering if their academic struggles are a reflection of their inadequacy as a person. Is it any wonder that a child, after a few years of this type of experience, decides that it simply isn't worth making the effort to conform to the demands any longer? Better, surely, to put his or her efforts into other more interesting and rewarding activities like disrupting the class, spoiling someone else's work or finishing the set task in rapid time with minimum effort in order to move on to an interesting activity. Other children resort to daydreaming or adopt a detached approach to work and may be diagnosed as having an 'attention deficit'; yet put the same children with so-called attention deficit disorder in an environment of their choosing and their concentration span is apparently endless.

If adults find failure hard to cope with, it is not surprising if children need help if they are to avoid spiralling into an attitude of negativity towards schoolwork and teachers (see, for example, Pye 1987; Varma 1993; Roffey and O'Reirdan 2003; Lloyd 2004). Dalton and Fairchild (2004) offer helpful comment in respect of maintaining a positive climate:

> Some of your best teaching flows spontaneously from your deepest intuition. At its core, teaching is the artistry of creating experiences that lead people into greater awareness. It's an artistry of knowing the moods, needs and expectations of your pupils, while staying fully aware of your own. (2004: viii)

Perceptive and caring teachers, by their attention to the children's individual needs, can play a major role in preventing children from becoming despondent and losing motivation to learn. Houghton and McColgan (1995) suggest that adults can help alleviate children's anxieties by being calm when dealing with their fears, trying to avoid giving the impression that the child is somehow to blame and sensitively encouraging them to 'approach what they fear' (1995: 41). Grossman (2003) stresses the need for genuineness of character in teachers, arguing that the pupils soon detect whether they can trust a particular teacher. By ensuring that you are one such trusted teacher, you will be in a strong position to reassure all children that you have their interests at heart.

Good practice

Speak informally over a period of time to a small group of sensible children who are willing to talk naturally about their views of school and other aspects of life. As the conversations unfold, listen carefully to the comments they make that give clues to the insights they possess and the things that matter to them. Reflect upon the impact that such awareness might make on your attitude to the children in your class.

Friendships and conflicts

From the most immature nursery child to the boldest adolescent, friendships are a significant element of school life. Some children rely heavily upon their friends for companionship and assistance with work. Young children often feel more secure when sitting by their best friend; older ones like to be accepted as one of the gang. Although these patterns of relationship are evident in the classroom, it is often during activities that take place outside the classroom that we see the most obvious examples of relationship failures, such as when choosing partners or team members. While some children are sought for and cheered enthusiastically when chosen, others are regularly ignored, chosen last or grudgingly accepted.

The intensity of friendship patterns and preferences is evident from an early age but intensifies across the primary phase. As alliances and rivalries develop over the years, older children can become entrenched in their views of individuals and sometimes the animosity spills over into aggression. Whereas most reception class children will accept their allocated partner, the emergence of prejudice towards children who are 'different' from the majority needs firm, sensitive handling as children move through the school. Negative racial stereotypes are relatively rare during infant days but can become rampant during the upper stages if left unchecked. Most schools have policies to ensure equal opportunities but the teachers' attitudes are an essential factor as they seek to engender a caring and positive environment.

Common challenges for Foundation Stage and Key Stage 1 teachers include children who:

- Become distressed if separated from a friend on whom they rely
- Physically cling to a friend
- Become upset when someone they want to be their friend chooses not to be
- Do not appear to have a close friend and use the teacher or classroom assistant as a substitute.

Teachers of older children face other challenges with children who:

- Opt to work alone and resist collaborating with others
- Will only select an activity preferred by their friends
- Become over-reliant on a friend for academic support
- Try to enter a friendship group and are rejected
- Become separated from friends when classes move up at the start of a new academic year.

And the problem which faces teachers of all ages – children who behave out of character when sitting with a particular friend and need to be separated, yet get upset when this happens. A friendless child is one of the saddest sights in school. You can help the situation by fostering a climate of 'united we stand', of which friendliness and helping each other is an integral element. Children will always have special friends, of course, but a classroom in which everyone is respected helps to create an *inclusive* environment in which no child is excluded or marginalised (see also Chapter 9). Many schools foster a system of *peer mediation*, by which there is a school-wide system of mutual support and pupils trained and designated to act as peacemakers and arbitrators to work alongside adult workers to diffuse conflict and reconcile differences.

Despite your best efforts, there are bound to be times when children fall out with one another, disagree and get upset. Adults have an important role on such occasions to provide a calm and reassuring presence and encourage harmony. This process is not always straightforward, especially when children have become over-excited or intensely angry, but there is little point in adding to the conflict by becoming fierce yourself. A calm presence pours oil on troubled waters. As a new teacher you may even find yourself feeling a little intimidated, especially if older pupils speak aggressively and walk away when you are speaking to them or, in rare cases, attack one another. There are guidelines for action contained in the school's policy but you do not have the luxury of consulting the relevant documentation and must rely on exercising sound judgement on the spot. The key is to deal with the primary behaviour (i.e. the first offence) and protecting children from injury, and not worry too much about the secondary behaviour (i.e. subsequent behaviour arising from the first offence), such as foul language, abusive remarks or defiant body language. These issues can be referred to in due course when things are calmer. See Chapter 8 for further details.

Bullying

The word 'bullying' is used to describe a range of circumstances in which the child's welfare is at risk (Sharp *et al.* 2002). Murphy and Lewers (2000) point out that bullying is not confined to mainstream school but can also apply to the pre-school. It is sometimes difficult to discriminate between high spirits and bullying and all children have squabbles that to adult eyes look more serious than they are. Within a short time, the animosity is forgotten and the two opponents are the closest of friends. On the other hand, there are situations that can cause long-term distress and unhappiness for children. Rigby (2001) argues that it is important to deal with bullying because it has three potential adverse effects. First, it lowers mental health. Second, it induces social maladjustment. Third, it creates physical illness. Sanders (2004) offers the following observation:

> Most definitions of bullying categorise it as a subset of aggressive behaviour that involves an intention to hurt another person ... Not only can it be displayed physically but it can also be subtle and elusive. (2004: 4)

However, Sanders goes on to warn that 'emotional harassment is much more difficult to identify and prove but should still be included under the definition of bullying' (2004: 5). Barton (2006) is more expansive in her definition of bullying as 'any behaviour that results in physical or emotional injury to a person or animal, or one that leads to property damage or destruction. It can be verbal or physical' (2006: 6).

Regardless of subtle differences in interpretation, bullying is one of the most difficult experiences of a child's life. The impact of deliberately hurtful behaviour, repeated over a period of time, where it is difficult for those being bullied to defend themselves, cannot be over-estimated. Forms of bullying tend to be described under one or more of three headings: (a) Physical bullying, including hitting, kicking and theft; (b) Verbal bullying, including name-calling and racist remarks; and (c) Indirect bullying, such as spreading rumours. Lawson (1994) suggests that there are three types of bullies: aggressive bullies, anxious bullies and passive bullies.

- The *aggressive bully* is the most serious, as weaker children may be injured. Aggressive bullies are often badly behaved in school and require close supervision and monitoring throughout the day. Controlling aggressive bullying must involve the whole staff to ensure that the malefactors are made to adhere to a strictly enforced set of rules governing their behaviour. Parental involvement is also essential in setting targets for improvement.

- *Anxious bullies* see themselves as failures and vent their frustrations on other children by saying unkind things and undermining their achievements. It is often younger, vulnerable children (unlikely to retaliate) who are subjected to their taunts. This type of bully needs to be helped to gain self-esteem by placing them in a position where they can succeed. Paradoxically, these pupils often relate well to younger children in a structured environment, supervised by an adult who can monitor the situation and offer encouragement and direction.

- *Passive bullies* are the 'support' members of bullying groups but not the principal perpetrators. The term 'passive bully' is not wholly satisfactory as it implies that such types are less guilty than their leaders. Nevertheless, it is probably true to say that many passive bullies do not particularly relish their role and would prefer to spend their time in other ways. Their fear of losing credibility with the aggressors and perhaps becoming victims themselves if they don't go along with the more assertive partner deters them from breaking free. Teachers and assistants need to help them to develop new friendships by providing them with positive alternatives and ensuring that they have a busy, interesting schedule, especially during break times. Needless to say, the principal characters in any gang need to be dealt with firmly.

Thankfully, aggressive bullying is rare in primary schools, but it is important to remember that the types of behaviour which emerge during primary school are likely to be continued once pupils transfer to secondary education and create a climate of fear and uncertainty for the victims (Balding 1996). Parents and adults in school need to be alert to common signs that children are victims of bullying; the symptoms include regular headaches, stomach-aches, anxiety and puzzling phases of irritability. Parents who suspect that their children are suffering are encouraged to contact the school immediately. All adults are keen to promote not only a bully-free classroom but a safe school environment (Varnava 2002; Lee 2004). Teachers can make a considerable difference by modelling behaviour which shows that they value individual children and by actively confronting any unsatisfactory situation using strategies such as:

- Listening carefully to explanations, especially from the victim
- Offering opportunities for children who have been bullying others to become involved in positive, supportive activities
- Clarifying expectations about mutual respect and tolerance
- Monitoring the bullied children to ensure that they do not, in turn, bully others.

Although there are some children who always seem to be in scrapes, it is not always helpful to refer to them as 'bullies' as this can become a label or stigma which hinders them from throwing off their bad reputation and establishing a more positive image. It is better to speak about 'bullying behaviour' with reference to a particular circumstance. Child 1 may bully child 2 who then bullies child 3. In these particular cases, some children are victims, some are bullies and some are both. The situation is made more difficult in that bullying tends to be selective and the pupil who causes grief to one child may be delightful with another.

One of the problems facing teachers in knowing how to deal with aggressive acts (physical or verbal) is that bullying becomes a learned behaviour that eventually acts like a stimulant; in short, bullying becomes enjoyable for the perpetrator. If bullying is not dealt with sooner rather than later, it becomes habit-forming and intervention to stop it being repeated becomes more difficult. Although pernicious bullying and frequent unsatisfactory behaviour which brings distress to others cannot be tolerated, the children concerned must also be shown that there are benefits attached to kindness, consideration and self-sacrifice that cannot be experienced by tormenting someone weaker than themselves. For some bullies this is a hard lesson to learn. Racist bullying is an unpleasant area of school life that has received a great deal of attention in recent years. All schools have to demonstrate that they not only have a policy to combat such behaviour but they are active in ensuring that it is implemented and monitored.

As teachers become aware of the power of friendships and the fears, frustrations and joys of complex child–child relationships, they discover that it is essential to pay attention to its consequences, for better or worse. Children do not attend school solely for developing friendships but attention to the implications arising from the quality of relationships is important in the quest for a good teaching and learning environment (Pollard and Filer 1996; Mosley and Sonnet 2006; Hewitt 2007) Bullied children, whatever the cause, will underachieve and be miserable not only in school but in life generally. They deserve and expect protection from adults.

Activate your thinking!

Which children tend to be marginalised in the playground? What practical steps can be taken to help?

Children's curriculum entitlement

Every child in a maintained school in the UK is entitled to receive an appropriate education as prescribed by the National Curriculum (NC) and associated statutory requirements (see Figure 1.1 for common acronyms). The curriculum experienced by the children must reflect the agreed whole-school plans and offer a properly weighted content that reflects the NC and externally imposed requirements, notably in mathematics and literacy. Schools must be able to show that every subject area is receiving an appropriate amount of time and that they are accommodating the needs of each child within the teaching and learning programme, with additional adult support where deemed necessary to reflect the need to provide targeted and individualised coaching (see also Chapter 3).

The word 'curriculum' may be thought of as a specified course of study (*Collins Dictionary*) but its interpretation and implementation is far more complex. Indeed, there is not even a consistent view about how curriculum translates into practice. For example, contrast the following:

> The curriculum should be thought out in terms of activity and experience rather than knowledge to be acquired or facts to be stored.

> Consultative Committee, 1931

> The term curriculum is used to describe everything children do, see, hear or feel in their setting, both planned and unplanned.
>
> *Curriculum Guidance for the Foundation Stage* (QCA/DfES 2000)

Acronyms

AST	Advanced skills teacher
DfES	Department for Education and Skills
DCSF	Department for Children, Schools and Families
ET	Excellent teacher
GTC	General Teaching Council
HLTA	Higher level teaching assistant
ITE	Initial teacher education
ITT	Initial teacher training
LA	Local authority
LSA	Learning support assistant
NC	National Curriculum
QCA	Qualifications and Curriculum Authority
SENCO	Special educational needs co-ordinator
TA	Teaching assistant
TDA	Training & Development Agency

Figure 1.1 Common acronyms

> The school curriculum ... should equip (pupils) with the essential learning skills of literacy, numeracy and information and communication technology, and promote an enquiring mind and capacity to think rationally.
>
> *NC2000*: 11

And the concept of a national curriculum that has to apply across all schools offers yet another interpretation of the word:

> An effective National Curriculum ... gives teachers, pupils, parents, employers and their wider community a clear and shared understanding of the skills and knowledge that young people will gain at school.
>
> *NC2000*: 3

Although at one level the curriculum can be thought about as everything that a child encounters that might affect learning, the *formal* curriculum for schools consists of the Foundation Stage for children aged three to five years and an NC, separated into Key Stages (1, 2, 3 and 4) for children after the age of five years. Arrangements for statutory assessment at the end of each Key Stage are set out in detail in Qualifications and Curriculum Authority's (QCA) annual booklets about assessment and reporting arrangements. The relevant stages are summarised thus:

Foundation Stage from three to five years
The Reception year is the last year of the Foundation Stage in which the children reach statutory school age (five years).

National Curriculum

■ Key Stage 1 from five to seven years (Year 1 and Year 2)

■ Key Stage 2 from seven to eleven years (Years 3, 4, 5 and 6).

And in the secondary phase:

- Key Stage 3 from 11 to 14 years
- Key Stage 4 from 14 to 16 years.

Subject areas in the NC consist of core and non-core subjects as follows:

Core subjects
English.
Mathematics.
Science.

Non-core subjects
Design & Technology.
ICT.
History.
Geography.
Art & Design.
Music.
Physical Education.

In addition, there must be a programme of Religious Education (RE), which varies from school to school, depending upon its status. Schools with a religious foundation have more flexibility in determining the RE curriculum than secular ones. Citizenship is only statutory in Key Stages 3 and 4 but is receiving considerably more attention in primary schools than hitherto, including the availability of detailed non-statutory guidance. (See also later in this chapter.) Primary schools must also include a Modern Foreign Language (MFL) as part of the curriculum, and all children will be required to learn a language from the age of seven, commencing in 2010.

The NC is broadly organised into three parts: programmes of study, attainment targets and six key skills:

Programmes of Study (PoS)

- PoS set out what content pupils should be taught in each subject at each Key Stage
- They also provide the basis for planning schemes of work.

Attainment targets (AT)

- ATs set out the knowledge, skills and understanding which pupils of different abilities and maturities are expected to have by the end of each Key Stage

- They consist of eight level descriptions of increasing difficulty to assess pupils' attainment at the end of a Key Stage (including national tests that are commonly referred to as SATs).

Key skills across the curriculum

Communication

- Including speaking, listening, reading and writing.

Application of number

- Developing a range of mental calculation skills and the ability to apply them within a variety of contexts.

Information technology

- Using a range of information sources and ICT tools to find, analyse, interpret, evaluate and present information for a range of purposes.

Working with others

- Contributing to small-group and whole-class discussions.

Improving own learning and performance

- Reflecting on and critically evaluating their work and what they have learned.

Problem solving

- Identifying and understanding a problem, and planning ways to solve it.

The NC also states that pupils should be given opportunities to apply and develop their ICT capability through the use of ICT tools to support their learning in all subjects, with the exception of physical education in Key Stages 1 and 2.

In addition to the NC, the introduction of national numeracy and literacy strategies in the late 1990s had a major impact on the primary curriculum. The framework provided in the National Literacy Strategy (NLS) was intended to cover the statutory requirements for reading and writing in the NC, and also contribute substantially to the development of speaking and listening and have relevance across the whole of the NC. Consequently, skills in reading and writing non-fiction texts are intended to be relevant to every subject area. In practice, the original concept of a 'literacy hour' resulted in a self-contained lesson, incorporated into the daily teaching timetable as a distinctive learning episode. The suggested framework for the 'literacy hour' consisted of the following:

- About 15 minutes of shared reading and writing with the whole class
- About 15 minutes with the whole class on 'word level work' (word recognition, phonics, spelling, vocabulary; also grammar and punctuation in Key Stage 2)

- About 20 minutes of group and independent work (including guided reading and writing)
- About 10 minutes plenary (whole class brought together to share and critically reflect).

However, the rigid composition of the hour, in which attention had to be paid to set extracts from books at a word, sentence and text level, meant that areas of English received less attention, especially the opportunity for children to experience extended writing opportunities and the development of speaking and listening ('oracy'). Thankfully, the importance of oracy has now received closer attention as an essential element of becoming literate and there has also been a re-emergence of the 'showing and sharing time' (where children bring, and talk about, things of interest to them) that was commonplace in most primary schools in the recent past. Although the framework helped to concentrate teachers' minds on the fundamental skills that children need to be literate, some practitioners found the highly structured and objectives-driven nature of the hour did not allow for spontaneity and exploration of unplanned areas of learning, and constrained teachers' attempts to make lessons more relevant. There was also a growing outcry from authors whose books were used for extracts that such practices distorted the quality of their work. In 2006 the UK Government accepted that the NLS was an unsatisfactory way to improve standards in reading, writing and oral communication, and introduced a renewed literacy framework as an electronic version. To simplify the structure of the objectives and to incorporate speaking and listening, twelve strands of learning are now identified to give a broad overview of the curriculum for English in the primary phase. Thus:

1. Speaking.
2. Listening and responding.
3. Group discussion, interaction.
4. Drama.
5. Word recognition.
6. Word structure and spelling.
7. Understand and interpret texts.
8. Engage with, respond to texts.
9. Creating and shaping texts.
10. Text structure and organisation.
11. Sentence structure and punctuation.
12. Presentation.

There is also a greater focus upon teachers and practitioners using their assessment to personalise learning. The teaching of phonics has been highlighted as the principal strategy in word recognition to support reading and spelling.

The National Numeracy Strategy (NNS) was developed in 1998 to be used alongside the NC so that their contents would, it was claimed, be compatible. The principles underpinning NC2000 applied to the original NNS and, broadly speaking, to the new framework (introduced in 2006). Thus: 'Mathematics equips pupils with a uniquely powerful set of tools to understand and change the world. These tools include logical reasoning, problem-solving skills and the ability to think in abstract ways' (2000: 60). The NNS framework contained yearly teaching programmes for Reception to Year 6 and consisted of five strands, the first three of which linked directly to the NC: number, calculations and solving problems, the last two which did not link directly: measures, shape and space, and handling data.

The NNS framework placed a heavy emphasis on the assessment of children's work and their progress and recommended that a typical lesson would consist of about five to ten minutes of oral work and mental calculation (often referred to as the 'mental-oral' phase), about 30 to 40 minutes of the main teaching activity and about ten to 15 minutes of a plenary at the end. Although teachers were given a degree of flexibility in the way they taught, the NNS nevertheless prescribed that each lesson should include direct teaching and interaction with the pupils, and activities or exercises that pupils do.

The Renewed Framework is, like literacy, an electronic version that allows you to link quickly to a wide range of teaching and learning resources to facilitate planning, teaching and assessment. Another key difference from the previous version is that objectives in the 1999 Framework for mathematics have been slimmed down to give a clearer sense of the important aspects of mathematics that need to be taught to children. To simplify the structure of the objectives, seven strands of learning in mathematics are identified to give an overview of the curriculum. The objectives are aligned to the seven strands to demonstrate progression in each strand. The seven strands are as follows:

1. Using and applying mathematics.

2. Counting and understanding number.

3. Knowing and using number facts.

4. Calculating.

5. Understanding shape.

6. Measuring.

7. Handling data.

The Early Learning Goals have all been incorporated within the Foundation Stage objectives. These objectives are all embedded within the Area of Learning and Development structure: Problem Solving, Reasoning and Numeracy, all of which form part of the Early Years Foundation Stage Framework. The objectives under Year 6 progression to Year 7 are broadly targeted around level 5 to help to plan appropriately for children working at level 4 or level 5 and to help with transition from Key Stage 2 to Key Stage 3.

Citizenship

Another important dimension of children's education is covered through Citizenship, which in Key Stages 1 and 2 is non-statutory but, in reality, is pursued by all primary schools. The QCA provide a scheme based on 12 individual units, including topics as diverse as 'Choices', 'People who help us' and 'Local democracy for young citizens'. Under the banner of PSHE (Personal, Social and Health Education) and Citizenship, the NC non-statutory guidelines provide a framework for Key Stage 1 and for Key Stage 2 under two main headings:

1. Knowledge, skills and understanding.

2. Breadth of study.

The first of these, knowledge, skills and understanding, incorporates four sub-areas:

- Developing confidence and responsibility and making the most of their abilities
- Preparing to play an active role as citizens
- Developing a healthy, safer lifestyle
- Developing good relationships and respecting the differences between people.

For each sub-area, there are details about what pupils need to be taught. For instance, under *developing confidence and responsibility*, younger primary children should be encouraged to recognise what they like and dislike, what is fair and unfair, and what is right and wrong. They are also to be taught ways of sharing their opinions, to deal with feelings positively, to recognise what they are good at, and to set themselves simple goals to achieve. Older primary children are to be invited to express their opinions and explain their views in writing, identify positive things about themselves, to make responsible choices and be responsible about the use of money.

In *preparing to play an active role as citizens*, younger primary pupils should be taught how to take part in discussions and debates about topical issues, and to recognise choices and follow group decisions. They also have to helped to realise their responsibilities to others, to be alert to environmental effects of their actions, to contribute to class and school life, and to understand the place and purpose of money. Under the same heading, older primary children have to be taught how to discuss and debate topical issues based on research evidence, to understand rule-making, to realise the consequences of antisocial behaviour and to recognise their responsibilities to the community. They should also be helped to reflect on spiritual, moral, social and cultural issues, to make informed decisions, to understand the meaning of democracy, to recognise the place of voluntary and pressure groups and to appreciate ethnic and religious diversity. Finally, older primary children should have a grasp of economic realities and explore how the media present information. Quite a challenge for any teacher.

Under *developing a healthy, safer lifestyle*, younger pupils should be taught how to make simple choices that improve health and wellbeing, maintain personal hygiene and to understand how diseases spread and can be controlled. They also have to be alerted to the ageing process, names and parts of the body, harmful household products and rules for keeping safe (including road safety). Older primary pupils should be told about the benefits of exercise and healthy eating, safe routines for minimising the spread of disease, changes to the body as puberty approaches and the availability and effects of common drugs. They also have to be taught about risk assessment, appropriate physical contacts, resisting pressure to do wrong and where to get help.

Under *developing good relationships and respecting differences*, younger primary pupils should be taught to recognise how their behaviour impacts upon others, to listen, play and work co-operatively, to identify and respect differences and similarities. They should also be taught about the importance of caring for friends and families, that all forms of bullying are wrong and how to get help to deal with bullying. Older pupils should be alerted the impact of their actions, to think about the lives of people in other places and times, to be aware of different kinds of relationships and to realise the effect of racism, teasing, bullying and aggressive behaviours. They should also be taught to recognise and challenge stereotypes, understand differences between people groups and where individuals, families and groups can get help and support. Full details of the curriculum programme are available through the National Curriculum website.

Finally, for Key Stage 1 and Key Stage 2, there is information about the opportunities that pupils should experience to be taught the Knowledge, Skills and Understanding under the heading *Breadth of Study*. Thus, younger primary pupils should have opportunities to:

- Take and share responsibility through, for instance, being given specific classroom tasks as a monitor
- Feel positive about themselves through, for instance, celebrating their own and others' achievements
- Take part in discussions through, for instance, making decisions about class rules
- Make real choices through, for instance, selecting which piece of equipment to use during break time
- Meet and talk with people through, for instance, organising pairing with older children in the school as buddies
- Develop relationships through work and play through, for instance, collaborative investigations and problem-solving
- Consider social and moral dilemmas through, for instance, the use of story in which the principal character has a difficult decision to make
- Ask for help through, notably, adult approachability and a learning climate in which pupil questions are welcomed and encouraged.

Older primary pupils should have opportunities to:

- Take responsibility through, for instance, assisting with the management of outdoor equipment or assisting younger pupils
- Feel positive about themselves through, for instance, being provided with the necessary skills to produce a high quality practical product
- Participate through, for instance, giving a short presentation about an area of interest from outside school

- Make real choices and decisions through, for instance, setting their own work targets

- Meet and talk with people through, for instance, inviting guests (e.g. older members of the community, artisans, local celebrities) into lessons

- Develop relationships through work and play through, for instance, team-building exercises

- Consider social and moral dilemmas through, for instance, organising discussions about child-relevant issues

- Find information and advice through, for instance, use of information technology

- Prepare for change through, notably, orientating to new situations (e.g. moving class or school).

For some parts of the knowledge, skills and understanding, there are recommended cross-curricular links with other areas, such as science, DT, ICT, PE and history. *Assessment* of children's progression in Citizenship is in terms of what knowledge and understanding most children should have to become informed citizens. Thus, Key Stage 1 children should be able to talk about and consider topics and issues, to begin to show understanding of simple citizenship (e.g. fairness and rules) and begin to show understanding of values (e.g. concern for others). Children in Key Stage 2 should be able to investigate topical issues, show understanding of some citizenship concepts (e.g. rights and responsibilities) and show an understanding of values. In respect of demonstrating skills of enquiry and communication, Key Stage 1 children should be able to respond to simple questions and explain their views and to listen to the views of others. Key Stage 2 children should be able to take part in discussions and debates, talk and write about their opinions, ask and respond to questions and understand different viewpoints. Finally, assessment of progress can be made by pupils demonstrating skills of participation and showing responsible action.

You could be forgiven for thinking that if the non-statutory guidelines were followed thoroughly, there would be little time for anything else to be included in the curriculum. In practice, a number of elements of Citizenship are incorporated into assembly times, special projects (such as those dealing with neighbourhood issues, see Hicks 2001) and the warp and weave of daily school life governed, for instance, by behaviour policy and inter-personal relationships. See Alderson (1999) for further insights into issues concerning children's rights.

The teacher's role

Teaching is not the seamless robe official publications present as normal and achievable, providing the advice is followed. Owing to the fact that pupil learning is often unpredictable and difficult to assess formally, the teacher's role is a demanding one and every teacher has to be alert to the moment-by-moment needs of each child. Despite the fact that staff room shelves are groaning with the weight of numerous publications and policies, all claiming to help teachers understand the way that brains function and the implications for classroom practice, the truth is that all teachers rely to a large extent on a cultivated instinctiveness to guide their actions, nurtured and honed through months and years of direct experience with children. External forms of advice and knowledge about learning is, of course, to be sought and evaluated, but teachers and assistants know 'their' children and organise things accordingly. This simple truth explains why every class and classroom is subtly different. A casual visitor will be aware that classroom 'atmospheres' differ, but there are important differences between teaching situations that appear, superficially, to be almost identical.

Whatever the nature of the curriculum, the teacher's own role is critical to the process of pupil learning. Teaching effectiveness results from many varied factors (adult knowledge, pupil dispositions, resources, teacher personality, etc.) but the central factor will always reside in an understanding of what makes 'this' child tick. During a single session, teachers can play a variety of different roles, which closely relate to the need for children to learn in particular ways and to deepen their understanding over time. Teachers may act as informer, demonstrator, facilitator or interpreter. Each role carries with it a special emphasis (see Figure 1.2). As these teaching techniques are refined, the children's learning will also be enhanced and enriched (see Figure 1.3).

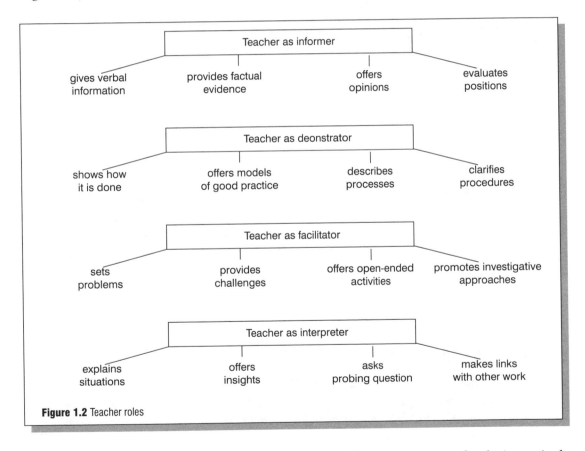

Figure 1.2 Teacher roles

The stages presented in Figure 1.2 are not in watertight compartments, for during a single lesson there will be opportunities for all of them to be woven into the fabric of the learning process. For instance, if the teacher's role is principally that of *informer*, the children's understanding will be limited by the information that the teacher provides. As a *demonstrator*, the teacher not

Figure 1.3 The relationship between teacher role and child experience

only tells but provides evidence to support the claims. In the role of *facilitator*, the teacher provides the circumstances and active support through timely interventions and guidance for children to explore and experiment and investigate processes for themselves. If the role is extended to incorporate *interpreter*, then children's understanding will be deepened as the teacher helps them to make sense of all their learning opportunities and explains its wider knowledge context. All four roles may be evident during a single session, though one will normally predominate (Dean 2001) Sometimes, a child will only be ready to receive direct information and not be ready for more challenging situations. On other occasions, after apparently grasping the concept, a child will unexpectedly require reassurance through (say) teacher-demonstration or further hands-on experience. Judging which role should be adopted with which children requires sensitivity and care, and is one of the more important strategy decisions teachers have to make.

Activate your thinking!

Watch experienced teachers carefully. Note how they subtly vary their tone of voice, body language, speed of speech and length of explanation according to the child concerned. Watch how they move backwards and forwards across the roles in response to the needs of the moment.

Promoting play

All children love to play, such that if a child stops playing, adults become anxious about the situation. Playing is an essential element of child development and wherever children are found – in every home, park, pre-school, nursery – play of some sort is evident. Most teachers of young children use play as a vehicle for enquiry-based learning; teachers of juniors tend to encourage play within the confines of a controlled learning environment such as drama, which, as we noted earlier, is the fourth of the 12 strands in the new framework for literacy.

In school, the significance of play has sometimes caused disagreements between teachers and parents, and even between teachers. Expressions such as 'She went to school but only played' and 'We didn't do any work, we only played', indicate the way in which play is perceived: that is, as a time-filling activity without educational value that has no place in the school curriculum. The vast majority of teachers, on the other hand, view play as an essential part of the educative process and a powerful learning agent. Chapter 4 contains further details about this crucial aspect of pupil's experience.

One of the challenges facing teachers of younger children in particular is the extent to which play should be directed or should be spontaneous. Left to their own devices, children play unprompted and create imaginative situations out of the most ordinary conditions (Duffy 1998). Some teachers argue that play is not play unless it is free of adult contrivance, arguing that even if they try to intervene in a play situation, they receive short shrift from assertive five year olds. For these teachers, manipulating play situations undermines its purpose and produces an artificial learning environment. They argue that children should be liberated to explore and come to terms with ideas without hindrance. In such classrooms, young children are found busily involved in a variety of activities: sand and water play, construction kits and toys, dressing-up. Noise levels sometimes become high and the teacher, who may be giving an individual pupil close attention or working with a group on basic skills, may choose to ignore the free play activity. Under such conditions, permission for children to spend time in free play is used as a reward for task completion or good behaviour.

Other teachers argue that the extent of the play should be closely controlled and monitored by the teacher. For example, a specific range of games is provided and activities are deliberately limited by the provision of certain resources and the exclusion of others. Play outcomes are targeted in terms of measurable learning outcomes that relate to social harmony, respect for property, tolerance and so forth. Play is seen as an opportunity for children to work through situations, solve problems, employ their imaginative powers to come to terms with new or exciting situations and exercise authority over confusing circumstances, bewildering paradoxes or worrying uncertainties. For these teachers, children use play to confirm ideas, create solutions and extend their thinking. Teachers use the opportunity to interact with the children, listen to their language and questions, and determine the extent of their understanding. Play thereby becomes a teacher-influenced strategy for learning rather than a completely child-directed one. Drake (2003) provides advice about implications for the Foundation Stage. She offers suggestions about key areas of learning, resources, preparation, use of vocabulary and activities. Crucially, Drake refers to the role of adults and follow-up ideas that build on the basic play activity.

The place of play in the school day will depend upon the age of the children and the teacher's education philosophy. Very young children enjoy the freedom that comes from playing without restraint and a teacher may decide that this reason is justification in itself, in which case the children are offered the opportunity to play whenever it is practicable and desirable. Younger children, who are familiar with school routines and able to cope with more structure, may be allocated play opportunities on a rota basis or as a reward for working hard, though there is a tendency for children to rush to complete the formal task if they know that extra time to play is an incentive. Sometimes a Foundation Stage teacher needs the space to concentrate on the academic learning needs of a particular group and allows the others to play as a 'holding task'. Older children, too, need a chance to play, and although this normally has to be reserved for timetabled break-times, the skilful use of improvisation and role-play in drama offers them the chance to relax and enjoy the spontaneity while performing an academically purposeful activity. However, Cohen (2006) warns that we cannot assume that play is necessarily beneficial; thus, 'at what point does larking about start to seem threatening' (2006: 139). Adults need to be alert to occasions when children's natural liveliness and testing of social situations deteriorates into bullying.

Whatever form of organisation pertains, the chance for children to take control over their learning with minimal adult intervention and imposed structure is an essential element of young children's social and intellectual development. This fact is probably truer for play than any other experiential learning.

Making decisions about, for and with children

Despite a lamentable tendency by some adults outside school to treat children as miniature versions of adults, they are not. It is true that, like adults, children get confused, bewildered, overwhelmed and elated; sometimes they excel; sometimes they struggle with work and their emotions; sometimes the world can seem a confusing, contradictory and rather scary place. However, unlike adults they do not have the life experiences, wisdom and broad perspective to make well-informed decisions, so as the responsible adult, you often have to make decisions on their behalf. This supportive intervention does not mean that children should have no voice or that they cannot offer their ideas, insights and suggestions; on the contrary, such contributions should be fostered and encouraged. Your role is one of guardian, guide and guru: as guardian to protect pupils from harm; as guide to point them in the right direction; and as guru to use your superior understanding and knowledge to help shape their thinking.

There are occasions when a pupil will be perplexed by a situation and needs your active intervention to resolve the issue or untangle the mess. If children trust you, they won't be afraid to ask for your advice and check that what they are doing is appropriate. In recent years there has been a trend towards teachers concentrating on the planning, teaching and assessing dimension of the job and TAs taking responsibility for what might be broadly termed the 'pastoral' side. Such distinctions are often unhelpful. To a child you are the key person in the classroom and although you will often have to delegate tasks to assistants, it is counter-productive to give children the impression that while you are concerned with their achievements, you are unconcerned about their general welfare. This approach is rooted in the fact that a contented child invariably makes better progress academically than a restless or unhappy one. That principle is true for all of us. The following list is typical of the experiences and situations that require such decisions, with suggestions about how you might respond:

- *A child is perplexed because she has lost an envelope containing money.*
  First, make sure that the money really is lost, as apparently lost items are often in the bottom of a bag or a pocket. If possible, check with an older brother or sister or ask an assistant to oblige; ask the school secretary or administrator to contact the parent or try to make contact directly. It is commonly argued that teachers should not deal with such trivial matters; but the matter is not 'trivial' to the child concerned.

- *A seven-year-old girl complains that a 'funny man' shouted at her outside the school gate.*
  Ask gentle questions about the circumstances; find out without fuss if any other children saw the incident; ask if the man has been there before; if uneasy about the matter, make sure the incident is reported to the head teacher immediately; if reassured, mention it to a senior colleague and log the incident in due course.

- *A top junior boy is sulky and refuses to work because he has not been chosen for the school team.*
  Talk the matter through with the boy; ask the games teacher concerned to speak to him; allow him time to get over the disappointment; at a later time speak to him again; monitor any subsequent reaction. If you are in a position to do so, offer some guidance about how he might improve his football skills. Suggest that the best way to be noticed is to be encouraging towards those who are selected and cheer them on. It won't be easy for him. Such matters are of major significance in some children's lives and can adversely affect their work and social relationships if unresolved. Be patient, but if the behaviour persists make good work a condition of selection.

- *A reception age child continually cries because he wants to go into his older sister's class.*
  This phase usually passes quite soon. An arrangement can normally be made with the other class teacher to allow occasional access for the purpose of reassurance. Playtime offers more opportunities for interaction, so help the child to look forward to this time. A sensitive assistant will often play a 'surrogate sister' role until the child is calmer. At all costs avoid dismissing the child's concerns as silly; try instead to involve the child in interesting work with other children and foster friendships in the classroom.

- *A girl who is weak academically produces a wonderful clay model.*
  Celebrate! Contact parents as soon as possible through a congratulatory note, telephone call or personal encounter. Take a photograph of the girl holding the finished model. Ask her to write a large label to accompany the model (if necessary assisted by a more able helpful child). It is important not to miss the opportunity that these critical incidents afford, so milk them fully, then move on and encourage the child to gain further achievements to boost her self-image.

- *A boy who was formerly well behaved suddenly begins to behave erratically.*
This change of behaviour may well have more profound causes. Seek advice from senior colleagues immediately. It is quite likely that the cause lies outside school and contact with the parent is needed. Children sometimes exhibit erratic behaviour if they are victims of bullying, though a more common reaction is withdrawal and sullenness. If you feel that the child is behaving that way because he is seeking entrance to a gang and wants to 'prove' himself, make a special effort to praise sensible behaviour, introduce discussions about people who were brave enough to say no, and keep a diary of incidents.

- *A four-year-old boy starts to soil himself.*
Soiling is a humiliating and frightening experience for a child. Provide reassurance and ask an assistant to deal with the matter discretely. Make contact with the parent the same day; ascertain from colleagues whether there have been previous incidents; inform the head teacher if the problem continues. An isolated incident is probably not significant but repeated instances may indicate that there is a more serious issue as the root cause.

- *A ten-year-old boy with a good voice won't join the school choir.*
Many older boys lose interest in singing, much preferring sport. The more that singing is a fun element of classroom life, the more likely that boys will retain their enthusiasm for it. Teachers responsible for choirs do well to consider the choir's image and give serious thought to its repertoire and the way it is perceived by all children throughout the school. Mention it to the parents next time you see them if necessary and cheerily encourage him in their presence but without pressure.

- *A nine-year-old girl is crying because (she claims) her mother won't let her have a birthday party.*
Listen carefully to the child; explain that you are sure there is a good reason. If you are on good terms with the parent, quietly mention the matter to her. Generally speaking it is not worth becoming embroiled in domestic matters of this kind unless you have a concern over the child's welfare or conduct. Perhaps you can mark the occasion in class, though be careful not to exceed what would normally be done for other children or it might trigger envy or set a precedent that cannot be maintained.

- *An 11-year-old boy is heard describing a video 'nasty' in graphic detail to his friends.*
Ask the child directly and unthreateningly whether he saw the video; ask whether he had permission from a parent to see it; discuss the issue with the head teacher before taking any further action. The head teacher will know the family and, if relevant, be in a position to gain informal advice from social services. Unless you suspect that there is abuse, it is difficult to do much more other than tackle it indirectly through the personal, social and health education curriculum. Quite often an older brother is the source of the problem.

- *Money goes missing and one boy is accused by several classmates.*
Calm the situation; do not allow pupils to make loud and public accusations. Gently but firmly ask the child if he knows anything about the matter but avoid making accusations; insist that he looks into your eyes when he answers, unless the child is from a culture where direct eye contact is considered impertinent. Inform the class teacher or a senior colleague immediately. Treat all instances of theft seriously, including those of children's snacks.

Persevere with exploring the circumstances with the help of an assistant or colleague until the matter is satisfactorily resolved. Once a child begins to steal it can become an obsession and difficult to stop.

■ *A 10-year-old boy starts to draw weird doodles on scraps of paper.*
Chat informally to the child about the drawings before deciding whether to seek advice. Images of this kind may be a short-lived phase or can indicate deeper psychological problems. If the child has a talent for drawing it may be possible to divert his efforts more constructively and use his creativity in a positive way (e.g. to design a class logo). Some children learn best through visual means.

■ *An 11-year-old girl, through silliness, breaks an expensive piece of science equipment.*
Console the child rather than condemning; after the lesson speak to her and explain your disappointment with her behaviour. Sensible children who behave out of character will normally confide in their parents about an incident of this kind, so don't be surprised if the parent contacts you first. Although a school can insist that a breakage be paid for, it is often not worth the trouble unless there is a serious matter of principle involved. Again, a senior colleague will offer advice about such matters.

■ *A six-year-old boy, new to the class, swears when the teacher rebukes him for aggressive behaviour.*
Firmly explain that such language is not used in school; reinforce this from time to time during the coming days. When younger children use unsuitable language, they have normally acquired it from home in the first place. A child new to school will need time to adjust to the differing expectations. The aggressive behaviour is a more urgent issue and the school's discipline policy will come into play, which may involve the special educational needs co-ordinator (SENCO). In the meantime persevere with a 'we are kind to each other in this school' approach. If other children are being hurt or intimidated it is essential to take immediate action and, as so often the case, involve a more experienced colleague and/or assistant.

■ *An eight-year-old girl is regularly a few minutes late in the morning.*
Ask the child why she is arriving late; consult with teachers of her brothers or sisters to see if they are also arriving late. If you are a new teacher to the school or a trainee, find out if there is a history of poor timekeeping. In some families, especially where parents leave for work early in the morning, the eldest child has the responsibility for ensuring that the younger ones get to school, with the resulting problem about lateness. If there are concerns about the children's welfare, the head teacher will pursue the case and may suggest that the parent takes advantage of the 'wrap-around' facilities, if available.

■ *A reception child frequently falls asleep during the afternoon story.*
Speak privately to the parent as soon as possible. Some small children simply get tired and need to sleep. Even adults have this problem. Other children stay up too late due, perhaps, to being the youngest in a house full of noisy siblings. Falling asleep may also indicate the presence or imminence of ill-health, so it pays to log the occasions and work closely with an assistant where possible to monitor the child's level of activity throughout a day.

As a guide to appropriate action, the child's immediate safety is always of prime concern. Once this is secured, the child's longer-term security needs to be considered. From this point onwards, any decisions will depend upon the circumstances of the case, bearing in mind agreed school policy, previous experience of similar incidents and the teacher's own judgement. It is usually better to err on the side of caution. The 'funny man' outside the school gate may have been a harmless passer-by with an unusual appearance or a child molester. The boy describing a video nasty might be unsupervised at home or have been told the story by his older brother and was showing off to his friends when he related the story. The reception-aged child falling asleep might be kept awake at night by noisy neighbours or suffering the effects of a hot and stuffy classroom. Suspicions that a parent might be the cause of the distress or responsible for a child's unsettled behaviour means that it would not be appropriate to contact that person directly. Always take advice from the head teacher and monitor the situation informally while advice is sought from the appropriate social service, such as the child protection agency. Trainee teachers do not need to become embroiled in the detail of procedures and processes but have the same responsibility as every other adult to ensure the physical and emotional wellbeing of young lives. You wanted to be a teacher; this is part of the job.

Case study

In many ways Jonny was the ideal pupil and just the sort of nine-year-old that any teacher would want in the class. He related well to his peers and also to adults. He worked hard and used his natural intelligence to maximum effect. Jonny always strove to achieve a high standard, was sensitive to people's feelings and would apply himself to sporting events with great enthusiasm and competitiveness. Jonny was socially aware in that he fitted in well with any group and was popular with his classmates. Jonny was a capable footballer and a member of the cross-country running team. At the end of the year the teacher, Geoff Anscot, was genuinely saddened when Jonny moved on to the next class.

Twenty years later Geoff was walking through an indoor market when he heard a voice call out to him from behind one of the stalls. It was a beaming Jonny, who to Geoff's eyes did not look all that different from the pupil in shorts that he remembered. After they had exchanged pleasantries, Jonny told Geoff proudly that he was now the owner of three small businesses that he ran from different markets. Jonny laughingly described himself as an entrepreneurial market trader. Geoff wondered what Jonny would remember from his days in the class and hoped that he might say something positive. (Even the best teachers need to be reassured sometimes.) Although Geoff recalled the time when Jonny had been in his class as if it were yesterday, for Jonny the same time period composed the majority of his lifetime. It was not long before Jonny's eyes glazed over as the memories flooded back.

'You used to play your guitar in assembly.'

'Yes, that's right, we had some good fun.'

'Mmm. We practised the play for Christmas.'

'Yes, I remember', the teacher replied.

'And you used to run the football team.'

'Yes, I was a bit slimmer then. You were a good player.' Geoff waited, hoping that Jonny might refer to the excellent learning experiences he had in class, but Jonny's priorities were different. Instead, Jonny's mind was saturated with the fun he had experienced, the personal interactions, the joy of being part of a team, the excitement of public performances in front of the rest of the school, parents and friends. Jonny reminisced about the times that the teacher took them out of school on short trips to explore the lanes and bring small treasures back to examine in class, mount them on displays, create large books with pictures and photographs, and include snippets of writing and photographs. Jonny's memories were full of the things that still served to motivate and inspire him.

What will today's children remember of their schooldays? What will be of value to them in five, ten or 30 years from now? School-based education must be an enabling process that creates a desire in children to discover more about the world and to learn skills and attitudes that will ensure a more productive and harmonious society. Education should excite in children a belief that life has purpose and liberate their imaginations and creativity. Every adult in school is making an important contribution to each child's present and future. As Geoff said goodbye to his former pupil, he felt quietly satisfied that at least some of his aspirations had been fulfilled in Jonny.

Further reading

Casey, T. (2007) *Environments for Outdoor Play*, London: Sage.
Contains ideas for developing play environments and deals with issues such as inclusion and playground management.

Eaude, T. (2006) *Children's Spiritual, Moral, Social and Cultural Development*, Exeter: Learning Matters.
Makes direct links between children's attainment and aspects of personal development, beliefs and values.

Robson, S. (2006) *Developing Thinking and Understanding in Young Children*, London: Routledge.
Combines introductions to theories about thinking with observations taken from classroom practice.

Smidt, S. (2006) *The Developing Child in the 21st Century*, London: Routledge.
Provides a multi-disciplinary global exploration of childhood, demonstrating how children from a variety of backgrounds make sense of the world.

Willan, J., Parker-Rees, R. and Savage, J. (eds) (2007) *Early Childhood Studies*, 2nd edn, Exeter: Learning Matters.
Reflects the multi-professional, multi-disciplinary scope of early childhood studies.

The Teacher

Introduction

Schools are not just places for children. Effective education relies on committed and conscientious teachers and support staff collaborating in this vital endeavour. This chapter offers a kaleidoscope of perspectives on the joys and challenges of being a teacher in school: a role that extends well beyond the act of teaching. The role of other adults in school is dealt with more fully in Chapter 3.

Becoming a teacher

Some people have a sentimental view of the task that teachers face. Visions of children's gentle, eager faces lifting their trusting eyes to gaze expectantly towards a much-loved adult, waiting on every word, are sometimes far removed from reality. Teachers have to be tough, persevering and determined. The rigours of daily classroom life and the demands of 30 or more children of varying abilities and enthusiasm can be a daunting business for even the most capable and committed.

On the other hand, teaching is an important job offering great reward and satisfaction. There is probably nothing to compare with the thrill of introducing children to new and exciting worlds of learning, to see the glow on their faces when understanding dawns. Not all teachers are loved, but many are and deserve to be. It may sound like rhetoric, but teaching really is a way of life; once a person has entered the world of school, things will never be quite the same again. Equally certain is the exciting truth that most children do not forget their teachers. Fifty years and more from now, many children will still speak some of their teachers' names, refer to their character and the effect they had upon their lives. When much else is forgotten, the memory of a teacher lives on. In a quotation from one of his respondents, Cotton (1998) offers an example of the essential characteristics that teachers must put across to the children if they are to earn a special place in pupils' memories:

> All have human qualities; they made us feel good about ourselves; they made us see things are possible and they justified our existence as unique human beings, not simply faceless pupils. (1998: 42)

Building a relationship with children takes time and perseverance. No one can claim the automatic right to be a respected teacher; it has to be earned and, for a trainee teacher in particular, there is little time in which to do so owing to the short-term nature of a school placement. If there is no mutual respect, then little account is taken of what a teacher or assistant says or demands unless the adult coerces the child. Some inexperienced teachers become despondent when their attempts to establish good relationships with the children are initially rejected. Yet it may be that the class has had some unpleasant experiences with adults and will take some convincing that they can be trusted. Or perhaps they were very happy with their previous teacher and are less certain about the new teacher's ability to take that place. It may be that particular children are shy or fearful and can't respond naturally, so they adopt a passive or aloof posture until they feel more secure. In a small number of cases, it may be that certain children are using emotional blackmail – 'I'll give you the satisfaction that comes from seeing me happy and responsive in exchange for staying off my back and not expecting too much from me.' Wright (2006) describes the consequences attached to being a 'passive' teacher:

> The passive teacher is characterised by efforts to be popular that include ingratiating herself. She will have fragile feelings and will take criticism badly. She will plan her lessons in great detail but is not a forward planner in terms of managing the behaviour of her class. She ends up having to react to incidents and usually does it badly because she has not worked out her responses. (2006: 58)

Teachers have to discriminate between children's tentativeness and their wiles. A demonstration of integrity and consistency will convince most children that a good relationship with a teacher is worth the effort, though there may be one or two children who are dismissive of the teacher's overtures despite trying to establish a bond with them. If you meet such children it is unwise to dwell unduly on the situation, but rather to persevere to establish a working relationship with them by being natural, showing flair in your teaching and being clear about where the boundaries of acceptable behaviour lie. Children who are initially reluctant to reciprocate are sometimes the ones with whom you ultimately develop the closest bond, so don't despair.

Procedures and rituals

Every school has its codified and unwritten rules and regulations, and trainee teachers and newly appointed teachers to a school have to make sure that they do not unwittingly contravene them. It is worth keeping a record of the procedures and rituals that you observe in the classroom and elsewhere to avoid too many embarrassing moments when you inadvertently cross the boundaries owing to your ignorance of situations that others take for granted. Most children are ready and willing to offer you information about specific aspects of classroom life, and a friendly member of the support staff will usually alert you to school-wide issues if you ask. It is important not to underestimate the significance of these 'concealed assumptions' in a school, as adherence to them is sometimes unfairly used as an informal measure of a trainee teacher's suitability for teaching.

In particular, knowing about the school policy for discipline and the use of sanctions may avoid problems of inconsistency occurring between you and the class teacher. Children may alert you to the mismatch when they protest by saying something to the effect, 'Miss lets us/does not let us do that'. Whoops! If you feel strongly about an issue it is best to tell the children that you will talk about the matter to the teacher and then make a decision, rather than publicly face down the protests on the spot. If you are a newly appointed teacher you might encounter a similar situation but the children will then refer to what their previous teacher allowed. In such a situation you can say that the new conditions pertain because the children are older now, or something similar. Similarly, if there is an accepted way for children to move around the school (to assembly, for instance) it is essential that you uphold the required code of behaviour. There are also more subtle issues, dependent on relationships between different adults, that are harder to identify but necessary to discern.

Guiding principles

If anyone suggests to experienced primary teachers that the job is quite straightforward providing they follow standard procedures as laid down in a government document or in a book or theory, they will probably show the speaker the door (once they have stopped laughing). The job of teacher is extremely complex and the act of teaching cannot be reduced to a formula. It requires an array of skills and strategies, thorough and ongoing reflection and no small degree of trial and error. Teachers are also learners, and the best teachers show a hunger to find out more about what works best and how they can be even more effective. Once teachers stop thinking about their work, they quickly slip into a dull routine. To stay bright and alert you should regularly review the following areas:

- Attitude to learning
- Reputation
- Commitment and enthusiasm
- Children's welfare
- Establishing a working relationship
- Attitude to achievement
- Encouragement and praise
- Equal opportunities.

Each of these areas is now considered in turn.

Attitude to learning

Learning does not happen in a vacuum. Teachers need to be clear about the conditions that contribute towards a satisfactory learning environment. Decisions about five key issues are needed.

The best conditions for learning

Learning takes place when pupils are motivated, clear about why the lesson content is worthwhile and clear about what is expected of them by the teacher. If the work is intrinsically interesting there is less need to explain why the learning is necessary; if the work content does not have immediate appeal you will need to work hard to convince pupils that it is worth trying hard (if only to finish and get on with something more engaging). Children make most progress when the challenges they face are manageable and allow them to use their knowledge, skills and understanding to achieve the lesson targets and, ideally, to use their initiatives to delve further. Children learn best when sessions are fun or, at least, not boring. They like working with their friends where possible and respond to an enthusiastic, committed teacher who introduces ideas in an original way through use of visual aids (not just whiteboards), drama, poetry, telling a story, asking a question, and so on. At the risk of being simplistic, it is fair to say that learning happens best when pupils want to learn and happens less when they do not.

The degree of co-operation and competition

Nearly all children want to do well at school. The only exceptions are a small number who are thoroughly miserable or emotionally unsettled. In some classrooms there is a notable co-operative spirit and children are generally courteous and kind to one another; in others, there seems to be an underlying tension and unhealthy rivalry that leads to sullenness and resentment. The ideal situation is one in which pupils are mutually supportive and celebrate other children's success as well as their own. Teachers who achieve this happy state do so through perseverance, modelling an appropriate attitude to their pupils, and valuing children over and above their ability to attain academically. The majority of pupils are eager to please adults; make sure that you don't disappoint them.

Motivation strategies

One of Aesop's Fables concerns a dispute between the sun and the wind as to which could make a man walking along the road remove his coat. The wind tries desperately to get the man to oblige by blowing harder and harder; but the man simply wraps the coat more tightly around him. The sun shines brightly and within a short time the man has taken off his coat. Motivation rarely increases as a result of threats or compulsion. The child who is motivated to learn will be more influenced by the warmth of a teacher's personality and encouragement than by icy threats. The greatest motivator is a desire to learn.

The criteria used to evaluate success and failure

One child works hard and achieves little; another makes minimum effort and achieves a lot. A teacher's attitude to each child will reveal a great deal about the criteria that the teacher is using to evaluate success; praise for the latter and dismay for the former will send a signal that attainment is singularly important as a measure. It is all too easy for teachers unintentionally to make children feel that their worth as a person is directly linked to their success in their schoolwork. Some children like to experiment and do things in a non-conventional way. As a result, they may make more mistakes than their conventional peers but enjoy a richer learning experience. Teachers have to be careful to credit children for showing initiative as well as achieving the correct results. It is said that the great inventor, Thomas Alva Edison asked his teacher so many questions that the teacher became exasperated and Thomas was branded as 'impossible' and had to be taught at home.

Acceptable behaviour

It is important for teachers to establish basic classroom rules so that every pupil is clear about what is acceptable and appropriate. This does not mean that there will not be infringements from time to time. Teachers have to decide almost instantly whether a particular behaviour warrants a warning or scolding or whether it is best ignored. Inexperienced teachers find it hard to know what to overlook and what to act upon. Though some behaviour is wholly unacceptable, many forms are merely expressions of children's immaturity. Whatever teachers decide, they should remind themselves that it is children's co-operation that is sought, not their indulgence. Firmness in the early stages may avoid the need for strictness later on. As a rule poor behaviour should never be overlooked other than in exceptional circumstances. It may be that you will decide to speak quietly to the child than to utter a public rebuke.

A more sophisticated consideration of factors involved in effective learning is considered fully in Chapter 4.

Reputation

It is said that a reputation is what others think of us and a character is what we are really like, so perhaps the sub-heading for this section ought to be 'character' rather than 'reputation'. Nevertheless, as a new teacher in school you will need to build a reputation quickly: among adults, so that you are treated with respect; among children, so that they grow to like or even love you.

Pupils frequently talk about their teachers. Parents ask their children searching questions about how their day has been and what their teachers are like. Any teacher who wants to play a positive role has to recognise that reputations grow as a result of incidents and responses to situations over a period of time. It is not easy to be a new teacher in school and establish yourself as equal to the existing staff, but it is worth considering the impact that your presence has on the classroom situation. For instance, the way that you dress and conduct yourself, the tone of voice you use, the way that you react to challenges and your attitude to other adults all contribute to the sort of impression that you create. Although you may be more concerned with lesson planning and the mechanics of teaching than you are about how you are perceived by others, the advantages gained through building a good reputation are considerable:

- Children are proud of you as their teacher and develop a healthy attitude towards learning
- Children talk positively about you at home, thereby encouraging their parents and constructing a climate of confidence

- Gossip at the school gate about your competence is passed from parent to parent so that they are eager for their children to be taught by you

- The host teachers relate to you like a colleague as much as a student.

For a qualified teacher in school, there are additional benefits:

- Parents and children look forward to being in that teacher's class

- The head teacher is able to speak of the teacher in warm terms to governors, visitors and prospective parents.

A good reputation is not easily established, especially if you are only in the school for a short period of teaching experience. Nevertheless, factors such as appropriate relationships with children, adequate preparation for lessons and a positive personality are all relevant. The comments of five different groups of people on the subject help to illuminate some of the key issues:

1. *From a four year old:* 'I like my teacher. She lets us do painting and tells us stories.'

2. *From an eight year old:* 'My teacher's good. She teaches us to do things and doesn't mind if we talk to her. We do science and make things and we have a laugh sometimes. She's not exactly strict but she doesn't like us to muck about or she can get really cross. She's alright, though, and I like her because she likes us.'

3. *From an 11 year old:* 'My teacher's quite cool. He does sports and stuff with us and tells us really terrible jokes! He's good at helping us with maths and gives you a chance to explain if you're stuck. I don't like it when he gets mad, but it's quite funny sometimes!'

4. *From a parent:* 'Lisa's teacher, Mr Andrews, is very nice and friendly. He said at parents' evening that he was really pleased with Lisa's progress and that her maths was improving. He said she was near the top in some subjects and one of the best readers. They went on a trip to the zoo and Lisa really enjoyed it. And when Lisa was unhappy about swimming, he phoned me up and asked to have a chat so we could sort things out and Lisa was fine afterwards. He's strict, sometimes, but the children think he's great.'

5. *From a teaching colleague:* 'Bella's a super teacher. She's got a marvellous way with the kids, somehow, and she really knows her stuff. She's also very creative and seems to have the ability to get children to think deeply. She and the TA did an incredible display for parents' evening, but she still had time to help the newly qualified teacher sort out her reports. The thing about Bella is that she's always got time for you. It doesn't seem to matter how busy she is, you always feel that she's interested in what you've got to say. She's the same with everyone – kids, staff, visitors, cleaners – I don't know how she does it. Even when she's stressed out, she can always raise a laugh! Hope she stays here.'

6. *From one of the ancillary staff:* 'Mr Ryan's lovely. He always speaks to you and smiles. He treats you fairly and remembers to say thank you. He's really appreciative if you do something and doesn't mind a joke every now and then. Mind you, he's a good teacher and keeps order.

I was with Mrs Burton last year and it was terrible. She's very nice and friendly but can't control the class at all. I can work with Mr Ryan; you know where you stand with him.'

7. *From the head teacher:* 'I appointed Lela four years ago and she settled down well. She got stuck in straight away and wasn't afraid to ask for advice. Even when she was struggling a bit last year with a difficult class, she was very tenacious and kept going when many of us would have been tempted to give up. Parents like her because she's friendly and efficient and says positive things about the children. She's great at fetes and open evenings because she takes an interest in people and always has an encouraging word to say. In fact she's very much a "people person" but doesn't patronise them. As the head teacher, I'm happy because the children learn well with her, she works hard, plans thoroughly, keeps her records up to date and is popular with parents. It's good to have someone so reliable on the staff team who is also willing to learn and take advice. Her performance during the concert last term was memorable!'

Reputation also has implications for the quality of your class discipline, not least because children quickly decide between themselves which teachers are 'soft' and which teachers have to be obeyed. The most formidable reputations are based on a combination of teaching effectiveness (including an emphasis on interaction with pupils and collaborative activities) and personal qualities. Gill (1998) captures the essence of the issue: One of the best ways to eliminate discipline problems is to have a reputation as a good teacher who tries to make learning enjoyable but who will do what she says she is going to do (1998: 42). Sarason (1999) suggests that both teachers and pupils (the audience) should participate in what he calls 'the performance'. Thus:

> Audiences are silent performers. They are silent but not passive; at least they did not come expecting to be inwardly passive. They come expecting to see themselves and a slice of life differently. They do not expect to be bored, unmoved and sorry they came. (1999: 14)

Sarason's description of an audience and performer is easily transposed to the classroom. Pupils have to *believe* in the teacher and be engaged in the proceedings. They are not passively going through the motions of 'being taught' but active learners trying to make sense of concepts, ideas and situations for themselves. In doing so they need to be interested (if not fascinated) by the curriculum, drawn into the lesson through the enthusiasm and authenticity of the teacher and contributing to the proceedings. The use of dialogue in classrooms to explore, test, shape thinking and tease out the unexpected is one such way to ensure that the audience of children is transformed into performers (see Chapter 4). Other methods include free play, experimenting with materials, working co-operatively, collaborating on projects and developing new approaches to familiar pathways. However, in fulfilling these aspirations for effective learning, it is important to be alert to the fact that giving children opportunities to explore and be creative does not guarantee satisfactory outcomes. Children can spend hours in aimless pursuits; they can respond to teachers' questions superficially; they can avoid taking risks; they can cloak shallow thinking in a frenzy of activity that yields little in positive learning.

Commitment and enthusiasm

We have noted that it is important for teachers to set a good example to pupils and impress parents by the way they present themselves in school and their general conduct. A small number of teachers spend time complaining about poor working conditions, the government, the head teacher and (sometimes) the children. It is wise to politely avoid being drawn into the conversation, even if you have some sympathy with what is being said. Wise teachers allow themselves the occasional moan but do not let it become a habit. It is surprisingly easy to slide into a negative spiral and depress both yourself and colleagues by constantly complaining, so it is worth persevering to make sure that the majority of your comments are positive ones. It takes effort to develop a healthy outlook on life, but the effect can transform the atmosphere and give hope to you and to others. As a trainee teacher you must strike a careful balance between listening sympathetically to colleagues' comments, yet maintaining a purposeful outlook on life. Do not be fooled into thinking that you will endear yourself to this glum minority by being as miserable as they are sounding. You will simply gain a reputation as a complainer and may be perceived as a burdensome hindrance. By contrast to the despondent practitioner, Fried (1995) promotes the concept of the 'passionate teacher'. Thus:

> To be a passionate teacher is to be someone in love with a field of knowledge, deeply stirred by issues and ideas that challenge our world, drawn to the dilemmas and potentials of the young people who come into class each day – or captivated by all of these. A passionate teacher is a teacher who breaks out of the isolation of a classroom, who refuses to submit to apathy or cynicism. (Prologue)

Research into attitudes of host teachers in primary schools who work with trainee teachers indicates that they value a number of characteristics in trainee teachers who are placed in their schools (Hayes 2002). These include the following.

Adopting a forthright attitude

Trainee teachers should make sure that they get 'stuck in' from the very start, show a genuine interest in what the children are doing, stay calm, poised and vigilant. They should volunteer for jobs where appropriate, including the messy ones. They should not, however, give the impression to the children that they are content to be assistants or parent helpers. Trainee teachers should let the teacher see that they mean business but avoid becoming frantically active that they unsettle the classroom atmosphere.

Staying focused

Trainee teachers should offer help and expertise to the children whenever possible and make every effort to concentrate their attention on the work in hand. If children start to show off or behave in a silly fashion while they are attempting to help them, trainee teachers should walk away and help another child. They should not allow the children to tease them, treat them like a favourite cousin or distract them from the main purpose of teaching. Schools value serious students of education that are dedicated and resolute.

Showing concern about the children

Trainee teachers should show that they like the children by establishing bright eye contact and taking an interest in their activities, but avoid being sucked in to childish conversations. When children approach to speak to them, a trainee teacher should smile invitingly and offer help willingly but also take care that they do not end up doing the work for the children. Children quickly sense if you really care or are putting on an act.

Enjoying the work

Trainee teachers should make it clear to the teacher that they are enjoying their time in school and appreciating the opportunities it presents. Those who speak and act to show that they are keen to be in the school will receive a sympathetic response from the staff.

Behaving courteously

As a visitor, trainee teachers are expected to be polite, helpful and well mannered to colleagues and to the children. They should not, of course, be patronising or stuffy, just thoroughly professional in outlook and conduct. Small acts of kindness and courtesy impress staff considerably. Don't always wait to be invited to do something; instead, volunteer to assist others.

Having a determined attitude to their own learning

Trainee teachers should regularly ask the teacher how they can improve their teaching and should not be fobbed off by general comments to the effect that they are 'doing fine' but ask instead for specific advice. All trainees should be encouraged to monitor their professional progress and acknowledge both weaknesses *and* achievements. You should maintain a log of key issues that emerge during your time on placement and an indication of what action you took or advice you sought to address the situation.

Extending the professional role

Teachers spend as much time working outside the classroom as they do inside it, so trainee teachers should be ready to get involved with other duties. However, in their eagerness to participate, it is important that they take care not to abandon common sense about how much they can cope with.

Expressing appreciation

Learning to thank the teacher regularly for her or his help and support, and showing that they appreciate the effort that has gone into making them welcome and giving them opportunities to gain experience of teaching is seen as a vital aspect of a trainee teacher's responsibility. They must give the firm impression that they value and appreciate what the teacher does but without being patronising or fawning. If you appreciate what a colleague (teacher or assistant or support staff) does on your behalf, say so.

There is much for trainee teachers and host teachers to learn about relating effectively to one another and establishing a partnership for the benefit of the children. Generally, if trainee teachers are willing to learn, respond to advice and make up their minds to be a positive influence in the school, they will receive nothing but support and encouragement. It is obvious that the better that trainee teachers and host teachers work together, understand each other's needs and accept the limitations of their different roles, the more rewarding life in school becomes for all concerned. This ideal state is more likely to happen if teachers and students agree to speak openly and honestly to one another about their feelings and expectations.

Good practice

Each time you respond to a situation, ask yourself if your response is contributing to your reputation as a decisive, forward-looking person.

Some schools have developed strategies to stimulate staff and lift spirits. Mosley and Grogan (2002) suggest that high morale is essential if a school community is to prosper, injecting mystery into the proceedings, having fun together, establishing a 'cheer-up' board and a 'words of inspiration' board, and bringing in outside support. Achieving a work–life balance is now seen as an essential pre-requisite for health and welfare, though in reality teachers seem to work as hard as ever. Mosley and Grogan also suggest that just as children's self-esteem and mutual respect can be enhanced through circle-time (see Collins 2001, 2007 for numerous practical suggestions), the same principles apply to adults in school. Thus:

- Taking care of oneself as well as taking care of others
- Learning to draw the line and not continually bend over backwards to be helpful
- Recognising that everyone has particular and special needs
- Learning to decline requests without feeling guilty
- Accepting that everyone can only do their best
- Expecting to be treated with consideration and courtesy and as someone with intelligence
- Refusing to be dependent on other people's approval
- Recognising that time for relaxation is not wasted time.

The position is well summarised by Suschitzky and Chapman (1998): 'The ways that children view themselves are influenced by the ways others respond to them' (1998: 8). And one of the most significant 'others' is you. That is why adopting an affirmative posture is good for you as well as being good for them.

Activate your thinking!

All teachers are entitled to the equivalent of one half day to attend to preparation, planning and assessment, commonly referred to as PPA time. These occasions may be ideal opportunities for you to take responsibility for the whole class, possibly in harness with a TA. Note that although PPA time has freed up teachers from some teaching responsibility, it has also placed on them an onus to be more thoroughly planned and carry out more detailed assessments than was hitherto the case.

Good practice

Make a deliberate effort to gradually introduce a larger proportion of positive comments into your conversations. Monitor the impact of your changing attitude on pupils and colleagues.

Children's welfare

All teachers must have a working knowledge and understanding of teachers' professional duties, legal liabilities and responsibilities, so it is essential to be aware of the extent and limits of your duty towards the children. They are protected by the Children Act (first published 1989, updated in 2004) that forbids adults to exert unreasonable psychological pressure upon them, such as shouting in their face and hectoring, or physical chastisement and force. There are obvious exceptions to this rule; for instance, screaming out loud may be the only means of preventing a child running in the road, and physical containment may be the only way to prevent one child from injuring another. However, these occurrences are rare and the general principle of treating children with respect and using reason rather than rage is contained within the Children Act 1989. These sentiments are explored more fully in the *Every Child Matters* agenda (DfES 2005; see earlier and Chapter 9). The Children Act 2004 aims to encourage integrated planning, commissioning and delivery of services to children, as well as improve multi-disciplinary working (notably education and social services) and improve the co-ordination of individual and joint inspections in local authorities.

In practice, it may take you a lot of self-discipline to avoid infringing the spirit of the legislation, especially with children who persistently and wilfully take advantage of their freedom and seem determined to push adults to the limits of their patience. Nevertheless, you must learn to remain calm and exercise self-control, regardless of the provocation or personal slights you receive; try hard to ignore the sense of injustice and anger that you feel with a child who is unreasonable and concentrate on a solution. The purpose is resolution, not retribution. If you are an inexperienced teacher it is unwise to try and deal with difficult situations without support and advice. If you are uncertain about what constitutes an appropriate response towards children, consult senior colleagues at the earliest opportunity, and keep them informed of subsequent developments. It may feel to you that the child has 'got away with it' because of your hesitation but this is not the case. It is preferable, though not always possible, to get advice from the host teacher and then deal with the matter yourself, based on the advice, than to bring in the other teacher to sort out the matter, while you stand back and admire her work. There are two reasons for adopting this approach; first, bringing in another teacher puts you in direct conflict with the child and second, handling the issue helps you to gain credibility with pupils and boosts your self-assurance.

Children need to feel at ease with one another and also confident about their place in society. The development of personal, social and health education (PSHE) in the curriculum is an important element of effective schooling, as it helps to develop positive attitudes, address issues of significance to children and stimulate an active interest in society and citizenship. There are many occasions when a teacher wishes to develop a more intimate atmosphere by gathering the children together in a smaller, well-defined area in which they can all sit comfortably. The children sit in a circle with the teacher to discuss key issues, share ideas and celebrate events (e.g. Roffey 2006; see also Further Reading). The circle-time approach depends upon everyone agreeing in advance about procedures (such as only one person speaking at a time) and conduct (such as speaking kindly). It is non-threatening (children only contribute when they wish to do so) and is intended to increase co-operation and allow for positive reinforcement, thus raising the self-image of every child. On other occasions, carpet time can be used for book sharing, or the teacher or a capable child reading aloud to the class or simply sharing the fun things that children have seen and done. For instance, a recent exciting television programme can stimulate great enthusiasm and promote speaking and listening skills. Although some teachers and their classes make fruitful use of circle-time each week, it should be seen only as a component of the overall teaching method. As with any other approach, its value has to be monitored and evaluated to ensure that the child is left with higher self-esteem and confidence as a result.

Timing can also influence the circumstances under which you gather children together. For instance, it may be unwise to gather children into close confinement immediately after a long assembly or inactive playtime. Although the end of the day is frequently used for a story and sharing, other times should also be considered, particularly towards the end of a session when children's minds are buzzing. At the end of the day, especially, it is essential to calm the children, relax the atmosphere and send the children from the classroom with a song on their lips and in their hearts, eager to return for more the following day. Some teachers stand at the door and say a personal goodbye to each child; others have small rituals, such as using a chant or getting each child to name (say) a town or country before they leave.

Health and safety

Pupils' safety must be a priority for every adult working in school. Health and safety factors depend on the nature of the activities, the age of the children and adult–child ratio. For very young children, basic cleanliness training may be the priority; for older ones, correct use of tools and equipment may be most important. There are also some common issues such as ensuring that:

- Each child is clear about what has to be done and the time constraints involved

- Children have sufficient space to do the task or activity
- Children are aware of others in the vicinity that may be affected by their actions (such as being sprayed by paint)
- There is a minimum of hazards on the floor (such as spilled paste) that might be perilous
- The procedures for movement about the room and the correct place for each piece of equipment have been explained to the children beforehand
- There is a well-labelled place for every resource.

Of course, prevention is always better than cure, so it is essential to think ahead. Sensible health and safety precautions are not for the purpose of limiting what children attempt to do or suppressing their enjoyment of practical activities. On the contrary, good working practices liberate the children to work confidently and assuredly. As the responsible adult, you have to make the final decisions about what is permissible.

In science, warn the children about:

- The hazards of cuts from split plastic and sharp edges. Cuts should be treated by holding the damaged area under free-flowing cold water, direct from the tap, into an empty sink
- The need to wash hands thoroughly after contact with soil and outdoor activity. Thoroughly washing hands in warm soapy water is recommended. Of course, children can wear plastic gloves when handling natural objects, though a small number of children find them unpleasant to wear and handle. They are also extremely difficult to put on and take off
- The danger of cord or wire being wrapped tightly around a wrist or tangled around the neck. A pair of wire-cutters should be readily available should instant release be necessary. Unless there is physical damage to the skin, it is usually sufficient to massage the affected area
- The effect of bright light on eyes and high volume sound on eardrums. Some flashing lights can trigger epileptic 'fits' in a small minority of children, so a warning should always be given.

In physical activity guard against:

- Over-exuberant 'warm-up' activities that involve children charging around and the potential for nasty collisions. Instead use more 'on the spot' activities and controlled short sprint activities
- Body movement that may cause strain without suitable 'warm-up' activities. Instead, ensure that you have led all the children through the required muscle-loosening exercises
- Unstable or damaged equipment. It is essential to check beforehand or, if this has not been possible, to put to one side any item that is in an unsuitable state. If you find the time spent in carrying out this check to be onerous, console yourself with the thought that it is better than having an injured child and explaining to a parent and the head teacher why you did not check

- Hard equipment, especially wooden or solid plastic bats that may hit a child in the face. If bats are necessary, you should not be afraid to enforce strict conditions for their use, especially maintaining a distance between the batter and the rest of the team. One way to achieve this is to insist that the batter stands at a point that is located at the centre of a concentric circle of outer hoops or a chalk/tape ring. No one else is allowed beyond the perimeter of the hoops until it is their turn to bat

- Equipment that allows children to climb beyond the limits of their capability. Such decisions are not straightforward; while you want to protect children from injury, you also want to encourage them to be adventurous. It's better to err on the side of caution initially

- Long breaks between bouts of physical exertion. If a lengthy break is necessary, a further warm-up should be used before proceeding. Ideally, it is better to increase the physical demands gradually and equally gradually reduce them

- Allowing the noise level to rise too high such that the children cannot hear your commands. Useful strategies include clear instructions, regular reminders (not nagging) about the need for a sensible noise level and a signal on a whistle or tambourine to indicate the need for quiet

- Stopping a lesson abruptly before the children have been led through some 'warm down' activities.

Art, design and technology presents a range of challenges, not least issues relating to resources, grouping and adult supervision of children. Monitoring of activities also makes heavy demands on the teacher. If the whole class is engaged in targeted arts activities, you will need to plan well in advance of the event to ensure that there are adequate resources available and children have been taught the necessary skills to make the best use of their time. Many TAs are willing and able to assist in the organising of resources and teaching children specific skills. Parent helpers can be tremendous assets but they are unimpressed if they have been invited to participate in something that is poorly organised or asked to carry out duties that are properly the province of trained and salaried staff.

Good practice

A basic rule is that the complexity of an activity should never be greater than the educational benefit that the children gain from carrying it out.

Although it is impossible to guarantee that children will never have an accident or suffer some type of emotional trauma, it is important to take every reasonable precaution without becoming obsessive about it or creating an atmosphere of fear and uncertainty. Casualness about safety issues may result in damage to children and stress for you. For instance, you can be sure that the one time you assume that the equipment is in good order or that all the children are safely away from danger will be the one time that something unforeseen happens. Experienced teachers develop a keen sensitivity to where danger and hazards lie and take steps to minimise risks. If you are new to teaching, however, you cannot rely on such awareness, so it is important to get into the habit of thinking through in advance where things could go wrong and taking preventative action to ensure that children can get on with their learning without undue hindrance. Simple procedures such as ensuring that classroom walkways are free from bags and keeping items within easy reach, rather than children having to stretch for them, make a considerable difference both to the safety of the classroom and its smooth running.

Safeguarding children does not mean that they should be wrapped up in cotton wool like fragile ornaments. It does mean that teachers have to undertake a risk assessment about the possible consequences of their work with pupils, especially in less familiar situations such as during out-of-school activities and swimming. However, even in regular lessons there may be instances in which special care must be taken. Electrical (mains) equipment should not be used unless it has been checked by a qualified electrician and labelled safe for use. In other words you cannot bring in your own electrical equipment unless a qualified person has certified it to be safe. If children are involved in any process requiring heat or blades they should be properly trained and organised to use the equipment. Some practical lessons requiring the use of tools necessitate close adult supervision, a point to bear in mind when planning lessons, ensuring that the assistant is fully briefed.

Although accidents are rare in primary classrooms, you should be aware of the correct procedures for dealing with casualties. A course of first aid training, regularly updated, will give you the confidence you need to act promptly in the case of an emergency, though you are not normally permitted to give medicines in school or carry out procedures which require specialist expertise. Should there be an accident in a situation where you are the responsible adult, make sure that it is recorded in the 'accident book' that is often kept in a school's main office or first-aid room. If you are unsure about any aspect of safety law, check with the head teacher and refer to the school's policy and practice documentation.

Health and safety is not only concerned with physical wellbeing, as every adult also has a responsibility to be alert to children's *emotional* condition. This concern should not be confused with the crude notion that taking an interest in children's welfare makes a teacher a social worker. Education involves more than simply teaching facts. It involves helping children to understand their place in the world, the contribution that they can make to society and their responsibilities to one another. Taking time to listen to children, to understand their needs, hopes and desires should not be seen as a burden for teachers, but as a privilege (see, for example, Corrie 2003). O'Quinn and Garrison (2004) insist that 'empathy, compassion, commitment, patience, spontaneity and an ability to listen are all closely connected to the trust necessary for creating the conditions for loving relations in the classroom community' (2004: 63).

Establishing a working relationship

Establishing a working relationship with a class of children requires patient perseverance. In particular, the first few weeks with any new class are always a time of adjustment, identifying established conventions and the creation of mutual understanding. Children who are themselves new to school, are also having to make the transition from the relative security of home, playgroup or nursery to the vagaries of school life. Those who may have received exclusive attention at home have to learn to accept that they are only one amongst many other children vying for an adult's time and attention. Those who are transferring to a different class in September will have at least a year of routines and procedures behind them which will differ to some extent from those preferred by the new teacher. And in addition to these changes, a trainee teacher now joins the social mix, you.

Although this process of establishing a working relationship is rarely smooth and unhindered, awareness of the likely course that the process will take allows you to be better prepared and less likely to be thrown by the circumstances. It is helpful to think of the route to a working relationship in terms of three stages: preliminaries, courtship and partnership.

Preliminaries

It is rightly claimed that first impressions count for a lot. It is also true that appearances can be deceiving. Nevertheless, early encounters with pupils strongly influence the quality of your future relationships with them. A poor start can jeopardise the remainder of your time in school, so it pays to be diligent from the start. Even qualified teachers who change schools take time to assimilate the culture of their new school, so trainee teachers are bound to struggle in the first days or weeks of a fresh school experience as they grow accustomed to the host teachers' expectations, the class procedures and the 'unwritten laws' of conduct that only become apparent after being immersed in the daily life of the classroom for some days (see Chapter 1). Preliminary encounters with children are often very demanding owing to the need to strike a balance between establishing a rapport and ensuring that you are not overwhelmed. Although a degree of sparring is inevitable, new teachers can help themselves by taking account of the following:

- *Do not allow yourself to be bombarded with questions by pupils.* If necessary, a curt refusal to answer all but the most basic questions is needed. Otherwise, a pleasant smile and 'that is mine to know and yours to find out' or similar will usually dissuade all but the most persistent questioner

- *Do not court short-term popularity.* You may be the most exciting thing that has come into the children's lives for some time, but the novelty will quickly wear off. It is wise to ease into the new situation and gradually to become absorbed into classroom life, rather than to imagine that the initial enthusiastic welcome will be maintained

- *Do not attempt too much too soon.* It is better to build up gradually than attempt too much and struggle to cope. Some trainee teachers want to take major responsibility from an early stage, but it is generally more realistic to work alongside the class teacher for a time and gradually increase the breadth and range of your teaching. Some trainees negotiate with the class teacher to take a proportion of the lesson initially and build up expertise in that area, rather than changing from having no responsibility to all of it in one move.

On the other hand there are strategies that help to ease you through these early encounters:

- *Learning names as quickly as possible.* Discipline is so much easier if you can use children's names when addressing them. It is invariably the case that teachers learn the names of the mischievous and assertive children first, but be careful not to use their names too much and reinforce their 'rogue' status. Quieter children probably hear their names far less often, so may deserve to hear them more. Aim to associate a pupil's name with a commending comment where possible

- *Thorough lesson preparation.* Pupils soon sense any insecurity that exudes from unprepared teachers, so make sure that you have prepared in such a way that you do not need to stare at the lesson plan and, importantly, have thought through the practicalities attached to the session. The more that you are clear about what you are trying to achieve, what the children are trying to learn and how this will all take place, the more likely that they will settle and respond positively. As we noted earlier, regardless of your lesson aims, children sometimes learn things that you did not intend or expect

- *Promoting success for pupils.* Nothing facilitates a smooth passage more than when children receive genuine approval for work well done. However, it is worth remembering that children will not automatically celebrate your positive tones until they have learned to trust and respect you. It is better to slightly understate your praise initially than to be unduly exuberant.

The preliminary stage demands a lot of bridge-building between adult and pupils, who must learn to relax together as trust is slowly gained through regular interaction, resulting in better understanding through the vagaries of classroom life. Teachers have to be willing to persevere and hold their nerve through the difficult days. If you refuse to be unsettled, continue to offer interesting lessons, take a genuine interest in individuals, remain alert and maintain a good balance between listening to children's views and insisting on basic conformity to agreed behaviour, you won't go far wrong. However, achieving this state of affairs requires persistence, so don't get discouraged if things take time to fall into place. Expect some ups and downs.

Courtship

It is not possible to get to know all the pupils straight away. Some children prefer to weigh teachers up and others almost jump into their laps. Some children remain aloof because they are shy or suspicious of teachers or because they are contented with life as it is and do not want to be influenced too much by the presence of another adult. Children's coolness towards new teachers is not an indication that they hold something against them; similarly, effusive children do not necessarily like teachers. Sometimes you will find that the relationships with children that take longer to establish prove to be the most fruitful in the longer term. You must try to be even-handed with the children and give them the opportunity to speak when they want to express something and remain silent when they prefer to listen or reflect. Children do not mind a firm teacher, but they despise a gullible, domineering or weak-willed one.

As the courtship continues, boundaries between acceptable and unacceptable behaviour can be clarified. Children will test the limits to see how far they stretch. If teachers are too lenient, they may find that the boundary walls are made of elastic. On the other hand, rigidity may lead to resentment. It is important for you to explain to your pupils why things are permitted and refused, but done so as matters of fact, not as issues for negotiation. Children may not always approve of a teacher's methods but providing they are seen as fair, relationships will gradually settle and consolidate. As a guest in the classroom with a limited time in which to make an impression and learn from your experiences, it is sensible to adopt the class teacher's approach as closely as possible until you feel more confident. Subsequently, you can discuss variations in approach with the teacher and offer your own perspective. In the meantime you may have to persevere with implementing the existing policy.

Partnership

The ideal teaching and learning situation is one in which teachers and pupils are at ease with one another and respond easily and naturally, so that learning is purposeful, children are motivated and discourse is more of a conversation between adult and child, than a monologue dominated by the adult. Exactly how this state is achieved defies easy explanation but it can be recognised instantly by a visitor to the classroom because of the shared trust that exists between teachers and pupils as they work harmoniously, celebrate success and handle setbacks resolutely. In such an environment, children will have confidence to ask questions and express an opinion without being dismissed before they have had chance to finish speaking. Rules will be adhered to sensibly, though there will be opportunity to discuss their application. The work will be meaningful and, though there may be spells when the children find the work tedious, they will persevere in the sure knowledge that more exciting moments are never far away. The most striking characteristics of the partnership environment will be the sense of mutual respect, good eye contact and natural use of the voice. Both the teacher and the children will find fulfilment in their work. Listen to the enthusiasm that oozes from a trainee teacher's comments as she records her experiences on audiotape:

> Things are going really well. I'm feeling quite happy. I'm really enjoying the school experience, really enjoying the teaching and the teacher has been very, very supportive. I realise that she's been under pressure with the national tests and other things, and she's been worried that she hasn't supported me enough, but it's fine. She's leaving me to my own devices but she's there if I need to ask her any questions and I'm actually enjoying it because it's just as if they are my own class.

There are always ebbs and flows in the struggle to achieve a partnership but the effort is well worthwhile. Perseverance, a willingness to evaluate your work as a teacher and a thirst to gain advice from experienced colleagues will help you in your quest for an enduring, positive relationship with the children and the enhancement in learning that accompanies it.

Some teachers never get beyond the first two stages (preliminaries and courtship). In exceptional cases the sparring will continue for so long that the classroom climate deteriorates and the teacher resorts to harsh tactics to maintain control and coerce rather than persuade the children to conform. Such circumstances are, of course, very disappointing for those involved. Instead of being relaxed and encouraging, the teacher's relationship with the class is tense and unsatisfactory, with the result that learning is ponderous rather than joyful. The teacher feels little satisfaction with the job and goes home feeling jaded and discouraged. Partnership pays.

Activate your thinking!

Consider your responses in the following situations:

1. A 10-year-old girl keeps asking you if you are married.

2. A five-year-old boy wants you to help him all the time and jealously pushes away other children who seek your assistance.

3. An eight year-old girl sulkily tells you that you are not her 'real' teacher.

4. An 11-year-old boy angrily accuses you of being unfair when you insist that he stays in to complete a piece of work because, he claims, you did not keep in other pupils who had been naughty.

5. A 10-year-old girl spends ages producing work that is inferior in quality to that from other children in the class, yet you know that she is capable of doing better.

6. 6. A five-year-old boy produces a colourful painting in half the time allotted and begins to take his apron off.

7. An anxious eight-year-old girl constantly seeks your approval and commendation for her work.

8. An 11-year-old boy brings a page of very neat work to you that he has copied from a page on the internet.

Here are some suggestions about an appropriate way to respond to the scenarios described in the 'Activate your thinking!' box. Discuss the suggestions below with your mentor:

1. Answer the question and immediately change the subject. If the girl asks the partner's name say that he or she would not like you to reveal it to her. If she asks why, say that if ever he comes into school, she can ask him herself.

2. Discuss the situation with the other adults; explain patiently to the child that he must take turns. It is likely that the boy is insecure and hankers for exclusive attention. It may be appropriate for an assistant to spend more time with him for a period of (say) one week and monitor progress. If the behaviour persists, mention it to the parent.

3. Do not take offence. Smile and say that it is true that you are not the teacher but you are *one* of her teachers. Some children are highly protective of their teachers, so you may want to add that you are working hard to see if you can become as good as the class teacher one day.

4. The boy may be genuinely cross or trying to undermine your confidence. Do not get into an argument with him; instead, repeat that he will not go out until he has completed the work and walk away. If he mutters threats about not doing the work or telling his parents, simply write down (or pretend to) the time and date and read aloud as you write: 'Billy stayed in to finish his work today', then add (as if he had never made any threats) 'hurry up Billy, your friends are waiting for you'. When he completes the work, thank him and usher

him out for the break. You may want to consider whether keeping children in at break time is an appropriate sanction, especially if Billy is hyperactive.

5. There are many reasons for poor quality work: weak motivation; uncertainty about what has to be done; fear of failure; illness; friendship problems; laziness. It is worth finding an opportunity to speak one to one with her and explain that you are puzzled about the low standard. Ask if she has any ideas. If she refuses to respond, you may want to write down the six options mentioned above and ask the girl to put them in rank order. Conclude positively by reminding her that you are here to assist her and want her to feel free to ask her any questions. Quite often, this intimate, non-threatening conversation is sufficient to trigger improvement.

6. Younger children will often rush to conclude an activity if they think there is something better to follow it. A lot depends on the purpose of the activity; if it is to employ specific skills that the children have learned you can be gently insistent. If you gave pupils free reign to paint in any way they chose, there is little to be done. Perhaps you needed to be more specific about what you required from the children in the first place.

7. The classroom can be a scary place for trainee teachers, but also for some children, who are daunted by the constant need to interpret adult's requirements and accomplish what they want. Government publications are replete with statements about 'driving up standards' and phrases such as: 'Our children deserve the best', forgetting, perhaps, the pressure that this creates for pupils as well as teachers. Be sympathetic and clear when she is anxious about procedural matters but also offer the girl choices whenever possible, so that she gradually gains confidence in her ability to be decisive.

8. It is important to clarify for pupils the difference between information and knowledge. It is easy to access information; it is more difficult to transform it into something meaningful for the child. Commend the boy for his hard work and ask him to make up a quiz for a friend to use consisting of (say) five questions based on the information he has gleaned, two of which are factual, two of which ask for an opinion and one of which asks for an alternative or option. In this way he is forced to think about the facts and their significance.

Attitude to achievement

Picture the scene. Ben and Angie, identical twins, come out of school clutching their recently acquired swimming certificates. Ben thrusts the creased card under his mother's nose and explodes in mock glee about the 10 metres award he has recently achieved. Angie saunters up a few moments later, quietly confident about her coveted 50 metres success. How will the mother respond? Ben knows that his sister is a better swimmer but had secretly hoped that he might match her accomplishments. He had never in his seven years of life shown more determination than in his frantic efforts as he struggled through the final moments of that seemingly eternal swim. The teacher had congratulated him but Ben had shrugged it off, all too aware of his sister's sparkling success a short time before. In his mind he pictured the scene when they met their mother – Angie receiving fulsome praise for her achievements. For himself, the sincere but consoling 'You've done well, too, Ben'.

Achievement is an important aspect of life and some people obviously achieve more than others do. Children need goals as much as anyone else. It is sometimes difficult for grown-ups to remember the thrill and excitement of scoring a goal in a games lesson, winning a prize for a special painting, enjoying a glass of orange after helping the teacher with a job or having a star placed on the chart for finishing another reading book. These are the moments when children's achievements are openly and publicly acknowledged and savoured. A more difficult challenge for adults is to know how to respond to children whose achievements are limited; where success has only ever been partial and exhilaration has depended upon a surrogate basking in the reflected glow from others.

Central to this matter is the importance of the teacher's concern not solely for children's performance but for children themselves. Liston and Garrison (2004) regret recent trends in education that place more emphasis on meeting the mandates of the state than to satiate children's hunger for learning. They go on to insist that:

> Teaching and learning are activities that work best when we work through our hearts as well as our heads. Teachers have known that [fact] for a long time. It is time for the academy to allow, even invite, the emotions, and more specifically, love, into our understanding and practice of teaching. (2004: 2)

Achievements are notoriously fickle. Children who depend upon tangible evidence of their own worth can become equally unhappy when achievements remain elusive. The hero of the hour is quickly forgotten. Certificates fade and crinkle. Sparkling reports become an archive. It is the children themselves who are the only consistent factor, and their wellbeing and contentment must outlive the pleasure of achievement. To base the worth of individuals on these certificated or measurable successes while ignoring the other qualities that characterise their lives is to burden children with the need to gain ever further achievements as a means of recognition and approval. That route can be a recipe for heartache and ultimate low self-esteem as the success and the approval that accompanies it diminishes.

There is a need to get this issue in perspective. Achievement is important. It is good to do well. Some children work extremely hard and persevere to attain their goals. They rightly receive recognition and our congratulations. No, it is not the achievement that's at fault but rather our attitude to it as adults if we give children the impression that their personal worth depends upon coming out at the top of the pack. Success should not be measured solely through identifiable and visible outcomes but also in how the outcomes affect the child's character, ability to cope with life, confidence and attitude to others. The child that trails in last at the end of the race, red-faced and sweating but determined to finish, deserves every bit as much recognition as the county long-distance champion who happens to be in the same school. Both children, in their different ways, deserve praise: the winner because of her victory, the loser because of her willingness to try. Both deserve encouragement: the winner to compete for coveted prizes, the loser to take pride in her sporting attitude and gallant endeavours. And we must not forget those between the extremes. It is easy to overlook the also-ran, the average child and the steady-but-unspectacular pupil. Teachers must ensure that the genuine efforts of every child are recognised and acclaimed.

You should aim to communicate to all children, regardless of ability and aptitude, that they are precious and loved. Of course, some children are lazy and cannot be bothered to make an effort, but they still require encouragement to improve and our commitment to helping them do so, or they will never be any different. At the same time, promote the need for perseverance and use the motto: 'With my help you can!'.

Activate your thinking!

Consider these comments from children, the adult responses and the extent to which they conform to the criteria of being positive, honest and encouraging:

Child 1: I'm rubbish at this.

Teacher: Well, that's the best I've ever seen you run; I don't suppose you'll ever catch up with mile-a-minute Mandy, but even I can't run that fast.

Child 2: Sir, John only beat me 'cause he cheated.

Teacher: Well, I'm sorry if that's true, but the important thing is that you didn't give up. You kept going and didn't cheat, so well done.

Child 3: Miss, I was almost last. That's the worst I've ever run.

Teacher: Yes, I expect you feel quite disappointed. But I know that you can do better and you know that you can, so you'll just have to keep trying. What's more, you haven't made any excuses for doing badly, which proves to me that you're a good sport and makes you a winner as far as I'm concerned.

Good practice

Looking the child in the eye, regularly use affirming expressions such as:

Well done, Ben. I'm proud of you.
Top of the class, Vernon.
You should feel very pleased with yourself, Junior. I certainly am.
Champion effort Jenny. Well done.

Snippets of conversation reveal a great deal about a teacher's attitude and the adult–child relationship based on whether:

- The adult took a personal interest in each child or was merely going through the motions
- The adult's comments were positive and truthful, while still affirming genuine effort
- The child was willing to confide in the adult in the first place (a strong clue about previous adult–child encounters).

Contrast the positive teacher attitude in the 'Activate your thinking!' box with the following negative one:

Child 1: I'm rubbish at this.

Teacher: Stop moaning and get changed.

Child 2: Sir, John only beat me 'cause he cheated.

Teacher: I don't want to hear about it.

Child 3: Miss, I was almost last, that's the worst I've ever run.

Teacher: You'll just have try a bit harder next time then, won't you?

The teacher in this second set of conversations was unable to discern the deeper motives that underpinned the children's comments. Child 1 wanted to be reassured that her poor performance mattered less than genuine effort. Child 2 was upset over the unexpected reverse of fortune and needed a calm adult response to give him space to come to terms with the disappointment. Child 3 was finding failure difficult to handle and looked for confirmation that a single setback was not setting a precedent for all time. The first adult looked beyond the immediate comment to the child's real needs and responded in a sympathetic yet constructive manner, which assisted the child to come to terms with the reality of the situation without humiliation or condemnation.

A teacher's attitude to achievement influences the creation of a healthy classroom climate and helps children develop a positive attitude towards learning. Teachers who are intolerant of low-achieving or under-achieving children bring about a deterioration in self-concept and, consequently, invite even lower achievement or acute anxiety, so as teachers we have serious responsibilities and need to ensure that we:

- Take every opportunity to give praise where it is due
- Encourage children who have tried hard, even if the end product is poor relative to others in the group
- Ensure that our relationship with the children is one of respect and tolerance.

A proper attitude to achievement for all children is an important element of school life and all teachers must think carefully about where they stand on the issue. A child who struggles with academic work ('cannot do' as opposed to 'will not try') may excel in an area of life that is not represented in the curriculum. For instance Kelly (2007) cites an instance where a pupil diagnosed the problem he had with his car before he had consulted a mechanic. Being positive and encouraging should not, however, be confused with giving children a false sense of their achievements. Pupils who do not or will not try and make minimal effort should be left in no doubt about your feelings on the matter.

Encouragement and praise

A small number of people seem unable or unwilling to encourage, but prefer to criticise and look for opportunities to find fault instead. Others want to be encouraging but somehow can't find the right words. But what is encouragement and what is its place in teaching and learning?

First, encouragement isn't the same thing as praise. *Encouragement* can be given to children at any time to help them improve on their present efforts, complete a difficult piece of work or concentrate harder in order to achieve a higher standard. Teachers can use a variety of expressions to cajole, chivvy, motivate and offer support, accompanied by sparkling eye contact, clapping, smiles, open faces and close body positions. *Praise*, on the other hand, is offered for achievement: good quality work, real effort, instances of sensitivity and responsibility. Praise is usually given with great enthusiasm, openly announced.

Encouragement recognises that the present situation is acceptable but the prospect of better things awaits the child who is willing to try harder, seek advice and show determination. *Praise* recognises that the very best has been achieved in the circumstances and nothing more could reasonably be expected. Children won't accept encouragement or praise from someone they don't respect but will see it rather as a subtle form of coercion. It is better to bide your time and be gently approving rather than let loose a flood of commendation in your earliest encounters with the class. You may discover that the efforts and product that you enthused about is below the child's ability level, so it pays to be cautious in making definite judgements before you have a clear view of a child's potential and previous attainment. At all stages it is important to invite children to comment on their own work and suggest possible improvements, though you should avoid spoiling the joy of the moment by implying that their present best is not in fact good enough. Additional advice about assessing achievement can be found in Chapter 7.

Despite these caveats, it is certainly the case that both encouragement and praise can help children in at least three ways:

1. By revealing that the teacher is interested in what they are doing

2. By helping them to understand the teacher's expectations about acceptable standards

3. By opening a dialogue that will help them to consider their attainment and monitor their own progress.

This third point is important. Children must learn to evaluate the quality of their own work regularly and explicitly and gain a sense of self-satisfaction rather than to rely wholly on adult approval. Do not try to be too sophisticated about the process; a simple 'good in these ways, less good in those ways' will suffice. Although there is great emphasis on pupils establishing and monitoring their own learning targets, you should not imagine that this process circumvents the need for accurate adult assessment and feedback.

With these issues in mind, teachers need to think carefully about the forms of encouragement they use. For instance, to tell a child in a dignified monotone that they can 'do better than that' is unlikely to inspire greater effort or determination and is more likely to engender disaffection in the pupil. The unspoken message from the teacher's utterance is one of dissatisfaction and the threat of further criticism if there is no improvement. Of course, an indifferent child with a poor attitude to work needs to be carefully watched, and clear, short-term work targets set, but nine times out of ten children (who are often their own worst critics) will admit if challenged that the work is not their best. This sort of admission opens up the way for you to make specific and non-threatening suggestions about improvement while maintaining an effective level of communication with the child. When children accept that you are trying to understand them rather than looking for things to criticise, they are more likely to confide their reasons for the lower than hoped for quality of the work. Perhaps they are bored or uncertain about what's expected or finding it too difficult. Perhaps they are unhappy about their partner. A sympathetic but firm approach unlocks doors that remain tightly shut to adults who adopt a stiffer approach that carries a strong hint of disapproval and reproach. Teachers who constantly carp about how disappointed they are with results should first look at their own teaching methods and relationship with pupils.

Similarly, most children will spot insincere praise. The unthinking 'That's good' or dismissive 'Yes, fine' (without paying any real attention to what the child has done or said) is likely to lead to a general malaise as children see how little they can get away with and still receive praise from the adult. Praise has to be merited and should not be offered lightly.

Encouragement is most effective when it is used constructively, without rancour and in the context of clearly defined tasks and expectations. Praise, publicly and sincerely given, should be reserved for genuine instances of quality work and effort. For children who trust their teacher, there is no greater source of satisfaction for them and no greater incentive to continue persevering.

Equal opportunities

> In free countries, where the safety of the government depends very much upon the favourable judgement which the people may form of its conduct, an instructed and intelligent people must surely be of the highest importance.
>
> Adam Smith, 1776

> When planning, teachers should set high expectations and provide opportunities for all pupils to achieve, including boys and girls, pupils with special educational needs, pupils with disabilities, pupils from all social and cultural backgrounds, pupils of different ethnic groups including travellers, refugees and asylum seekers, and those from diverse linguistic backgrounds.
>
> *The National Curriculum* 2000: 31

It is important to understand that discrimination is not allowed in schools on any basis whatsoever. Thus, deliberate or unintentional bias towards pupils which can be construed as discriminatory leaves teachers open to charges of unprofessional conduct, so it is important to be as impartial as possible at all times when dealing with children. Not only must pupils be granted the same opportunities, support and encouragement, but it is not appropriate to label children due to circumstances beyond their control such as home background or physical appearance. A teasing pleasantry about a child's looks or domestic situation may be more hurtful and do greater damage than you imagine at the time. A useful antidote to discriminatory attitudes is to develop a positive attitude towards achievement and to adopt a 'you can do it' working atmosphere in which all children can fulfil their potential. Remember, too, that it is part of your responsibility to foster an environment in which children treat each other respectfully. Yours is the model behaviour to which they should aspire.

In addition to the statutory and moral requirements, children like teachers who exercise consistent control and are fair in their dealings with everyone in the class, so fair-mindedness also pays dividends in terms of fostering a settled learning environment. By contrast, adults who exhibit favouritism or indifference towards certain groups or individuals are resented and pupils who are so treated cannot be expected to make an effort to progress. Teachers must therefore regularly interrogate the ways in which their own attitudes towards children might affect learning. In particular, ask yourself whether your reaction, voice tone and response changes significantly when dealing with different pupils under similar conditions.

At one time, boys were steered towards the skills and subjects that would provide them with a foundation for working life; girls were expected to become homemakers and were taught accordingly. Today, teachers have to be aware that both girls and boys have an important role in the workplace and in the home and it is important to treat each child as an individual, rather than make blanket assumptions about temperament, ability and life chances based solely on gender. Teachers also have a considerable responsibility to use teaching approaches that appeal to lively children, as well as to the compliant ones.

Sometimes gender and not ability or potential appears to be the controlling factor in judging academic potential and progress (Brown 1998; Yelland 1998; Francis and Skelton 2005). However, results from national tests indicate that the position is more complex, and girls are forging ahead of boys in most areas of work, especially in language and topic work. The experience of many reception class teachers is that although most girls tend to persevere with reading, take their books home faithfully each night and seem to pick up the necessary skills and strategies with little difficulty, the picture with boys is more varied. Some boys are slower, fail to organise themselves as well as the girls and are attracted more by computer games, construction kits, practical activities and competition than by desk-bound exercises. It is also ironic that despite girls' tendency to socialise more naturally than boys, it is the independent tasks associated with reading that many girls find fulfilling. Paradoxically, the more independent image frequently attached to boys is counteracted by the unease shown by many of them with the solitary work tasks and their preference for collaborative practical work. It is the common experience of teachers that boys who display antisocial behaviour in school often struggle with the basic academic skills.

The spiral of failure now becomes clear. The boy who has experienced constant failure in reading and other aspects of English is marginalised from many of the everyday classroom activities that bring commendation and praise from teachers and peers. Because of his difficulties, he is offered increasing amounts of support in elementary skills by an adult, usually a TA, sometimes at the expense of involvement in the more attractive practical and creative tasks. This double deprivation (loss of approval for academic success, fewer exciting activities) leads in turn to frustration and resentment and a negative attitude towards school. Teachers, despairing of what to do with these recalcitrant youngsters, resort to strong control strategies or conclude that they are beyond the school's available expertise and are in need of external specialist expertise. The impact of the *Every Child Matters* agenda may assist in offering such children appropriate one-to-one coaching in areas of weakness and, perhaps, the involvement of parents and external agencies (such as social workers) but should not be seen as a simple solution to a complex problem. Pupils that present the greatest challenge to teachers have to be disciplined when necessary but also understood as to the source of their academic and relational difficulties.

Although school inspections show that girls outperform boys in almost every area of academic work, some schools and teachers seem better able to help boys achieve their potential, especially in the problem area of writing. The issue of schooling boys (Skelton 2001) has assumed a higher profile for teachers in recent years, though 'quick-fix' solutions are unhelpful (Epstein *et al.* 1998). Eaude (2006) suggests that boys find social development especially hard. Thus:

> The reasons are very complicated but because gender identity is, at least in part, socially constructed, both girls and boys experience strong pressure to conform to the gendered expectations of the family, the peer group and society. Put crudely, boys tend to be encouraged not to express their emotions, to be wary of intimacy and either to interact through emotionally 'safe' activities, such as sport, or to be less dependent on relationships; while girls interact more by developing close relationships. (2006: 46)

By using the expression 'socially constructed', Eaude and other writers mean that girls and boys behave the way that they do because we ('society') expect it, the implication being that they would behave differently if we held different expectations. Note, however, that Eaude qualifies his statement with the phrase 'in part' because recent research suggests that gendered patterns of achievement might be due to natural differences between the sexes 'as a consequence of hormonal, chromosomal or brain differences' (Francis and Skelton 2005: 75). The Francis and Skelton proposition is an interesting case in point, in that while the one author (Skelton) is willing to accept that brain structure research 'offers some potential explanation as to why there are more boys who are autistic, have special needs, or even why boys generally are less adept at literacy than girls', the other author (Francis) 'supports the view that gender is completely socially constructed' (2005: 76). The choice is yours.

Wherever the truth lies in the 'nature/nurture' debate, in schools where boys progress well there is a culture where intellectual, cultural and aesthetic accomplishment is valued by boys as well as by girls. Progress is most pronounced where positive incentives, respect and encouragement for boys to pursue their own interests; these elements also help to combat the 'laddish' anti-intellectual culture. In schools where boys perform well, they are encouraged to read widely and offered choice about the content of their writing, even when the form or genre is prescribed, and the children are encouraged to write to real audiences where possible. Frequent and formative assessment of boys' writing, with helpful feedback and guidance, enables them to take pride in the outcome. Teaching and learning is further enhanced when there are opportunities for the boys and girls to write at length ('extended writing') and tackle non-literary texts, poetry and narrative, both as readers and writers. There appears to be a clear link between the development of independent reading habits and enthusiasm for writing on the part of the teacher and the pupils.

Activate your thinking!

How can you accommodate reluctant writers into a standard lesson by allowing them the opportunity to pursue their own interests, yet still ensure that learning is well focused?

Some boys, capable of communicating effectively through speech and visual means find themselves out of favour with teachers due to their reluctance to commit ideas to paper. Wise teachers try to harness their enthusiasm, while firmly insisting that they apply themselves to recording ideas and results, though in practical subjects the children's reluctance can become a significant issue. Such pupils are often highly motivated to achieve a result, active in organising the team and apply themselves wholeheartedly in completing the task. However, at this point they find any excuse to avoid writing or due so casually. Perhaps, unwittingly, these children are conveying an important message, namely, that active forms of learning do not *always* have to be accompanied by a literacy task. As the teacher you may decide that occasionally it is better to concentrate on the practical task and allow verbal feedback to dominate or, if you are anxious that the children must have something to show for their efforts, encourage the use of diagrammatic representations.

Although expectations and role-orientation are woven into the fabric of society and are hard to disentangle, relatively small instances may reveal deeper assumptions about gender roles. For example, grouping all the girls' names beneath the boys' names on a register may simply be a method of organising, or it may reflect a belief that boys are more significant. Similarly, in the choice of team leaders, allocation of the order in which children take a turn and selection for prestige positions (in a presentation to parents, say) it is necessary to make decisions based on competence, fairness and academic priorities, not gender or assertiveness. Knowles (2006) warns that one 'lingering stereotype about boys is that they are innately clever, but unwilling to work, whereas any success that girls have is frequently put down to hard work and diligence rather than brilliance' (2006: 102). Similarly, a sweet smile from a charming girl should not result in a lesser sanction being imposed on her for a misdemeanour compared with that for an untidy boy with a permanent scowl. Knowles argues that it is easy for teachers to fall into the trap of interpreting the same behaviour differently, based on gender. She offers the example of a misbehaving girl being described as 'a bad influence' or 'spiteful little madam', while the boy is simply described as 'mucking about' (ibid.).

Although impartial decisions are needed as far as possible when dealing with children, male and female, this fact should not be confused with a need to take account of individual differences in children. Children respond differently to situations and circumstances and adults must be prepared to adjust their responses and actions accordingly. However, this axiom results in a dilemma. On the one hand it is necessary for teachers to be consistent in their treatment of children. On the other hand one child will respond to a lighter 'touch' than another child. Teachers are not judges in a court of law handing down sentences regardless of whoever stands before them. They must exercise wisdom in the way that they approach all interpersonal encounters. Nevertheless, the need for discernment is far removed from a blanket stereotyping of children on the basis of gender or any other defining characteristic (such as background, sportiness or even physical height). The key is to treat every case on merit and use a large dose of common sense in making decisions. One of the key skills that you must develop is to evaluate a situation rapidly and make a response that is not only fair but also seen to be fair by the children. You will sometimes get it wrong.

Although the majority of concerns about equal opportunities have focused on gender issues, there are studies that suggest that stereotyping may be associated with pupil personality. Teachers can develop expectations about achievement (and behaviour) that are related to their perceptions of pupils' apparent willingness to learn rather than a child's true capability. Thus, the child with a bright personality who volunteers to do tasks and errands, and who is comfortable chatting with the teacher, may or may not be a capable, committed learner. On the other hand, the shy, passive children can be perceived as less capable than they really are. This description is, of course, also in danger of becoming stereotypical. Some articulate children with a bright personality are also clever. Some under-confident, diffident types are strugglers (which is part of the explanation for their timidity).

Our awareness of these interwoven factors suggests that it is foolish for teachers to jump to conclusions about their pupils' ability and potential. The outgoing child may, despite an apparently carefree approach to life, be concealing a deep unease that leads to underachievement. The shy child may be lacking self-confidence or may be an uncomplicated and contented person who does not feel the need to be assertive. As a newcomer it is sensible to observe carefully and get to know the children before making a judgement. As a rule and without being naïve, it is good to assume the best and not the worst about a child.

To further complicate matters, the outgoing non-academic children are sometimes skilled in 'losing' themselves in a group of more capable children and benefiting from the reflected glory of their expertise and talent. Against this, the less confident children may lose out in two ways. First, they are unable to articulate their needs, and second, they lack the social and communication skills to find suitable collaborators. Such children often end up being paired with unsuitable individuals who are the remnant after more popular children have been absorbed into the more stable groups or chosen first for teams and collaborative groups. If teachers are to avoid the pre-disposition that may exist that denies children their rights as learners, they must step back from making spontaneous decisions and look objectively at the evidence from outcomes, such as completed work, comments made during question-and-answer sessions, and engagement with tasks.

In every class, therefore, there are children – girls and boys – with varied personalities, talents, ideals and potential. Teachers have a responsibility towards all of them and need to employ different teaching strategies to:

- Ensure that passive children are given as many (though not necessarily any more) interesting tasks as their assertive peers

- Allow children who do not find it easy to learn in traditional ways to have opportunity to experience different forms of learning

- Make allowance for ebullient behaviour born out of enthusiasm for the task in hand rather than mischievousness

- View basic skills, such as reading, as a socially welding activity through group work and collaborative strategies.

It is essential to avoid situations in which a compliant group of passive children (more often girls) are given repetitive tasks while a few very assertive children (often boys) are kept occupied with the exciting practical activities with which they are most content as a means of keeping them content and better behaved. Teachers have to learn to strike a balance between accommodating children's natural preferences and pandering to their stubbornness or unwillingness to toe the line by allowing them excessive opportunities to enjoy favoured options. The best teachers are clear about what they expect and how much flexibility and negotiation they are willing to countenance. Heavy-handedness results in resentment; too much accommodation leads to pressure from pupils for increasing concessions. Beware!

Teachers should also be aware of how many left-handed children are in the class and how to help them, including the provision of softer-leaded pencils, left-handed scissors, a left-handed ruler, an ergonomic left-handed mouse or a mouse set up for left-handers and a sloping board beneath paper to assist correct writing and drawing. There is no proof that left-handed people differ from right-handers in terms of educational attainment or IQ and various organisations exist to assist children and teachers, including a club for children. You are advised to watch out for children who sit 'side on' as this may indicate that one eye is weaker than the other, or that the child has a particular spatial preference. Left-handed children tend to write 'into' their bodies and may develop an awkward posture.

A teacher's assumptions about children's ability to learn and make progress may have a direct influence upon their attitude to school in general, their willingness to co-operate and persevere, and ultimately their achievements. Attention to equal opportunities yields unexpected rewards.

Activate your thinking!

- Do you pay undue attention to the more articulate and outgoing children?
- Do you make unwarranted assumptions about certain groups of children without evidence?
- Do you have a prevailing view of boys as naughty, girls as biddable?

Good practice

Although the practice of adjusting the curriculum and teaching approach to 'match' the child's needs is contestable and in many ways, unrealistic, it is nevertheless worthy of attention.

Teaching children with special educational needs

There have always been and always will be some children who struggle with certain aspects of school work or suffer from some condition which prevents them from fulfilling their potential (see, for instance, Heeks and Kinwell 1997). Arthur, Grainger and Wray (2006) remind us that 'teaching in a primary school is a self-giving enterprise concerned with the betterment of [all] pupils' (2006: 3). When considering how best to teach and support learning it is helpful to distinguish between children with special needs and those with special *educational* needs (SEN). The terminology is quite confusing: sometimes under-achievers are referred to as 'slow learners' or pupils with 'special learning needs'. The term 'disability' is most often used to denote that the child suffers from a physical impairment, but it is also used in conjunction with the word 'learning'; thus, learning disability. The term 'handicapped' is now more often employed to indicate that the circumstances are hindering pupils from reaching their potential. Most often the handicap is resource-based and pupils cannot achieve things of which they are capable because equipment is not available or damaged or inappropriate for use. However, the handicap can also be a lack of time, poor working conditions (such as a stuffy room) or poor teaching. Consequently, children may have physical disabilities that do not, with appropriate support, handicap their educational opportunities or advancement, while some children have congenital problems that impact strongly on their capacity to learn. The remainder of this section is concerned with children who are falling behind in their academic work for a variety of different reasons, and who may or may not suffer from a medically diagnosed disability.

Pupils labelled as 'less able' tend to fall into one of four categories, though more than one of the factors below may be relevant:

- Children who do not possess the intellectual capacity to keep pace with the majority of children

- Children who are of such a high intellect that they find it difficult to fit in to the familiar learning structures and may be unsettled in class

- Children who are capable of average to high achievement but under-achieve due to their erratic or uncontrolled behaviour. Such children are often referred to as emotionally disturbed or having behavioural difficulties. More recently, the term 'attention deficit and hyperactivity disorder' (ADHD) is employed when referring to children who struggle to concentrate, though its broad definition makes it problematic (see also Chapter 8)

- Children who, though intellectually capable, possess physical disabilities that tend to hinder their ability to attain to full potential.

Effective learning and teaching should ensure every child succeeds by providing an inclusive education (see Chapter 9) within a culture of expectations and build on what learners already know by structuring and pacing teaching so that pupils know what is to be learnt, how and why. Teachers are encouraged to make learning vivid and real by developing understanding through enquiry, creativity, e-learning and group problem solving. Learning can be made more enjoyable and challenging if you respond a range of preferred learning styles (e.g. pupils who learn more effectively through use of visual stimuli or by practical 'hands-on/kinaesthetic' application; see Chapters 4 and 5 for further information) in your teaching techniques and strategies. You can enhance the richness of the experience by making links across the curriculum and inviting children to be partners with you in their learning by clarifying the task purpose, inviting their comments, taking their views seriously and providing specific and constructive feedback.

However, Claxton (2004) alerts us to the danger of taking learning styles too seriously as a rigid attitude can be to the pupil's detriment. Thus:

> The idea that we can find out someone's general-purpose 'learning style' is debunked, and the idea that having done so, we then have to treat it as immutable and teach them as if they were always and everywhere a 'visual learner' or had 'a high level of logical-mathematical intelligence' is not only false but pernicious. It locks [pupils] into a view of themselves, rather than encouraging them to grow. (2004: 9)

The Code of Practice (DfES 2002) is a document with which every teacher should be familiar. An equivalent Code operates in Wales but not in Scotland, which has different procedures. It contains detailed information about the identification of children with SEN and suggestions for appropriate action. It is designed as a positive way of responding to the individual needs of children by means of a systematic process that draws upon expertise from inside and outside the school, and places great emphasis upon parental involvement (see Figure 2.1). Children with SEN have a strong right to be educated at a mainstream school and the local authority (LA in England) has to arrange for parents of children with SEN to be provided with relevant advice and information, together with a means of resolving disputes. Schools and nursery education providers have to inform parents when they are making special educational provision for their children, and can request a statutory assessment for a child who is causing concern. It is fair to say that even with the new synergy between schools and other services the assessment procedures are lengthy and cumbersome. You may hear teachers complaining that more urgent action is required on behalf of a particular child with SEN but an interim measure will sometimes rely on the allocation of a TA for part of the time to support the 'personalised' curriculum.

Every maintained school must have a member of staff who acts as a SENCO and a responsible person (usually the head teacher or a governor) who acts as a point of reference for the process. A school governing body has a sub-committee to take a particular interest in such educational provision; it is obliged to report to parents about policies for children with SEN and their implementation.

The Code recommends that in order to help match education provision to children's needs, schools and LAs should adopt a graduated approach through the two-stage process of *School Action* (when matters are handled internally) and *School Action Plus* (when outside agencies are involved). The same advice pertains to the early years' process, namely, *Early Years Action* and *Early Years Action Plus*. The stages of the Code of Practice within 'School Action' and 'School Action Plus' are not necessarily sequential. A child can enter the process at different points, depending upon his or her circumstances. While all this is going on, class teachers have to do their best to cope with the children in question. The interim period of time can be stressful as events often move more slowly than expected. Long delays prove exasperating for over-stretched teachers as they struggle to help children who may, in certain cases, also suffer from hyperactivity or attention disorders with the accompanying discipline challenges they bring. All this takes place against a backdrop of government demands for higher standards of achievement in core subjects for every child, including those with SEN.

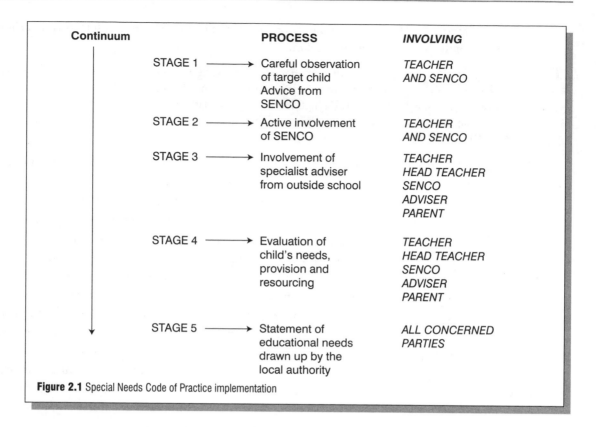

Figure 2.1 Special Needs Code of Practice implementation

Future provision for children with SEN emphasises *preventative* rather than remedial action and promotes effective school-based support and monitoring. Key principles for provision need to take account of the following:

- Having high but realistic expectations for all pupils

- Greater support for parents through information, advice about learning at home and liaison with outside agencies (such as educational psychologists)

- Further inclusion of pupils in mainstream schools by providing appropriate resources, including staffing

- Close liaison between schools and the support agencies, ensuring that parents are informed at all times except in cases where child abuse may be involved.

All teachers, including trainees, have to work hard to ensure that all children, regardless of status and previous history are given the opportunity to learn, enjoy school and make best use of their educational opportunities. The increase in TAs to support children with SEN now involves teachers in more sophisticated patterns of classroom management and organisation as they take account of the additional adult help and a wider ability range of pupils (Fox 1998; Jacklin *et al.* 2006: 99–103). The greatest challenges for teachers come from pupils whose educational problems are rooted in their emotional instability and antisocial behaviour. If you find yourself situated with a class of children that includes a high proportion of pupils with learning or behavioural challenges it is essential that you regularly seek advice and support from the regular staff. Don't struggle on nobly in the mistaken belief that you have to perform miracles: leave those for the saints. See Chapter 9 for fuller details about issues relating to inclusion and special educational needs.

Teaching minority ethnic children

In recent years there has been a large influx of immigrants from the EU and Commonwealth countries, together with asylum seekers from many different places in the world. Their arrival has strengthened the diversity of cultures, knowledge and expertise in the country but also created some serious challenges for the communities in which they are located. Particular pressures have fallen upon the education system (and social services) as children arrive in school with little understanding of the indigenous norms and, in most cases, with English as an additional language (EAL). Once in school, children quickly pick up the language but their parents – especially mothers – may only speak their first language and struggle to adjust. In practice, there are issues about contacting parents, providing information and other forms of communication that tax teachers' ingenuity and test their resolve. There is a considerable amount of advice for school staffs from different groups with an interest in the welfare of immigrants but it is far from easy to generalise, as each class contains such an exclusive and particular range of pupil needs. Sometimes only one child from a particular country of origin will be in the class and receive individual attention; sometimes a number of pupils of similar origin will be in the class but vary in their grasp of English; again, there will sometimes be a large proportion of pupils speaking the same language, allowing for the formation of groups to receive targeted teaching or coaching in reading and writing. Perhaps the greatest challenge for a new teacher is to co-ordinate the many activities and adults involved in the special educational provision.

One of the major issues concerns the variation in achievement across ethnic minority groups. The following characteristics are amongst those identified as significant for helping to improve the educational attainment of minority ethnic pupils:

- Having an agreed strategy that applies across the whole school
- Effective learning and teaching, especially for bilingual pupils
- Promoting an ethos of mutual respect and tolerance.

National surveys reveal a complex picture of minority ethnic attainment and participation, suggesting that the involvement of parents and the community in the life and development of the school is highly significant. Generally, it appears that Black, Bangladeshi and Pakistani pupils perform less well than other ethnic groups during the period of compulsory schooling. By contrast, Indian and Chinese pupils perform better than other ethnic groups. Proportionately more Black, Pakistani and Bangladeshi pupils are recorded as having special educational needs, though there are notable exceptions in individual schools.

Explanations about the reasons for underachievement of certain minority groups are partly explained by the social and material deprivation that characterises those groups, as indicated by the incidence of free school meals. For instance, about one third of Pakistani and Black pupils, and over half of all Bangladeshi, Gypsy/Roma pupils are eligible for free school meals, compared with under 15 per cent for White pupils. However, there isn't a simple relationship between these figures and academic achievement, as the biggest gap in attainment is between White pupils with, and White pupils without free school meals. Clearly, then, there are other factors that need to be taken into account when addressing issues of under-performance.

It is one thing to be aware of the trends noted above, it is quite another to have strategies for improving the situation. The most successful schools in raising ethnic minority attainment have high expectations of staff and pupils, and ensure that they initiate and maintain close links with parents. Every teacher and trainee should be asking a number of important questions about their teaching approach and attitude towards all pupils, including:

- Are all children achieving their potential and gaining individual benefit from their education? As a visitor to the classroom, trainees are in a good position to see the situation with fresh eyes and, perhaps, offer insights that will help the regular teacher

- If some children appear to be underachieving, what factors seem to be contributing to this state of affairs? You may be able to modify classroom practices that are contributing to this state of affairs, though do not assume that you have all the answers or you will be perceived as arrogant

- Are some children underachieving because of lack of access to curriculum opportunities? This is one of the more straightforward areas of difficulty to address, as a simple process of recording which child does what activity quickly reveals injustices

- What steps can/should be taken to address the unsatisfactory situation? Regular monitoring and assessment of children's progress will assist in identifying specific problems being experienced by children and begin to remedy them. However, pupils may be academically capable but socially immature or unhappy

- Would some identifiable groups of children benefit from exclusive attention from an adult or a modified curriculum? This question is one for senior staff to answer but it may be that a trainee is asked to offer such exclusive attention to a child. If this useful experience happens to you make sure that you don't find yourself playing the role of assistant for too long.

Gardner (2006) summarises ways to improve the quality of learning for all children, including children for whom English is an additional language. Thus, they should 'encounter an element of problem solving if their learning is to be effective. They need to be able to build on prior knowledge, not to be overloaded in terms of the number of objectives for any one lesson, be able to interact with others and be given time to complete tasks' (2006: 78). Gardner goes on to suggest that using puppets, verbal games involving pairs of children, role play, and rhyme and story, and visual tactile resources are strategies likely to enhance learning and create a language-rich environment.

The application of an agreed school policy to combat racism and unfair behaviour can only be effective if adults in school examine their own attitudes. Every teacher must be honest in confronting covert beliefs about the breadth of issues embraced by inclusive education and address areas of prejudice. This process is a testing one and sometimes uncomfortable, but unless you are willing to face up to your own disposition, it is difficult for you to make a positive difference to the situation and influence others.

As a new teacher you need to be aware of any circumstance in which you may unwittingly show prejudicial attitudes. For example, children may be highly competent in their own language but struggle when expected to use English. It is possible to lower your expectations of the children and assume that they are far less capable than in fact they really are. While it may be tempting to allocate a child with limited English easy tasks to allow for his or her language deficit, it is important to limit the length of time that this happens, for two reasons. First, the child may become the butt of teasing from classmates owing to the simple nature of the tasks. Second, the child quickly becomes under-stimulated and disillusioned with the undemanding work. The strategies you employ to ensure that the child is given appropriate tasks depend upon the extent of the adult language support available and the age of the child. Young children benefit from plenty of play activity, where they can immerse themselves in their imaginations, interact naturally with children their own age and become absorbed into the fabric of class life. Older children may struggle to orientate because they are more acutely aware of their language limitations and may not pick up a second language as easily as their younger brothers and sisters. A variety of approaches are commonly used to promote practice that is rooted in positive and high-expectation practice. Thus:

- Taking account of children's special needs in literacy sessions by implementing individual education plans (IEPs; see Chapter 9) and utilising opportunities to develop language across the curriculum

- Promoting respect and understanding of diverse cultures, languages, ethnic groups, faith groups, travellers, asylum seekers and refugees in regular interaction with the class and the interest taken in (for example) cultural diversity and special occasions

- Working with parents from different community groups, both informally (e.g. as a classroom helper) and during planned events

- Ensuring that display work reflects the diversity in ethnicity

- Discussing issues relating to prejudice with the children, being careful not to unintentionally excite prejudice as you do so or merely load them with lists of things they should and should not do.

One of the keys to successfully integrating all new children into the classroom is to assess their academic competence as accurately and swiftly as possible. In her work as a teacher of younger children, Heyda (2002) describes the strategies she employs when dealing with the arrival of new children in the class who speak little or no English:

- Welcome the child with a big smile and a warm friendly voice

- Assign a 'buddy', preferably someone who speaks the language, to accompany the child throughout the day

- Take care not to use 'baby talk' that might embarrass the child or speak too loudly as if the child has a hearing impairment

- Utilise support staff at an early stage

- Be encouraging and positive

- Use the child's mistakes as starting points for progress

- Use lots of visual aids to get across concepts, such as drawing pictures next to vocabulary and using photographs and diagrams to explain things

- Give the child plenty of hands-on experiences

- Label the room with key words.

Heyda's sound advice applies in many respects to work with children generally. In a multi-lingual situation in which there are numerous children who speak the same first language, the challenges of incorporating a newcomer into the class are usually less severe than if the child is the only pupil who speaks the language. In such circumstances the school is likely to have additional adult support for EAL, though the proliferation of different languages in the school and the involvement of various language assistants present formidable organisation and management issues.

Children for whom English is an additional (often a second) language should, ideally, be assessed by an adult who speaks the same tongue and can thereby give a better-informed picture of their abilities. If such a person is not available, the process will obviously take longer and involvement of a bilingual child is the next best option. In the absence of adult or child to act as interpreter, parental or family help may be called upon, as it is likely that at least one person has a sufficient grasp of English to explain the new child's needs, strengths and limitations.

The Commission for Racial Equality website (www.cre.gov.uk/pubs) contains a useful, though extremely detailed set of guidelines for schools in the form of two audits to monitor whether the curriculum, teaching and assessment and pupils' personal development, attainment and progress are sensitive to ethnic diversity and cultural factors. The curriculum audit contains 14 statements for the staff and governors of schools to consider whether they are fully, mostly, partially met, or not met at all. As a teacher in training or a new teacher you will not be responsible for decisions concerning the audits, but they provide a useful reminder of the principles of fairness and justice that should underpin the work of every teacher in all schools. The curriculum audit contains a range of useful key words and phrases to help teachers understand better their planning, teaching and assessment of pupils' progress. Thus, paraphrasing some key expressions:

- 'Needs of all pupils'

- 'Appropriate curriculum'

- 'Fair and equitable'

- 'Assessment methods are checked'

- 'Assessment outcomes identify needs and inform'
- 'Teaching takes account of needs'
- 'Teaching encourages positive attitudes'
- 'The curriculum draws on areas of interest'
- 'Diversity is promoted'
- 'Resources are inclusive'.

Similarly, from the personal development audit, the emphasis on caring for and valuing individuals so that they can make the best use of their educational experiences provides a model that has applicability for all teaching situations. With the constraints of the NC programmes of study and the use of literacy and numeracy strategies in schools, it is far from easy for teachers to respond to all of the expectations made of them by special interest groups, however laudable their motives. However, the essence of helping all children to achieve their potential, respect and care for each child and the promotion of a secure and relevant learning environment is something to which every teacher can and should aspire.

Activate your thinking!

The following extract is a modified version of a more extensive one offered by Watkinson (2003a: 33). Examine the list and respond to the questions: (1) on the basis of what you have seen in school; and (2) on the basis of what you would like to see in school:

- What books are available in the school to show different cultures and ways of life?
- Are there books that show people with disabilities as heroes?
- What resources in terms of musical instruments, fabrics, pictures or artefacts does the school possess?
- Where does the recorded music that is played during assembly originate?
- What sort of artwork is displayed on the walls?
- What relationships does the school have with the local community, voluntary organisations, churches and other places of worship?

Good practice

Go to the CRE website and follow the trail: Publications/Good practice/Sectors/ Education/Learning for all/audit form (look for hyperlink)/'curriculum teaching and assessment' and also 'pupils'. Take special note of: (a) item 7 under C, T & A; and (b) item 5 under Pupils.

Being a child in your class

What will it be like to be a child in your classroom: a delight, a misery, an endurance test, a laugh, a puzzle? Much depends upon whether you see the pupils as the enemy to be subdued or a group of inexperienced youngsters with whom you will need to develop a working relationship to ensure that they gain the most benefit from their schooling. To help you decide what it is like for pupils in your class, consider the following questions:

- *Which children do you get to know first?*
  Is this because you are working closely with them or because they are the noisiest or the tallest or the prettiest?

- *Do you tend to ignore some children?*
  Perhaps because they are shy or you feel uncomfortable with them?

- *What kind of behaviour upsets you most?*
  Is this because you don't know how to handle it or because it affronts your dignity?

- *How interested are you in children's opinions?*
  Do you really care or do you go through the motions of appearing interested?

- *How much do you want children to like you?*
  Will you be too soft, try too hard to be nice or perhaps be too fierce and unreasonable? Cullingford (1997a) suggests that successful teachers 'will be fair and consistent, will praise more than blame, will be clear and patient, will ask questions and listen, rather than shout and present repetitive exercises' (1997a: 113). Wyse (2001) recommends the acronym REG, where the R stands for Respect, E for Empathy and G for Genuineness. Thus; 'Respect can come from your positive attitude to children … Empathy is about really trying to understand how the child is feeling and appreciating their point of view … Genuineness is about being honest with the child …' (2001: 9).

In the light of these points, it is worth thinking about the children you know in your class or groups and how you relate to them:

- The children who show the greatest self-confidence
- The children who are ill at ease and in what contexts
- The children who co-operate
- The children who gain most of your approval
- The children who seem to have a bright future in school
- The children who seem to have the odds stacked against them.

And most significantly, what your answers reveal about you as teacher. Remember that children like teachers who are firm but fair, willing to explain things patiently and have a positive attitude to work and people. They are ill at ease with adults who hector, complain, agitate and fulminate.

Making progress as a trainee teacher

Fitting in

Every successful teacher has established routines, procedures and patterns of interaction with pupils that contribute to what may be described as a 'classroom rhythm' and do not take kindly if this hard-earned efficiency is disrupted by a well-meaning trainee (or anyone else). Classroom rhythms are developed through successfully creating a positive learning environment, convincing the children that it is in their best interests to co-operate in maintaining the ethos and providing a thirst for knowledge that gains a life of its own. Class teachers need to establish their priorities or pupils will attempt to do it for them, leading to disharmony and unnecessary tension as the children vie for influence. Although school policies are useful in broadly establishing the way things happen in a particular classroom, final decisions about day-to-day interactions and routines still belong to the individual teacher.

Trainee teachers are obliged to adopt the supervising teacher's general approach to routine and procedural matters, regardless of whether they agree with the philosophy underlying them. If you are operating on someone else's 'territory' you will soon discover that it is far from easy to implement someone else's decisions and remain true to your own beliefs. Nevertheless, that is precisely what you must endeavour to do. It is helpful if teachers are able to explain to trainees the rationale for decisions rather than merely expecting unthinking compliance. Any changes that a trainee teacher wishes to make should be discussed with the teacher first and introduced gradually. Children quickly become alert to any inconsistencies they detect between their regular teacher and the newcomer and may react adversely, usually to the trainee teacher's cost. Sometimes your (apparently) obvious improvement or solution to a problem has already been tried by the resident teacher and found to be unsuitable. You can console yourself with the thought that when you have a class of your own you will be in a position to implement some of the things that were denied to you while in training. You will discover how difficult it is to relinquish control when you are qualified and have to host a trainee teacher.

An essential quality for the development of a successful teaching and learning environment is the ability to organise and manage classroom affairs (see Chapter 6). All teachers want to maintain an orderly environment to facilitate progress but order should not be confused with rigidity or passivity for, as Desforges (1995) points out, 'Parade grounds are often associated with firm discipline, clear control and immaculate performances' (1995: 183) but that graveyards are also orderly places. Neither venue, however, is noteworthy for the quality of the learning that takes place there. It is possible to be efficient without being effective.

At certain times of the year, carefully organised lesson structures are disrupted by events such as a block of the timetable allocated to swimming, play rehearsals, music practices, fire drills and educational visits. Although it is not possible to anticipate every eventuality, an awareness of wider school happenings is essential. Fitting in to your new school is smoother when you take account of these and the other issues noted above.

Professional learning

All teachers need to think carefully about their practice, seek advice from more experienced practitioners and try to keep abreast of research findings that provide insights into effective teaching and learning. This process is commonly referred to as 'professional learning' and trainee teachers are normally required by their colleges to maintain a written record of their progress across the weeks of school placement as evidence of their development. This type of review should not be confused with providing evidence to show that formal teaching standards have been met. The reviews are intended to be reflective commentaries on school experience to demonstrate an ability to analyse situations constructively as a means of adjusting practice for the benefit of the children you currently teach and those that you will teach in future classroom situations. The best commentaries combine an awareness of immediate requirements with general principles of practice. One trainee, Helena, wrote at length about the first two weeks of her placement, including the following extracts:

Week One

I found week one fairly challenging because of discipline problems. The class has a number of lower ability children and one child with special educational needs who is on medication to help control his behaviour. My previous experiences in school had not prepared me to deal with anyone like him. However, by observing the strategies used by the class teacher and spending time in a one-to-one situation with the child, I began to feel more confident. I have already begun to change my previous ideas on discipline, as I realise that shouting and constant telling-off is not the best option. Discussion with the class teacher helped me to begin to work out the most effective strategies to use with the class. I am also struggling with managing my time. I have spent every night over the past week preparing literacy and numeracy lessons, leaving me quite jaded. After talking to the teacher and tutor, they convinced me that the pressure would grow easier as I get into the swing of things. I can hardly wait! I have identified three target areas next week: (a) improving my time management for lesson planning, (b) developing my discipline strategies, (c) observing how the teacher copes with troublesome children. I also want to teach part of a PE lesson and have a go at organising practical science.

Week Two

This week was much busier than the last one. I spent more than a third of the time teaching literacy and numeracy and learned a lot from the experience. Each lesson flew past and what felt like ten minutes was in fact half-an-hour and work that I thought would be completed was not. The class teacher assured me that this was a common problem. During Friday's literacy hour I did not check the finishing time and had to rush to assembly. In future I must not make assumptions about times. Each morning I take registration. Although this seems a simple task I found it quite difficult. I had to take the lunch time register and add up all of the totals in front of the children at the same time as keeping good order. It made me feel quite insecure with all the eyes looking up at me from the carpet, with the whispering getting louder! During sessions that I taught, the children were less attentive than with the class teacher and I was shocked when some of them back-chatted when I told them what to do. However, I used some of the class teacher's strategies and found that the situation improved slowly. For instance, I separated children if they were noisy together, wrote the names of persistent offenders on the board and made children stay in at break time if they did not respond and concentrate on their work. When I first dismissed the class there was a rush for the door and general pandemonium, so I became much stricter, stood by the door and dismissed them row by row, which improved the situation enormously. I have also come to appreciate the importance of getting resources absolutely ready. I forgot to put spellings examples in order for Thursday's lesson and so produced the difficult words first, which meant that the less able children struggled and became frustrated. Next time I made sure I started with the easiest ones! I have found that annotating my present lesson plans, thinking positively about failures instead of getting miserable, and modifying my plans so that they took more account of children's needs is starting to have an effect on the quality of my teaching. It is all taking time and, unlike the impressive lists we are given in the documentation from college, nothing is straightforward!

Helena did not continue to write at such length. However, she started as she meant to go on by taking time to evaluate her progress, gain advice from the class teacher and tutor, and amend her approach on the basis of what she had observed and learned. After the first two weeks Helena began to summarise points, note critical incidents, refer to key decisions and give an indication of the action that she was taking to remedy weaker areas and further strengthen weaker ones. Nonetheless, she was careful not to spend too much time being introspective and certainly did not allow herself to mope.

The community of practice

It used to be said that if teachers weren't exhausted by four o'clock and on their way home by a quarter past, they hadn't been doing their job properly. Today, with the many different demands upon a teacher's time, most teachers consider themselves fortunate to leave before five, having worked throughout the day with little or no break. After-school and lunchtime clubs and activities are commonplace and almost every teacher has a curriculum or related responsibility. In small schools each teacher may have oversight of more than one curriculum area. Paperwork has increased considerably, and the emphasis on assessment for learning has required that ever more detailed records are becoming the norm. Accountability to parents and the local community has become a key focus as funding increasingly depends upon numbers of children in school and the traditional safety net of the old local education authority has been replaced in many schools by managerial (though not curriculum) autonomy. In short, at one time the local authority 'carried the can'; now it is shared with head teachers and governors.

We may agree that children need to feel secure in school but forget that adults, too, need to be comfortable if they are to achieve peak effectiveness in their work. Teaching has always been a demanding and sometimes exhausting job but in the recent whirl of national legislation its demands have increased. Many teachers complain that they have been scrutinised more closely than any other profession and expected to cope with an unreasonable rate of imposed change (Cockburn, 1996; Woods, 1997). As Day *et al.* (2007) sadly describe, 'After a decade of relentless reform in a climate of shaming and blaming teachers for perpetuating poor standards, the attractiveness of teaching as a profession has faded fast among potential new recruits' (2007: xi). However, it is important to note that all jobs involve some stresses and strains, especially those that involve close contact with people, but teaching seems to stand alone in its potential for exhaustion and, paradoxically, for rich reward. One of the reasons for this tension between benefits and losses is the extent to which teachers consider themselves to be responsible for children's learning and personal growth. Teachers' self-identity is partly rooted in their classroom competence, so any perceived failures (real or spurious) on their part can leave them feeling demoralised. In addition, the external imposition of targets has done little to relieve the belief in the profession that teachers are losing their autonomy. The whirlwind of initiatives from Government has left some teachers feeling breathless and guilty that they are unable to keep abreast of all the changes. Opportunities to 'stop and stare' are few and must be treasured. Even so, without creating these havens of stillness, teachers burn out and lose their sharpness.

Another danger for teachers is that they can grow cynical as they struggle to accommodate the many new requirements into their busy schedules of planning, teaching, assessing, marking, recording and filling reports. The intensity of teaching can easily lead to over-commitment and increased vulnerability (Cox and Heames 1999; Bubb and Earley 2004). In the midst of this, a school's prime resource – reflective and enthusiastic teachers – must be safeguarded and *self-management* is crucially important in this regard (Thody and Bowden 2004). The situation for trainee teachers is particularly acute. As noted earlier, they have little control over where they are placed and enter a school that is largely unknown to them in respect of its ethos, personalities and patterns of behaviour. Trainees have to cope with the effort required to adjust to the prevailing expectations, establish and maintain relationships with staff, learn procedures and adapt to the school's priorities, some of which may be abstruse and difficult to interpret. In addition, as Maynard (2001) describes, trainee teachers have to adopt to the class teacher's practices and priorities. Even if they quickly orientate, it takes time before they become fully aware of the reasons underpinning the teacher's actions. Thus:

> It was through acting like a teacher, initially through becoming someone else, that students [trainees] began to develop an identity as a teacher. In addition, trainee teachers appropriated their teachers' discourse, even though they did not appear to be aware of doing so, nor initially share the same conceptual understandings as their teachers. The use of this discourse enabled trainee teachers to gain acceptance into the community of practice, the approval of their class teacher, the means by which they could negotiate richer and more appropriate understandings. (2001: 49)

Medwell (2007) suggests that acting like a teacher is part of the contract between a trainee and the placement school. She offers two reasons for children respecting a teacher. Primarily, 'because teachers act like teachers, sending out subtle signals that indicate they know what they are doing, have authority and expect children to behave well' (2007: 110). Medwell then provides some 15 strategies to assist the process of 'acting like a teacher', including knowing the children by name as quickly as possible, dressing suitably, moving confidently about the room and sounding confident, having an appropriate signal for gaining pupils' attention and, crucially, knowing the systems and procedures that operate in the particular setting. However, Medwell also alerts us to the sorts of pitfalls awaiting the unwary trainee teacher (indeed, *any* teacher) including inappropriate tasks, poor explanations, dilly-dallying, using inducements to gain popularity and imploring rather than insisting. Notably, the author warns against over-praising, ignoring bad behaviour, using sarcasm, acting inconsistently and failing to employ your personality to full effect (for the complete list, see Medwell 2007: 111–12).

If you want to enter fully into this community of practice you have to make rapid adjustments and learn the unwritten rules that are taken for granted by the staff in the school. You may not fully grasp the reasons for teachers' actions and priorities but be assured that understanding will develop as you become absorbed into the school community. You will also become aware that subtle differences of approach and emphasis exist within a staff that is apparently wholly united and agreed.

Emotional adjustment

The significance of emotions in the work and motivation of teachers has long been recognised. The concept of *Emotional Intelligence* draws from the work on multiple intelligences by Howard Gardner. The author suggests that the traditional notion of intelligence, based on IQ testing, is far too limiting. Instead, he proposed seven, and later nine different intelligences to account for the range of human potential (see Figure 2.2). Gardner defined the first seven intelligences in his book *Frames of Mind* (1983) and added the last two in *Intelligence Reframed* (1999). He claims that all human beings have multiple intelligences. These multiple intelligences can be nurtured and strengthened, or ignored and weakened.

Descriptions of the intelligences vary slightly in the literature but the following is based on the original texts (with a shorthand description in brackets):

Verbal-linguistic intelligence ('word smart'):
well-developed verbal skills and sensitivity to the sounds, meanings and rhythms of words

Mathematical-logical intelligence ('number/reasoning smart'):
an ability to think conceptually and abstractly, and capacity to discern logical or numerical patterns

Musical intelligence ('music smart'):
an ability to produce and appreciate rhythm, pitch and timbre

Visual-spatial intelligence ('picture smart'):
a capacity to think in images and pictures, to visualise accurately and abstractly

Bodily-kinesthetic intelligence ('body smart'):
an ability to control one's body movements and to handle objects skilfully

Interpersonal intelligence ('people smart'):
the capacity to detect and respond appropriately to the moods, motivations and desires of others

Intrapersonal intelligence ('self smart'):
a capacity to be self-aware and in tune with inner feelings, values, beliefs and thinking processes

Naturalist intelligence ('nature smart'):
the ability to recognise and categorise plants, animals and other objects in nature

Existential intelligence ('philosophy smart'):
demonstrating sensitivity and capacity to tackle deep questions about human existence, such as the meaning of life, why we die and how we got here.

Figure 2.2 Multiple Intelligence Theory

Gardner argues that while there is a good case to be made for *spiritual* intelligence, he rejects it as a distinctive form of intelligence because people's capacity to grasp cosmic and transcendent truths ultimately depends on affective characteristics and we have no scientifically reliable way of investigating such traits. Similarly, he rejects *moral* intelligence on the grounds that morality involves value judgments and intelligence is by nature value-neutral (though this point of view is an issue of some dispute). As for *naturalist* intelligence – defined as the ability to recognise and classify natural species and understand ecological relationships – Gardner says that it deserves to be recognised as a genuine intelligence, similar to the seven described in the original theory. He argues that *existential* intelligence qualifies as 'an intelligence' in its own right, while admitting that there does not appear to be a specific part of the brain dedicated to dealing with such profound questions about deep human issues.

Schools focus most of their attention on linguistic and logical-mathematical learning (see the first and second descriptions above), sometimes at the expense of other areas; as evidence of this tendency, we esteem the highly articulate and mathematically inclined people in our culture. However, Gardner argues that we should give equal attention to individuals who learn better by other means: for example, artists, architects, musicians, naturalists, designers, dancers, therapists, entrepreneurs, and others who enrich the world but may not be recognised in school.

Gardner is largely correct when he complains that many children who possess gifts don't receive much reinforcement for them in school, though in the UK there have been efforts to improve the status of these subjects; for instance, by requiring schools to teach PE regularly. There is a danger that some children that have a propensity towards the 'Arts' may end up being diagnosed as having a learning disability or attention deficit disorder or simply being underachievers, when in fact a curriculum programme dominated by literacy or mathematics is not aligned to their ways of thinking and learning. The theory of multiple intelligences implies a major transformation in the way schools are run. It suggests that teachers be trained to present their lessons in a wide variety of ways by using music, co-operative learning, art activities, role play, multimedia, field trips, inner reflection, and much more, though good teachers have always employed such diversity of method.

Emotional intelligence (EI) is often measured as an *emotional intelligence quotient* (EQ) and describes an ability, capacity or skill to perceive, assess and manage the emotions of one's self, of others and of groups (based on Wikipedia, The Free Encyclopaedia). As a relatively new area of psychological research, the definition of EI is constantly changing, but it has been made popular by Goleman (1995; 1999; 2005) who has been instrumental in promoting the central role played by the emotions in decisions and actions. It is fair to add that Goleman's work has not been universally accepted and others in the field regard some of his claims as rather suspect (e.g. Eysenck 2000). Nevertheless, regardless of where the truth lies about the concept of emotional intelligence, three general principles should underpin your practice as you focus on recognising that:

1. *Your role is important in helping children feel safe.* Without secure and confident teachers and other adult workers, children are unlikely to gain maximum benefit from their education. You and the rest of the adult staff are undertaking a vital task in helping to educate the nations' children and provide for the future stability of the country and, ultimately, the

world. This notion is not a fanciful one. You do not know whether a child sitting in front of you is a prospective genius, leader or entrepreneur. And even if most pupils end up in unexceptional situations, they are unique individuals with their own special contribution to make to society. Let that thought motivate you.

2. *It is essential to use every means to encourage and support colleagues.* Teachers who spend time praising and helping children to feel positive about themselves and their classmates may need to offer the same level of support to their co-workers. There is a saying that you should not judge a book merely by looking at the cover. In any staffroom there are folk who need reassurance, a word of comfort, a kind smile and a pat on the back. Even apparently confident and assured characters can be inwardly vulnerable. Schools rely on active collaboration across the whole team, and even if you are a trainee teacher with little direct control over events, a word of appreciation, a short note of thanks or willingness to listen can help to transform someone's day and give that person hope. Such actions not only demonstrate compassion for fellow-humans but also provide a foundation for a successful school placement and establish an attitude of mind that you can carry throughout the rest of your career.

3. *It is better to focus on your achievements and successes than dwell on failures.* Teachers possess and exhibit daily a range of skills and knowledge that are taken for granted: organising, planning, summarising, public exposition, dealing with children and adults, curriculum expertise and so on. A bad day often simply means that the call upon these skills has been excessive or you lacked the experience to cope. It is frequently the case that what you consider to have been 'a bad lesson' was, in fact, simply less good than it might have been. In evaluating your progress as a teacher and the distance yet to be covered, don't lose sight of how far you have already travelled. Remember that many successful people in other professions would quake at the knees at the thought of being left in charge of a class of children.

Teaching is rewarding and occasionally thrilling but as noted earlier in the chapter there are also physical (sheer exhaustion), psychological (rooted in concerns about being good enough to succeed) and emotional stresses and strains. A number of warning signs exist to which all teachers need to be alert in their own experience and in those of others that signal potentially injurious negative emotions and the likelihood that stress is affecting health and the ability to carry out tasks efficiently:

- *Persistent anxiety:* this emotion is deeper than worry and eats into every aspect of life in and outside school. Some people say that they are unable to 'switch off'. They fall asleep straight away at night but find themselves wide-awake in the early hours. Sometimes a persistently anxious person takes on more and more responsibilities, well beyond the ability to cope, as a means of blocking out feelings of distress. If this description characterises your experience, it is sensible to seek professional help urgently. Do not imagine that you can somehow 'pull yourself together' or that you will be thought the worse of by asking for assistance

- *A lack of enthusiasm for the job:* every teacher entertains feelings of doubt. Every trainee teacher has times when fervour diminishes and may even entertain vocational uncertainty. These emotions are commonplace and are often due to fatigue and poor health. Schools are places where an easy transmission of germs is possible, owing to the close proximity of adults and pupils, and the propensity of children to share their bugs. During such debilitating periods of time the quality of lessons may suffer (or at least that is how it feels to you), which in itself creates additional anxiety. At such times it is essential to remind yourself of two things. First, no teacher is perfect and everyone has off-days. Second, children will learn despite your feebleness. A good night's sleep and a talk with a sympathetic friend will usually remedy loss of appetite for the job. If humanly possible, avoid the work-sleep-work syndrome, where your life revolves around school to the detriment of all else

- *Resentment towards pupils:* it is undeniable that some pupils are more troublesome than others. Occasionally, a child gets 'under your skin' and you find that it is hard to resist becoming irritated or convinced that your professional identity is being undermined. A small minority of teachers become disillusioned with the job and express their concerns publicly and bitterly. Others fall into the trap of compensating for their own shortcomings and difficulties by criticising others. Such behaviour quickly becomes endemic and wise head teachers and senior teachers act quickly to stop the spread of disillusionment. It is often the case that a teacher who makes negative comments is merely letting off steam and does not normally feel that way at all. However resentful you feel, try hard not to view unco-operative children as your enemies

- *Unnatural ill-temper or intolerance:* the most even-tempered adults sometimes become unsettled by children's or other adults' behaviour and overreact. For the most part the reaction consists solely of a strong word or impatient remark and is soon forgotten. However, if you find that you are regularly employing authoritarian tactics to enforce discipline or getting tetchy with adults with whom you work, it is time to take yourself in hand, step back and coolly evaluate the source of your impatience. If the situation does not improve, seek help from your tutor or mentor or a trusted friend. It is likely that those who know you will be aware of your irritability and relieved that you are facing up to the problem. Sleep deprivation is probably the main reason for such anti-social behaviour

- *Reluctance about going to school:* even experienced teachers admit that their confidence can sink to a low point prior to going in to school, but that once they are there they feel completely different. Although as a trainee teacher you are probably not earning a salary (or, at best, just a small remuneration) teachers are paid to teach! Sometimes the pleasure that teaching engenders can cause us to forget that it is a form of employment and, like any other job, requires effort and perseverance and a reasonably consistent standard of performance. On the other hand if you start panicking at the prospect of school, consult medical help without delay.

Although these stress signs are often associated with a time of ill-health or other unsettling life experience (such as financial or relational problems), their recurrence signals the need for rapid action (Woods and Carlyle 2002; Hayes 2006). Day *et al.* (2007) claim that a teacher's identity consists of competing interactions between professional, situated (socially located) and personal factors. *Professional* identity is 'open to the influence of long-term policy and social trends as to what constitutes a good teacher, classroom practitioner, etc'. *Situated* or socially located identity within a specified school, department or classroom is 'affected by pupils, support and feedback loops from teachers' immediate working context, connected to long-term identity'. *Personal* identity is 'based on life outside school; it could have various competing elements, such as identity of being a father, son, partner, etc'. Day *et al.* explain that feedback from family and friends 'often become sources of tension as the individual's sense of identity could become out of step' (all quotes from 2007: 106–7). The authors conclude that although pressures are an inevitable part of work and life:

> there are likely to be times when everyday pressures turn into pressures that make teachers more vulnerable which, in turn, can have adverse emotional effects. These can impact on teachers' well-being, which can be positively and negatively affected by a number of issues, such as management of the school, the school ethos and culture, staff morale and opportunities for CPD. (2007: 121–2)

A teacher who works in a school where such feelings and attitudes can be openly expressed and discussed is fortunate. However, many teachers find that the opportunities for such openness are few, either because the school ethos does not espouse it or because life is too busy and colleagues too preoccupied with their own worries to listen. Good team spirit, however, comes from support and encouragement (see Wilson 2004).

The skills of listening carefully, sympathising and affirming should not be reserved for work with children; every adult needs to hear that they are needed, valued and trusted, too. Publicly expressed statements of gratitude for advice, guidance or example can enliven an ailing colleague. Teachers who are at ease with school life should support those who presently are not. Comradeship and empathy can strengthen and heal. Just as children's experiences and attitudes affect their performance in school, it is similar for adults, though they are usually more skilled in concealing their feelings and often see it as part of their professional responsibilities to carry on regardless. If consolation and encouragement are not available within school, it is essential to spend time in building an informal network of confidantes outside school as an alternative. Lawrence (2006) offers some sensible advice on keeping things in perspective when he suggests that while teachers should be careful to take their work seriously they should never take themselves so seriously that they lose their sense of humour. Life in school relies on every member functioning efficiently, so effort expended in supporting others benefits everyone, including you.

Activate your thinking!

On your way home every night make a mental list of your many achievements during the day. If you allow negative thoughts to dominate your thinking, they will squeeze out everything else.

Whatever the stage of your career, you will be aware that being a teacher is a demanding, exhilarating and emotionally charged experience. There will be good days and not-so-good days, outstanding lessons and mediocre ones. Learn to take it in your stride, reflect upon your practice, keep buoyant and don't allow the job to become such an obsession that it dominates your life.

Care of the voice

Your voice is probably the single most valuable teaching resource that you possess, so it pays to take good care of it (Kovacic 2005). Teachers should avoid placing undue pressure on their voices by sudden switches from a normal speaking tone to a fierce or forced one. In addition to avoiding smoke and polluted atmospheres, teachers are encouraged to breathe carefully through the nose (and out through the mouth) refrain from eating unsuitable foods (such as very spicy ones) and use alcohol and dairy products sparingly. General health can be improved through humming quietly before speaking (making the lips vibrate), standing upright (not slouching) and taking regular pauses for breath. Teachers should also keep to a minimum the amount that they clear the throat, which causes the vocal cords to collide with accompanying wear and tear, talk too quickly (which leads to inadequate breathing and increases chest tension) and use an unnatural pitch or forced whisper. Teachers can help themselves by sipping water during the lesson – it is recommended that you drink at least a litre of water each day and avoid excessive drinks that contain caffeine – breathe deeply into the furthest recesses of the lungs and make a determined effort not to push the voice when it is tired or hoarse.

It is important to support your voice with deep breaths from the diaphragm, the wall that separates your chest and abdomen, so it pays to persevere in practising good breathing techniques when talking (and singing). Once you get into the habit of practising correct breathing, it quickly becomes natural; but it is surprisingly easy to lapse into bad old habits. Singers and speakers are taught exercises that improve breath control, because you place a great strain on your system if you talk from the throat without the help of 'supporting breath' from lower down in your body.

Forcing the voice so that it becomes a 'bark' will cause serious damage if prolonged. It goes without saying that the ability to relax the whole body during teaching assists the health of the voice, too, with the accompanying improvement in speech clarity that results. It is also important to exercise regularly, as this increases stamina and muscle tone, and provides for good posture and breathing, which are necessary for proper speaking. Getting sufficient rest is essential, as studies show that physical fatigue has a negative effect on your voice. Some voice specialists recommend including a lot of whole grain, fruit and vegetable in your diet, as these foods contain important vitamins A, E and C, which help to keep the mucus membranes that line the throat healthy. Your voice is your powerhouse, so treat it with the utmost respect (Grant-Williams 2002).

Good practice

- Warm up by humming and freeing your jaw, tongue and lips
- Stand upright when speaking
- Breathe deeply from the bottom of the lungs
- Drink plenty of water
- Talk regular breaks from talking
- Speak naturally.

Case studies

Martha

Martha's classroom seems to flow with paper. Her desk is littered with exercise books, worksheets and half-finished drawings. The walls drip with numerous charts, pictures, unmounted writing and the remains of an earlier display. Tables are pushed together in groups of three and some chairs are touching the wall. There are corners: a play area, large construction, a dressing-up box and a row of CD players strewn about the shelf. Two computers and printers are greatly in demand and children jostle for position. The atmosphere is exuberant, with children moving freely about the room, chattering, laughing and busy. After a few minutes observation, it becomes clear that much of this activity is rather purposeless. The noise level rises as Martha, immersed in a queue of children, calls out instructions and general warnings that many children appear to ignore or respond to for a short time before resuming their unsatisfactory behaviour.

Martha likes the children to get down to their work quickly. She regularly uses photocopied sheets full of tasks that the children have to work through and hand in when completed. The tasks are varied, some requiring the application of library skills and investigation, the majority desk-bound and requiring a single correct answer.

To cope with the constant flow of queries and questions, Martha and her flustered assistant spend much of their time dealing with children on a one-to-one basis, repeating answers to the same query from different children. Occasionally, she stops the class to remind them of the need to behave or of what they are supposed to be doing.

Although the tasks are not differentiated, the worksheets gradually become more demanding so that although all the children can attempt the first one, less able children find later ones too difficult. As the session continues, some children become restless as they tire of the work and begin to copy from more confident neighbours; others work very slowly, choosing the easiest elements and avoiding anything conceptually difficult; a few hurry through to be ahead of friends. The standard of work is variable. Martha often warns individual children to 'get on with your work'.

At the end of the lesson, she tells the class to clear up and put the completed sheets in a box on her desk and the uncompleted ones in their trays. There is a scramble to do so and some sheets are crumpled. Martha raises her voice and tells the class to 'be more sensible'; one child is strongly rebuked and told to sit down on his own in the corner. Children find their snacks, chatter about card 'swaps' and playground activities as they noisily leave the room; no one remains behind to talk to the teacher about the work. She sends out the last child after saying that she is 'tired of your behaviour'. She walks down to the staffroom and is the first to make a drink before flopping down in an armchair. When the head teacher mentions that it is her turn to have a trainee teacher next term, Martha pulls a face and says that she hopes that this one is 'a bit better than the one I had last year; she was useless; couldn't keep control'. The head teacher smiles to herself but says nothing, secretly hoping that Martha will apply for the vacancy in a nearby school in which she has expressed interest.

A few weeks later, Martha comes across the uncompleted worksheets and throws them away. During the tidying-up prior to a parents' evening, several children ask her what they should do with their completed work from earlier this term found in their trays. The teacher collects them all in and, when the children have gone home, hurriedly ticks the best of them and helps the TA mount them on an empty display board together with some colourful, bold labels and an impressive title.

During parents' evening, Martha speaks loudly to parents, extolling the merits of their children and offering comments about their achievements, edged with inferences about their potential 'if they concentrated better on the work'. She regales the parents with impressive talk about assessment for learning, layered assessments, targets and individualised learning. Parents are quite pleased to hear positive things but feel unaccountably troubled as the teacher's report does not square with their children's diminishing enthusiasm for school.

Diane

Diane's classroom, with its interactive displays, selected examples of children's work, due regard to safety and easy access to equipment is the envy of her colleagues. Children's work is mounted with bold labels that enhance the room's appearance. Most displays consist of children's contributions, though here and there the teacher's artistic touches are evident. Photographs of the children in a variety of formal and informal poses, together with dates of birth and a list of their favourite foods and animals, are arranged on a small board. Well-thumbed documents in carefully labelled folders are in place on a shelf behind Diane's desk. The room is orderly but not clinical; the atmosphere is purposeful yet relaxed.

The class always seems business-like without being rigid; children work singly and in groups and relate together comfortably. There is little acrimony and many moments of genuine laughter and smiles. On other occasions, there is a serious intent about the children as they concentrate on the task. Peer support is powerfully evident

Diane has a brisk but friendly manner. She begins a session by reviewing previous work and asking thought-provoking questions, trying to involve as many different children as possible. The children sit up straight in anticipation of what the teacher might say and don't seem afraid to venture an answer even if they are unsure. In turn, Diane treats every response seriously and tries to make a positive comment about its merits; children are encouraged to speculate and offer their own thoughts. She insists that other children respect what is said by others. The overall impression of these whole-class times is one of mutual respect and a healthy learning environment.

Diane introduces the lesson by telling the children what she hopes they will learn and do, explains the activities and gives some specific instruction to each group. It is clear that the children are used to showing initiative as they sort themselves out, gather resources, settle to work and discuss the activities. Different children are engaged in similar tasks but there are subtle differences between the groups: some are using an open-ended worksheet as a starting point for discovering new facts by way of a library search; others are using books pre-selected by the teacher to check some facts; a further group is using a computer databank to extract information. While offering close guidance to one group of children, Diane nevertheless spends some time with each group in turn and tries to give each child some personal attention, even when a TA is supervising them. It is clear who is in charge but Diane relates so easily to people that it doesn't cause any tension. Some pupils wander out of their place to see her but generally the children persevere and appear to have a shared sense of purpose. When a child occasionally becomes over-excited or silly, Diane stands and looks hard at the culprit without saying anything; other children alert the transgressor to the teacher's concerns and normality resumes. Once the situation is calmer, she walks across to the group and quietly enquires if she can assist with anything but does not mention the incident.

From time to time, Diane stops the class to point out an instance of good work or to commend someone who is trying hard; the children listen attentively. Towards the end of the session, she tells the class that in a few minutes there will be opportunity to share with others; one or two children explain anxiously that they have yet to finish and she reassures them that they do not need to rush. About five minutes before the end, the teacher stops the class and invites the children to turn to someone nearby and explain what they have done or discovered; a hum soon fills the room as children share together. After a minute or two, Diane stops the class and asks a few children to tell the rest of the class about their findings. Several children do so with confidence and enthusiasm; others listen carefully, occasionally thrusting their hands in the air to indicate their own willingness to add something. After each contribution, the teacher thanks the person warmly and briefly summarises what has been said. When she tells the children that they have to finish, there is a quiet groan of disappointment and several children ask her whether they are going to continue after the break; several more ask if they can stay in to finish during playtime.

After clearing up thoroughly, the children slowly slide out of the class, some still talking about the work, others engaging the teacher in animated conversation. Diane stops one noisy girl at the door and gently places her finger on her lips. The offending child smiles an apology and saves her exuberance for the playground. Diane is often one of the last into the staffroom and one of the first out; she always asks if anyone else wants her to make them a drink and has time to offer a brief word of encouragement to a trainee teacher who is struggling with his class.

At the open evening, she does as much listening as talking. When she speaks, she impresses parents with her sincerity and knowledge of each child. Diane speaks considerately and positively about the children but does not try to conceal their shortcomings or weaknesses. She has detailed notes about the children, each pupil on a separate page to which she occasionally refers for fuller information, but she seems more interested in the child than the statistics about the child. When parents make a significant comment, she notes it on her pad and promises to follow it up; parents feel confident that she will.

The head teacher overhears two parents talking as they cross the playground later that evening: 'I wish our Becky had Diane Jones again this year', sighs one parent wistfully. The other parent nods in agreement.

Further reading

Acker, S. (1999) *The Realities of Teachers' Work*, London: Cassell.
  Based on research, highly informative and to the point.

Deed, C., Bellhouse, B. and Johnston, G. (2007) *Using Circle Time to Learn about Stories*, London: Sage.
  Helps teachers who want to use collaborative and co-operative circle time learning methods in other parts of the curriculum. Includes a CD-ROM.

Holmes, E. (2004) *Teacher Well-Being*, London: RoutledgeFalmer.
  The author presents strategies for teachers who want to be proactive in dealing with their own welfare.

Weatherhead, Y. (2007) *Creative Circle Time for Early Years*, London: Sage.
  Uses music, songs, poetry and practical activities to engage children in circle time activities.

Zucker, J. and Parker, D. (1999) *A Class Act*, London: Sapphire Publishers.
  A book that is fun to read and opens up the mystery of a teacher's world.

Working with Parents and Other Adults

PARENTS

Introduction

Parents are the first educators of their children. Once formal schooling begins, teachers assume some of the responsibility, but the closer the partnership in learning between school and home, the more that children benefit. The first part of the chapter explores the relationship between teachers and parents, including professional boundaries, informal and formal liaison, parent meetings, coping with difficult parents and the role of parents in the classroom. The second part of the chapter considers the increasingly important role of other adults in supporting and enriching children's education.

Home and school

Studies show that one of the most important in a child's academic performance in school is the quality of parental involvement. Some parents seem to assume that it is sufficient to send their children to school and pop in to see the class teacher once or twice a year. In fact, a great deal more is necessary if children are to make good progress in all kinds of learning. A report by Desforges and Abouchaar (2003) about the impact of parental involvement on pupils' education found that what parents do with their children at home is the single most significant factor. They quote from Kreider (2000) that the greatest success occurs when parental development is integrated fully into a school's development plan. Although a few parents will not always be able to help with homework tasks, they all have the potential to contribute to their children's learning in other ways (Burnett and Jarvis 2004). Some schools provide training evenings for parents who are interested in knowing more about how they can help directly.

Adults in school spend a great deal of time working with children, so much time, in fact, that it is possible for teachers to believe that they are the sole educators. In truth, parents may not teach their children much of the formal curriculum that they engage with when at school, but they impart other forms of life knowledge. They teach them about living in a community, learning to cope with different sorts of people, discriminating the good from the harmful and spending time wisely. Parents teach their children particular sets of values. They set boundaries for behaviour and the consequences of not obeying the rules. Most parents take children out into the open air to experience nature, observe the changing seasons and marvel at the wonder of creation. They take them into the city to savour the sights and sounds of urban life. They share books, introduce them to games and offer them opportunities to play alone or play and talk with friends. A parent can give close attention to an individual, whereas in school 30 or more pupils have to share one or two adults. In fact, children are being educated at home, either implicitly by absorbing what happens without being consciously aware of it and explicitly by having their consciousness raised and their attention drawn specifically to items (Stern 2003). School helps them to make the implicit learning become more explicit.

All parents want the best for their children, though some do not have a clear understanding of what 'best' means in terms of school-based learning. School reports offer them a limited amount of information about specific aspects of their children's learning, but parents also want to know about their children's behaviour, attitude, friendships and potential. If their children are unhappy in school, parents will be concerned, regardless of academic results. If children are seriously underachieving, then this obviously requires urgent attention, normally commencing through the school's Special Educational Needs Co-ordinator (SENCO), who will ensure that parents are aware of the problem and involved in its solution.

It goes without saying that some parents do a better job of educating their children than others do. When children arrive in school they vary in the extent and quality of their experiences and so-called 'baseline' assessment of their capability is a standard procedure for teachers of reception age children at the end of the Foundation Stage (see below). This initial assessment is not only an evaluation of children's academic ability but of their social skills, and it is often in this area that teachers soon become aware of the differing ways in which children have been prepared for life in school. McEwan (1998) claims that 'skilled teachers can often identify several children with problems before the first week of school is over' (1998: 42). Nevertheless, Hutchinson and Smith (2003) are among those who stress the importance of remaining positive and inclusive about young children's behavioural disorders. The growth of pre-school education has helped to compensate for the minority of children who have not received adequate parenting, but no strategy can wholly redress the limitations placed upon children whose parents are uninvolved in their education. Nevertheless, children do have a life outside school and it is important for teachers to recognise that theirs is only one of many influences upon an individual child's learning.

By the time 'rising five' Sharmilla joins the reception class, she will already have had four years of experience of adults, most of it helpful, some of it confusing or frightening. A few of these adults will have carried out a teacher role – playgroup leaders, nursery assistants – but most have simply been 'the grown-ups' who have, in one way or another, influenced Sharmilla's life. The likelihood is that she has spent most time interacting with a few close family members – mum, dad, brothers, sisters. Her own behaviour will reflect their attitudes, preferences and personality, and affect her willingness to learn and her satisfaction with school life. Parents, in particular, will remain the most important influence in Sharmilla's world, a world that she carries into school with her every morning (Tizard and Hughes 1984; Hughes *et al.* 1994; Hallgarten 2000; Weil 2003; Sclafani 2004, Chapter 5).

The vast majority of parents co-operate fully with teachers to ensure that children receive the best education in the most pleasant environment. However, two of the major changes in parental attitudes in recent years have been an increasing awareness of their rights and a willingness to express their views about school individually or through group pressure. Wise teachers are not intimidated by these changes but take account of them in their dealings with parents (see later in this chapter). Part of the formal inspection programme requires that inspectors take account of parental views. Whatever your opinion of parents, you can't ignore them.

Activate your thinking!

Consider what it means for your relationships and professional attitude to see parents as *clients* or *customers* or *partners*. Reflect upon how parents may perceive the relationship.

Home–school contacts

Over recent years, legislation has established the rights of parents to be well informed about the curriculum offered by each school and to know about their child's progress through reports and informal access to teachers (see, for example, Hughes *et al.* 1994, Chapter 8; Vincent 2000; Beveridge 2004). With each school's budget depending in large measure upon the number of pupils on the roll, there is extra incentive for head teachers and governors to ensure that parents are welcomed and made to feel part of the school community. Inevitably, this new relationship has caused schools to re-evaluate home–school links and to establish procedures for coping with parental concerns. Parent areas are a common feature of primary schools and almost every school has regular meetings with groups of parents in a parent–teacher forum. This often provides the impetus for fund-raising, school events and (sometimes) policy decisions.

The greatest level of interaction between parents and school staff is commonly found at nursery, reception and Key Stage 1 (Stacey 1991; Lindon 1997, Part 4; Fitzgerald 2004; Crozier and Reay 2005) owing to the fact that parents tend to bring their young children into the classroom and meet them after school. Although every school has its own particular ideas about establishing and maintaining good quality relationships with parents, contact in the foundation years (for children aged three to five years) and at the start of Key Stage 1 often includes:

■ Home visits by the reception class teacher close to the start of a child's formal schooling

■ Visits to and from nursery schemes and playgroups by teachers from the mainstream school

■ Informal meetings between teacher and parents at the start and end of the day when they are leaving or picking up their children

■ Involvement of parents in the classroom, both to assist, and in some cases to help ease the transition of their child from home to school.

Many head teachers actively promote home–school liaison through invitations to participate in aspects of school life from practical and mundane tasks such as mending library books, making tea for special events or tidying classroom cupboards, through to an active contribution to teaching and school effectiveness (Wolfendale and Bastiani 2000; Campbell and Fairbairn 2005).

As children progress through the school, contact with parents tends to become less regular. Older children may travel to school on their own or with friends. Parents, freed from the demands of caring for young children, may find a job or decide that they have 'done their stint' as parent-helper and look elsewhere for fulfilment. Junior-aged children sometimes find their parent's presence in the school an embarrassment and ask them to stay away. So although it may appear that parents lose interest in their child's education over time, in reality parental interest merely changes perspective (Tizard *et al.* 1988). Early on, parents are chiefly interested in basic considerations such as:

- Is my child happy in school?
- Is my child being properly cared for?
- Does my child have friends?
- Is my child getting on well with basic skills such as reading?
- Is my child behaving satisfactorily?

Later on, when parents are satisfied that these basic needs are being met, they are more likely to concentrate on specific aspects of teaching and learning:

- How is my child progressing in his or her work relative to others in the class?
- Is my child being offered a full range of educational opportunities?
- Is my child excelling or falling behind in any area?
- Does my child have the ability to achieve success in future education?

Parents of all children are also concerned that their children are not disadvantaged at school, that teachers treat them fairly and that they are encouraged to do their best. It is worth remembering that when adults in school interact with a child, they are not only affecting the child but indirectly influencing the parents, families and friends, too.

Parents and homework

Parents are able to assist their children in various ways outside the school day, including support for assigned homework. If you are advising parents about making the most of their opportunities, first of all encourage them to communicate by talking about the curriculum, friendships, activities and the nature of the homework assignment. Some parents assume that if the children want to tell them about an aspect of the work, they will do so. In fact, many children wait for an invitation and older children in particular are surprisingly coy about sharing openly with a parent. Nevertheless, unless parents talk naturally and without pressure to children they will find difficulty in helping them to set realistic goals, organise their schedule and check progress. Like a good teacher, parents should praise genuine effort but not be gushing about things that would be expected from the child; otherwise, the child's expectations are lowered. A number of parents will feel unskilled in supervising homework, on the basis that the child knows more than them – which may be true. Other parents may take some persuading to be a surrogate teacher and complain that's what they pay you to do, but if you point out that they were the child's first educator (from birth onwards) then monitoring homework is merely an extension of this role.

You are bound to get some parents who are unable or unwilling to participate in a home–school agreement or scheme, but this problem is for senior staff to deal with and you don't need to be unduly concerned about it.

It is worth remembering that children from certain backgrounds will be used to the continual presence of family members at home and may have had little experience of separation from them until they enter school. Some cultures emphasise the importance of maintaining close family ties and several generations may live in the same household or close to each other. In addition, close chaperoning of children (girls in particular) mean that the concept of complete privacy, so cherished by many in the Western world, is largely unknown to some children from different backgrounds. Such factors may explain, for instance, why some children are uneasy about going to the toilet on their own or have reservations about changing in the presence of boys.

Professional boundaries

There will be a variety of parents represented in a single class of children, including a few teenagers and the occasional set of grandparents who are the guardians of their own grandchildren. Some parents will have enjoyed their time at school, others will have unhappy memories, and this experience has a strong influence on their attitude. Certain parents are constantly in and out of school; others are never seen. A few parents will be keen to give their time helping the school in whatever way possible. The majority will be too busy earning a living to afford such luxury.

Parents who are struggling with life will occasionally come into school to seek comfort or reassurance from a sympathetic teacher but it pays to be cautious about being drawn into delicate social situations. If a distressed parent approaches you, the general rule is to listen a lot and say little. If there are sensitive issues involved (especially about a teacher in the school or another parent) take particular care not to say anything that might be relayed to the person in question or misconstrued as being critical. It requires a disciplined approach to avoid being swept into an ongoing dialogue with anxious or unhappy parents who begin to see you as their ally. On the other hand, a few moments spent listening and showing some interest in their plight is an important humanitarian role. If possible, try to steer the conversation away from personal issues and towards the progress currently being made by the child of the parent in question. Think of something positive and optimistic to say. If you find that a parent is keeping you from your duties, it is perfectly in order to say something to the effect that you are sorry to have to interrupt them but you will be in trouble if you don't get back to work. A cheery goodbye as you walk away may provide the spark of encouragement that the parent requires. If the parent repeatedly comes to see you, ask for advice from a more experienced colleague. It is important that you never release information about another child or discuss his or her progress to anyone other than the parent or legal guardian (carer). If you feel uncomfortable about an episode, mention it to the head teacher and make a brief record of your conversations with the parent in your private diary. Any interactions that leave you feeling uncomfortable should, of course, be reported to a tutor or colleague as soon as possible. There is a fine line between liaising with parents and being at their beck and call.

Communicating with parents

Head teachers and governors are always anxious to ensure that parents are kept well informed about aspects of school life that impact upon their children's education and the move towards integrating education and social services has highlighted the importance of establishing and maintaining good relationships. As an important part of the communication network, class teachers are often given the responsibility of ensuring that information reaches home and helping to ensure that parents don't receive conflicting or confusing messages about school life. Information is usually conveyed in one of three ways:

1. Printed correspondence, such as a school circular or letter, if the issues affect the whole group or class
2. Verbal messages given to an individual child
3. Handwritten notes.

A number of practical points are worth noting.

Printed correspondence

Printed correspondence in the form of general circulars normally come from the head teacher and sometimes unexpectedly arrive on the teacher's desk or are brought in by an assistant or administrator. It is a sensible policy always to check the instructions about sending them out and to follow the head teacher's wishes precisely. A delay (or sometimes premature release) in sending a letter home can cause problems if some parents receive notification and others do not. In the busy end-of-day activity, it is easy to overlook a letter intended for home.

If there is time, and particularly in the case of younger children, each child's name should be written neatly at the top of the sheet: classroom assistants will often carry out this task. Many circular letters never reach parents, and, although they usually emerge some weeks later from a deep coat pocket, it is useful to be able to tell the parents that the circular really was sent home with the child's name on it.

It is sensible to maintain a file to hold copies of all circulars; this ensures that they are available for parents who arrive to complain that their children never received the letter. A quick photocopy, pleasant smile and gentle apology can diffuse the situation. Many schools have a special noticeboard for copies of important circulars, such as those from the school governors. If you are especially busy and liable to forget to send the letter home, ask the children or a TA to remind you. One of them is bound to remember.

Written messages often have to be produced in a variety of languages. Although the child may speak good English, parents do not necessarily do so. This situation makes the distribution of letters more time-consuming and you will need to take this into account when organising sessions, so leave a few additional minutes at the end of the session and where possible ensure that an assistant is on hand to help with the practicalities.

Verbal messages

Adults tend to speak quickly when they get excited or time is pressing and although a child may nod when asked if the message is understood, there remains a good chance that it will not have been heard properly or will not be remembered. This fact is especially true in the case of younger children.

It is therefore important to be careful when relaying verbal messages. If you hear yourself saying, 'Tell mummy that …' or 'Ask at home to see if …' then you should not be surprised if the next day a bewildered parent contacts you to ask what the school can possibly want with a pair of grandpa's old socks or why David has to bring sausages for the school rabbit. Children do not alter a message deliberately; they simply mishear or forget what is said and become confused. It is like the game of Chinese Whispers in which the message becomes distorted out of all recognition by the time it reaches the person for whom it was intended. More significantly, a special effort should be made to communicate effectively with parents for whom English is not their first language. Imagine if you were that parent trying to make sense of it and reluctant to come into school to check owing to embarrassment about your poor grasp of English.

If circumstances oblige you to send a verbal message home that relates to one particular pupil, then the child should be asked to repeat what has been said before leaving. It is sometimes appropriate to use an older sibling to act on the younger child's behalf. Generally, though, it is far better either to write down the information or to contact the parent directly. It can be worrying and irritating for a parent to receive a jumbled verbal message in the evening and have no idea whether it is urgent or important.

Handwritten notes

Teachers do not often have the time or inclination to write notes to parents, but if you do it is important to remember that parents expect teachers to maintain high standards, so scruffy handwriting will be viewed badly and any spelling errors jump out of the page and become a topic of conversation. When such errors occur, a teacher's carefully polished image can be damaged. The same is true of everything teachers write that is placed on public view, such as labels for displays or lists of words around the room.

If you feel it necessary to send a personal note home, take great care to be accurate and thoughtful. Many inexperienced teachers have caused themselves considerable anguish by writing to a parent about a child without giving the matter adequate consideration. It is one thing to drop a note to Meena's mum to ask if she would mind coming in to help in the classroom on Friday instead of Wednesday; it is quite another to send Sam's parents a formal-sounding letter to say that he is banned from recorder club because he hasn't bothered to practise. If in doubt about taking action that has implications for a child's learning or for relationships with parents, it is always worth consulting a tutor or senior member of staff first. Whereas an ill-advised off-the-cuff remark can usually be smoothed over, a letter in the teacher's own handwriting is harder to dismiss and acts as primary evidence if a complaint is made.

If you write home to parents, use the opportunity to compliment the child who has tried hard or made a special effort. Parents are pleased to receive those personal comments. Children are equally delighted. Studies suggest that this form of commendation is more important than any number of house points ot merit cards.

In any communication home, it is essential to be careful about addressing letters. If in doubt, the safest way is to ask the child discreetly what you should write or simply put: 'To the parent (or guardian) of Jody Adamson, class 4E, from Miss Eddis' and seal the envelope. If you are a trainee teacher it is unlikely that you will need to send a note home, but following the common-sense guidance outlines above may save you a lot of trouble if you do. In any case, you need to be aware that attention to detail pays dividends when dealing with parents.

The quality of communication with parents can help or hinder a teacher's attempts to build a good working relationship and may even adversely affect the child's attitude towards school. One of the greatest challenges comes when a new teacher meets parents, often for the first time, in the formal circumstances of parent interviews.

Face-to-face with parents

Face-to-face formal encounters with parents take many forms. Some schools operate a rota system, in which a set of appointment times is drawn up for parents to come in to the school during the late afternoon or evening. Other head teachers like to foster a less formal approach in which parents are encouraged to wander in and out of classrooms during the teaching day and chat to the teacher. Some schools have experimented by encouraging parents to have their child present during the discussion with the teacher as a means of giving the child some ownership of the process. A small number allow parents to attend lessons and see first hand how the teacher fosters learning and how the children respond, though this option is not always successful because the adult presence impacts on behaviour; in addition, young children may want to sit with their parents, creating logistical problems. Each of these (and other) systems has various advantages and shortcomings, but whatever the form of parent interview adopted, all teachers find their first few formal meetings with parents rather nerve-racking and stressful. With time, the experience becomes easier, but never easy. Teachers have variously described it as frightening, exhausting and exhilarating – sometimes all three – but ultimately very worthwhile. If you are still training, then you probably won't have to undertake anything more than a practice event with (say) a TA playing the part of a parent. However, you should take every opportunity to sit alongside the teacher during a formal event, both to learn and to experience the strong feelings and sense of responsibility attached to the occasion.

There are ways of reducing the sense of burden and making the experience positive and beneficial for all concerned. First, the groundwork for a parents' evening is done well in advance of the first parent entering the room. The teacher's personality, attitude to children in the classroom, pleasantness during informal contacts, willingness to take time finding out something of a child's interests and approach to learning will already have made a mark. Teachers are talked about regularly at home and at the school gate; their reputation goes before them and influences parents' reactions and inclination when they visit the school. It will be the same for you.

Second, some parents are nervous about school and (occasionally) have a negative attitude towards teachers in general, which is often a reflection of their own unsatisfactory schooling or fear of adults when they were pupils. Little wonder that the parent concerned can find it difficult to relax and act naturally, and is either rigid and hesitant or unnecessarily abrupt. It helps to understand that merely entering the school premises requires a considerable mental effort for the small number of disillusioned parents and may not be easy for many others. Most parents come into school because they are deeply interested in their child's education and want to find out more about their progress, both academically and socially. Teachers have access to this information and therefore something of value to share with them. Very few parents want to trip you up or be intimidating. It is worth viewing parent interviews as a wonderful opportunity to share knowledge, ideas and concerns, in addition to giving facts and figures about a child's academic attainment. Consider it a privilege rather than a chore.

Activate your thinking!

Fostering positive relationships with parents:

- Make your classroom a welcoming place in appearance and the way that you greet visitors
- Use informal opportunities for developing positive relationships with parents in the weeks leading up to the meeting
- Give advice to parents about helping with their children's education at home, especially concerning ways they can assist with homework
- Utilise parental help as partners in education: directly in school or indirectly through providing items of interest such as photographs.

Questions parents might be asking themselves:

- Is the teacher taking a personal interest in my child and providing appropriate opportunities for learning?
- Is my child happy and doing well?
- Can the teacher maintain good order and control?
- Does the teacher have an interesting and lively personality?
- How well is my child doing compared to others in the class?

Preparing for parents' meetings

Every meeting with parents has the potential to enrich the existing situation and strengthen the home–school partnership in learning. There are a number of practical and organisational points that can facilitate a more successful meeting and increase the likelihood that parents will go away feeling satisfied and that you will also be pleased with the outcome.

Check that the classroom is in good order

Parents are only partly aware of what happens in a classroom from day to day, so it is the teacher's responsibility to offer evidence of the vitality and effectiveness of the learning that takes place. Trays should be tidied, marking completed, wall displays arranged, examples of children's work named clearly and boldly. View the meeting as an opportunity to show off your expertise and express your personality. Neatly labelled cards with useful information about the nature of projects focus parents' attention on important elements of learning. As parents enter the room let them be impressed by the marks of industry and creativity. Put yourself in the visitor's place and see what impression you get. If you are a trainee, take the opportunity to wander around the school and chat with other teachers and assistants about the practical and psychological preparation they undertake prior to the visits.

> ## Good practice
>
> Invite a friend into the classroom before the parents' meeting for an objective opinion about its appearance.

Prepare thoroughly

In the hurly-burly of school life, even important events like parents' meetings can arrive with alarming speed and find teachers ill-prepared. It is said that great wartime leader Sir Winston Churchill was the best prepared impromptu speaker the House of Commons has ever known. This paradox (well prepared yet apparently spontaneous) has an easy explanation, as the great man prepared so thoroughly that he could speak with authority without constant reference to his notes. This gave the impression of mastery and spontaneity. Teachers should emulate his example.

Thus, when a parent comes to talk about her son, Tom, the teacher ought to be clear about Tom's general strengths and weaknesses without the need to fuss about searching for notes and files. It is important to begin the meeting with a clear, positive statement about Tom as an individual that will help to create a bond with the parent. The amount of detailed information needed will depend upon the purpose of the meeting and access to notes may be necessary to look up specific test results and levels of attainment but it is essential that your detailed knowledge about Tom as a person as well as a scholar comes across clearly.

At the start of the school year, a parent will probably be satisfied to hear about how Alice has settled down, whether she has made some friends and if she is making good progress overall. Later on, the same parent will look keenly into Alice's exercise book, scan the wall for examples of her work and make rapid comparisons with other children's work. If the teacher needs to disclose or discuss test scores, it is essential to give clear explanations about the circumstances under which the test was carried out, the status of the result and the implications for Alice's future progress. It is important to be honest with parents but not brutally so. If there are serious concerns about a child's work, do not leave it until the formal meeting before revealing them or parents will rightly ask why you waited so long to inform them.

Know the child

It may seem unlikely, but in the intensity of the moment it is surprisingly easy to confuse the progress of two different children. It is helpful to have a photograph of each child on a separate page in a folder and write down brief notes for every child prior to the meeting. Having a separate page that you can turn over after each interview also prevents parents reading information about other children. Generally, parents are always impressed by a teacher who takes a close and personal interest in their child. The author once confused the parents of two boys, both called Nicholas. The first boy was tall, blond and sporty; the second was short, suffered from a minor physical disability and was much less academic than his namesake. Readers can only imagine my horror and desperate backtracking when the truth dawned.

Keep things orderly

Assuming that the background preparation is satisfactorily completed, two guiding principles are important during the meeting: (a) keeping to time by adopting a systematic approach; and (b) keeping the conversation focused on the key issues.

Keeping to time is essential if an appointments system is used. Parents rightly become cross if they have to wait for an unreasonable length of time because a teacher is running late. Sometimes it can take a few minutes before the conversation 'warms up' and the allotted time is used up before the serious business begins. Thinking through in advance about the way the meeting will be handled is invaluable and can both help avoid over-running and keep the conversation focused on the relevant issues. The following procedure often proves successful:

- Stand up as the parents approach

- Make immediate eye contact, smile, extend your hand, greet them by name (or, if in doubt, say: 'You're Andrea's parents, aren't you?') and invite them to sit down

- Tell them that it is good to see them and thank them sincerely for coming

- When you need to refer to the child's performance, make sure that you have already turned to the page on which their child's photograph and details are noted. Don't leave another child's details open in front of a different set of parents

- Begin positively and truthfully: 'I'm really pleased with John's progress this term; he's made a terrific effort' or 'Richard is so persevering. I won't pretend that he has found the work easy, but I have tremendous admiration for the way he refuses to give up' or 'Where did Ling learn to play the piano? She was wonderful in the class assembly the other day'

- After this item of conversation has run its course, change direction and state the purpose of the meeting. For instance: 'In the next few minutes I've got to tell you about Stephen's progress in the core subjects' or 'We've got just five minutes to chat about Astra's report and another couple of minutes for you to ask me any questions about the class visit next week'. It is, of course, important to be clear about the purpose of the meeting or you and the parents will either stare at one another blankly or indulge in small talk

- When the time is nearly used up, begin to bring an end to the conversation by saying something like: 'I'm sorry we haven't more time to discuss this. I'm happy to talk again on another occasion if you need to do so. Perhaps you can let me know when you've had chance to think about it but we'll have to draw to a close now'. Stand up and extend your hand.

As you conclude, close with a positive summary comment that gives the parents something to take away with them:

> Mihail's a lively young man and certainly keeps me on my toes. We're doing all we can to help him and there are already signs that things are improving.

> We want Amy to grow more confident in her own abilities because there's no doubt that she can do well.

> Alisya is doing her best and I'm convinced that with a little extra help in maths she'll start to make real progress. We love her sense of humour.

> David's a bit anxious about the trip but we'll keep our eye on him, so don't worry. If you've got any concerns, don't hesitate to contact us.

As the parents walk away, thank them again for coming. Note the name of the next parent and turn your file to the appropriate page.

Notice how often these examples include the plural forms 'we' and 'us'. This strategy reinforces the teacher's own comments by emphasising the team effort in what is said and gives parents confidence that the issues are being addressed. Parents expect teachers to act and behave like professionals but also to show compassion and understanding. As the meeting proceeds, make a brief note of any parental concerns, action needed or points of interest. Parents can see that you are taking their child's needs and their comments seriously and are more likely to go away feeling happy and satisfied.

Case study

Restawhile Primary has been refurbished and given a cash injection after coming through several years of disruption owing to staff changes. Your class, Year 3, is drawn mainly from a white, working class population, with a small but growing minority ethnic community and a few middle class families who want their children to attend the school because it is representative of 'the real world'. The aim of the Parents' Evening at the end of September is for the teacher to let parents know how their children have started the year and begin to cement a working relationship with them. Detailed information about children's progress is not on the agenda for this 15-minute meeting. Consider how you would deal with the following parents:

Parent 1: Miss Smallways, a shy, retiring person, did not have a successful time at school when she was young. Her daughter, Charlaine, is also timid and underachieving but has shown a growing ability in gymnastics. Miss Small has several younger children and regular contact with Social Services for support. Charlaine has a small cohort of quiet, compliant friends.

Parent 2: Rupert's parents are among the wealthiest in the school. They are professional people and well aware of their rights, but have agreeable personalities and understand that teaching is a challenging job. They also have high expectations for their son, who is a bright cheery lad but not a high-flier. Rupert is passionate about football, sensitive to his parents' aspirations for him and has a growing awareness of his academic limitations. Rupert has a highly intelligent older sister.

Parent 3: Mr and Mrs Singh are very proud of their eldest son, Gulwar, and desperate that he should do well in school. They have considered moving him to another, more academically successful school, but are afraid he will lose his friends and become miserable if they do. Gulwar excels in mathematics but is ambivalent about literacy and restless during formal teaching sessions. He is an enthusiastic, popular boy and prefers to work unaided.

Parent 4: Mr and Mrs Tuffnutt have twins in the class, Marty and Ocean. Marty is a sharp-tongued, irritating child who often succeeds in getting under a teacher's skin. He is adept at being subtly rude (especially to the support staff) yet charming at the same time. He is always on the fringe of trouble. Ocean is a sad-looking child with few friends, who would, given the chance, spend all her time drawing and colouring. She rarely initiates conversations with adults. Mr Tuffnutt is a loud character and can be dismissive of other people's opinions. Mrs Tuffnutt seems to be a little in awe of her husband.

Parent 5: Ms Monroe has five children, allegedly by three different fathers. She has a gushing, breezy manner and teachers consider her to be a genuinely nice person, very willing to help out with school events. Her son, Brixton, is far more intelligent than anyone else in the family but chooses to mask his abilities for fear of being thought of as 'a swot' by his mates. He is very helpful in class and completes his work without fuss.

Guarding your words

It is obvious that a person who wishes to be treated like a teacher must behave like one. This particularly applies when parents are present. Parents do not expect teachers to be casual or indifferent, but rather to be pleasantly professional. Many teachers enjoy chatting with parents and sharing a joke with them, but it is important not to get carried away with the friendliness. Even informal comments from teachers are remembered and taken very seriously by a lot of parents, so careless remarks should be avoided. Teachers in staffrooms may sometimes say outrageous things about serious matters but it is unwise to do this publicly. A pleasant smile and responsive laugh at the right moment is helpful when dealing with parents, but witticisms and subtleties should be saved for when you are mixing with friends outside school.

In a small number of cases, a parent will befriend you in the hope of gaining inside information about the school and staff. Some parents may wish to know about the current state of thinking in the school about issues where a firm decision has yet to be made and probe your knowledge by asking an innocent question. It pays to be cautious and say as little as possible about controversial issues, without giving the impression that there is something to hide. Even if you feel strongly about a particular matter, resist the temptation to vent your feelings in front of parents, as rumours about staff disharmony spread rapidly. Gossip can be fuelled by a throwaway remark from a teacher in an unguarded moment, so be careful that you do not allow yourself to be ensnared in this way. Special care and wisdom is required in discussing matters in front of parents who regularly help in school (as mealtime staff or TAs). It is naïve to think that they operate within the education equivalent of the Official Secrets Act. There is the world of difference between involving support staff in discussions that impinge directly on their work (a commendable thing) and divulging confidential matters that are the sole concern of the teaching staff (a foolhardy thing).

The intensity of parents' meetings and the heavy demands they make on a teacher can easily lead to elementary blunders. These can be avoided with a little forethought and discipline. The following are five common mistakes in teacher–parent dialogue to be aware of.

Saying too much

Teachers must learn to listen as well as speak and not become carried away by the sound of their own voices. Nerves can sometimes make a teacher too talkative but take time out to pause for breath occasionally and allow a parent to clarify a point or ask a question.

Patronising the parents

Parents may or may not know much about formal education but they know a lot about their own children. Even if teachers feel that parents are not doing a very good job in bringing up their child, it would be unwise to betray such thoughts in conversation. The key is to listen sympathetically to parents wishing to share their private thoughts but avoid passing judgement. If parents ask your advice, offer a thoughtful response without sounding too assertive, always leaving the final decision with them.

Promising to do something that cannot be done

Parents will sometimes come to a meeting with their own agenda relating to what they want for their children from academic work, extra-curricular activities, sports events or relationships. The frequency with which parents mention these matters reinforces the important truth that they see their own child's needs extending beyond the academic. Teachers try to be as accommodating as possible in responding to parental requests, but there is a danger of promising too much. For example, it is unrealistic to offer to establish an individualised teaching programme for a child that cannot be maintained due to the demands of teaching 24 other pupils. Teachers put under pressure to pay special attention to a child should check with the head teacher or suggest that the parents do so. Whereas it is an admirable thing to 'personalise' the curriculum or even offer one-to-one coaching, you should recognise the limits of your own competence and the attention you must give to other priorities. Promises are easy to make to a parent in the intensity of the moment but much more difficult to keep. As a trainee, of course, you can always pass the parent on to the class teacher; but remember that one day *you* will be that class teacher.

Imagining that parents are full of ill-intent

The vast majority of parents are not teacher-consuming monsters. Some are critical and others are not easily satisfied, but most are supportive and as keen for their child to do well as anybody. It would be a mistake to be defensive when meeting parents. Assuming the best, trying to be positive and enthusiastic, and looking upon the parents as allies and partners in teaching and learning provide the basis for happy encounters.

Parents need reason to be optimistic and have confidence in you and it is unusual for them to be negative or abrasive. It is important to give parents hope and the clear message that you can be trusted with their child's education. If you are an inexperienced teacher or do not have children of your own, you may not realise what a transformation a good report can make to the atmosphere in the home. Once the parent has left the classroom after the meeting you immediately forget about what was said; the parent, however, continues to think deeply about the significance of your words and talks to family and friends about them. Never underestimate the power of a teacher's opinion.

Difficult parents and parents with difficulty

From time to time, teachers come into contact with challenging or unco-operative parents; this likelihood is increased with parents of children who are struggling educationally (Greenwood 2004; Jaksec 2005). However, there is a difference between 'difficult parents' and 'parents who have a difficulty with an aspect of school life'. Difficult parents may feel intimidated in the teacher's presence or have bad memories of school or be experienced parents who are hoping unrealistically that their younger child can emulate an older child's success. Sometimes the parents may have had a bad experience with another teacher in the school. Of course, they may just be nasty people. On the other hand, 'parents who have a difficulty' often signal something important about the school or the teacher's own teaching, skills of communication or attitude towards the children.

It is uncomfortable to be confronted by a parent who seems intent on finding fault and very difficult to remain detached from the issues. However, it helps to remember that only teachers have the power to influence the classroom situation directly, whereas parents do not have. Always listen. Never be tempted to belittle parents or, at the other extreme, allow them to intimidate you. Keep the channels of communication open. Maintain a professional attitude at all times but don't tolerate abuse or threats. A more positive way of viewing parents who express dissatisfaction is that they are taking the time and trouble to become involved in their child's education, however clumsily it may be expressed. Nevertheless, when faced with sour or indignant parents, it is important to think through the practicalities:

■ If the confrontation is public, the parents should be asked to accompany the teacher to a more private spot, but not out of sight. If they refuse, ask whether they would like to arrange another meeting in the near future. Quite often, the parents have already 'had their say', will refuse the offer and march off. In this case, it is essential for tutor, mentor, senior colleague or, if it is serious, the head teacher to be informed as soon as possible. The head teacher will probably want to contact the parent directly and clarify the nature of the grievance. Don't allow matters to remain unresolved in the hope that they will somehow fade from sight. A disgruntled parent will talk to others about the grievance and a small spark can easily become a conflagration

■ If the parents agree to sit and talk about their concerns, the teacher should maintain eye contact and show interest in what is said, resisting the temptation to refute any allegations or become defensive. The teacher may want to summarise the parents' concerns in order to clarify the nature of the grievance. In most cases, a simple explanation will suffice and the parents will go away satisfied. The teacher should thank the parents for taking the trouble to come and encourage them to return should there be any further concerns. If you are a young new teacher (as opposed to a more mature one) you may feel that the parent is scorning your youth and inexperience; however, you should push such thoughts to one side and concentrate on the issues that are being raised

■ In the unlikely event of parents becoming very agitated or threatening, the teacher should state that the conversation is terminated, stand up and inform the parents that the matter should be shared with the head teacher (or the most senior person available). It is important (though far from easy) to maintain a calm demeanour. Walk quickly away and find a colleague to assist.

Aggressive behaviour from parents is extremely rare and is normally avoidable by following the advice given in the earlier part of this chapter. It is quite possible that you may never experience such unpleasantness. Remember that an increasing number of children live with only one parent or with a substitute parent and this can sometimes create additional pressures for all concerned. Bear this fact in mind when tempted to be judgemental or deride someone who behaves oddly. Most parents, whether in a stable relationship or not, are keen to offer their support and will do all in their power to ensure that they maintain a good relationship with their child's teacher. An aggressive parent can leave you feeling vulnerable and shaken, but console yourself with the fact that you have 29 other satisfied customers.

Parents in the classroom

Over the past 20 years, the number of parents working alongside teachers in the classroom and around the school has increased significantly. There are many reasons for this:

- The publication of numerous reports stressing the importance of closer home–school links
- A recognition of the useful skills possessed by parents
- The need to have more adult support in the classroom.

Most schools will have a policy for parental involvement and teachers need to work within these guidelines. Parent helpers are volunteers and could, under other circumstances, be receiving payment for their work. Parents in the classroom can be a bonus or a problem depending on the care with which they are selected and the skill with which they are deployed. When a parent approaches a teacher with an offer of help, it is essential to check first with the head teacher, as some parents are unsuitable for reasons that may not be obvious to the teacher. Once a teacher is committed to accepting an offer of help, it is difficult to tell parents that they are no longer wanted. Good parent helpers are worth their weight in gold: they are an extra pair of hands and probably possess expertise (including life experience) that is invaluable in promoting learning; poor ones can cause problems by being over-assertive, critical or casual in attendance. Older parents and grandparents provide stability and a different perspective on matters of concern; they are also a calming influence for careworn teachers.

If you hope to recruit parental help, first make sure that you are aware of the school policy, if such exists. If not, speak to a senior member of staff before initiating proceedings. As a trainee, it is unlikely that you will actively seek parents to assist, other than in the short-term to support the development of a specific theme or topic, in which case you will work with the class teacher to organise the arrangements. Assuming that all else is in order, the following procedures may be adopted:

- Make a list of the jobs suitable for parents
- Find out what prospective parent helpers have to offer
- Discover specifically what each prospective helper is willing to do
- Ascertain when the parents are available and how regularly
- Invite potential parents into school to discuss the implications of assisting. Prepare in advance a summary of principles governing adult–pupil relationships (encouragement, listening carefully, eye contact, etc.).

It is important to understand that a parent who is in and out of the classroom and staffroom picks up a lot of information about individual children and staff, so care about disclosing information which may or may not remain private beyond the school gate is essential. Further discussion about the deployment of TAs is found later in the chapter.

Remember that a large percentage of a school's budget depends upon the number of children attending the school. The loss of just a few children, especially in a small school, can make a substantial difference to the overall financial position and put pressure on governors and staff to cut resources. Establishing harmonious relations with parents is not simply a matter of good educational practice; it is necessary to ensure that they are sufficiently satisfied to keep their children at the school and recommend it to others. Don't forget that the views of parents (and pupils) are sought and are reflected in school inspection reports.

OTHER ADULTS IN SCHOOL

As noted earlier, parents provide the emotional and practical bedrock for pupil progress, by stimulating interest in learning, encouraging the children to persevere, assisting with homework and, in some cases, working as a volunteer helper. The next section deals with the different roles of the many other adults apart from parents who form part of the school community and contribute to the teaching and learning programme, and to the nurture and care of children.

Working together

Children have their own views on who matters in school and who does not. For instance, mealtime assistants are rarely accorded the same respect as teachers, whereas the school administrator is seen as being very significant. Nevertheless, in different ways, every adult makes a contribution to school life and their co-operation, support and encouragement are vitally important in shaping the school ethos and the children's progress (Mills and Mills 1995; Vincett *et al.* 2005). The more successful schools are usually those in which there is a high level of collaboration and a good team spirit (e.g. Nias *et al.* 1989; Beaudoin and Taylor 2004), both between members of the same group (such as ancillary staff) and across groups (such as the relationship between teachers and assistants). Teachers, in particular, as the most influential people in the children's education, have a responsibility to consider ways in which they can develop positive links with other staff members, outside agencies and volunteers for the benefit of children's learning.

Trainee teachers are included in the variety of adults who contribute to this complex amalgam of influences. It is not easy for them to go into a strange school and begin to establish a good working relationship with children and colleagues that they have never met. This adjustment is, however, exactly what has to happen in most school placement situations. The skill of trainees in relating to their class teacher and mentor can make the difference between an effective and a disappointing school experience. This fact does not mean that trainee teachers have to like the teacher or fully approve of his/her methods. It does mean that they have to make every effort to show that they appreciate what is being done on their behalf and support the teacher fully in helping pupils to fulfil their potential and grow up as responsible members of society. The large majority of host teachers value the presence of trainees in the classroom and want to see them succeed.

Because of the commitment of the host teachers to trainees, under no circumstances should you ever admit to having doubts about your vocation. Teachers are understandably dismayed if they think that they are wasting their time helping trainees to succeed when they have little intention of teaching after qualifying. All members of staff involved with the trainee teacher's placement will give their full backing if they perceive that you are determined to be a positive influence in the classroom. They expect you to be willing to listen, learn, respond, acknowledge mistakes and do all that you can to improve your classroom practice. Teachers will judge your commitment by the thoroughness of your preparation, awareness of opportunities to enhance children's learning, positive contribution to classroom decisions and resolute attitude. Although it is important to demonstrate a willingness to be an active member of the team, it does not mean that you have to passively accept all that is said to you without ever questioning or offering your own opinions. Trainee teachers have to be prepared to question, reflect, ponder and establish an intelligent dialogue with those who are responsible for their mentoring and training. Always bear in mind, however, that the final responsibility for the children's welfare and achievement lies with the class teacher.

Developing a supportive attitude

When you are qualified and have responsibility for a group of children, you will understand more fully the concerns that teachers have about allowing a stranger to take charge. Every teacher has some idiosyncratic practices and ideas which others find difficult to accept. However, at the heart of the collaborative endeavour must be a strong inclination on the part of trainee teachers to co-operate with the host teachers for the benefit of the children, even when they don't fully approve of some of the things that are done. For instance, you may not feel that you want to use the same system of rewards and sanctions as the teacher. You may want to do more listening and less speaking than the teacher does. You may wish to give children more freedom or less freedom to make choices, and so on. However, it is important for every trainee teacher to take an unprejudiced view of these sorts of issues, as the more that teachers at all stages of their career can develop an open dialogue with colleagues and mentors about the managing and organising of learning, the more confident they will become in adjusting their approach from the basis of a well-informed and considered perspective. However, in undertaking such forms of dialogue, it is particularly important to be courteous and non-judgemental because even well-intended comments may be construed by the teacher or assistant as subtle criticism. A school ethos founded upon positive attitudes and affirmative comments towards pupils should also apply to adult–adult relationships, and facilitate open discussions about serious issues. You must still try your best to be positive and supportive, whether or not you are sympathetic towards the host teacher's priorities. On the other hand, many teachers are so busy implementing the latest government initiative that they scarcely have time to stop and think about fundamental issues. Your insights about issues can awaken fresh awareness and enthusiasm in your jaded host.

Activate your thinking!

Take time to raise interesting questions, such as: What is education for? What is the difference between assessment and evaluation of learning? How detailed should records of progress be? What is the difference between collaboration and co-operation?

Fostering understanding among school staff

As a means of gaining a better understanding of other adults in school, it is important to consider some of their roles and examine the ways their work impinges on others. The rest of this chapter provides a synopsis of the work, needs and priorities of some key personnel.

The head teacher

Every report about schools stresses the importance of the head teacher in the success of the school. Together with governors, the head teacher is responsible for the whole running of the school. For instance, the head teacher has immediate responsibility for achieving agreed aims, safeguarding curriculum entitlement for pupils, maintaining links with the community, involving parents closely in school life, informing parents about their children's progress and establishing appropriate forms of pupil assessment. All these responsibilities are in addition to oversight for staff welfare, training, development and appraisal, with a view to making decisions about Expert Teacher status and other promotions.

Head teachers work long hours and this exacts a high cost, which is now reflected in enhanced salaries. Local management of schools (LMS) brought with it new demands for control of the school budget and associated financial decisions. A large proportion of the head teacher's day is spent dealing with administrative tasks, meeting people and attending meetings. Unless the school is very small, it is unlikely that the head teacher will have a substantial teaching commitment. While it is true that head teachers are often less informed about the detail of the curriculum than their class teachers, they are certainly interested in what goes on in the classroom. A good head teacher will spend a lot of time encouraging staff to work as members of a team, to attend courses to enhance their work and promoting high standards of pupil attainment and discipline. The numerous education initiatives of recent years, legislation covering the so-called 'work–life balance' and closer links between the education service and social services have made heavy demands of heads and their governing bodies (see later). In addition, head teachers have had to manage the introduction of extended school hours, the *Every Child Matters* agenda, changes in inspection regimes and the introduction of TAs and HLTAs into the classroom, plus a raft of training and qualifications for staff at all levels. It is not surprising, perhaps, that numbers of applicants for headship have slumped.

Whatever head teachers' strengths and weaknesses, they are entitled to anticipate every teacher's support and enthusiasm. Some new teachers are in awe of the head teacher, but need to remind themselves that the head was once a classroom teacher and only asks that staff work hard, respect their colleagues and help to promote the school's reputation and achievements.

Teachers are most likely to have contact with the head teacher during assembly, at staff meetings, when specific decisions are being made or when their advice is sought. Head teachers also write references for teachers who apply for other jobs, so it is in every teacher's interest to maintain an open, courteous and professional relationship with them. In turn the head teacher expects staff to:

- Be trustworthy and hard-working
- Prepare lessons thoroughly and teach efficiently
- Show enthusiasm and determination
- Relate well to parents
- Show respect towards colleagues and visitors
- Have a bright and tidy classroom with evidence of good quality children's work on display.

Governors

The role of governors has changed considerably in recent years (see, for instance, Doust and Doust 2001; Adams 2002; see Adamson, 2007 for a summary of key responsibilities). At one time, they were merely figureheads and rarely involved in school life other than for special functions and emergencies. Until the 1980s, governing bodies had few powers and relatively little influence in schools. The head teacher determined most school policies, and teachers decided what they taught their children. The Education Acts of the 1980s and 1990s drastically altered the responsibilities and status of governing bodies, all of which must now include representatives from the teaching staff, parents and local community. The governing body's main role is to help raise standards of pupil achievement. Governing bodies are responsible to parents, funding providers and the community.

People become governors for a variety of reasons. The majority have a desire to help the school community. A small number get elected so as to wield influence on behalf of a particular social or religious cause. They are normally people of considerable ability and experience, and although they may not have a background in education, they normally have other skills and attributes that allow them to offer a different perspective on issues. Many governors are delighted to offer their help and support wherever possible, and although they may not have the time or inclination to give regular classroom support, the best sort of governor will always listen and provide sound advice. Governors have become increasingly significant in ensuring that the school operates efficiently. They are accountable for the performance of the school to parents and the wider community; they help plan the school's aims and policies and make appointments, including the head teacher. They also make decisions about the school's budget, monitor the curriculum and determine how the school can encourage pupil's spiritual, moral and social development. Governors also have a legal responsibility to ensure the school provides for all its pupils, including those with special needs. Every trainee teacher should take the opportunity to meet governors, as they have responsibility for every aspect of school life, including the work of trainees.

Each year, a formal meeting of governors and parents is held at which governors produce a report for parents to discuss the manner in which the school has been and is to be conducted, plus any other matters relating to the school that are raised by parents of registered pupils. Although in practice only a small percentage of parents attend, this annual meeting highlights the governors' accountability and significance in the life of the school. Commonly, the head and governors use the evening as a celebration of achievement as well as fulfilling the formal requirements. Governors have the right to enter the school at any time and examine aspects of its life and work, though convention and common courtesy dictate that this should only be done with the permission of the head teacher and, if teaching is to be observed, with the consent of the teachers concerned. Governors are not inspectors or local authority advisers and are generally not equipped to conduct a formal evaluation of teaching quality; this task is within the head teacher's remit. Many head teachers arrange informal gatherings of teachers and governors each term to help cement relationships and celebrate successes. These meetings form an important element of professional life. It is also reassuring to know that at least one colleague will be representing the views of staff by being elected as the 'teacher governor'. The full composition of a governing body normally includes the following members:

- Local authority governors
- Teachers elected by their colleagues
- A governor elected by support staff
- Parents elected by other parents at the school
- A governor co-opted by other members of the body
- The head teacher (normally)
- Representatives of churches in schools with a religious foundation.

Governor elections

Numbers vary depending on the school's type or size and appointments are for four years. Parent and teacher governors are elected. Ballot forms are distributed to parents of the children in the school and the candidate with the most votes is elected. If a number of parents wish to stand for the vacancy, they have a right to circulate their views and win over support; this is sometimes carried out by the simple expediency of allowing each candidate a given number of words in which to set out their position. Their manifestos are then copied to all parents. Ballot papers have to be carefully monitored and returns counted carefully. Governors (often the chairperson) have to be involved in the process to ensure that procedures are correctly followed. Procedures for appointing the teacher representative are less complex, though equally rigorous. In very small schools with only a handful of staff, there is sometimes a problem in finding a teacher willing to stand.

The head teacher can opt whether or not to be a governor, though nearly all do so. When school inspectors visit, their report is sent to the governors, who are charged with the task of ensuring that the recommendations are followed and perceived shortcomings dealt with. Head teachers often refer to 'my governors' indicating the close relationship which ideally exists between them. A school in which the governors and head teacher have a harmonious relationship is likely to prosper. Head teachers who enjoy this level of security know that when there are difficulties and problems, they will be assured of support and encouragement from the governing body.

Governors' responsibilities

Whatever their motivation, the role of governor is a demanding one and requires people with stamina, determination and the ability to grasp fairly complex issues and make sense of a large number of government missives and local authority circulars. Governing bodies are responsible for the upkeep of the buildings, curriculum development, staff, finance, special needs provision and maintaining satisfactory community relations.

Governors also have the responsibility for ensuring that school policies and decisions accord with the large number of government edicts which have been issued in recent years, including managing the curriculum, publishing an informative school brochure for parents containing test results and other information about the school, staffing, health and safety, special needs provision, employment contracts, disciplinary procedures, buildings and numerous other aspects of school life. Governors also receive, comment upon, and act upon inspection reports and other consultation exercises. They are expected to be involved in establishing and monitoring 'target setting', relating in particular to the percentage of pupils who reach level 4 in the National Curriculum Tests (commonly referred to as SATs from a time when they were Standard Assessment Tasks) in core subjects (notably Literacy), which is supposed to improve year upon year. In theory, the head teacher is responsible for the day-to-day running of the school and the governors act as an executive. In practice, the roles can overlap and there may be uncertainty about where the head teacher's role ends and the governors' role begins. The line between governing bodies offering adequate support to a teaching staff and becoming intrusive is a fine one, but the trend is towards more, rather than less, governor involvement (Dean 2001; Sallis 2007). In fact, the responsibilities carried by governors make it among the most demanding voluntary jobs in education.

Most governing bodies are sub-divided into groups responsible for different areas of school life: curriculum, fabric, finance, community, and so on. The groups report back to the main body at each governing body meeting. Some decisions can be made by sub-groups, but there are guidelines on which decisions require the full governing body and which do not. In some schools, governors take a particular interest in one curriculum area or age-phase. For instance, a governor may be attached to mathematics, another to science; similarly, a governor may develop links with the nursery class or with classes at the end of Key Stages. In other schools all the governors target a particular curriculum area over a given period of time; for example, they may focus on the teaching of mathematics. Governors do not have the right to interfere with curriculum planning and implementation but the more they know about the detailed situation, the more able they are to argue the case for additional resources for it. Schools should have a governor with a brief for monitoring the implementation of policies for special educational needs (SEN).

In the past, governors have not paid much attention to trainee teachers. However, as their contribution has come to be seen as part of the teaching and learning, and forms an element of the inspection process, governors now need to show more interest in what they do. If appointed as NQTs, of course, they become the subject of intense interest because:

- Governors appointed them and will want to feel that their decision was a correct one
- In any inspection the performance of every teacher (recently qualified or otherwise) is significant
- Governors regularly talk about the school staff, their needs, concerns and aspirations
- One of the parent-governors may have a child in their class or will know several people who do.

Teachers are most likely to have contact with governors:

- During specially organised meetings for the purpose
- When a governor has been delegated to collect information about a given curriculum area
- Through teacher-governor colleagues
- Informally with parent-governors who collect children and attend parent teacher association meetings.

Things that governors expect from teachers:

- To do the job to the very best of their ability and be willing to learn how to do it better
- To support and be enthusiastic about all aspects of school life
- To be willing to develop and extend their expertise and influence within the school and community.

Over and above the regular issues, governors' chief concerns are about the head teacher's welfare, financial considerations, parental satisfaction, individual teacher's welfare and school inspection. Governors are also charged with making important decisions about internal promotion, the head teacher's salary and, as noted above, ensuring that teachers are able to enjoy a reasonable balance between work and home commitments.

Teaching assistants

There has been a considerable expansion in the use of teaching assistants (TAs) in primary schools over recent years. Each TA has a job description to which she or he needs to conform, though flexibility is considered to be a great asset. TAs have been employed in larger primary schools over many years for general duties but they are gradually assuming more responsibility for pupils' learning and the large increase in their numbers is to support the work of class teachers in boosting standards of achievement. However, TAs share with teachers motivation that is driven by a desire to work with children and help them to do well in all aspects of their lives: personal, social, academic and spiritual. The concept of the TA as the education equivalent of an extra locomotive to help pull the train up a gradient is far removed from the way that TAs view their role.

Some TAs are responsible for the needs of one child, for whom the term Learning Support Assistant (LSA) was often used in the past. However, assistants are now graded as a TA or as a Higher Learning Teaching Assistant (HLTA) so labels like LSA tend to be associated with their role rather than their status. HLTAs in particular are likely to work more closely with the teacher with respect to teaching and learning, though all adult assistants can be used in one or more of a variety of ways (see Waters 1996; Burnham 2006). Although some assistants have a job description and hold their own clear view of what they are and are not prepared to do, it is up to you to be specific about your expectations from day to day, and from session to session. The need for clarity is especially relevant in early years' classes where additional adult support is often interwoven into the fabric of the teaching day. With older children the TA may be involved in intensive coaching of children who have fallen behind or struggling; they may be allocated to supervise a group of children and guide them in task completion. Whatever the specific responsibility, the principle of working closely with the TA and valuing her expertise is fundamental to a healthy working environment. To use an extreme example, it would be a waste of the TA's time to wash paint brushes, when she could be leading a group of able children in mathematical problem-solving.

Nearly every class teacher who has the services of an assistant is grateful for the help and support offered. Salaried TAs tend to be more common in younger age classes than in the upper primary range, though the emphasis on providing low achievers with intensive additional support to 'boost' their attainment in Key Stage 2 has required the services of many more trained staff. Increasingly, all paid assistants possess a qualification and nearly all attend additional in-service courses to develop their expertise (see Watkinson 2003a, 2003b; Cousins *et al.* 2004). About 10 per cent of TAs are former teachers who no longer wish to teach but who possess a range of suitable skills. Many assistants are local people who enjoy working in school, have their own children there and have been appointed to support the work of teachers with larger classes. Due to funding limitations, assistants may be employed on temporary contracts or work strictly to their hours, making liaison with teachers difficult.

In many primary schools TAs have been principally used to work alongside children in core subjects rather than in the more creative and aesthetic areas, with the result that some of their traditional responsibilities (such as assisting with basic practical tasks and putting up displays) have assumed secondary importance. However, the situation is dynamic and a new breed of better-trained and remunerated assistants is gradually emerging. The recruitment of tens of thousands of support staff and exploit their expertise in the classroom is supposed to mirror the situation in hospitals where a senior professional (such as a consultant) is involved only with key decision-making and advanced practice, leaving the subordinates (junior doctors, nurses) to carry out the orders and perform most of the regular work. However, for those assistants wishing to pursue further study there are career routes into teaching. The strategy of employing more TAs has implications for classroom work, including:

- More flexible models of teaching and learning, such that teachers can use professional judgement in leading support colleagues
- Teachers becoming principally responsible for learning outcomes than every aspect of the teaching and learning process
- Teachers can be freed from more routine tasks and concentrate on the more specialised elements of their role, such as planning, preparation and assessment of pupils' learning
- Support staff gain appropriate skills and knowledge to complement and enhance the work of teachers.

It is evident that additional support staff must be flexible and able to respond rapidly to a teacher's requests. Although a lot of lesson planning is done in advance, a great deal of a teacher's day consists of making spontaneous decisions and sometimes adjusting plans at the last moment to fit the events of the moment. On the one hand a TA is not a lackey, waiting obediently for the teacher's command; on the other hand a TA must accept that effective teachers modify and adjust priorities and that not everything can be predicted. Any action that might upset the delicate balance of mutual trust and endeavour that is the mainstay of effective schools must be assiduously avoided. Thus, it is essential that the relationship between teacher and assistant is comfortable for both parties and responsive to changing events. Primary schooling involves an array of rich learning opportunities, such as the visit of a theatre company, outdoor pursuits, educational trips and school productions. The value of mature and appropriately trained adults to help administer and organise such events is invaluable, though there are important legal implications for schools and teachers with which you must become familiar, perhaps through your Union or the relevant Teaching Body (notably, the General Teaching Council, GTC).

The strategy for involvement of large numbers of TAs is posited on the assumption that having additional support staff is advantageous in releasing the teacher from onerous tasks and supporting children's learning. However, there are specific management skills that you need to develop, both in knowing how to relate to TAs and how to use them profitably. There are many routine tasks that teachers have carried out in the past but are now deemed more suitable for classroom support staff. Not all of the items in the list are equally important or relevant to primary schools. The full range of tasks is shown in Figure 3.1.

The most relevant tasks for TAs in primary schools are predictable ones Thus, assistants may be involved in activities that involve putting up displays, administering money, organising paperwork and pupil records, photocopying, ordering equipment and maintaining essential resources. On the other hand, it is clearly a waste of time and money to employ capable assistants and fill their time with menial tasks when they have other talents to offer, so some of the more skilled TAs might be involved in assisting with ICT or acting as counsellor in conjunction with the school's child advocate (who is the named person responsible for dealing with children who wish to share a particular concern or grievance, especially if it concerns an adult).

Good practice

When you start work in a new school it is important to ascertain the particular roles occupied by the different assistants.

1   Collecting money
2   Chasing absences
3   Bulk photocopying
4   Copy typing
5   Producing standard letters
6   Producing class lists
7   Record keeping and filing
8   Classroom display
9   Analysing attendance figures
10 Processing exam results
11 Collating pupil reports
12 Administering work experience
13 Administering examinations
14 Invigilating examinations
15 Administering teacher cover
16 ICT trouble-shooting and minor repairs
17 Commissioning new ICT equipment
18 Ordering supplies and equipment
19 Stocktaking
20 Cataloguing, preparing, issuing and maintaining equipment and materials
21 Minuting meetings
22 Co-ordinating and submitting bids
23 Seeking and giving personnel advice
24 Managing pupil data
25 Inputting pupil data

Figure 3.1 Possible tasks for teaching assistants (based on DfES 2002b)

Although TAs carry out these tasks, they still have to be co-ordinated by a teacher. In addition, whereas a simple job such as photocopying does not require specialist expertise, it is not acceptable (for example) for an assistant to carry out minor repairs to technical equipment without full training. Similarly, it is useful if a TA can relieve you of important but time-consuming jobs in the area of health and safety (such as checking the state of games' equipment) providing that legal responsibilities are met. In other words, if a TA says that all is well and the equipment proves to be unsafe, the teacher and not the assistant, takes final responsibility. Again, it saves a teacher a lot of time if an assistant carries out the administration of ordering (say) consumable resources, but the teacher still has to spend time in being familiar with what is needed and liaising with the assistant before the order is sent. In other words, the mere availability of an assistant does not of itself free you to concentrate on the tasks that require more sophisticated professional skills such as planning and preparing, teaching, assessing children's progress, marking and reporting. It is also the case that an assistant will not always be available when you need assistance, so there are bound to be times when you have to do the task yourself. Consequently, although you may want to delegate jobs, it is important that you do not lose touch with them entirely or allow yourself to become deskilled. Although an experienced teacher can usually cope with the unexpected absence of a TA, you may find the situation more challenging.

Good practice

Working with reception-age children, one TA's responsibilities included the following:

- Hearing children read orally and maintaining records
- Assisting with a maths extension group
- Assisting during the lesson time, working one to one with particular children
- Mounting and displaying children's work around the room and corridor
- Producing some resources for teaching as requested by the class teacher
- Taking children to the library to select books and other general library duties
- Assisting the teacher when children were moving around the school and being taken outside the premises
- Keeping accident report records and overseeing health and safety requirements
- Designing and producing scenery for school plays
- The collection and distribution of refreshments, including drinking water
- Voluntarily running an after-school craft club.

The number and level of involvement of support staff will be affected by the size of the school. In particular, very small schools (of which there are many) with fewer than 100 pupils do not have the infrastructure, physical space or finance to operate like a secondary school of (say) a thousand pupils, with dedicated spaces and specialist support staff. Small schools are more likely to utilise voluntary adult help or employ part-time assistants, often shared across several classes. Consequently, the deployment of support staff involves considerable flexibility and close teamwork to ensure consistency and equity.

The need for developing expertise becomes even more essential when HLTAs take responsibility for teaching a group of children or even the whole class under the general guidance of the teacher. See, for example, Rose 2005; Cullingford-Agnew 2006. However, in assuming greater responsibility, part of their essential skills' training is to gain more experience in behaviour management (Bentham 2005).

One way and another, the involvement of assistants in a variety of activities previously considered the sole province of qualified teachers is likely to become increasingly significant in schools but is not of itself a panacea for reducing teachers' workload. The most important factor is that the benefits that accrue from having an assistant outweigh the additional demands that managing another adult involve for the teacher.

Activate your thinking!

Imagine that you have responsibility for managing two TAs, one of whom works with a blind child, the other on general duties, shared half-time with the adjacent class. What factors will you need to consider in managing the situation?

Special needs assistants are now subsumed under the general title of 'learning support assistant' and undertake a specialist role in working alongside children whose learning needs are sufficiently acute to have been formally identified through a 'statementing' procedure involving the parents, school, educational psychologist and local education authority. The statement is a formal document in which the child's needs and an action plan to support these needs are identified. The local authority, through the school, is legally charged with providing the resources (human and practical) to assist in supporting the child's emotional and academic shortcomings or, quite frequently, addressing a combination of both these problem areas.

Due to the policy of placing all children into mainstream schooling, the status of learning support assistants has been enhanced over recent years. Ideally, if there is a child who has been formally identified as having special needs, an assistant will be available for part or all of the day to offer additional learning support or provide an extra adult presence to channel poor behaviour into something more constructive, depending on the nature and severity of the need. However, the concept of one adult clinging like a leech to a single needy child throughout the day is becoming outmoded; rather, the child works intensively with an adult, either inside or outside the main classroom base (see Chapter 9).

Almost all TAs are hardworking and dedicated. They may not have the teacher's level of professional expertise – though around 10 per cent of TAs have qualified teacher status – but will often have a store of experience about what happens in and around the school and life in general. Every assistant has an agreed job description but most enjoy some variety in their routine and are happy to undertake other tasks when it is appropriate to do so.

TAs rely on the class teacher to direct them and provide support for them when they are unsure or wish to enhance their expertise. It is, of course, entirely wrong for TAs to be allocated tasks and responsibilities for which they are poorly prepared. If class teachers fail to provide adequate support and direction, support staff understandably become frustrated or insecure and begin to create their own patterns of working which may not suit the teacher.

It is essential for you to maintain good and open relationships with all support staff. If an assistant has been at the school for a long time and has become attached to a particular way of working, she or he will possibly be resistant to change. Under such circumstances, you need diplomacy and patience to introduce new ways of working and make adjustments to the assistant's responsibilities. However, it pays to listen to advice from experienced TAs, as they often possess insights that you lack. If the assistant is a parent, the teacher's reputation can hinge on the informal conversations about the teacher that the assistant has with other parents outside school, so be warned.

Good practice

To ensure that your TA contributes effectively to classroom life and gains satisfaction from doing so, it helps to incorporate the following good practice into your weekly schedule:

- Take time to clarify her duties and your own expectations
- Offer her the chance to develop her skills and be involved in those aspects of classroom life she finds enjoyable and fulfilling
- In addition to regular communication, set aside a time each week to discuss matters of mutual concern
- Take every opportunity to thank her for her efforts and acknowledge her contribution.

TAs are not assistant teachers and this fact must be taken into account when deciding the tasks they are asked to undertake. For instance, if you ask an assistant to hear children read aloud, it is essential that she has enough knowledge about learning how to read so that she can make a positive impact on the pupil's progress. One of the quickest ways to damage a TA's dedication is to make unjustified assumptions about her capability and level of responsibility or to take advantage of her goodwill (Balshaw 1999; Fox 1998; Hancock and Collins 2005). Teachers have to take care to assign to their assistants appropriate duties and responsibilities rather than burden them with the mundane tasks that no one else wants to do. TAs expect from teachers appropriate respect and understanding, clarity about the nature of their work and being kept informed. TAs' chief concerns include opportunities to engage with tasks that use their expertise instead of lower level activities, and the positive responses of the children they supervise. In common with every other adult in school, assistants merit and enjoy sincere praise and encouragement, so don't disappoint them.

Caretakers and cleaners

Over the past few years, the demands upon caretakers and cleaning staff have grown. A school that once had three or four staff to safeguard and clean the premises may now make do with one or two on reduced working hours; some larger schools employ security firms to protect the premises. Such is the world in which we live. There has been a tendency over recent years to employ contracted staff, who may or may not have a personal commitment to the particular school and are probably on minimum wages. Caretakers work prescribed hours and are possibly also on call, which means that they have to be available beyond their normal duties. For instance, if a child is sick over the classroom floor, it is normal policy that only the caretaker clears it up, using specific procedures and designated chemicals. Unfortunately, the caretaker may be unavailable or live at a great distance from the school, in which case there will be a school policy about the appropriate procedure. Although such instances may sound trivial, they can be highly disrupting and a health hazard, so it pays to be informed. Caretakers are not allowed to perform certain tasks such as climbing ladders above a certain height, lifting heavy weights and carrying out property maintenance. Although many caretakers will loosely interpret these rules and bend over backwards to be helpful, it is important to remember that an innocent request for assistance may meet with a reluctant refusal if the request means breaking the contractual terms. The first rule for teachers who hope to develop a good relationship with the caretaker is to discover what duties are specified and which ones are favoured. Why not ask?

One of the caretaker 's most demanding tasks in a larger school is to supervise cleaners. Cleaners sometimes work in the early morning before school begins or, more often, for two or three hours after school. In that time they have a lot to do and the caretaker is responsible for ensuring that the work is carried out satisfactorily. In a very small school, one person may be both cleaner and caretaker and will have to do everything from locking and unlocking the school to mopping floors, collecting and depositing rubbish, and controlling stock. Even in a medium-sized primary school, there may be as few as two persons involved.

All teachers should be sensitive to the pressures on cleaning staff and bear in mind that the most frequent complaints about the state of classrooms made by cleaning staff include the mess made by clay and sticky products trodden into carpets, inappropriate use of paper towels, chairs not stacked according to the school's agreed procedure, messy sinks and graffiti on table tops. As cleaners need to come into the room after school, a little consideration to allow them access to your room is both courteous and practical. A little effort to train the children to clear up and follow sensible rules will avoid irritating cleaners as well as improve your organisational skills.

Activate your thinking!

What does the cleaner say to colleagues about the condition of your room? How does your attitude to the caretaker help in generating a positive working relationship?

Good practice

If your caretaker has an interesting background, extend an invitation to talk to your class about it. Remember that this volunteer may not be used to addressing children and will need your support and guidance. It is usually better to have two short sessions on different days than a lengthy monologue. The caretaker (or any other adult you invite to speak to the children) may be loquacious with adults but feel constrained when addressing children.

Caretakers expect respect and courtesy from teachers, an acknowledgement of the demands of their job and advance notice about forthcoming events. Caretakers' chief concerns are receiving a visit from their supervisor, cleaner absenteeism and a lack of basic resources to do the job effectively. Every time you make an effort to be co-operative you will receive double the reward in return.

Mealtime assistants

Many people feel that mealtime assistants (MTAs) have the least enviable job in schools. Playground supervision, in particular, places great demands upon them as they attempt to control large numbers of excitable children, sort out squabbles, mend damaged knees and broken relationships, and direct children to the right place at the right time. Inside the school, there are lunch boxes to open, tables to wipe, slow eaters to encourage and poor manners to correct. Although the majority of MTAs are dedicated and conscientious, their lack of authority can cause them to struggle with unco-operative children, and the sound of strained adult voices is a familiar one in some schools.

An increasing number of head teachers and governors have come to recognise that as MTAs play an important role in the life of the school, it is worth investing time in the provision of training and guidance. As a result, issues such as behaviour management, assertiveness, interpersonal relationships and first-aid are addressed through regular sessions. MTAs need to have a good sense of humour, plenty of stamina and a strong personality. Due to the low wages, most of them will be local parents and a number of them may have a second job. When MTAs are seen leaving school the moment the dinner break is over, it is tempting to think that this reflects a low level of commitment. In fact, they are likely to have other responsibilities or are (understandably) refusing to do unpaid overtime. Until relatively recently teachers were all expected to undertake a dinner duty and although in some schools there is still a voluntary rota of teachers who wish to help, very few do so. Larger schools may employ a more highly qualified person to supervise lunchtime arrangements, generate interest in traditional games and activities, and manage the other mealtime staff. Certain MTAs may be allocated to a child with special needs and most of them are encouraged or trained to learn more about the value of play and handling potentially combustible situations. It is noteworthy that Cohen (2006) claims that there is strong evidence that play has not only has a therapeutic function, but also that energetic, spontaneous physical play may facilitate neurological development. Cohen rightly argues that if this is the case, 'stopping children from playing, either by punishing them or medicating them might actually contribute to developmental abnormalities' (2006: 162). A large number of schools involve older, responsible pupils to assist through involvement in all-age 'family' groupings, monitoring a 'time out' space or even being trained as counsellors.

With the youngest children, it is quite likely that an MTA will come to the classroom a few minutes before the official end of the morning to take responsibility for the children who stay for lunch. If so, it is important that teachers consider the organisational implications of completing work and tidying up before she arrives. This last point is especially significant if the room is used for children to eat their packed lunches. If it is a wet day, the MTAs will be trying to look after the children all together in the school hall or flitting from classroom to classroom attempting to entertain and subdue the restless children. MTAs are only responsible for children who remain at school to eat their lunch, not for children who go home. Younger children who are going home for lunch have to be supervised by the teacher until an adult collects them. If children return to school too early from lunch, they are not, strictly speaking, the responsibility of MTAs.

When children are together in the playground, it is inevitable that there are disagreements and conflicts from time to time that require adult intervention. Occasionally, MTAs cannot cope unaided and may bring a naughty child to the teacher for admonishment. There are a number of principles to consider in evaluating your interaction with MTAs:

- As a teacher, MTAs believe that you are never fully off-duty

- MTAs expect teachers, however inexperienced, to be able to deal with instances of pupil misdemeanour

- It is important to remain detached from the emotions of the moment until explanations are sought and the situation can be properly resolved

- There is a need to balance the MTA's expectation that she will receive your support with the possibility that the child concerned may also have a genuine grievance.

Lunchtime conflict situations are never easy to deal with but teachers must expect to meet them from time to time. Frustration on the part of adult or child can lead to overreaction and a rapid deterioration of the situation; emotionally vulnerable children may become aggressive and require immense patience and calm insistence. A useful guide to the success achieved in deploying and training MTAs in a school is the length of the queue of children outside the head teacher's or deputy's room at the end of the lunch break: the longer the line, the more urgent the problem. Effective MTAs lead to happier children and a more settled start to the afternoon, so it pays to support them in their attempts to do the job well, as you don't want unsettled and resentful children in your class at the start of the afternoon.

Guidelines for managing lunchtime situations

- Do not jump to conclusions. Make sure of your facts first

- If in doubt about the appropriate course of action, delay in making a decision until you have chance to consult a more senior colleague

- In the case of serious incidents, always inform the head teacher or deputy as soon as possible. Make a brief note about the details of the incident as soon as practically possible

- Never use platitudes to placate an angry adult. Try to find out the facts and remain calm until the position is clearer

- Be constructive with your comments and search for a resolution or strategies to improve the situation

- Listen more than talk

- Always support the MTA where possible but remember that children have rights, too.

What MTAs expect from teachers:

- To be courteous and pleasant

- To acknowledge the demands of their job

- To take direct responsibility for situations when appropriate

■ To offer constructive support when necessary but not to undermine their position.

MTAs' chief concerns are individual mischievous children, uncomfortable relationships with fellow MTAs and worries that they have done or said too much to a particular child.

Good practice

Allocate some time in your schedule to get to know one other adult better each week. Decide how you can demonstrate your gratitude for their contribution to school life and to your own work without appearing patronising.

The role of adults on educational visits

Children love to go out of school on visits and many claim that it is the most exciting part of the school year for them. There are now strict rules governing charges made to parents for school visits and no child may be excluded from an educational visit on the grounds of cost. In other words, visits are for all children, regardless of status or a parent's ability to pay. Teachers have to consult with the head teacher about the procedures for outings before committing themselves or the school to any financial agreement. As a trainee you will not be expected to carry out this preliminary work but you still need to be aware that it happens.

School trips, educational visits and other field activities can be great fun and a wonderful opportunity to seal your relationship with the pupils. They can also be times of hazard and potential danger, so a lot of planning is required to ensure that a visit is safe and educationally worthwhile (Smart 1995; Salaman and Tutchell 2005). In addition to checking that the venue is suitable for the age group and is properly managed, trip organisers have to send letters home detailing the itinerary, receive permission slips from parents, order transport, confirm insurance and liaise with colleagues whose lessons may be affected. They also have to ensure that every part of the day has been considered in detail. A 'good practice guide' known as *Health and Safety of Pupils on Educational Visits* (DfEE 1998) was designed to help head teachers, teachers, governors and others to ensure that pupils stay safe and healthy on school visits. It includes chapters on Responsibilities for Visits; Planning Visits; Supervision; Preparing Pupils; Communicating with Parents; Planning Transport; Insurance; Types of Visit; Visits Abroad and Emergency Procedures. It also includes a number of model forms that can be copied or adapted. The guide is not intended to replace local or other professional guidance or regulations and local education authorities should be the first source of advice to clarify finer points in the guide. A three-part supplement to the good practice guide was produced in 2002:

■ Standards for Local Authorities sets out the functions of the educational visits co-ordinator in schools and the levels of risk management that Local Authorities and Standards for Adventure is aimed at the teacher or youth worker who leads young people on adventure activities

- A Handbook for Group Leaders is aimed at anyone who leads groups of young people on any kind of educational visit. It sets out good practice in supervision, ongoing risk assessment and emergency procedures

- Group Safety at the Margins is aimed at anyone who organises learning activities that take place near or in water, such as a walk along a river bank or seashore, collecting samples from ponds or streams, or paddling or walking in gentle, shallow water. Comprehensive official guidance containing information and guidelines on all aspects of health and safety that affect schools, including the medical needs of children, emergencies and school security is provided in a document, Health and safety: responsibilities and powers, issued to schools in 2001.

Even when all the planning and organising is complete, there is still a lot of work to be done in ensuring that the day runs smoothly. In particular, it is essential to anticipate problems or hazards and the action needed to respond to a situation should something go wrong. It is not only important to have access to a mobile telephone for making immediate contact with emergency services should this prove necessary, but to carry a list of key contacts. Clarifying the role of the different adults involved is vitally important in making the visit a safe and successful one.

In practice, most schools have a well-ordered programme of visits and new teachers will discover that there are well-trodden paths to museums, landmarks, ancient monuments and adventure courses. Nevertheless, thorough preparation is essential if the trip is to be a success, including the following.

Costs

Some visits are not viable due to the cost of travel (coach hire is expensive) or entrance fees. Providing the weather is reasonable, there are usually numerous outdoor opportunities that offer valuable educational opportunities, as well as having a lot of fun. Waite and Rea (2007) comment that if suitable clothing is worn and sensible precautions are taken, there is no end to the range of opportunities for outdoor learning at minimal cost.

Timings

Coach travel is slower than travelling by car and an apparently short car journey through country lanes can become a long jaunt as the coach driver is obliged to follow a much longer prescribed main road route. Always leave a few minutes leeway for the journey time at both ends of the trip. Parents are rightly frustrated and anxious if the coach arrives back later than planned. It is important for adults to have a mobile telephone and a list of contact numbers with them at all times.

Safety

Coaches must conform to minimum safety standards. Experience has shown that it is better to pay a little more and ensure a high standard of service from a reputable company. Regulations have become much stricter in recent years, but a few rogue companies still exist. Although it was at one time possible to put three smaller children per double seat, the requirement for coaches to fit safety belts means that this option is no longer available. The two pupils per double seat rule also has cost implications owing to the fact that fewer children can be accommodated on a single vehicle. If private cars are to be used, a list of experienced drivers with current licences should be compiled and checked with the head teacher. Check with the head teacher as to whether each parent is required to satisfy a police check requirement beforehand. If the venue involves any activity that carries some risk (such as adventure courses) then basic health and safety regulations must be observed and the Activity Centre's own safety procedures verified. Safety first means thinking ahead and following guidelines closely.

Communication with parents

Parents should be notified at least six weeks before the proposed visit. For standard visits, an initial note should first be prepared about the purpose of the visit and the intentions for the day, with information about clothing, lunch arrangements and possible physical demands, plus an invitation for parents to contact the teacher in charge with any queries. A detachable permission slip is normally included as an indication that the parent is willing to permit the child to take part. (Parents can refuse, though they rarely do so.) The form sent home should include space for the child's name, address, contact number and space for the parent to mention any special circumstances (such as the child's need to carry an inhaler, fear of heights or water, etc.). It is better to send two letters: one a preliminary note with the basic details requesting parental permission; the second, nearer the time, including more detailed information about the precise nature of the educational visit and journey times (see below).

Itinerary

Each stage of the visit should be allotted a time: setting out, stops and starts, breaks and arrival. Parents and children should be given a copy in advance of the visit. If the visit is likely to continue beyond normal school hours, it is important to stress this fact to parents beforehand.

Resources

Clipboards, paper, pencils, activity sheets, maps, measuring tapes, cameras and other necessary equipment need to be gathered in advance. Educational visits have a habit of creeping up unawares on busy teachers and it is very stressful to be scurrying about on the morning of the visit in search of an essential item when it should have been ready the previous day. TAs have an important role to play in the preparation and monitoring of equipment, supervision of children and support for learning – so make sure they are also properly informed.

Adult–child ratios

Local authorities have guidelines for the amount of adult help required for an educational visit. Younger children obviously require more supervision than older ones and under-fives need a large adult presence. The experience and competence of the adults involved should be taken into account and they should all be fully briefed before the visit. The other adults will vary in competence, so take account of this fact before allocating any vulnerable children to inexperienced helpers. Pupils who are emotionally temperamental should be attached to the more experienced staff.

School arrangements

It is essential to check whether canteen staff have been informed that children will be away during that day, in addition to the teachers who normally hold clubs and activities. A playground duty may have to be swapped with a colleague. Children bringing dinner money may need to bring money for one day less than usual unless the canteen is providing a packed lunch for them. Children whose parents do not have to pay for meals are entitled to a packed lunch. All these details need to be sorted in advance; leave nothing to chance.

Educational potential

The effort required to plan a successful educational visit demands that in the days and weeks following the visit there is opportunity for children to draw upon their experiences and utilise their new-found skills, understanding and knowledge in a variety of contexts. Many teachers use a visit as a starting point for innovative teaching and learning and the production of stimulating displays and events. No teacher who has planned an educational visit will underestimate the effort that is required. Trainees and new teachers are advised to collaborate with a more experienced colleague and plan the enterprise jointly. Visits are very hard work but immensely rewarding and a means of enhancing the pupils' social development and helping adults to gain insights into each child's disposition, interests, strengths and limitations. Pupils also get to know the adults better and trainees do well to note that the adults also learn a lot about you.

Case study (parents)

Grace was nervous about meeting parents. She knew it was irrational to be so fearful but had never found it easy to relate to adults, though she had a natural way with children and her gracious manner endeared her to her colleagues. It was a shock, therefore, to be placed with Foundation Stage children, where home visits and close liaison with parents formed an important dimension of the job. Grace was relieved to hear that she would be accompanied by an experienced TA for the visits, but was still daunted by the prospect. In addition, the head teacher had arranged a series of informal meetings for the parents of new school entrants at which they could ask questions, express concerns and provide information about their children. Grace understood the benefits of such gatherings but still wished that she could just be left alone to get on with the job of teaching the children. However, over the following weeks, Grace's attitude changed completely as, to her surprise, she enjoyed the meetings and found that she was able to relate well to the parents. Furthermore, the knowledge that she gained about the children helped her to understand parental and pupil concerns more clearly and respond to each child's social and academic needs more appropriately. In addition, Grace discovered that her self-confidence increased sharply and such was the excellent rapport that she established with parents that she found herself actively looking for opportunities to deepen relationships with them.

Case study (other adults)

Miss Burns is pinning up some children's work on the display board, when the MTA, Mrs Adams, marches in, tugging a reluctant nine-year-old boy by the sleeve.

'Miss Burns, I'm bringing Terry to you because he won't do as he's told. I said to him "Don't throw your trainers up in the air" but he insisted on doing it and now Vicki's got hit on the head and ended up crying. Then him and Shaun set to, and Shaun ends up in tears. And I can't find Mrs Carlevale [the head teacher] or Mr Halpern [the deputy] so I found you instead.' [Sullen looks from Terry.]

'Well, Terry, what have you got to say for yourself?' the teacher ventures. [Shrug of shoulders.]

'He's always the same, Miss Burns; I tell him and tell him but he takes no notice.' [Terry looks at Mrs Adams fiercely but says nothing.] 'Anyway, I'm sick of him.'

'I'm sick of you picking on me,' retorts Terry, provocatively and angrily. The mood is blackening. Mrs Adams and Terry begin to argue in what is clearly a continuation of a longstanding feud. Miss Burns has a few seconds to decide what should be done: shout louder than either of them; walk off to find a senior colleague; deal with it herself. She wisely decides to take firm action.

'Thank you Mrs Adams; you did the right thing; I'll deal with Terry now. Thank you very much.' Mrs Adams, much relieved to unload the problem, returns to her duties. Miss Burns sensibly stands still for a moment to allow Terry time to regain his composure, then quietly but firmly asks him what happened. Terry is on the verge of tears and clearly frustrated. As Miss Burns listens to his story unfold it becomes clear that the episode with the trainers was a secondary issue and that the real problem has its roots in an argument that took place between Terry and Shaun about team selection. As a result of Shaun's taunts and cutting comments born of superior intellect, the less competent Terry hit back in the only way he knew how. Mrs Adams observed the moment when Terry punched his adversary and, owing to Terry's reputation for fighting, took immediate action. Miss Burns did not blame the MTA, who was only doing her job, but had some sympathy with the boy as he stood in front of her, miserable, resentful and defiant. She told him that she would have to think about what should be done and told him that he must see her straight after the lunch break. She would also ask Mrs Adams whether he had tried hard to behave. After extracting a muttered promise that he would 'do his best to behave' Miss Burns let him go. She immediately started to worry about whether she had done the right thing. After all, the rule was that anyone seen fighting should stand outside the head's door. She did not want to appear to be soft or failing to support the MTA, but she was also aware that the circumstances were not as straightforward as they seemed and wanted to give Terry, who was a child from a very unsettled background, another chance. She is torn between conforming to school policy and using her instincts to guide her actions in the particular circumstances.

Good practice

To reduce confrontations, take account of the following:

1. Stay calm, even if your insides are churning
2. Take charge of the situation by speaking with authority
3. Insist that one person speak at a time
4. Listen more than talk
5. Avoid making judgements about rights and wrongs
6. Ask the alleged perpetrator to confirm his or her actions
7. Do not allow any 'yes but' comments initially
8. After the facts have been established, allow the individual an opportunity to explain his or her actions
9. Ask the main perpetrator what he or she thinks should happen
10. If no answer to point 9 is forthcoming, offer alternatives
11. Offer strategies to avoid further problems to those involved
12. Make it clear what action you now intend to take.

Activate your thinking!

Imagine that you are Miss Burns: What next for Terry? Whom else will you involve? What will happen tomorrow lunchtime? Terry goes home and tells his mother that Mrs Adams is picking on him at lunchtime. His mother comes in to find out from you what is going on. What will you say?

Further reading

Kay, J. (2003) *Teaching Assistants' Handbook*, London: Continuum.
   Contains primary school examples, including the role of assistants in helping to teach English, mathematics and science.

Rose, R. (2005) *Becoming a Primary Higher Level Teaching Assistant*, Exeter: Learning Matters.
   A practical guide that provides a combination of theory and practice for TAs on training and assessment routes in achieving HLTA status.

Stern, J. (2003) *Involving Parents*, London: Continuum.
   A concise exploration of the potential benefits associated with parental involvement in children's education.

Whalley, M. (2007) *Involving Parents in their Children's Learning*, London: Sage.
   Offers ideas about how early years practitioners can collaborate effectively with parents, including case studies.

PART

2

Teaching and Learning

The Process of Learning

Introduction

This chapter concentrates on the ways that children learn and the way in which a teacher's decisions and priorities affect its quality and effectiveness. Throughout the chapter there is a recognition that learning relies on motivation, working relationships and curriculum relevance. By carefully considering these issues, teachers are better equipped to help children achieve their potential. The value of dialogue in learning and the needs of gifted and talented children are also explored.

Learning

The process of learning is complex and unpredictable and no one fully understands how it takes place, though there have been many attempts to do so. Robson (2006) argues that it is difficult to differentiate between learning and thinking, though claims that it is important to try. She offers one example (based on Perkins 1992) that 'learning is a consequence of thinking'. Robson also suggests that it is necessary to take a broad view of learning, 'which includes use of the imagination, a playful disposition, persistence and the ability to learn with and from others' (1992: 3). Crucially, success in learning is not solely concerned with things that can be measured (as promoted by Government and its agents). There are occasions when even the slowest children amaze everyone (including themselves) by grasping a difficult concept, mastering a skill or retaining some knowledge when their more illustrious classmates struggle to do so. Although teachers' enthusiasm and commitment play an important part in bringing about the best conditions for learning, it is essential that they consider things from a child's perspective if effective progress is to be made. Children are not merely recipients of learning but active partners and initiators of it. Three inter-dependent essential elements of learning are knowledge, understanding and the development of skills.

Knowledge

Knowledge has a safe ring to it but can be slippery and deceptive. There are many different forms of knowledge, including knowledge of facts, of controversies, of situations, of procedures and of people.

Knowledge of *facts* involves more than memorising. It needs to take account of new understanding; for instance, we now know that the earth is more or less round, not flat. Knowledge of *controversies* requires an awareness of the disputed information; for instance, whether Columbus discovered America. Knowledge of *moral dilemmas* demands a wide view of the relevant factors and an ability to make judgements about their significance. Knowledge of *procedures* is necessary when a task has to be completed or decisions made about effectiveness. Knowledge of *people* is needed to prosper in social situations. And so forth.

Although at one stage of a child's development it may be sufficient to 'know' something is 'true' it may subsequently be appropriate to point out that things may not be as straightforward as they appear. For example, seven-year-old children can be told that all objects fall towards the ground at the same rate, but 11 year olds also need to be aware that the principle only holds for objects over a certain density and under normal atmospheric conditions. A 15 year old may be interested in the variations according to air pressure, the effect of a vacuum, and so forth. Knowledge evolves and deepens with age, experience and a greater facility with language use.

Knowledge may also be thought of in terms of being *transitory*, such as remembering a telephone number for as long as it takes to dial it but no longer. It can be *accessible*, such as recalling a spelling rule for use when writing but not holding the knowledge at the forefront of thinking for regular use. It can be *immediate*, such as knowing a friend's name or the route to school without needing to think deeply about it. Sometimes, children seem to remain locked in the transitory knowledge zone. They appear to have learned something during the morning lesson but cannot remember it during the afternoon. Sometimes the knowledge is locked into a child's recall system but cannot be accessed, either because it is too deeply stored, the child is tired or circumstances (such as stress) create a barrier to remembering. Knowledge that does not relate to previous learning is no more than mechanical repetition or 'rote learning'. For instance, a child could learn a list of Latin names off by heart and get full marks in a test, but have no idea about their meaning.

Finally, children gradually need to gain wisdom about the use of knowledge, its appropriateness, its relevance and its application. Teachers therefore have the challenging task of helping children to locate what they learn in social contexts or at least using case studies to exemplify the principles involved.

Many of our teaching techniques rely on children's immediate access to knowledge. A teacher may use a question-and-answer session to draw out what pupils know and understand. One child has her hand flapping in the air every time a question is asked; another remains as still as a statue, eyes lowered, hoping that the teacher does not choose her. We may reasonably conclude that the enthusiastic child has a higher level of knowledge than her timid classmate, but this is not necessarily the case. The second child may have stored the knowledge and, in the intensity of the moment, been unable to draw it out of her memory bank. She may be weighing up other options rather than the obvious response or simply hate answering questions publicly for fear of being wrong. Teachers should be careful to ask both closed questions that test immediate recall, and open questions in which a variety of answers are acceptable. There are numerous other types of questions, all of which rely on the purpose for asking it. The child who has prompt immediate recall may or may not be able to offer a more considered and thoughtful response. Able children are often the most successful in responding to open questions but all children benefit from being given time to think. The best teachers have fun shooting out closed questions to a class, but also ask speculative types of questions that test a child's ability to reflect and perhaps suggest unlikely possibilities. When working with children, it is helpful to think of knowledge from their perspective:

1. *Received knowledge*: I know because I can repeat what you have told me.

2. *Descriptive knowledge*: I know because I can tell you about it.

3. *Explanatory knowledge*: I know because I can explain why it happened.

4. *Applied knowledge:* I know because I can understand the implications for its use.

Walker and Soltis (1992) use the term 'knowledge in use' and identify three forms: associative, applicative and replicative. *Associative* knowledge allows links to be made with previous learning. *Replicative* knowledge is being able to remember and reproduce facts when required. *Applicative* knowledge is for use in solving questions. Walker and Soltis argue that applicative knowledge is the most significant of the three as it 'requires seeing the connection between what one knows and what one wants to achieve' (1992: 41). Thinking about how knowledge is used allows pupils to move from basic comprehension to being able to analyse and evaluate situations. The most powerful forms of knowledge involve higher levels of understanding that permit its use in a variety of contexts. Knowledge without understanding is merely information. Knowledge that cannot be applied may be superfluous.

> ## Good practice
>
> Keep an informal record of the types of questions that you ask. Try to shift the balance away from closed types that rely on memory to ones that require deeper thinking.

Understanding (conceptual development)

One of the most common questions that teachers ask their pupils is whether they understand something. In the majority of cases, the children chorus 'yes' and the teacher, pleased at her skill in explaining, proceeds to the next stage of the lesson. But do the children really understand? And what does 'being able to understand' mean? These are complex questions. Having asked if the children understood, the teacher might usefully say: 'Well done; now will everyone please whisper to the person next to you what I have said'; and after a suitable time has elapsed: 'Now put up your hand if you think that your partner really understands'. The chances are that a number would be less clear than they imagined they were before having to explain it to a friend.

Understanding is normally gained gradually. Like knowledge, it operates at a variety of conceptual levels and requires considerable reinforcement and testing out in real contexts before a thorough grasp of the issues has been accomplished. Understanding comes initially through *raising awareness*, as many children simply do not properly realise that there is anything to be understood. Raising awareness is followed by *raising interest*. Children are naturally inquisitive, a characteristic which needs to be exploited (by the teacher posing relevant questions or wondering out loud about a situation). The inquisitiveness results in children raising their own questions, and this is the point at which the teacher's skill in explaining is important as queries are dealt with and misconceptions are corrected. Subsequently, children should have opportunity to explore, discover and test propositions, experiment with ideas and raise fresh issues. This cycle of raising awareness and interest, followed by further questions can be continued until pupils reach the limits of their understanding.

Knowledge and understanding are inextricably entwined. For instance, a young child may understand through observation that seeds grow into plants with roots and a stem. The teacher will probably have to supply the terminology and, as the process takes place, enthuse with the child at the visual growth, raise significant questions about how it happens, and speculate about what might happen next. Older children not only understand the significance of the root system and the influence of different types of soil but can also offer explanations as to *why* it happens. The five year old who gazed in wonder at the bean plant's speed of growth becomes the 11 year old who can not only describe what is happening but also use evidence to prove underlying principles. The steady progression from five-year-old Karoline who wonders at what she sees happening, to the 11-year-old Karoline who can provide insights about the unseen biological processes at work, is testimony to the levels of understanding that children reach. Examples of this progression can be found in every area of the curriculum. For example:

- *In moral and social development*, children's understanding of ethical issues, social justice and fairness emerge over time as they gain a more complete picture of the prevailing circumstances and conflicting claims of varied viewpoints

- *In mathematics*, a child may initially understand concepts such as 'smaller and bigger than' but will later apply more varied terms which involve expressions such as 'multiples and factors of'

- *In science*, the use of a coloured dye in the water used to sustain the plant (such as a piece of celery) results in a gradual discoloration. Young children talk about the colour change; older ones will, if provided with the necessary vocabulary, discuss issues relating to capillary action and metabolism

- *In art*, the four year olds' random dabs of paint are gradually replaced by rainbows of colour, which lead to paint mixes and experimentation with other substances. Older primary children draw from their knowledge of techniques and combine these with their own spontaneity.

The development of understanding (concepts) therefore involves a combination of intellect, maturity (especially the ability to think abstractly), the opportunity to explore ideas and 'play' with alternatives, combined with the teaching skills of teachers who give children appropriate information, strategies and encouragement to speculate, make discoveries, articulate their claims and uncertainties, and eventually reach firm conclusions.

Continuity of learning experiences through concept development is a foundation stone of the National Curriculum (NC) and the different government strategies for literacy and mathematics (formerly referred to, inaccurately, as numeracy) strategies. It is facilitated by lessons that build on previous knowledge and experience, encourage children to explore and question, and allow time for understanding to grow and consolidate by using it in a variety of contexts. Higher levels of understanding come through experimentation and opportunities to explore ideas, discuss findings and investigate possibilities. It is now easy to see that asking children if they understand something is hopelessly inadequate. You must specify precisely what it is you are referring to.

Good practice

A poor question to children: 'Does everyone understand what they have got to do?'. A much better question: 'Put your hand up if you can tell me how I want you to do your work?'.

Activate your thinking!

Consider how the following statements might apply to some of your lessons:

- I hear what you say and understand a little
- I reflect upon the ideas and get them straight in my mind
- I explore the ideas for myself and understand more fully
- I ask questions to clarify the issues and my mind becomes clear
- I gain confidence by explaining to others using my own words
- I speculate about possibilities and grasp the implications
- I use my understanding to some purpose and grow eager to find out more.

Skills

The term 'skills' is used to describe a wide range of abilities that children need to function effectively in their lives. Skills may be considered under two broad categories: (a) abilities that children need so that they can find out things for themselves and enhance their existing knowledge and understanding; and (b) abilities and attributes that children will need to acquire if they are to take learning forward. Skills can also be thought of in terms of those that are principally *cerebral* (mainly to do with active thinking) such as the skill required to present an opinion, and those that are *manual* (mainly to do with physical co-ordination) such as throwing a ball accurately or kneading a ball of clay. This distinction is not to suggest that manual skills do not require thought and judgement, but that the predominant form of learning is represented by an immediate outcome in such cases.

Mastery of skills is necessary to support learning. For instance, there is little to be gained from a child being able to open a book and find the index, but then being unable to use it effectively. Similarly, it is interesting to study the trajectory and flight of a ball in the air, but this does not ensure that the child will hit the target. Every skill involves judgement, decision-making and evaluation as to the effectiveness of the procedure and the quality of the end result. Skills sometimes need to be exercised in conjunction with discernment or wisdom if they are to be most effective.

The NC originally used the word 'skills' to denote transferable abilities in areas as diverse as communication, numeracy, problem-solving, personal and social relations, and information technology. These skills are intended to be used across the curriculum and apply to every subject area. For example, children should be able to express themselves in speech across the whole curriculum and use computer software to produce visual representations of findings. The importance of promoting speaking and listening has received closer attention in recent years after being allocated a marginal position in the original NLS of 1999. Concerns that children were unable to express themselves clearly have been given greater urgency by the fact that studies suggest that some parents are talking less to their children due to working long hours and the dominance of television and electronic games. The NC specifies six 'key skills' that are intended to help learners to improve their learning and performance in education, work and life as follows:

1. *Communication*, using speaking, listening, reading and writing. Skills required include the ability to take account of different audiences, to understand what others are saying and to participate in group discussions. Pupils should be able to read both fictional and non-fictional texts fluently and with understanding. Although most direct development of communication skills takes place during literacy lessons, consideration should be given to the development of language across the curriculum. The development can be enhanced by promoting a climate whereby children's comments, suggestions and ideas are taken seriously. There are also more formal opportunities to enhance communication skills through drama sessions.

2. *Application of number*, including the development of a range of mental calculation skills and their application. The use of mathematical language to process data, solve problems and explain the reasoning behind solutions also forms part of this skill.

3. *Information technology*, developing the ability to use a range of information sources and ICT tools, and to make critical and informed judgements about when it is appropriate to use ICT to access information, solve problems and for creative expression.

4. *Working with others*, including the ability to contribute to small-group and whole-class discussion, and to work collaboratively. The interaction requires the development of social skills and an awareness of other people's needs and perspectives (see Cohen 2006). The importance of identifying and understanding their own and others' emotions has assumed greater urgency in recent years following unwelcome violent trends in society.

5. *Improving own learning and performance*, involving pupils in reflection and critical evaluation of different aspects of their work, assessing their own performance and establishing targets for learning. Most schools involve pupils in establishing and monitoring their own progress, both through setting targets and assessing outcomes. It has also become fashionable to encourage peer assessment, whereby pairs of pupils co-operate in assessing the quality of one another's work.

6. *Problem solving*, including identifying and understanding problems, planning ways to solve them, monitoring progress and reviewing solutions.

Five 'thinking skills' are also identified in the NC as important in assisting children to know how, as well as knowing what. These skills are: information-processing, reasoning, enquiry, creative thinking and evaluation skills. The NC also offers explanations about each of the skills. Thus:

1. *Information-processing skills* enable pupils to locate and collect relevant information, to sort, classify, sequence, compare and contrast, and to analyse part/whole relationships. These skills require that pupils are not satisfied with gaining a single piece of information but draw from a variety of sources, including electronic, human and book-based.

2. *Reasoning skills* enable pupils to give reasons for opinions and actions, to draw inferences and make deductions, to use precise language to explain what they think, and to make judgements and decisions informed by reasons or evidence. These skills encourage children to express their beliefs and opinions, guided by sensitive adults and an agreed protocol.

3. *Enquiry skills* enable pupils to ask questions, to pose and define problems, to plan what to do and how to research the problem, to predict outcomes and anticipate consequences, and to test conclusions and improve ideas. These skills require that children think beyond the immediate circumstances and project into new possibilities and opportunities.

4. *Creative thinking skills* enable pupils to generate and extend ideas, to suggest hypotheses, to apply imagination, and to look for alternative, innovative outcomes. The key word in this definition is *imagination*, where the children are actively encouraged and liberated into fresh modes of thought and activity (see, for example, Carter 2002 for ideas for creative writing; Craft 2005 for a more comprehensive review of issues).

5. *Evaluation skills* enable pupils to evaluate information, to judge the value of what they read, hear and do, to develop criteria for judging the value of their own and others' work or ideas, and to have confidence in their judgements. These critical skills (Quinn 1997; Haynes 2007) are considered to be amongst the most difficult for children to grasp, as they require considerable experience and maturity if they are to be anything more than superficial, spontaneous responses.

Skills do not exist in isolation from knowledge and understanding. Children need knowledge and understanding in order to consolidate what they have already grasped and open up fresh areas for enquiry. For instance, the skill of being able to solve problems systematically can provide insights that may not be gained by other means such as direct instruction or information served up in neat chunks from a database.

Skills, therefore, involve both thinking and dexterity through words and physical means. To possess thinking skills is important, but without having the necessary skills to complete the task, children quickly become frustrated. The application of practical skills that involve only a small amount of thinking leads to inertia and passivity, limiting children's capacity to think more widely and imaginatively. Thus, knowledge, understanding and skills are mutually dependent. Wenham (1995) graphically expresses the relationship between the three elements: 'Without understanding, experience is blind; but without experience, knowledge and understanding are empty; and without skill, all of them are dumb' (1995: 133).

Forms of Learning

Learning is a word that rolls easily off the tongue but it is difficult to define and even harder to explain the processes that combine to produce a learning outcome. Over the past few years a lot of emphasis has been placed on what is sometimes referred to as 'meta-learning', which is a sophisticated way to say 'learning how to learn'. One of the key principles is that learning is a skill to be acquired, mastered and improved, not a once-for-all 'hard-wired' trait that pupils (and adults) possess or do not possess. Further, by learning about learning, children find out about themselves: their preferences, desires and the things that enthuse them. If the concept is extended to collaborative settings, it also offers children insights into how others in the group learn.

Although learning comes relatively easy to some children, others find that they have to work hard over a long period of time before things fall into place. Some children seem unable to master quite elementary principles and are adjudged to have special educational needs and require a considerable amount of adult help in remedying the situation. By the time children leave the infant sector (Key Stage 1) and join the big boys and girls in the juniors (Key Stage 2) teachers are normally in a position to predict with some certainty which pupils will succeed academically and which will not. In fact, most playgroup leaders and nursery staffs will claim that they can spot danger signs early on: poor vocabulary, difficulty socialising and solitary play. It is not unusual for children who struggle academically to exhibit symptoms such as lack of motivation and general dissatisfaction with life. Some of these children may also have few friends and, occasionally, exhibit erratic behaviour. In addition to academic achievement, therefore, the learning process has implications for children's emotional and social wellbeing.

When asked by the teacher how she understood what was happening when she was working out a problem, Cordie, a five-year-old girl thought for a moment before replying: 'When I want to understand something I draw a picture of it in my mind'. This small insight into a child's thinking suggests that definitions of learning must be rooted in the effect that the process has upon the learner, rather more than the actions of a teacher (teaching). With this principle in mind, a number of suggestions have been made to describe learning; for instance:

- The process of making sense of information and creating something new from it
- A process that transforms our current understanding into fresh and more elucidated understanding

- The process of utilising the knowledge and insights that we have gained from our previous experiences to respond effectively to new ones

- The process of taking risks and moving away from the security of certain knowledge and exploring less well considered areas.

None of these definitions offers a complete picture, but they share a common thread in emphasising the transformation that takes place in the learner. The teacher's role in the process is to provide the resources, guidance and wisdom that facilitate the learning. Such teaching recognises that learning does not consist merely of the linear transfer of an adult's superior intellect to a less knowledgeable pupil but rather children's accommodation of fresh understanding into their existing conceptual framework. As such, the teacher must be aware of the child's present understanding, not in order to 'tailor make' the teaching programme to fit the needs of all the children (as this would require 30 different approaches and curricula) but to graze contentedly across the pastures of knowledge. The grazing metaphor promotes the idea of 'sampling' from the variety of food available as opposed to being force-fed. The concept of a learning objective, popularised through the NLS, is more accurately a learning *intention*, as it is impossible to predict what sort of learning will take place in each child's mind.

Activate your thinking!

Think of a time when each of the four types of learning definitions indicated in the bullet points above has taken place in your *own* experience.

Although it is natural to emphasise the importance of making sure that children have 'learned' something after exposure to a planned educational experience, the term has a variety of different meanings, depending upon the context in which it is used. For instance:

- Learned for now but likely to be forgotten very soon

- Learned, never to be forgotten

- Learned within defined limits

- Learned but requiring updating and reinforcement to be secure

- Learned and understood so thoroughly that the learning can be used successfully in different situations.

Thus it is possible for children to learn how to use a piece of computer software early in the school year but without regular practice they are likely to forget the procedure by the next term. In this case, the learning has been functional and the fourth of the statements given above is relevant. A child may 'learn' how to multiply two numbers by using a certain technique but flounder when given the same problem in a different form. In this case, the third of the statements is relevant. The ideal is for children to have such a grasp of knowledge, skills and understanding that they can use their existing abilities to forge ahead confidently into new areas of learning (the final option in the above list). Furthermore, if learning is only *functional*, it relates solely to the work in hand and has little value outside the immediate context in which it is being used; if it is *pervasive*, it moves outside the boundaries artificially imposed by the task or activity, and has wider applicability.

Learning, then, may be of the restricted type (merely functional) or the transferable type (usable in different contexts). Take, for instance, the earlier example in which children learn to use a software program. Some children will doubtless become adept at using the program and may even be used by the teacher to tutor other children about its functioning. However, only a proportion of the same group of well-informed children will make connections with the implications for using other, similar programs. The first group, knowing only how to operate the program, will possess a restricted form of knowledge. The second, who can use their knowledge, skills and understanding in less familiar contexts, are of the transferable type. Again, children who learn a set of spellings for a test may get them all correct, yet misspell some of the words in free writing. The aim is, of course, to ensure that children not only master the word list but can also utilise their learning in a variety of active, writing situations where spelling is only one of the required skills. To say that something is 'learned' always requires qualifying.

Some learning is short term; other forms need to become embedded and for all practical purposes permanently etched in the memory (long-term memory). The child who learns lines for a drama sketch in front of the school will memorise them carefully, prompted no doubt by an anxious parent who is keen for the child to do well. This learning may require repetition, frequent reminders, and a move from artificial to more natural speech as the words become familiar. A few months after the performance, the words may be largely forgotten, though odd phrases may spring to mind for a while. Contrast this temporary memorising with the ability to interpret words on a page for the purpose of reading, in which the regular use of the words in a variety of contexts (books, work sheets, text on a whiteboard, screen) will ensure that they are never forgotten and can be produced at any time.

Every teacher is keen for their pupils to learn in such a way that they can use their abilities widely and thereby achieve intellectual freedom (or 'conceptual autonomy'). Conceptual autonomy allows children to free themselves from reliance on the teacher as they develop the skills, confidence and determination to be self-motivated, ask suitable questions and evaluate answers. Children will always need teachers, but learning should be an adventure in roaming through the woodlands, not a predictable walk down a straight path.

Activate your thinking!

You can teach a child, but the child being taught is not always learning what you teach.

Enhancing learning

Most learning is gained or enhanced by 'experiencing' for which no amount of direct teaching will substitute. For example, pupils' understanding of industrial change is brought to life through a visit to a working museum. Similarly, listening to poets and authors read from their own work, enjoying practical drama, playing with construction materials, touching unusual objects and buying vegetables from a market stall, all help children to understand the world better. Children's learning is also improved through 'investigations' in which the outcome is uncertain. For instance, science experiments, paint mixing, library searches and computer simulations all involve investigations that assist conceptual understanding, skills acquisition and factual knowledge.

Enhanced learning also depends upon the opportunity for children to ask questions and raise issues in the expectation that teachers will respond positively (Wragg and Brown 1993; Morgan and Saxton 1994; Hayes 2006). Most children are extremely curious and will, if their interest is aroused, ply adults with queries and questions about how and why. Teachers sometimes need to understand the reason for a child asking a question. An apparently innocent question from a five year old about 'Where did I come from?' may be the first sign of a wish to understand the wonders of human reproduction but is far more likely to relate to the fact that her friend said that she came from Birmingham. Interpreting children's questions is time-consuming but essential if teachers are to help them in finding answers to things that are of real interest to them. Whatever the age of pupils, teachers need to capture their curiosity, encourage a questioning attitude, engage with issues that concern young minds and provide enough stimuli to arouse fresh interest.

It is important to be mindful of ways to help pupils to be creative in their work. That is, to encourage diverse thinking, risk-taking and innovative practice (see, for instance, Jeffrey and Woods 2003; Starbuck 2006; Best and Thomas 2007). Bowkett (2005) argues that creativity 'is as much an attitude as it's a set of mental processes. It incorporates playfulness, curiosity, sensitivity, self-awareness and independence' (2005: 3). Inspection reports about creativity in schools seem to agree that it is most likely to be found in schools where teachers did not feel bound by orthodox teaching methods, but rather made use of cross-curricular themes and spent time developing an enlivened physical environment. Creativity did not emerge by simply giving children time and space to 'create something', but by generating enthusiasm and offering appropriate adult support within a culture of self-expression where new ideas were actively sought and encouraged. Grainger (2003) argues that teachers should spend more time on discussing literature, oral storytelling, poetry performances and improvised drama if children are to be offered the chance to 'interpret, communicate and *create* meaning for themselves' (2003: 44, author's emphasis) in their learning. She stresses that a willingness to take risks with creative and artistic activity enhances teachers' confidence and pupils' imaginative engagement. Teachers who are excited and personally involved with the literacy curriculum are much more likely to communicate its joy and wonder than a plain transmission of the necessary facts.

Children need to be given some ownership of their learning. After all, it is they who have to use it in their present and future lives. Learning is not, therefore, principally about accumulating sufficient information, knowledge and understanding to gain high scores in national tests and examinations; rather, it is about empowering pupils to live their lives more productively and successfully. Examination success is likely to assist this process of self-fulfilment, but there is a danger that anxious teachers may see scores gained during a test as the sole yardstick of achievement. Williams and Ryan (2000) argue that teachers should view the tests as an opportunity to gain information that will help to improve their teaching and raise standards. A wide range of other eminent educationists disagree; for instance, Kohn (2004) argues from a US context that twenty-first century children are tested to an unprecedented extent, yet standardised test scores often measure superficial thinking.

Ransom (1993) contends that curriculum entitlement and rational planning are inadequate unless pupils are adequately motivated within a community context. He argued that teachers need to develop an 'empowerment curriculum', characterised by the following elements:

- Citizenship in learning
- Active learning through practical reasoning
- Democratic and public organisation
- Partnership.

The issue of pupil empowerment is also seen as important. Smith (2006) argues that all pupils, including those with a special need, should be involved in decision-making at two levels. First, and principally, by contributing to decisions about the effectiveness of their own provision. Second, pupils 'can also participate in decision-making at a wider level and thus influence school policy' (2006: 146). Although the establishment of pupil 'school councils' and 'focus groups' are an important element of the process, it is more common for children to initially say something to a parent, which is fed back into school via a variety of formal and informal routes. Nevertheless, the principle of the 'pupil voice' is now well-established in schools and is a feature that is noted during formal inspections.

Consequently, pupils' learning can be enhanced by the following.

Valuing pupils' capability

By celebrating the untapped reservoirs of capability in individuals in order to create active rather than passive learners, endowed with skills to make responsible choices and co-operate with others.

Offering a comprehensive curriculum

By providing a broad and balanced curriculum, relevant to learners, enabling them to draw upon their experience of living within the community.

Promoting active learning

By involving pupils, thereby engaging their interest, sustaining their motivation to succeed, and encouraging them to take responsibility for their learning experience and that of others.

Creating partnership with parents and the community

By promoting education within the community, notably by involving parents and local people. This aspect of education, once seen as relevant for younger pupils only, has assumed much greater significance for children of all ages, notably supporting reading and homework.

A lot of children seem to have a 'product' attitude to learning, often abetted by adult expectations. They are set tasks for completion or activities to perform, and they strive to finish the work to the teacher's satisfaction. The children soon become aware that they will be rewarded with praise and approving comments from adults if they accomplish precisely what is expected of them. If children deviate from the set task, they are guided back onto the right path or scolded if they insist on pursuing their own preferences. Fisher (2005) argues that if children become obsessed with an objectives-driven agenda, they tend to display some of the following characteristics:

- Success is viewed as absolute, being either achieved totally or missed completely. There is no halfway position for such children and they become upset if they do not fulfil or exceed expectations

- Excuses are given to explain away shortcomings in their work. Children view anything less than perfect or below the achievements of their rivals as a personal affront

- Ability to learn certain things is seen as fixed rather than something to be improved. Children will say that they are 'no good' at some things and brilliant at others. In response to a teacher's prompting they will resist being coached or trained to get better at something

- Difficulties dominate their thinking rather than possibilities and solutions. Two men looked through prison bars; one saw mud, the other saw the stars. Such children see the mud

- Initial failure or problems result in depression. Children with a product orientation evaluate success only in terms of achieving the objective. They do not regard the process as significant; only the end result matters.

Focusing exclusively on an objectives-driven agenda can lead children to become anxious about making errors, which in turn paralyses their minds and creates a form of mental stagnation. Fisher also comments that pupils often resist the invitation to think for themselves. It is easier for them to be told than to think but also that extended contact with a child gives a teacher opportunity to become a significant and influential model in that child's life. One means by which this can be achieved is through the teachers modelling the behaviour that they want the children to imitate, such as listening to one another, taking time to think, allowing other points of view, thinking things through properly, being curious, questioning and keeping setbacks in perspective.

Lessons have to be properly organised, of course, and in the pressure of school life there is a limited amount of time that can be spent exploring and interrogating a given area of work. Teachers also have to be reasonably clear about the things they hope that children will learn (indicated through the learning objectives) and provide a facilitating structure to make it more likely that they will do so. However, learning encompasses more than children satisfying the designated objective. Just as children can convince themselves that they must have learned something if they get the right answer by an approved method, so teachers can slip into the same way of thinking and believe that task-completion is the primary goal. In fact, finishing a task may or may not involve deep learning. Too many so-called experiential lessons, for instance, consist of little more than mechanically 'predicting' and 'testing' and 'recording' without properly engaging with the principles underpinning the work or employing problem-solving skills. Completing pages of sums may or may not demonstrate that the underlying principles have been mastered. In this regard, MacGilchrist (2003) makes five important points about the nature of learning that have implications for classroom practice:

1. Learning is an active process of meaning-making. Learners construct and integrate new knowledge in a way that makes sense to them.

2. Learning about learning (meta-learning) and making sense of experience is a hallmark of effective learners. Learners become increasingly aware of the thinking and learning processes that are taking place and thereby assume greater control over them.

3. The relationship between learning and performance is complex and is influenced by motivation and self-image. Some children are capable of completing tasks ('performance orientation') without thinking hard about the implications of the work and gaining personal satisfaction other than through a tick at the bottom of the page.

4. Learning involves the understanding and mastery of emotions, both personal and viewing things from other people's perspectives. Learning can be enhanced through developing a variety of social skills and a willingness to persevere and stay on task.

5. Learning is situational. The social contexts of the school and classroom are significant in promoting or inhibiting learning.

The implications for classroom practice can be summarised as follows:

1. Pupils need the opportunity to discuss what they are doing and understand where it fits into their overall understanding. The teacher needs to spend time explaining the context, where the present lesson content fits within the larger picture and the links with previous learning. The use of familiar examples and experiences will help children to grasp the concepts more easily.

Good practice

When discussing the lesson with the children, use phrases such as 'You remember that last time …' (making links with previous learning) and 'It is the same as when you …' (linking with familiar experiences).

2. Pupils will often complete tasks and engage in activities solely because they are set before them by a teacher. Meta-learning encourages children to talk about what they are doing and express how they feel about learning, both verbally and through different media (such as drawings).

Good practice

Spend small amounts of time regularly talking to the children about ways in which they can approach the work in hand, probing alternatives and encouraging them to speculate about the challenges and opportunities. These conversations should be underpinned by a positive 'can do' attitude and an acknowledgement that trying different approaches and searching for creative solutions sometimes results in failure/setbacks.

3.   Pupils should be encouraged to satisfy their own aspirations rather than those of the teacher and be self-motivating rather than compliant.

Good practice

Make a habit of asking children what particularly pleases them about the work that they are undertaking. Encourage them to think about their achievements and share their excitement with others.

4.   Some pupils fear failure and worry about getting things wrong and 'being in trouble' as a result. Other pupils are unwilling to persevere when faced with challenges, either because they are unable to cope with the situation or try to avoid making more than a nominal effort to achieve a satisfactory outcome. As these negative responses are the result of emotional insecurity, teachers' reactions need to focus on finding solutions to the root cause rather than merely treating the symptoms. In other words, it is important to make a priority of strengthening children's emotional security.

Good practice

Make it clear that children can use an adult or another child as a source of advice, confirmation or guidance, but that as far as possible, they should persevere with work and not be afraid of making genuine errors. At the same time, use mistakes positively by expressing an interest in how the child has gone about the work, explaining the alternatives and using the opportunity formatively to assist understanding.

5.   Teachers should put themselves in the child's place. Is the classroom environment stimulating or depressing? How does the attitude of adults (teacher, assistants) serve to motivate or discourage? How do patterns of social interaction, such as friendship patterns, grouping of children and peer support, impinge upon children's appetite to engage with tasks?

Good practice

Observe a child unobtrusively throughout a full day and try to evaluate his or her experience with regard to classroom environment, adult attitudes and social interaction. What does it 'feel' like to be that child? How does s/he perceive the learning experience?

It is preferable for children to have an 'adventurous' attitude to learning, where they are eager to try things out, experiment and find solutions to problems. Challenges are seen as opportunities to use their ingenuity and determination to break through the uncertainty rather than obstacles. Children with an adventurous spirit towards learning are not fazed by setbacks. They are persistent and willing to approach the problem from a variety of positions. They are reluctant to take 'no' for an answer and will seek ways to improve their abilities.

The term '*praxis*' is sometimes used to describe action that is informed by reflection, with the aim to free those involved into more productive forms of learning. Some educators (notably Jurgen Habermas) argue that the teacher's role involves emancipating pupils through the curriculum and developing a liberated and fair world. The curriculum then becomes as much about 'uncovering' fresh truth and insight as it is about 'covering' pre-determined content. With regard to classroom teaching, Morrison (2001) refers to the eight principles of pedagogy (the principles and practice of teaching) that Habermas and others propose:

- The need for co-operation and collaborative work
- The need for discussion-based work
- The need for autonomous, experiential and flexible learning
- The need for negotiated learning
- The need for community-related learning to explore a range of environments
- The need for problem-solving activities
- The need to increase [pupils'] rights to employ talk
- The need for teachers to act as 'transformative intellectuals'.

This critical form of pedagogy is built upon a belief that 'educators must work with, and on, the lived experiences that [pupils] bring to the pedagogical encounter rather than imposing a curriculum that reproduces social inequality' (2001: 219). Setting aside the social equality issues that these educators argue can be addressed in part through the curriculum, the eight principles outlined above provide a useful basis on which to develop a positive teaching and learning environment. Thus, pupil collaboration facilitates a 'fusion' of minds as children grapple with problems and combine their intellects. Discussions allow issues and contradictions to surface and demonstrates that nearly every situation has a multiplicity of perspectives. Experiential learning allows children to touch, sample, feel, manipulate and handle substances, equipment and circumstances directly. Negotiated learning encourages children to advance their own ideas, priorities and suggestions about what is important. Community-related learning promotes the value of involvement in the local environment and draws on the expertise of those who live there. Problem-solving helps children to see that the skills and knowledge they acquire in school have a practical outworking. Children's right to venture their own opinions and ideas, when coupled with an appropriate sense of responsibility, encourages self-confidence and a willingness to be innovative. Teachers who view themselves as such 'change agents' approach their work with children with a greater sense of purpose than those who merely see themselves as curriculum technicians, systematically engaging with predictable intentions and outcomes. You must decide where you stand along the technician to change agent continuum.

The learning context

It is clear to anyone who works in school that learning does not take place in a vacuum; it is powerfully influenced by three factors: situation, motivation and emotion. If it were not so, we could dispense with schools and teachers and send 'electronic teaching machines' to do the job. Every learning experience is 'situational' and affected by the physical and social context. Thus, within the physical environment, the numerous interactions that take place daily between child and adult, and between different children, impact upon the quality of learning because: (a) we learn from one another; (b) energy is generated through human interaction; and (c) mutual endeavour leads to a sense of team work and raises aspirations (sometimes through competition). The nature of these interactions depends on the power relationships and authority structures that exist in a classroom. If children feel relaxed and confident when seeking adult help, they can channel their energies into the task rather than worrying about doing or saying the acceptable thing and avoiding adult wrath. Similarly, if there is an ease of relationship between children, they can concentrate on their work and not on worry about friendship patterns or being marginalised. It is the teacher's responsibility to establish a facilitative and co-operative climate such that learning can proceed unhindered by social conflict or emotional insecurity. There is also the broader social context to consider, not least the fact that technological and social changes have influenced the skills needed for daily living, people's priorities and their expectations. As Turner-Bisset (2003) argues, classrooms must move with the times and consider the teaching and learning needs of primary education in this century rather than those that existed in the last. To ignore such factors can cause learning to seem less relevant and to become less interesting. On the other hand, there are some teaching and learning needs that remain unchanged across the generations: the need for security, affirmation and respect, set within a framework of fundamental skill acquisition (such as reading and communicating effectively) and mutually beneficial moral boundaries.

Teachers' attitudes to the work also affect learning. The depth of a teacher's motivation and expectations about pupil achievement make a profound difference to the way in which children approach the work. A teacher who is enthusiastic about the tasks that the children are engaged with, clarifies what is expected from them and gives clear guidance about what can be achieved, will not be disappointed with the outcome. Children respond well to an adult who displays a positive attitude and belief about attainment and celebrates small successes rather than highlighting minor errors.

Pupils' attitudes towards themselves influence the quality of learning and the impact of these emotional factors on learning is increasingly viewed as being of crucial importance. Although a degree of anticipatory tension can spur children to success, too much anxiety hinders learning. It is a common experience in classrooms that some children adopt a very positive attitude despite their limitations, while others are doubtful despite their obvious ability. By contrast to fearful anxiety, enthusiasm pumps oxygen to the brain and stimulates its operation. There are three sets of conditions that assist the promotion of pupil confidence in learning: to feel secure, to know the rules, to be clear about the lesson. Thus:

Children need to feel secure

This is particularly important when teachers are asking questions or inviting responses from the class. Timid children are unlikely to risk answering if by doing so they are met by the teacher's exasperation. Teachers who treat all answers seriously (including incorrect ones) and encourage the children who give them by praising their efforts will soon have the class clamouring to participate. Similarly, if a new skill or concept has to be mastered, the teacher's patience and understanding can transform children's tentativeness into boldness. The maxim to 'have a go and find out what happens', if promoted and practised within a safe environment, will act as a springboard for progress.

Children need to know the rules

Teachers who spend time explaining and clarifying the details of an activity or the procedures for involvement at the start of the session will have to spend less time during the lesson in reminding children of the expected standards, repeatedly answering queries and rebuking transgressors. Boundaries for behaviour and action allow children to explore with confidence. Learning has more chance to be effective when everyone understands the rules of the game.

Children need to be clear about the terms and conditions of the lesson

Some lessons are specifically for the purpose of gaining knowledge. Others are more concerned with understanding processes, and yet others demand skill mastery. Many lessons involve all three dimensions. Children should be told about the lesson purpose as well as what they have to do or complete. Some classrooms have a small whiteboard affixed to the wall on which the teacher writes the lesson purpose prior to commencement; other teachers print out the objective and ask children to affix it to their work, though this practice seems unduly laborious and, frankly, not worth the effort. That's a decision you will have to make. Although sharing the lesson/session intention(s) is important, it is a mistake to place too much emphasis on predicted outcomes if it acts to disregard other unintended outcomes. Pratt and Berry (2007) even argue that sharing the learning objectives (using mathematics as the example) in too much detail can be counter-productive, as it reduces the joy of discovery. A lot depends on the lesson purpose: if it is dominated by information and factual knowledge that can easily be defined and assessed (such as memorising key events in history) then a fixed learning objective is more relevant than if the purpose is exploratory and involves play, investigation or problem-solving, in which case the final outcome is likely to be more diverse. Teaching and learning cannot be neatly packaged into a linear process from introduction to conclusion. Nevertheless, the more that teachers are prepared to involve children in their learning and make learning explicit, both in its purpose and usefulness, the more the learning climate will be enhanced.

Reinforcing learning

It is important for teachers to seize every opportunity to reinforce learning. For example, during question-and-answer sessions it is useful to repeat a good or thoughtful answer for the benefit of all the children, some of whom may not have heard the original response. In appropriate cases, an answer can spark ideas and open possibilities that may not have occurred to you. At key moments during the task phase a brief comment to the whole group or class about a specific point can focus the children's attention on improving their work. And of course the final few minutes of a lesson or session is normally a good time to extract key points and emphasise them or offer examples and extend thinking by providing a challenging question about 'where next?' or 'what if?'. You can also promote learning by noting impressive practice, employing individually targeted praise and then disseminating the information; for example:

> 'Yes, Toby, well done. Did you hear what Toby said, everyone? He said that ...'

> 'What a lovely idea, Georgia, I hadn't thought of counting them in that way. I think we could all have a go at ...'

> 'Now that's a brilliant suggestion, Raj. I love the way you used the things we've been doing and added your own ideas. I hope that everyone heard when Raj explained how we could ...'

> 'Alice, what a clever technique! Come and stand by me and show everyone else in the class what you did, please ...'.

In addition to positive comments about children's attitudes and willingness to persevere; for example:

> 'I'm pleased with the way you have kept trying, Mustafa. Well done!'

> 'Thank you for helping Greeta, Sara; I'm very impressed.'

> 'You haven't quite finished, Alan, but you are a star for working so hard.'

Teaching style and retention in learning

Suffice it to say at this point that the methods employed strongly influence the effectiveness with which children are able to learn. For instance, Koshy (2000) refers to the fact that different teaching approaches in mathematics have markedly different outcomes in terms of retention rate. Thus, whereas only about 5 per cent of the information presented in a formal lecture is retained, the figure increases with other strategies:

- 10 per cent retention when the same words are read
- 20 per cent retention when audio-visual aids are used

- 30 per cent retention for a demonstration
- 50 per cent retention for a discussion group
- 75 per cent retention for practising by doing
- 90 per cent retention when teaching others the immediate use of the learning.

Although retaining facts is only one dimension of learning and the above figures are only approximations, they suggest that direct transmission of information to children is unlikely to be effective if it is the sole means to present knowledge. The opportunity to read relevant text, listen to sounds or see images, watch an adult showing how something is done, discuss the lesson content with others, engage in practical activities and make use of peer tuition, can all enhance the quality of learning. In addition, children learn best in different ways. Some children find it easy to understand written information, others prefer to hear it explained verbally, others like pictorial representations and yet others benefit from diagrams. Most children benefit from a combination of approaches, so it pays to bear this fact in mind when planning lessons. For instance, you may want to read an extract of text (with or without involving the children), explain the concepts/issues/key points, provide visual aids and use the board to demonstrate stages of progression. Recent claims that children can be neatly divided into (for instance) 'visual learners' or 'tactile learners', and so forth is at best naïve and at worst, positively harmful, because it can lead to an artificial and fragmented teaching style.

It is also helpful to allow children some degree of choice when it comes to presenting their answers. While you will not often want to give latitude to a child who dislikes writing to use pictures instead, a little flexibility on your part to encourage a little of both types of recording is sometimes worth considering. While some boys (in particular) are averse to writing things down and need to be cajoled into doing so, the value of employing alternative means is always worth considering.

Using homework to extend and reinforce learning

Teachers must provide relevant forms of homework and other out-of-class tasks that help to consolidate and extend the work that has been carried out during the school day, thereby promoting independence in learning and, where possible, the active involvement of parents. In setting homework tasks, bear in mind that it has to be just as appropriate to the age and ability of the pupil as the work in school is intended to be. Homework also has to be realistic and manageable (Kidwell 2004), as there is little point in having grandiose schemes that are impossible for the children to complete, even with adult support, or that require sophisticated equipment or expensive resources. For instance, tasks should not assume that ICT equipment is available in the house. Suitable homework might include giving the children an observation activity (such as noticing pattern formation on wallpaper and carpets), consulting with an adult about living history (such as life in the 1950s) or paper and pencil activities (such as learning key vocabulary or completing as many sums as possible in a given time). The most straightforward homework is when the same task is given to all children such that they are all able to engage with it at their own level, and the end product can be marked easily or shared with others. For younger children, additional reading, supported by an adult if possible, is frequently used, with an adult signing in a 'reading record book' to confirm that it has been done. It is wise to remember that homework has to be monitored and assessed if it is to be fully effective, so the more elaborate you make it, the more time and effort has to be expended in dealing with the results. It may be appropriate use of a teaching assistant (TA) to check that homework has been completed, offer advice about difficulties and (even) liaise with parents 'at the classroom door'.

Homework tasks need to be organised in such a way that children can cope unaided if necessary and, ideally, be directly linked to the learning objectives that you have established in class work. The tasks, therefore, provide consolidation and extension opportunities that would have been available in school had time permitted it. Formative feedback on homework tasks is not always possible, owing to time constraints and the many other demands upon a teacher. However, pupils can be inducted into sharing their work with a classmate, though this apparently simple procedure is more difficult than it sounds, as evaluation is demanding enough for adults, let alone for children. One way or another, comments must be made about the overall quality of homework tasks with indicators about improvements or implications.

Homework is most useful if it builds on previous school-based work or begins to open up new avenues of learning. Some homework consists of 'finishing off' incomplete work from the day; however, this penalises slower workers and does little to extend the more able. Other than familiar paper–and–pencil types, the best type of homework is of the 'project' kind, where children are given a number of activities that have to be completed over a period of time (a half term, say). Homework can provide a starting point for discussion and sharing experiences, the very heart blood of learning, and a useful spur in promoting dialogue in learning (see later in this chapter).

Good practice

For one week's homework ask the children to prepare a three-minute talk about 'my favourite toy/hobby/day out'. Younger children can base their talk on pictures; older ones can use more sophisticated means if they choose. Shy children can be asked gentle questions by an adult about their topic in front of their classmates. Make sure that the process is fun and non-competitive. You may be surprised at the depth of knowledge that some children possess.

Invigorating learning

Katz and Chard (2000) remind us that from a child's point of view, school is real life, not contrived or pretend, so children need to make learning an adventure that is sometimes challenging, sometimes perplexing but always motivating. Although some parts of the curriculum are less appealing than others, teachers should strive to create a learning environment that offers diverse experiences, excites children's interest and, wherever possible, builds on their enthusiasm. The following four principles apply to every age group and situation:

Help children to feel that learning is worthwhile

Learning becomes worthwhile when four factors apply: (a) the content is interesting and relevant; (b) the lesson is presented imaginatively, see second bullet point below; (c) the tasks associated with the lesson present a reasonable challenge; and (d) the learning climate is lively and encouraging. Teachers obviously have a vital role to play in each of these four factors. Thus:

- Even when the lesson content is mundane, you can explain its usefulness

- By the tone of your voice, the passion of your delivery and the incorporation of visual material, story, verbal exchanges and collaborative activity, you can stir the children's imaginations and engage their minds

- Differentiating tasks so that each child can succeed and feel pleased with her/his efforts helps to enhance self-image and motivation

- Your friendly but purposeful approach to teaching, emphasis on positive aspects of learning and patient explanations can transform the climate from one of stale conformity to energetic vibrancy in a short time.

In promoting effective learning, it is important not to dismiss underachievement by using tired excuses such as 'boys will be boys' or 'that sort of child never makes an effort' or 'well you cannot expect anything more' (see also Chapter 1). High expectations must be accompanied by adult enthusiasm and belief.

Feed and exercise children's imaginations

As noted in the second point above, stirring children's imaginations is important in learning and a key aspect of creativity. The root of the word imagination is 'imagine', which can be thought of as a 'mental picture' or 'seeing in the mind's eye'. Although the methods by which this can be achieved vary with age of child, there are a number of common stimuli that can be employed:

- Posing questions that cause the children to think deeply

- Offering real-life or fictitious scenarios to highlight key points or offer examples

- Using familiar objects in unfamiliar ways to offer differing perspectives on a subject

- Using unfamiliar objects as a source of awe and wonder

- Using powerful music, expressive poems or stimulating pictures to evoke an emotional response

- Giving children opportunity to share their own life experiences with others in the class.

Stirring children's imaginations may be an end in itself (for sheer joy) but is more often used as either a starting point or an accelerator in the learning process. As Napoleon Bonaparte is alleged to have commented: 'The human race is governed by its imagination'.

Answer a child's unasked question: 'Why are we doing this?'

It is not possible to ascertain how many children ask this question but unease about the lesson's relevance is sometimes expressed by younger children through their superficial commitment to the task, yawning or restless behaviour. Older children will also exhibit these tendencies but will often be more assertive and even ask directly about why an activity is necessary or its purpose. These misgivings can be minimised in two ways: (a) most importantly, by explaining the purpose to the children beforehand; and (b) by being honest with children when they express their doubts.

The process of explaining the purpose beforehand is rooted in the learning intentions for the lesson (see earlier) but more pragmatic explanations are sometimes equally valuable. For example, you may tell the children that they need to spend time practising their sums because you want to move on to a different topic and cannot do so until the job is completed. You might tell them that you want them to finish writing the story because it is parents' evening soon and you want to show mum what they have achieved. Being honest with children is not the same as being apologetic, though there are occasions when you will need to admit that although the content is not particularly interesting, it is a necessary prerequisite for subsequent, more exciting work. Your responses will vary according to circumstances but should be an explanation and not indicate that the child has a choice (unless, of course, this is the case). You may be faced with an option when dealing with a recalcitrant child about whether to insist or compromise, but dealing with stubborn children is an issue for Chapter 8 and will not be pursued here.

Convince children that they can be successful

The tone of the preceding parts of this chapter should have convinced you that whereas children need to develop self-motivation, this is often enhanced by an adult's attitude towards success. Merely encouraging a child to do well will not, of itself, produce a sudden transformation from uncertainty to optimism. However, a positive approach, coupled with appropriate support and direction will allow a child to persevere in the certain knowledge that there is an adult 'safety net' underneath. Over time the buoyant and cheerful mood you exude will spread throughout the class and, coupled with appropriate external rewards (such as stickers and merit cards) will influence the children's expectations and sense of determination. Your positive attitude may not affect pupils in the same way. There will always be occasions when, with your very best efforts, a child simply refuses to take an upbeat view of his or her potential and prefers to remain sullenly defeatist. Occasionally, a pupil who is inwardly quite confident will pretend to be downcast because it invites the teacher's close attention. Nevertheless, if the classroom exudes a 'we can' approach to learning, the increase in self-esteem, work of high quality and co-operation soon becomes tangible.

Activate your thinking!

To what extent do you sympathise with the following statements?

1. Each child learns in a different way from every other child.
2. Boys' and girls' learning needs differ from each other.
3. Adults can unintentionally constrain children's learning.
4. Children need time to observe, think, try and experience first hand.
5. Enthusiasm is contagious.
6. Teachers should learn to be skilled observers of children.
7. Self-belief is a necessary pre-requisite for effective learning.
8. There are times when it is difficult for children to learn and times of great significance.
9. Children's imaginations need to be activated for effective learning.
10. Pupils should be empowered in their learning.
11. If teachers convince themselves that they like children, they grow to like them.
12. Criticism is invariably damaging.
13. Children need to have something to hope for and look forward to.
14. The best teachers have deep personal humility.
15. Children are more likely to succeed if they feel welcome and valued.
16. Children have many things to teach one another.
17. Children benefit from having an accurate view of themselves as learners.
18. A fear of consequences constrains children's learning.
19. Children learn better if they understand the process of learning.
20. The heart is at the heart of education.

What are the implications for classroom practice?

Good practice

Read how one trainee teacher was able to enthuse all the children in the class. This sparkling description shows how an ordinary lesson can be transformed when children are liberated within a secure framework of adult support:

This week's session gave me a real sense of shared pleasure, with the children and I enjoying the music, each other's company, and creating real joy. We had worked hard listening to Vivaldi's *The Four Seasons*, thinking about what he was trying to say with his music and then, as the piece called 'Summer' built to a crescendo, the children were finding it hard to keep still. Toes were tapping, bottoms wriggling and heads moving. I encouraged them to take on the role of the conductor, using their hands and arms, but also moving with the music. We turned the music up really loud and got completely caught up in it. It was a wonderful sight to see them all enjoying the music so much. Hannah, a little girl with Down's Syndrome, had a huge grin on her face and was dancing around to the rhythm.

Dialogue for learning

Many experts have argued that pupils learn more effectively when they are given the opportunity to talk about their work, express their feelings and offer comment on issues. Killick (2006) even argues that young children 'can be observed to display a high degree of skill in organising groups, negotiating solutions and to have a high degree of insight into others' feelings, motives and worries' (2006: 51). Teachers who taught in primary schools during the 1970s and 1980s will be familiar with the term 'oracy', which was a shorthand for the speaking and listening that took place during collaborative sessions. A lot of emphasis was placed upon the potential for learning when children were given properly constructed opportunities to explore dilemmas, make decisions, experiment with ideas and draw conclusions through working together rather than singly. Oracy as a learning tool was predicated on a belief that by allowing children the space and time to talk together about a common interest their combined contributions, knowledge, skills, understanding and wisdom would lead to a more satisfactory outcome than one person working alone.

Teachers commonly interact with pupils by inviting spoken contributions to subjects that the teacher raises and the children respond appropriately. The teacher approves the response and comments further (or perhaps asks a question). The children respond again and the teacher confirms or casts doubt on the responses. The pattern is set: teacher speaks, children respond, teacher praises or redirects. Superficially, there is an active dialogue, especially if the teacher invites the children to provide alternatives, give another example or offer suggestions. Yet even this apparently rich learning environment may be less efficacious than it seems. For instance, it is the teacher who raises all the issues and asks all the questions. It is the teacher who determines the quality of the children's responses. It is the teacher who decides when to move on to the next point or lesson phase. In the practicalities of teaching lessons within a given time frame these practices are difficult to avoid if the session is ever to finish. After all, the lesson content has to be 'covered' and there is not an endless amount of time available for child-initiated talk. On the other hand, such a strongly teacher-led approach assumes that all ideas must be from adults and that children cannot learn without close guidance. Such assumptions merit close scrutiny.

Using pupils' talk for learning can be accomplished by identifying the nature of the talk and the conditions for its use. Three opportunities for talk are commonly used in classrooms:

- Discussion
- Debate
- Decision-making.

We will deal with each one separately.

Discussion

Discussion involves verbal contributions that approach a topic from a variety of directions and requires that pupils know enough about the subject to offer an opinion, suggest alternatives or summarise a position. To ensure effective discussion, participants must gain a variety of skills:

- Talk meaningfully to one another
- Listen carefully to one another
- Respond constructively to what others say
- Express their own views carefully
- Acknowledge that a variety of views exist
- Be determined to develop their knowledge, understanding or judgement.

As with all spoken language, discussion necessitates careful listening as well as marshalling and articulation of ideas. Such qualities are not easily acquired but can be shaped and steered by a teacher who is willing to give children the time and opportunity to express their thoughts. One of the challenges for teachers is to help children to understand that discussion is not merely an opportunity to put a point of view but to acknowledge and receive another person's perspective. Even adults find it hard to be disciplined in discussions, so little wonder that children also find it difficult. Dillon (1994) provides a helpful definition:

> Discussion is a form of group interaction, people talking back-and-forth with one another. What they talk about is an issue, some topic that is in question for them. Their talk consists of advancing and examining different proposals over the issue. (1994: 7)

Fisher (2005: 49) suggests that the word discussion has two common uses: (1) a general term to cover a wide range of informal situations where talk occurs between people; and (2) a specific meaning involving a particular form of group interaction where members join together to address an issue of common concern, during which they exchange different points of view in an attempt to reach a better understanding. Fisher refers to this second usage as a 'community of enquiry and stresses that seven moral principles need to operate to facilitate the discussion:

orderliness; reasonableness; truthfulness; freedom of expression; equality of opportunity; respect for others; and open-mindedness.

It is evident that pupils can only discuss something if there is something that merits being discussed. For instance, the worthiness of a cause, the correctness of a decision and the ethics of a controversial issue all provide fertile ground for talking to one another. Thus, younger children may discuss how best to take care of their 'snacks', ways to share toys or whether it is right to speak to strangers in the street. Older pupils may discuss issues of 'fairness', equality and classroom sanctions. Children of all ages can contribute to a discussion about local issues (such as a proposed road scheme) national issues (such as how to care for the elderly) and world issues (such as conservation). Opportunities also exist through personal, social and health education and citizenship. Teachers who wish to promote discussion should take account of four factors:

The physical environment

The context should be stress-free and settled but also purposeful, as additional noise and distractions detract from the concentrated attention that discussions deserve. Children should, if possible, work in natural light and the room temperature should be appropriate for the task.

The size of group

With older children it is sometimes better to split into smaller units of (say) four or five children to discuss the issues, with a subsequent report-back and plenary in which summary comments can be made by a child from each group. Younger children are usually better off working within a whole-class situation (such as 'circle time') where the teacher can exercise a more immediate influence upon the proceedings and ensure that timid children are included.

The sophistication of ideas

It is important that issues do not lie beyond children's experience or imagination. The best discussions deal with things that are of direct concern to the children involved but allow them to think beyond the immediacy of present circumstances. There is a place for drawing upon pupils' interest in the 'unseen', providing the discussion does not degenerate into silliness and trivia. Sometimes reading aloud an unusual poem, humorous story or intriguing extract can trigger excitement and an exchange of perceptions.

The teacher's role

A lot depends upon the nature of the discussion as to how intimately the teacher is involved. If the teacher intervenes too much, discussion will be stifled; if too little, discussion may move too far from the intended topic or dissolve into a series of unconnected comments. There are occasions when the conversation strays from the topic and you may be tempted to 'pull it back' by a sharp reminder about the main purpose of the task. However, it pays to be less hasty, for children need short bursts of relaxed talk before returning to the matter in hand.

Debate

Debate follows more closely prescribed rules than discussion and is more carefully structured. It therefore requires formal organisation and tends to be restricted to Key Stage 2 classes. Prior to the debate, pupils need time to research the given topic, talk informally to one another and, perhaps, record some of their findings in a form that can be later shared. The search for information can also be extended into homework tasks. During the debate, children who have volunteered to speak are given a period of time (say two minutes) in which to do so without interruption. The rest of the class have to sit patiently until the contribution has been concluded before being given about one minute to think about a helpful question or speculative comment. When the opportunity comes for questions and comments, no one is allowed to preface their comment with the words 'Yes, but …' or similar negative overtones. No responses are allowed at this point. Once the questions and comments are exhausted, another speaker is permitted the same amount of time to present information and ideas. Ideally, speakers should offer contrasting views so that when the process of contributing, questioning and commenting is complete, a more interactive plenary is able to take place. During the debate, the teacher needs to ensure that time is carefully monitored, issues are noted and contributions of all types are considered fairly by pupils. At the end of the lesson, teachers also have an important function in drawing together the different threads of the arguments, thanking the main participants and (most importantly) reminding the class about the significance of the debate in terms of the overall learning intentions. Although debate is of itself a valuable means of stimulating interest and inculcating children into mature thinking and a tolerant consideration of differing (or similar) viewpoints, it is doubly worthwhile if it can be seen as directly contributing towards longer-term curriculum subject goals. If you have established a relaxed and respectful relationship with the children, it may be appropriate to ask the participants how they felt before, during and after the session.

Decision-making

Decision-making is a strategy used principally in collaborative problem-solving and investigations in areas of science and mathematics, and in resolving ethical dilemmas. It is most effective for groups of about four children working towards a shared aim. Teachers sometimes give individuals specific roles to members of the group (such as chair, secretary, scribe, time-keeper), though it is normally more successful to allow children to sort themselves out or take turns in the different roles. Decision-making processes require a lot of teacher preparation in setting the scene, explaining the parameters of the task and organising groups. As with discussion and debate, teachers have a responsibility to encourage all children to participate, to discourage some pupils from dominating the talk and generate sufficient enthusiasm for children to feel that their efforts are worthwhile. Time must be allowed for feedback from selected children from each group and, where appropriate, questions and comments. If necessary, some 'overspill' time must be allowed to save rushing the concluding phase, which can reveal some powerful themes. Decision-making can be used to resolve genuine problems (such as the citing of waste bins), gain a consensus prior to a School Council meeting (about, say, how to supervise children who come to school early) or interrogate a fictional scenario (such as what action should be taken in the event of everything that is touched turning to gold).

It takes time to train children in making the most effective use of their opportunities for talk, and many teachers find that it is several weeks before the strategy is working smoothly. Your role is crucial in planning and organising, managing the lesson and maintaining a sense of purpose and direction without crushing pupils' enthusiasm or causing them to feel that they can only express opinions of which you approve.

Activate your thinking!

Consider the following questions:

(a) Do people naturally think first, speak later?

(b) What is meant by 'getting your brain in gear' before you speak?

(c) Is thinking the same as talking to yourself?

(d) Can you think without words?

(e) When do people talk to themselves?

Allowing children opportunities to talk to others enables them to move outside their familiar world and explore different avenues of thinking, recognise life's complexities through the eyes and mind of another person, and occasionally fantasise. The opportunity to hear their own voices and opinions taken seriously allows insecure children to gain confidence and can enhance their self-belief. Not only does dialogue help children to learn through sharing ideas with others but, with guidance from a sensitive adult, to learn to evaluate different opinions and, where appropriate, to offer their support in helping others to search for solutions.

There are many forms of talk that help children to master cerebral and social skills. They can recount an interesting experience, tell a joke, comment on what is said by others, wonder out loud and express concerns about a situation. Children can be taught how to debate, offer advice and disagree. They can provide information, explain how something is done and suggest alternatives. In other words, children's insights and present sources of knowledge are a rich resource waiting to be unearthed. However, it cannot be assumed that children will be able to handle all these elements of talk unaided, so you need to offer them wise guidance about doing so.

Promoting dialogue

Learning through dialogue does not and will not happen automatically simply because children are split into groups and given something to talk about. It needs to be developed in the same way as any other learning technique such as scientific enquiry, manipulating figures or shaping a clay pot. Dialogue is, perhaps, an inadequate word to explain the complexity of multiple interactions between a selected group of children and the learning that ensues. A more satisfactory expression might be 'critical dialogue' to indicate the interrogative nature of the happening or 'focused dialogue' to indicate its purposeful nature. Some children are naturally talkative and dominate conversations to the detriment of more passive types. Other children find it difficult to express themselves and may, therefore, prefer to remain silent rather than expose their inadequacy. Teachers need to take these factors into account when planning their strategies for teaching and learning.

If learning through dialogue is to be effective, a number of things need to be in place. First, as noted earlier, a suitably positive classroom learning climate must have been developed such that teacher and children are mutually supportive and encouraging. If, as a trainee teacher, you find that such conditions are not ideal, it does not preclude collaborative enterprises but means that you will have to work even harder to establish and maintain the right atmosphere by your accessible approach, approving manner and clear instructions. Second, children must be inculcated into thinking about their learning rather than passively receiving it from an adult. This process takes a lot of perseverance because a lot of teaching in the core subjects especially is dominated by a philosophy of 'teacher gives, pupil receives'. By posing interesting and speculative questions, encouraging children to think aloud and providing alternative explanations for events and phenomena, you can gradually foster a more inquisitive attitude and thirst for knowledge in your charges. Third, children must be given strategies for taking turns and offering an opinion. Even adults struggle to conform to the conversational 'rules of engagement', especially when the topic is controversial, so little wonder that some children blurt out what they are thinking at the first opportunity. Last, and importantly, children must be taught how to listen to one another. This apparently 'natural' ability is anything but natural for a lot of children. The skill can be improved and refined in a number of ways, including:

- The teacher models the importance of careful listening by repeating or summarising for the benefit of the whole class what a child has said

- Children are given opportunity to summarise what another child has said after being selected by the teacher to do so

- Play a 'repeat after me' game based on the US Marines' strategy of the group echoing the leader's statements (this is also great fun for the children).

Despite the growth in interactive teaching involving teacher–pupil exchanges, the incidence of extended dialogue has become less evident in primary teaching because teachers have been encouraged to inject 'pace' into the lessons and plan sessions under specific time constraints, most notably in literacy sessions. As a result, some teachers do not feel comfortable in allowing children room to pursue an argument, explore an issue or express an opinion unless it can be done succinctly and strictly within the constraints of the stated learning target. In addition, some younger children speak slowly and others need opportunity to deliberate, pause and retrace their steps. If time is taken up by a child's extended verbal contribution, the squeeze on the remaining lesson phases (e.g. group activity, recording, plenary) becomes a serious factor in managing the lesson. There is a balance to be struck between encouraging dialogue and observing the lesson conventions.

It is worth remembering that the partitioning of lessons into units of equivalent length, usually about an hour per session, is for convenience rather than necessarily being based on children's learning needs. Trainee teachers are sometimes fearful (with some justification) that they may invite criticism if they do not adhere to the normal lesson structure. However, if you are in a position where you want to develop children's verbal skills but are sensitive to time constraints, there are a number of ways in which the problem can be addressed:

- First, discuss the issue with the host teacher and find out whether there is any flexibility allowable in the length of session. It may be necessary to straddle a session before and after a break time

- Introduce the strategy of 'tell a friend what you think before you tell the teacher' during interactive and 'carpet' sessions

- Make stronger use of teamwork, where a number of children work together to discuss and solve problems

- Allocate specific slots in the timetable for the purpose of discussing issues. It is sensible to start with a familiar issue and introduce more challenging ones when the children become familiar with the process.

A scan of the above factors shows the difficulty and complexity of trying to promote learning through dialogue. As teacher, you have to model the attributes and carefully guide children's attitudes so that they gradually learn to speak and listen effectively. It is far from easy to involve all the children in a whole-class discussion, so if the children are inexperienced in verbalising their thoughts and ideas or tend to be excitable, it is best to begin with discussion in small groups. Once the children become more confident and understand the system, you can consider having a reporting-back time and wider debate.

The concept of learning through dialogue has been resurrected to an extent through the emphasis on adult/pupil verbal interaction that forms such a crucial part of formal literacy and mathematics sessions. More recently, attention has been focused on the significance of pupil/pupil interaction through the establishment of collaborative learning that can take a number of forms:

1. First, the teacher establishes a practical problem-solving situation related to the existing curriculum work for the children to resolve by discussing approaches and then acting upon the agreed procedure. For example children may be offered three possible ways to improve the tidiness of the playground, such as: (a) to erect a larger number of bins; (b) for each class to take a turn in being playground monitors; and (c) for the establishment of regular playground 'guardians'.

2. Second, the teacher establishes a theoretical problem-solving situation based on present curriculum work in which the members of the group have to discuss the options and arrive at an agreed solution or position on the matter. The teacher outlines the issues, invites preliminary comments from the children and presents them with the problem to be discussed in groups of (say) four or five children. For example, in the area of citizenship the issue may relate to an issue of *fair distribution*. Younger pupils might be asked to talk about ways to ensure that every child has an equal chance to use the classroom-based computers.

Older pupils may be asked to discuss ways in which money raised for good causes overseas will not be squandered through bureaucracy or the actions of corrupt leaders.

3. Third, the children raise an issue about which they feel strongly with the teacher during the teacher/class interactive session. The teacher then helps the children to shape their ideas into a proposition, which each group discusses. For example, children have firm opinions about friendship patterns, school rules, homework, children's television programmes, playground behaviour, and associated topics, all of which may provide fertile ground for exploring important principles.

In each of the three circumstances, the groups combine after a suitable time to contribute their ideas and, after further discussion, arrive at a consensus or the teacher summarises the conflicting positions. Children need to be shown that having different views about issues is perfectly acceptable, providing there is evidence to support their assertions.

Activate your thinking!

During the collaborative activity, which children were the thinkers and which children were the followers? How do you know?

Good practice

Think of a 'discussion topic for the week' and introduce it each Monday morning. Allow f opportunities throughout the week for discussion and on Friday afternoon gather hts and ideas in a forum.

ꞈner role in dialogue

In promoting the concept of learning through dialogue, it is important to keep your eye on the central purposes of the exercise, namely, to learn from one another by pooling idea and expertise, and enhance social cohesion through shared experiences. However, the teacher has an important role to play in the proceedings, expressed in one of three ways:

Acting as an expert

That is, you provide knowledge, information and advice, as and when you consider necessary. Being an expert may militate against free discussion and expressions of opinions if the children perceive that there is a 'right' answer and that you are the final arbiter of what is acceptable, but consider yourself a resource to be used as much as any other. There is a place for pupils to act as expert if the area of discussion is in their own field of interest (e.g. a hobby or pastime).

Acting as a facilitator

That is, you ensure that the conditions are right for children to learn through talking. The conditions must include mutual respect and an agreed method of proceeding, but also the provision of adequate time to delve into the area of interest and a pleasant working environment: airy, light and uncluttered. You keep a low profile in respect of what is being said but monitor the way in which contributions are made and pupil involvement.

Acting as a participant

That is, you take part as a 'temporary' member of a group or the class. In this role, you take your turn in the same way as everyone else. In such a case, there is no hierarchy and no imposed authority. You can only occupy this 'neutral' role when you have complete confidence in the children concerned.

Although it is tempting to set children to work in groups and stand back, thereby not interacting with them until work is finished or a child asks a question, your role in stimulating children's verbal contributions is significant. While you will not want to swamp the children so that they are unable to express their own ideas, it is overly optimistic to imagine that you have no part to play in the proceedings once the children are talking. However, it has been known for trainee teachers to become so engrossed in one group that they forget what the remainder of the class is up to, so stay alert and make sure that you scan the room regularly or go for a walk around.

A variety of practical considerations have to be taken into account in making the most effective use of time spent on dialogue:

1. First, it is better to put children into homogeneous groups initially (capable pupils together, less capable pupils together) rather than mixed ones. In mixed groups the dominant children tend to do all the talking and although you can monitor the situation to some extent, less confident children often merely sit and listen rather than participating. In homogeneous groups, a group consisting of assertive children is invariably loud and bold as the personalities compete for dominance. A group consisting of quieter children usually struggles to make headway but the under-confident children are more likely to have opportunity to say something.

2. Second, it is worth giving pupils something to talk about in the early stages by providing them with a subject for debate. As pupils grow more experienced and confident, you can allow them to raise their own topics, but probably within certain boundaries (e.g. relating to the present cross-curricular theme or topic). Sometimes the issue arises naturally from the curriculum work that you are covering with the children. Sometimes a national or international event will trigger considerable interest and you decide to 'catch the moment' (a necessary part of teaching at all times). However, you may decide that as a means of promoting dialogue and stimulating discussion you are going to set up a contrived situation and maintain close control over what happens, at least in the early stages. The close control

approach allows you to teach or reinforce the necessary skills for effective speaking and listening before exploiting other learning opportunities.

3. Third, children should be encouraged to think and organise their thoughts before speaking. There is a fine balance to be achieved between verbal spontaneity and talking nonsense. Saying the first thing that comes into their heads can lead to children being ridiculed. On the other hand, too much time spent deliberating can result in missed opportunities. It takes some children a lot of courage to make a verbal contribution, so it may on occasions be necessary to employ a strategy to facilitate it without causing embarrassment. For example, children can be taught to jot down a few ideas on paper prior to the main discussion or work in pairs/with an adult to compile a short list of key points.

4. Finally, it is helpful to encourage children to speak aloud what they want to say in their heads before opening their mouths. This is also a useful strategy for trainee teachers. Telling children to 'hear it in your head first' is particularly useful for diffident pupils and an alternative to writing ideas down first.

Classroom management considerations include the need to structure opportunities for one-to-one listening and group-to-group listening, to teach children to rephrase what others have said and ask them sensible questions and to enthuse about other children's verbal contributions as a means of encouraging them. In working with young children, skills can be enhanced through games and fun activities that foster listening. For example, well-known games such as 'Simon Says' and 'Chinese Whispers' require children to concentrate on what is being said by others. There are also opportunities through so-called circle time to facilitate taking turns and concentrating on what other children say.

Activate your thinking!

Write down some responses that a four, seven or ten year old might give to each of the following questions:

1. What do you like to talk about with your friends?
2. When do you talk to your teacher?
3. When does the teacher talk to you?
4. What do you mainly talk about during class lessons/sessions?
5. Who does most talking in class?

Good practice

Other organisational considerations for learning through dialogue include:

- Deciding how much (if anything) should be written down
- Having paper, pencils, computers or other recording instruments available and accessible
- Seating arrangements for the groups
- Roles for different group members
- Specific targets for achievement in the time available
- The way that ideas will be shared between groups
- The activity that follows the dialogue.

Play in learning

We noted in Chapter 1 that all children love to play and that a lack of desire to do so is viewed with anxiety by parents and teachers. Bruce (2001) maintains that play helps children to learn in a number of powerful ways (based on 2001: 8):

- To become symbol-makers by making one item stand for another (such as a stick becoming a wand)
- To think in abstract ways that take them beyond the here and now
- To develop theory of mind, an understanding of the way others think and feel, and relate to people
- To make changes, transforming their lives and events, using imagination and creating alternative possibilities
- To be flexible thinkers, so that intelligence continues to develop throughout life.

Smidt (2006) offers four explicit characteristics that define the concept of play: (1) play is something the child has chosen to do; (2) play is often pleasurable and always deeply engrossing, and we tend to see children enjoying their chosen activity, except when the play is 'acting out' a traumatic experience; (3) in play there is no risk of failure, as the child simply changes the agenda; and (4) the emphasis is on the process rather than on the product (adapted from 2006: 48). Robson (2006) argues that what she refers to as 'pretend play' may be 'particularly significant for the development of theory of mind' because in pretend play 'children step in and out of role, represent situations and transform objects, talk about mental states ... and have to negotiate meanings and actions with others' (2006: 79). However, as noted below, work by Cohen (2006) suggests that if learning is to occur, it is necessary for play to translate from the 'pretend' (or 'playful') state to a 'serious' state.

Most teachers of young children use play as a means of enquiry-based learning; teachers at Key Stage 2 tend to encourage play only within the confines of a controlled learning environment (notably in drama). For younger children, who are familiar with school routines and able to cope with more structure, play may be timetabled or used informally as an incentive to complete formal tasks. For older children, play can be a vehicle to explore issues and confront life choices through improvisation, and to be introduced to the demands and responsibilities of team membership. A teacher's planned intentions for a child of any age will always be limited by the child's enthusiasm for, and ownership of the task. This applies to play as much as any other form of learning.

Johnston (2002) stresses the importance of adult–child and child–child interaction as the basis for effective early learning. She suggests that adults affect children's learning through interacting with them in two principal ways. First, the adult provides a role model for the children and can show them by example (such as showing enthusiasm). Second, adults can focus the children's attention and raise issues by asking questions. Johnston underlines that by interacting with children, adults can learn alongside them, as 'It is important that children do not see adults as having a complete set of knowledge, understandings and skills' (2002: 29).

O'Hara (2004) suggests that there are four broad types of play: structured, free, exploratory and social. Structured play is planned and initiated by the adult. Free play is spontaneous. Exploratory play is when children experiment with tools, equipment and materials (including sand and water). Social play provides 'opportunities to learn about and practise the rules, rituals and norms of society' (2004: 79). Play as an essential part of the educative process and a powerful learning agent (see, for example, Griffiths 1998). Orr (2003) presents a compelling argument for play as a vital agent in the development of children suffering from disabilities. Garrick (2004) argues the importance of outdoor play. Texts that provide an in-depth analysis of the arguments supporting the educational value of play include Beardsley and Harnett 1998; Drummond and Pollard 1998; Manning-Morton and Thorp 2003; Kalliala 2004; Cohen 2006. Cohen, referring to work by Apter and Kerr (1991) views all play (adults as well as children) as a state of mind rather than a series of behaviours. He distinguishes between a 'playful' state of mind, in which 'the individual is able to explore and elaborate a variety of skills and test them to the limits in a free and imaginative way', and a 'serious' state of mind, which is goal-orientated. Cohen claims that in the playful state, the child is 'able to build up a stockpile of habits, skills and knowledge that is more extensive than it would have been in the goal-orientated state alone'. When in the 'serious' state, a child selects from this playful agenda and begins to articulate the ideas. The synergy between the two states is where learning takes place. In other words, it is not enough for you to simply let pupils play freely, but to do so in the expectation that the repertoire of skills and insights that they gain will be transformed into a better understanding of the world, increase self-confidence, develop new ideas, reduce anxiety and reinforce social relationships (Cohen 2006: all quotes taken from 82–3). Teachers need to be clear about a number of principles before they incorporate play into their repertoire of enquiry-based learning strategies. These principles relate to ways in which children learn, how they understand the world and their need to express themselves imaginatively. If teachers believe that children learn by engaging with issues and life-situations through play, then there needs to be evidence to support that view. If teachers are disparaging about play and see it as a holding activity to keep children happy while the real work goes on around them, then it is difficult to justify play as an essential element of a teaching and learning strategy.

Teaching gifted and talented children

A lot of attention is given to the needs of less able children: however, rather less has been paid to the needs of the more able (sometimes referred to as 'gifted'). There are numerous definitions of the terms 'gifted' and 'talented' though it is often employed in a single phrase: 'gifted and talented'. However, a commonly held view is that *gifted* is an exceptional ability in the literacy, mathematics, science, history, geography, design and technology, and religious education. The word *talented*, on the other hand, tends to be reserved for children who display exceptional ability in other curriculum areas where there is more of a public performance element: art and design, music, PE, dance, drama. Bates and Munday (2005) define gifted children as 'those who exhibit high ability across one of more academic subject areas', and talented children as 'those who excel in a specific subject area; either socially – in terms of leadership – or in sport, the performing arts or design and technology' (2005: 4). However, Knowles (2006, referring to Sternberg and Davidson 2005) offers a different perspective, claiming that giftedness is the potential a child may possess in an particular subject or area of human activity; it is characterised by the child's ability to learn in that area faster than its peer group. Whereas talent is seen by Knowles as 'the *realisation* of that giftedness; in effect, the performance of that giftedness' (2006: 150, original emphasis). Whatever definition we adopt, it is likely that gifted and talented pupils will typically comprise between five and ten per cent of the class. In other words, in a class of 30 children there are likely to be two or three children in the gifted and talented category.

One of your tasks after identifying the factors that separate outstanding ability from the good and very good is to be sensitive and flexible in the way that you prescribe learning outcomes. A characteristic of gifted and talented children is that they learn things that were unanticipated and may be unimpressed with teachers' priorities for learning. In such circumstances it helps to remember that many pioneers and entrepreneurs were headstrong in their determination to pursue their own ideas and dismiss more obvious pathways. Einstein rebelled when his tutors insisted on promoting old-style scientific theories. The great inventor, Edison was so single-minded that he drove his teachers to distraction and had to be educated at home. Effective teaching promotes independent learning skills and fosters creativity in very able pupils in primary schools, and schools are becoming more adept in early intervention and tailoring an education suitable for the needs of the gifted and talented. Nonetheless, it is important to realise that there is no single curriculum and teaching approach suitable for all gifted children: each case has to be dealt with on its individual merits.

When a task is challenging and interesting, gifted and able pupils will tend to self-select by their enthusiastic and wholehearted responses. Typically, gifted and talented pupils will be characterised by some or all of the following behaviours:

- Intensely focused on the task
- Asking insightful questions to probe and clarify concepts
- Seeing possibilities beyond the obvious solution
- Thriving on the challenges and complexity of the problem
- Making abstract connections between pieces of information

- Offering original and unusual solutions
- Posing questions beyond the immediate remit of the task.

The prominence of gifted or talented ability should not be considered as being either innate or absent; that is, either a child 'has it' or does not 'have it'. Although it is normally quite easy to distinguish the very able children (i.e. those possessing exceptional innate abilities) from the majority (i.e. those who do not have innate abilities) the learning environment can also have an impact on the *emergence* of the gift or talent (see Hymer and Michel 2002 for practical ideas and suggestions). Bates and Munday (2005) warn that 'children develop at different rates according to their home and school influences, and their potential for achievement may well remain undiscovered and untapped well into their teenage years' (2005: 8). Furthermore, it is possible to be so insistent that gifted and talented children conform to the pre-determined lesson format and learning target that they become dispirited and begin to under-perform.

Part of the challenge for teachers lies in the fact that as some gifted and talented children are unconventional, their behaviour might be interpreted as anti-social because they push the boundaries, ask probing questions and insist on being innovative rather than compliant. Some *talented* children may not shine at mathematics and literacy; as a result they are obliged to spend additional time on these subjects, which reduces the opportunity for them to display their creative abilities in areas where their natural abilities lie. Yet other children have latent talent that requires a stimulus before it is released. Unfortunately, children from less affluent homes may not have a chance to attend (say) out-of-school ballet, dance, craft or sporting sessions, at which they might have excelled. Again, the heavy demands made by planning, teaching, assessing, meetings, marking, reporting, extra-curricular activities, and so forth sometimes mean that a teacher is already stretched to the limit and has little time to identify individual talents; consequently, the child is not offered the support and encouragement to fulfil his or her potential. Despite the problems, you owe it to the child to make every effort to help them exploit their potential and every school is now required to have a policy covering such matters (see, for example, Eyre and McClure 2001).

Helping *gifted* children in core subjects is easier for teachers in that there is a considerable amount of time spent on them, so it is easier to spot exceptional ability and differentiate the work accordingly, particularly in literacy and mathematics. Recognising giftedness in science is more complex and may not become evident until secondary school.

Gifted and talented children may be emotionally sensitive and need time and opportunity to develop their knowledge within a secure classroom environment, though this advice applies to all children at every level. However, the learning culture should ideally take account of:

- The learner's own interest in the topic, theme or subject
- The learners' preferred style of learning, without becoming obsessive about it
- Opportunities for learners to be increasingly independent and autonomous, with appropriate training in necessary skills
- The need for openly sharing ideas and initiatives with others (through formally designed discussions and informally)

- The need to find cross-curricular links

- Opportunities for wider application of knowledge (preferably in 'real' situations)

- The use of a variety of resources, ideas, methods of approach and tasks

- The importance of encouraging a reflective and probing attitude of learning.

To make optimum progress, a learning climate has to be created in which mistakes are used constructively, children are encouraged to discuss their learning with adults and other pupils, and opportunities are afforded for them to explore challenging forms of learning. While it is unlikely that anyone would disagree with such sound advice, there are practical reasons why such an approach may be easier to say than to do. First, studies of more able pupils in larger classes indicate that teachers tend to leave them alone to get on by themselves or simply give them additional work to keep them busy rather than stretch their minds. The highest levels of performance are achieved when teachers interact with pupils in a way that encourages them to grapple with more demanding concepts and levels of understanding than other children. By contrast, the imposition of artificial ceilings in tasks result in pupil frustration. Dickinson (1996) found that able pupils wanted to be challenged and find fulfilment through active dialogue with the teacher. They wanted to be 'challenged within the curriculum rather than by special provision outside it' (1996: 8); that is, able pupils did not want to be isolated from the regular tasks and activities, but rather to be given the opportunity to extend their thinking and be innovative. More able pupils were motivated by teachers' comments more than grades and wanted to receive truthful, realistic and challenging feedback.

Able pupils of whatever type are not always easily identifiable because teachers sometime struggle to disentangle pupils' *potential* from their visible performance. Gifted and talented pupils can underachieve in the same way as other children, especially if they lack motivation or if, due to their quizzical attitude, teachers diagnose them as unco-operative instead of intelligent. Denton and Postlethwaite (1985) offer a useful list of characteristics that help teachers to identify very able (gifted) pupils (see Table 4.1).

The majority of able pupils take their work seriously and want to do well. Their attainment can be suppressed by teacher insensitivity, mundane tasks and being treated 'differently' from everyone else, thereby gaining a reputation as a 'swot'. The challenge of presenting academic success as desirable is most acute among a small percentage of older primary age boys, who may view sporting prowess and gang membership as more significant than gaining high grades. Disillusionment with schooling is an attitude that can easily be carried with them into secondary education and lead to underachievement, so you have an important task to persuade them otherwise. As part of this persuading process you may need to offer these under-achievers some 'earned autonomy', whereby they are allowed greater choice as a reward for satisfactory task completion.

Teachers also need to be aware that able pupils do not necessarily possess the full range of fundamental skills that may be assumed. For instance, Dean (1998) notes that boys, in particular, struggle to keep pace with the demands of writing and sometimes underachieve, and offers suggestions about helping able pupils to reach their full potential in reading and writing. Some very able pupils may exhibit odd characteristics that mark them out as being atypical and invite

TABLE 4.1 Characteristics of gifted pupils (based on Denton and Postlethwaite 1985)

superior powers of reasoning	intellectual curiosity
alertness and quick responses to new ideas	quick memorising
ease of learning	interest in the nature of humanity
wide range of interests	unusual imagination
broad attention span	able to follow complex directions
superior vocabulary	rapid readers
independence in working	enjoy a range of hobbies
advanced reading skills	wide ranging reading habits
keen powers of observation	effective users of the library
initiative and originality	superior in maths problem-solving

teasing from other children. Others will excel in every curriculum area (including sports) and thereby attract excessive admiration from their peers. Howe (1990) warns that although able children may not react in expected ways, close parental involvement, coupled with high expectations, yields rewards. Teachers need, therefore, to be alert to the possibilities and challenges that such children present. Few children are naturally good at everything but, with perseverance and determination, many are capable of achieving a higher level of success than was initially evident.

We noted in Chapter 2 that in recent years there has been an increase in interest in the principle of 'multiple intelligence' popularised by Howard Gardner (1983; 1999) This awkward phrase ('multiple intelligence') reminds teachers of two important principles. First, children can be successful in a variety of ways and not only in the more obviously measurable ones. Thus, Gardner suggests that we each have different intelligences for expressing ourselves and solving problems. Because we experience life in different ways and have different emotional responses to the same stimuli, it is appropriate for us to express those responses in a variety of ways. For example, emotions may be expressed through language or the employment of visual images or in movement. The second principle is that intelligence is not fixed and can be enhanced, developed and matured through appropriate teaching, high levels of motivation and determination. The stereotypical comment made by children that 'I am rubbish at such-and-such a subject' betrays a belief that they are either good at something or not good at it, and that this situation is irretrievable. However, the evidence does not support this gloomy prediction. Skilled teachers try hard to develop in the children a different attitude towards themselves and wean them off adopting such a negative viewpoint. Your enthusiasm, teaching skills, ability to motivate and close relationship with pupils may expose a larger number of gifted and talented children than you were initially aware of.

Activate your thinking!

All children are gifted. Some just open their presents later than others.

Anon

Garnett (2005) interprets the seven original forms of intelligence as described by Gardner (*naturalistic* intelligence and *existential* or *philosophical* intelligence were added to the list later) with regard to the ways in which the possession of such an 'intelligence' can assist pupils' learning as follows:

1. Verbal/linguistic intelligence: helps pupils to communicate and make sense of the world through language.

2. Musical/rhythmic intelligence: helps pupils to create, communicate and understand meanings made out of sound.

3. Logical/mathematical intelligence: helps pupils to appreciate abstract relations, use deductive and inductive reasoning and critical thinking.

4. Visual/spatial intelligence: helps pupils perceive visual or spatial information and to create visual images from memory.

5. Body/kinaesthetic intelligence: helps pupils to use all or parts of the body to create or solve problems.

6. Interpersonal intelligence: helps pupils to make and see distinctions in other people's feelings and intentions.

7. Intrapersonal intelligence: helps pupils to distinguish among their own moods and feelings.

Garnett (2005: 44–6) offers fuller descriptions for each of the Gardner 'intelligences', a selection from which include:

Verbal/Linguistic—reading, writing, listening and speaking…creating stories, using metaphors and similes, symbolism and conceptual patterning…humour, jokes, puns, play on words and the ability to quickly acquire other languages.

Musical/Rhythmic—tapping out intricate rhythms…[Pupils] might like to have soft music in the background to help them concentrate.

Logical/Mathematical—Pupils with a strong leaning to this intelligence may like to develop strategies, perform experiments, reason things out, work with numbers, and explore patterns and relationships.

Visual/Spatial—[Pupils] tend to have active imaginations and are good at expressing their ideas and thoughts through drawings, paintings, sculpture, patterns and colour schemes.

Body/Kinaesthetic—[Pupils] like to learn through touching, physical movement, manipulating concrete objects, interacting with their environment and 'making and doing'.

Interpersonal—[Pupils] like organising, collaborating and solving problems between people. They notice and react well to the moods of their friends.

Intrapersonal—[Pupils] are good at taking responsibility for their own learning. They typically enjoy working alone and are more uncomfortable in groups and will not usually volunteer to make whole class contributions.

With respect to the additional two categories, Fisher (2005) reasons that the eighth intelligence (naturalistic) can be defined as our capacity to investigate the physical world, which enables us to find out more about the outside world in a systematic way. The ninth intelligence, which Gardner calls 'Existential intelligence', Fisher refers to as philosophical, and states that: 'It expresses itself in the ability to ask deep questions about human existence, such as the meaning of life and why we die' (2005: 12). Fisher agrees that the concept of multiple intelligences is a contested one but that it seems to fit how humans respond to the world. He also makes the point that there may be other forms of intelligence, such as spiritual intelligence (a concept rejected by Garner but accepted by some other psychologists), that have not yet been defined. Furthermore, intelligences do not have to stand alone but can and do combine in different ways.

Gardner's work has value if it encourages us to identify special capability and build on natural strengths. There is, however, a danger attached to holding a rigid adherence to the principal of multiple intelligences. It is easy to envisage that in attempting to move away from the concept of a single intelligence (the Intelligence Quotient, IQ) towards multiple intelligence, the Gardner categorisation could become equally unhelpful if it is used as an alternative labelling system for children – which is quite contrary to Gardner's intentions. Thus, certain pupils might be deemed to possess only specific types of 'intelligence', with the net effect that expectations are raised in these areas but suppressed in the those areas where children are not judged to have such 'inclinations'. Indeed, it is quite possible to predict a scenario in which a child will simply refuse to try in the mistaken belief that *I don't have such and such intelligence, so it's pointless.* There is the world of difference between identifying natural strengths and ignoring the fact that weaker areas can become stronger with perseverance and application. An awareness of the fact that children have different learning preferences and potential that can be exploited and enhanced is obviously a positive approach to education. Ignoring the fact that every child is capable of improvement and even excelling in areas (intelligences) that do not appear to be naturally evident, is not.

Activate your thinking!

Use the list in Table 4.1 to identify the most able children in your class. Consider ways in which you can help them to achieve their potential.

Case study

The children in Year 4 were learning their five times table and every member of the class or group was able to chant the table without a mistake and give correct and immediate answers to individual computation questions asked by the teacher. Initially, the teacher was very pleased but quickly recognised that although superficially every child had 'learned' their tables, their conceptual grasp varied considerably:

- Shena could respond correctly when asked a straight question, such as the answer to four times five, but had little understanding beyond the immediate answer. For instance, she did not realise that 20 is composed of two tens

- Gareth could work out the answer by adding five and five and five and five very rapidly. He was a little slow in finding the answer but at least he understood that multiplication is equivalent to multiple adding

- Nicu knew the answer, too, but had grasped that five times four is also 20. He also realised that the total bill for four items costing £5 each totalled £20

- Skye not only knew the answer but could also tell the teacher what 40 times five equals.

Although the teacher was initially satisfied that each child was equally competent in their grasp of the computation, the reality was more complex. Once he spent time talking to the children about the work and setting them a variety of tasks to test their grasp of the concepts, he was able to structure future lessons in a more informed manner. Although all the children were able to respond at a functional level and get the correct answer to the computation problem, some had a sound conceptual grasp of the mathematical principles and a small number were able to apply their learning to other situations. The bare test result was insufficiently rigorous to expose the true situation.

Further reading

Alloway, T.P. and Gathercole, S.E. (2007) *Memory and Learning*, London: Sage.
Provides a coherent overview of the role played by working memory in learning during the school years.

Harnett, P. (2007) *Supporting Children's Learning in the Primary and Early Years*, London: Routledge.
Helps trainee teachers and newly qualified teachers reflect on the professional decisions they need to make, including making children agents of their own learning.

Lowe, V. (2006) *Stories, Pictures and Reality*, London: Routledge.
Follows two children as they probe the meanings of stories and the motivations of the characters they discover.

Reid, G. (2007) *Effective Learning Strategies for the Classroom*, London: Sage.
Focuses on recognising and meeting the individual needs of different kinds of learners and providing strategies for helping pupils develop their own successful approach to learning.

Simister, C.J. (2007) *How to Teach Thinking and Learning Skills*, London: Sage.
A series of ready-to-use lessons, using games, activities and group tasks. Includes a CD-ROM.

Watkins, C., Carnell, E. and Lodge, C. (2007) *Effective Learning in Classrooms*, London: Sage.
Provides insights into what makes learning effective and how it might be promoted in classrooms.

Planning and Teaching Skills

Introduction

In this chapter we focus on the range of teaching skills and strategies needed to develop effective classroom practice and enhance children's learning. Of the many teaching skills that teachers have to master, it is planning and the production of lesson plans that are among those of highest importance. Issues relating to differentiation, individual learning needs, body language and adult–pupil interaction, notably the use of questions, are also considered closely.

Lesson planning

When trainee teachers begin teaching, they go into their first session clutching a lesson plan like a lifesaver, fearful that it may slip from their grasp and leave them exposed and helpless. As they become more confident, they are able to set the plan aside and concentrate on improving their lesson presentation, interaction with pupils and exercising control. Over time, they think less of merely surviving to the end of the session and more about what the children are learning. They realise that the best laid plans can prove to be unsatisfactory unless they are clear about what the children already know, the most effective way to organise for learning and how to make an accurate assessment of what is presently being learned (so-called assessment for learning, AFL).

Inexperienced teachers gradually become aware that children take differing amounts of time to grasp concepts and remember facts, and that most children do not learn in a smooth, uninterrupted way but are like the tide moving up the beach in a series of waves; sometimes gaining ground, sometimes slipping back, occasionally surging forward. Trainees' lesson plans become more comprehensive as they make allowance for faster and slower workers, less able and more able pupils, and the vagaries of classroom life. They realise that a short lesson at the end of the day following an exciting PE session requires a different approach from one of normal length during the early part of the day. As the trainee becomes familiar with the class situation, lesson plans are developed with closer respect to pupils' previous learning and anticipated future progress. Both immediate and cumulative learning outcomes are taken into account in determining the structure and content of future sessions. Spontaneous opportunities are seized and 'milked' for all they are worth, even if they do not conform exactly with the anticipated lesson direction.

Lesson *planning* is an active process, requiring some knowledge of the school's existing plans and schemes of work (see, for instance, Butt 2006). In drawing up successful lesson plans, it is important for trainee teachers to do so in accordance with the school's medium-term school curriculum plan (often spanning half a term) and to collaborate with other teachers who have responsibility for the same age group or subject (often formally done weekly or fortnightly, though more regular informal liaison is normal).

At the start of a school experience, it is likely that you will teach 'one-off' lessons and there will be little chance of experiencing continuity from session to session. You may initially have little grasp of the overall curriculum direction for the class and feel slightly bewildered about priorities and longer-term goals. If so, do not be overly anxious, as most teachers concentrate the majority of their efforts into the immediate lesson patterns and the week or two that lie ahead rather than peering too far ahead. Over time, you will become more knowledgeable about the full curriculum and the selection of material from the extensive amount of information now available through online and paper-based resources.

As more teaching responsibility is allocated to you, you begin to perceive teaching and learning as a continuous unfolding of related knowledge, skills and understanding across days and weeks, rather than within a single session. When you start teaching a series of lessons rather than individual and stand-alone ones, each session should begin by rehearsing some of the key points from the previous one and linking the present one with them. Assessment of one lesson enables the next one to be planned more accurately by using evidence about the way that the children responded to the tasks, answered questions and completed the activities. The planning process supports progression in learning through continuity from one session to the next as the threads of learning are woven together and teaching is targeted using information from previous lessons. *Continuity* refers to the close relationship required between the learning objectives/intentions from lesson to lesson. It is achieved when there is a discernible thread of knowledge, skills and understanding running through a series of lessons. *Progression* refers to the need for children to build upon their existing knowledge, skills and understanding in a systematic fashion so that they achieve higher levels of attainment (though as we noted earlier, this process is often rugged rather than sleek). To be effective, every lesson plan should contain a number of key elements, as follows, notably:

Lesson purpose or purposes

These are often referred to in the form of 'learning objectives', though 'learning intentions' is a more appropriate term, as it not always possible to predict precisely what children will learn. Lesson objectives should be clear and specific. Vague ideas about purpose and broadly based aims are inadequate, especially in mathematics and literacy. Sometimes the same learning objectives apply to several consecutive sessions, requiring only minor adjustment over the period of teaching them. Although the objectives apply to every child in general terms, the specific needs of particular children must be taken into account through differentiation (see later in this chapter).

Lesson content

Normally, the lesson content should be set within a National Curriculum Programme of Study (PoS) or relate to the NLS or NNS. Schools follow a variety of subtly different programmes, using units of work or utilising guidance material from (notably) the Qualifications and Curriculum Authority (QCA). Many schools have incorporated the precise wording of the particular document source into their planning and even provided details of suitable tasks and activities to support learning in that area. The use of ICT enables the process of information transfer to be carried out more efficiently.

Knowledge

It is essential to note what pupils are expected to know factually (i.e. commonly agreed knowledge) and implicitly (i.e. knowledge that is shaped from individual thought and reflection) as a result of the lesson or, in many cases, series of lessons. This is often closely related to PoS ('knowing what') but may include less obvious forms of knowledge, such as 'knowing how' and 'knowing why'. In considering what knowledge children should acquire, it is important not to confuse it with 'information'. There is a surplus of information available through many sources. Children need careful guidance about ways to access information (through the internet, for instance) and how to be discriminating about the facts that are presented. For example, it is relatively simple to accumulate information about Queen Victoria and inventions of that era (a popular theme in schools) but more challenging to consider Victoria as a person and why inventiveness was such a characteristic of the nineteenth century. It is even harder to evaluate the merits of prevailing social conditions when measured against industrial development.

Concepts

These are composed of the main ideas and principles that are significant in the lesson, often referred to as 'understanding'. As with skills, the concepts from previous teaching that require reinforcing or revising and those that are being developed or introduced by means of the present lesson should be identified. Conceptual development is more difficult to pinpoint in a lesson plan than knowledge or skills, as it encapsulates a large number of variables and modes. Understanding something is rarely a one-off event for children. It requires careful and persistent explanation, engagement with practical tasks, talking about the issues, trying things out, making errors, adjustments, revision, rehearsal and repetition. Every teacher has experienced the frustration that comes when children appear to understand one day, only to have forgotten by the next. Some forms of understanding take years to mature, especially those with a 'values' dimension that require discernment and judgement.

Skills

Most learning requires the application of particular skills. These may be of a practical kind (such as knowing how to use equipment) or cerebral kind (such as knowing how to orientate a map or manipulate data) or social kind (such as working as a team member). Skills should be listed under: (a) those which pupils have already mastered that are needed to complete the tasks and activities; and (b) those which are being introduced, developed or revised through the activities. Note that ideas about knowledge, concepts and skills are explored in Chapter 4.

Links with previous lessons

As mentioned earlier, very few lessons happen in isolation. Mentioning to pupils the links with previous sessions enhances the feeling of continuity in learning and helps them to see the relevance of the present activities. Children are obviously not concerned with the details of lesson planning like their teachers are doing, so regular reminders about the whys and wherefores are essential if they are to engage fully with the process of learning and understand better how they learn (i.e. 'learning about learning', sometimes referred to as 'meta-learning').

Resources

Resources can consist of practical items or human assistance, so lesson plan details should include: (a) a list of the equipment needed by you to teach and for the children to aid their task completion; and (b) the role of the adult helper (TA or parent). If equipment requires special training or there are health and safety factors to consider, these must, of course, be taken into account when planning the lesson as even commonly used resources can pose dangers if procedures are not correctly followed. Resources should always be appropriate for the task. It is unwise to 'make do' if such action increases the risk attached to it. For example, using PE equipment that has loose parts would be reckless.

Vocabulary

Significant words and expressions, especially subject-related ones, should be noted on your plan. In some lessons it is useful to write down examples of sentences containing the key words to use as part of the teaching because this strategy reinforces pupil learning. If vocabulary is needed for written work and pupils' anxiety about spellings will detract them from the main lesson purpose, it is worth writing a list of the words in bold pen on a large sheet of paper and putting the list in a prominent position for children to use or producing cards for groups of children on tables. Children should, ideally, try to spell words for themselves first, but it is counter-productive if a science session (say) is dominated by literacy concerns instead of mastering scientific concepts. Subject-related terms may be a mystery to the children unless explained in context.

Special needs provision

Less able and more able children must be catered for in the lesson. This may entail them doing separate tasks from the majority of children or modifying the lesson so that the less able are able to find success in the elementary component tasks and the more able can extend their learning through open-ended activities that require higher level thinking skills, such as speculating, drawing comparisons and evaluating. If less able children are extracted from the lesson for tuition purposes, you need to take account of the way in which they will be incorporated back into the lesson on their return. In addition, it has become increasingly important to be sensitive to the individual needs of each child, which may, for instance, involve 'booster' sessions (one-to-one using a TA) or intensive 'coaching' through after-school classes and computer-assisted learning.

Questions

Questions that you will use with pupils, particularly in the opening lesson phase, should be listed under two broad headings:

- Those to assess pupils' knowledge ('closed' types)
- Those to make pupils think and reflect ('open' types).

    More details about questioning can be found later in this chapter.

Assessment criteria

Assessment of learning falls broadly into two forms: (a) assessment *for* learning (AFL) in which the teacher is often making rapid evaluations of pupil progress and feeding back information to the children to help shape their learning and achieve learning outcomes; and (b) assessment *of* learning (AOL) which takes the form of a spoken or written test of pupil knowledge and understanding. Assessment of learning should always relate closely to the original lesson objectives, for the simple reason that AOL is a means by which you ascertain how successfully the children have attained the hoped-for outcomes. Although it is not possible to employ all types of AFL during a lesson (see 'Good practice' below), careful observation of children's progress and purposeful use of the plenary will provide a lot of information about their understanding and progress. Although it is impossible to observe every child closely during each lesson, you should make it your aim to categorise the children under one of three broad headings in respect of the tasks they do:

- Coped comfortably
- Struggled to cope
- Required more challenge.

The use of the three categories is a starting point for more sophisticated assessment strategies. Assessment following the lesson (sometimes referred to as 'summative' assessment) usually relies on an evaluation of children's written or pictorial output after work has been handed in.

Good practice

Assessment for learning may take one or more of the following forms:

- Asking pertinent questions to see if a child has grasped the point
- Asking a child to explain something to another child
- Clarifying a misconception that is evident from what a child says
- Noting correct and incorrect written answers and exploring the misconceptions
- Asking a child to repeat a process (e.g. on the computer or with equipment) with an adult present.

Lesson review

The process of review is an important part of the learning process, as it allows the teacher to draw together some of the various task and activity strands that have characterised the lesson. The word 'plenary' is sometimes used to denote the fact that the whole class/group are present and involved in this review procedure. Sometimes a review requires the teacher to spend just a minute or two summarising outcomes. Sometimes it involves the teacher selecting children at random to tell the rest of the class what they have found out or done. Occasionally it involves one child speaking on behalf of the collaborating group to explain what they have found out together. Other strategies include children:

- Showing or reading aloud their work to everybody
- Saying what surprised or pleased them about their work
- Voting on which idea or approach they preferred
- Telling someone other than their partner about what they did.

Children normally love the opportunity to talk about their work and show off their models, charts, pictures and drawings. Teachers have a vital role to play in the process of gathering the class together and enthusing about pupils' achievements. Whichever method (or combination of methods) is used to involve pupils, it is important to ensure that every contribution is received enthusiastically by the teacher. Even comments from children that are self-evident or replicating what has already been said should receive praise and commendation. Very young or shy children also need to feel that they have contributed towards this phase of the lesson, even if they have not actually spoken. This can be achieved by asking for a show of hands about different aspects of the lesson and praising everyone. One way or another, a plenary session, however brief, should reinforce learning and provide encouragement and a sense of fulfilment. There are many occasions when the last moments of a lesson can be used to remind the children of what is coming after the break or during the next lesson in that subject. One way or another you should make a conscious effort to conclude the lesson on a positive note.

Effective lessons

It is worth noting that the most effective lessons are those in which teachers have high expectations, offer their pupils clear instructions, help them to identify their own learning targets and encourage an active, purposeful dialogue about the lesson content. By contrast, weaker lessons are vague, teacher-dominated, routine or repetitive and badly paced. The best lessons are those in which the teacher uses an appropriate range of teaching strategies, monitors and intervenes progress, and sets appropriate challenges with respect to the ability range of children.

It is useful for teachers to share with pupils the learning intentions and, perhaps, provide a visual reminder (often through a written notice displayed for children to see, though it is essential to use child-friendly vocabulary). Children need to reach a point where they understand that the activities are not an end in themselves but part of a wider learning intention. Contrast the following exchanges between a visitor and two children engaged in the same activity:

> *Visitor to classroom:* What are you doing?
>
> *Child 1:* I'm cutting out words and sticking them in the gaps in the sentences.
>
> *Visitor to classroom:* What are you doing?
>
> *Child 2:* I'm finding a way to use more interesting adjectives in my poem.

The first child was concerned solely with the activity in which she was engaged. The second child saw that the activity served a larger purpose. It is similar to the story of two men cutting stone for a building. On being asked what they were doing, the first replied that he was cutting bricks, the second that he was helping to build a cathedral.

Activate your thinking!

It is important to make it clear to children that their lack of understanding about what we intend is our failure to explain, not their failure to receive.

Planning for learning involves much more than finding appropriate activities for pupils to do, though they are usually much more interested in *what* they are doing than *why*. As noted above, it is extremely important to be certain about the lesson purpose (represented through learning objectives/intentions) and the method for carrying out an assessment of the lesson or, in some cases, series of lessons if they all contribute to the same broad goal. Furthermore, the lesson purpose will vary according to the class circumstances, as even tried and tested lesson formats have to be modified for different groups of children depending upon their previous experiences, the level of their knowledge and their grasp of the concepts to be learned. The lesson format that succeeded with one group may prove inadequate with another unless you take account of individual needs, current rate of progress and time factors. As Hart (2000) rightly reminds us

'Classroom dynamics are so complex that it is impossible to predict or fully control what will happen when decisions made at the point of planning are translated into practice' (2000: 7). Nevertheless, careful and detailed thought about the practicalities of lesson implementation prior to the commencement of the session, as well as during it, increases the likelihood of success. On the other hand, if some lessons do not turn out as expected it may be that they have taken a turn for the better, not for the worse.

Activate your thinking!

There's a difference between lesson objectives (your overall purpose), learning intentions (what you hope children will learn) and learning outcomes (what they *do* learn).

Lessons that span several sessions

Unless there is a specific and easily measured lesson outcome (such as whether the children can add in twos or spell certain words) it is usually not possible or desirable to try and 'achieve' learning objectives through individual and isolated sessions, though in some subjects the limited curriculum time makes it unavoidable. The unsuitability of trying to match closely a single task or activity with a single objective was explored in Chapter 4 and also referred to earlier in this chapter. Deep learning is best achieved in stages by being initiated during one lesson, developed in a subsequent lesson or lessons and concluded at a later stage after a lot of rehearsal, practice, discussion, problem-solving and investigation. Although the process of introducing the lesson, allocating tasks and evaluating outcomes during each teaching session is a useful method of managing lessons, it is also important to take a longer-term view of the teaching-and-learning process. Lessons do not always fit neatly into a one-hour slot (say) and the lesson purpose often requires more time to fulfil than a single timetabled session allows, other than at a superficial level. For instance, the main purpose may be to inculcate in children the skills of discernment about the value of primary sources as historical evidence. To accomplish this purpose, the teacher may wish to spend a whole lesson simply introducing the significance of historical evidence to the class through demonstration and transmission teaching, plus (say) the visit of an expert to the classroom, the use of video material, and so forth. This opening lesson in the sequence would not, therefore, involve any practical pupil activity to consolidate learning, though it is to be hoped that questions and comments would be generated. A second session might consist of subdividing the class into collaborative groups for the purpose of examining archival items. In this case, pupils would be involved in a lot of practical experience but, perhaps, require little recording of results. A third session might involve drawing together the threads of the two previous sessions, sharing findings, raising issues, drawing conclusions and recording results. In such a situation, the overall structure of the 'lesson' would involve a number of sessions, as no single session would be sufficiently long to incorporate all the features needed to achieve the stated purpose. Thus, the principal learning objectives would be achieved in stages; for instance:

Phase 1: Introduction to historical evidence (teacher-led).

Phase 2: Hearing from, and putting questions to, an eyewitness (guest speaker).

Phase 3: Collaborative tasks: to begin writing up findings and incorporate further information.

Phase 4: Complete writing up findings.

Phase 5: Publicly sharing results (initially in class, then more widely).

Three factors have to be taken into account when planning lessons which span several sessions. First, short-term lesson objectives (per single session) have to be subsumed within the overall lesson purpose. Second, the sessions should be reasonably close together to facilitate continuity. Third, children who have been absent will need to catch up. The introduction of tightly defined teaching sessions and the strong advice from school inspection reports about the importance of systematic lesson structures may deter teachers from thinking more imaginatively about the ways that learning can be organised. However, lessons that straddle a number of sessions provide the opportunity to explore ideas within a more natural and less rigid framework than attempting to cram every element into a single, artificially designated period of time. Although the principal learning objective will require a longer period of time to be achieved than a single session, the short-term objectives for each session all contribute to the final outcome. Encouragingly, advice from the Department for Children, Schools and Families (DCSF) and QCA has increasingly taken into account the need for such flexibility.

Spiral curriculum

All learning intentions must take careful account of pupils' existing abilities, experience and knowledge. It is important to recognise that there is often a need to rehearse, reinforce and restate ideas before a child's grasp of the ideas and concepts involved is secure. The term 'spiral' or 'cyclic' curriculum is sometimes used to describe the process of returning to an area of learning in order to remind children of previous learning and enhance their understanding. Sometimes the reinforcement will take place within a single session, but more commonly over a greater time span. Some concepts take years to mature. For example, imagine trying to explain to a class of six-year-old children about the change of state from a tadpole to a frog. Now consider doing the same thing with a class of 11 year olds. Although the learning objective would be similar ('understanding the process of change') the level of detail and complexity would differ greatly.

Although lessons are usually planned within an overall framework in which the learning outcomes are identified with reference to statutory documentation, it is essential to gradually allow opportunities for reinforcement and the development of new ideas through more demanding work and challenges. More able pupils can use these opportunities to forge ahead by using their initiative to explore fresh avenues of thought and build upon their existing knowledge in innovative ways. Less able pupils can gain confidence and raise their self-esteem by dealing with familiar concepts in novel ways, such as using diagrams instead of extended writing. Reinforcement is most effective when children are offered the chance to engage with a variety of stimulating tasks through which they can develop, practise and rehearse their ideas. Tedious repetition is not a substitute for imagination.

Reinforcement of previous learning is facilitated if you use the introduction to each lesson as an opportunity to remind children of what has gone before, ask some suitable questions to stimulate thinking, point out the implications of previous learning and so forth. Similarly, the end of some sessions is not only useful to rehearse the key points of the lesson but to draw together the threads from across a series of lessons and consolidate the key outcomes.

Differentiation

All classes and groups of children are of mixed ability. They contain slower and faster workers, less and more intelligent, keen and apathetic, confident and insecure. No matter how carefully pupils are divided on the basis of ability, each group will contain a range of different types of children whose learning and academic needs have to be taken into account during lesson preparation and teaching. In the light of this diversity, teachers are faced with a choice about the way they plan lessons. The first type is differentiation by *outcome* in which all pupils are engaging with similar curriculum material at a variety of conceptual levels. For example, differentiation by outcome may be appropriate when children are working independently or in matching pairs, when they will progress at varying rates, depending on their abilities. In this situation, the teacher's expectations for children differs according to their academic competence. Second, differentiation by *task* in which pupils of different ability work with separate curriculum material. For example, different groups (or 'sets') in mathematics will attend to tasks that are geared specifically to their competence. In this situation, the activities and tasks involved would differ substantially from group to group so that all the children in the group have a reasonable chance of keeping pace with others in the same group. For older primary children this system of organising for learning is frequently selected so that pupils of similar ability across several classes are taught together. This approach allows the planning to be more specifically targeted towards the academic needs of those particular pupils and requires less differentiation, though even within a single ability group there can be considerable variation in ability. There is considerable merit in restoring the system that existed a generation ago (especially in mathematics) whereby each child worked through a series of tasks and problems at his or her own pace, using adult expertise and guidance at key points as necessary.

Less able children will normally need more time to reach the same point in their learning than more capable ones. A small number of capable children are slow and methodical in their work, not because they lack the ability but because they are conscientious and anxious to avoid making mistakes. Some less able children complete work quickly because they can only engage with the concepts at a relatively superficial level and need to be encouraged to tackle more demanding tasks. More able children need opportunities to extend their thinking, rather than merely repeating 'more of the same' type of work, which, though it guarantees a high success rate, ultimately leads to stagnation in learning. It is important to ensure that planning allows for every child to gain initial success relatively easily and move on to interesting tasks that require determination to complete. There is general agreement that early success builds a firm foundation of confidence and understanding on which more advanced concepts can be built.

Some able children struggle to complete their work on time because they want to divert from the standard approaches advocated by an adult and try out their own methods; other children simply like to spend time pondering issues and are reluctant to conform to adult-imposed time pressures. Your introduction to the lesson must clarify the amount of flexibility you are prepared to allow, taking account of the fact that many children are stimulated and motivated by opportunities to consolidate their learning through open-ended activities (without any clear end-point), problem-solving (finding answers to a specified problem by various means) and investigations (identifying the problem before seeking a solution). See Figure 5.1.

- Open-ended activities
- Problem solving
- Investigations

Figure 5.1 Three strategies for consolidating learning

In addition, all children need to be given the opportunity to transfer what they have learned to new situations, as this is often the acid test for whether or not deep learning has been achieved. Even if all the group or class appear to have grasped the principles and ideas contained within a particular learning objective, some children will retain what they have learned, while others will require regular reminding and refreshing. However, the more that children see the relevance of their learning, the more likely it is that they will engage enthusiastically with the lesson content and retain what they have learned as they apply it to situations.

Every teacher has to take account of the resource and time implications of trying to develop too many tasks and activities for children in an attempt to cater for everybody's individual needs. Such a personalised curriculum is impractical other than for classes numbered in single figures. Planning must rely on a satisfactory grouping of children so that each group can cope with the demands of the work, and individuals can develop and enhance their own understanding, knowledge and skills in the subject. The allocation of TAs to offer a child specific training or coaching in an area of difficulty (e.g. reading recovery) is usually determined by the head teacher or member of staff with responsibility for standards of attainment in that curriculum area (e.g. the literacy leader).

Personalised learning

The concept of a 'personalised education' and 'personalised learning' has entered the lexicon in recent years. Their definitions are far from universally agreed, though Bird (2006) helpfully suggests that models of a personalised education can be compared with assembling a motor vehicle. The first model is a version in which every pupil has an *identical* main chassis, frame, engine, body and wheels; however, each pupil has a *stylised* section, unique to each child, and special. The second model is a version in which the basic composition of chassis, frame, engine, body and wheels, etc. are present in every vehicle, but the basic composition of the vehicle is slightly different. In this case each pupil's education is stylised, while superficially similar.

Bird goes on to explain that personalised learning is not the 'individualised' learning of the past, characterised by each child engaged on solitary learning paths – often dominated by work sheets – or letting children choose what they want to do, which runs the risk of them selecting easy tasks that fail to stretch their minds. Rather, it is encouraging pupils to be involved in establishing their own medium-term targets for learning, while recognising that the ultimate target of success in national tests is already determined nationally.

There is then a tension between personalised learning, pupil choice, curriculum coverage and national expectations. Teachers have to find ways to accommodate pupils' aspirations, while ensuring that test results don't suffer. In addition, they have to be cognisant of how 'learning styles' impinge upon the way in which teaching and learning are organised and managed. If, as claimed by some educationists, children have different styles of learning, teachers have to: (a) discern the nature of this preferred style; and (b) adjust their approach to take account of the different styles (see Chapter 10 for a discussion about special needs). Bird (see above) also notes the conceptual and practical difficulties facing teachers when they attempt to accommodate pupils' learning styles into classroom practice. He cites five different ways in which learning styles are categorised:

- Visual, auditory, kinaesthetic/tactile (note that the first three of these 'styles' are often referred to by the acronym, VAK)

- Reflectors, activists, theorists and pragmatists

- Innovative, analytic, common sense and dynamic

- Field-dependent and field-independent

- Sequential/global; visual/verbal; sensory/intuitive; active/reflective.

The VAK model of learning types (see first bullet point above) is based on the premise that every person learns best when exposed to one of three approaches, or a particular combination of them:

- Visual approach (in which pupils learn best by seeing)

- Auditory approach (in which pupils learn best by hearing)

- Kinaesthetic (in which pupils learn best by doing).

Visual learners are often characterised by rapid speech and making remarks such as 'it looks fine to me'; they enjoy writing, seeing and drawing diagrams and imagining possibilities. *Auditory* learners tend to be prefer to have information presented to them and enjoy explaining something to someone else; they might have a tendency to sit upright and look directly ahead; they may also make comments such as 'I hear what you are saying'. It is worth noting, however, Cullingford's comment that 'babies in the womb are constantly interacting with their surroundings which, in those conditions, consist of sound and sensation' (2007: 136). The unborn child has no choice but to rely on auditory learning. *Kinaesthetic* (tactile) learners often exhibit a restless temperament, with short concentration spans; they like to make things and 'fiddle' around with items; they also tend to avoid eye contact and get inspired by colour, movement and practical task completion.

A moment's thought will reveal the impossibility of organising your teaching in such a way that different groups of children are divided on the basis of an alleged preferred learning style (Franklin 2006). In practice, a more realistic approach is to enrich all the pupils' learning experiences through rehearsal and reinforcement by taking account of the categories listed above. In other words, use every weapon in your teaching armoury and don't rely on a single approach to promote learning.

Finally, some pupils fail to learn because their home circumstances and background limit their motivation or have an adverse impact on achievement. In this regard, the *Every Child Matters* agenda (see Chapter 10) attempts to align education and social service provision in such a way that these disadvantages are minimised and combated.

Good practice

It is far better to *cover* a little of the curriculum and *uncover* a lot of learning, than to do the opposite.

Body language

To effectively implement lesson planning, every teacher needs to have a repertoire of teaching skills to promote learning, including the effective use of body language, variously defined as the gestures, postures and facial expressions by which a person manifests physical, mental and/or emotional states, and communicates non-verbally (without speech) with others. Thus, head movements, eye contact, hand gestures, body position and tone of voice express an individual's emotions, feelings, and attitudes. Body language is significant because unintended communication takes place non-verbally on the part of one person to another, which may have an impact on his or her behaviour and conduct. Teachers are performers, not in the same way as a stage artist who aims to receive public acclaim, but rather as a means of improving the quality of their communication with the children. Although it is important for teachers to avoid artificial behaviour and react spontaneously in the classroom, there are techniques that can be useful in gaining and maintaining children's attention, particularly during interactive phases of a lesson, such as whole-class questioning. These techniques are based on the premise that variations in a teacher's body language (stance, voice tone, gesticulation, eye contact, etc.) can generate and maintain interest among the children, enhance pupil response rate, create enthusiasm and thereby excite a powerful learning environment. There are five principal areas in which body language is important:

1. Speech patterns.
2. Head position.
3. Eye movement.

4. Pauses.

5. Stance.

Speech patterns

Listeners use the quality of speech as an indicator of a speaker's competence and sincerity. Some inexperienced teachers make the mistake of thinking that they will endear themselves to the children by using casual or slang expressions. In fact, the opposite is true. If teachers want to establish and maintain their authority, they should speak plainly at all times and (other than with children who have specialised language needs) never attempt to modify it for the sake of effect. Some teachers gradually slip into using an unnatural tone when addressing children (and parents), which can sound patronising and false. Good speech comes through correct breathing and posture and, as the voice is of prime importance in teaching, it is worth taking care of it (Hayes 1998). A simple strategy such as relaxing the shoulders and breathing deeply into the lungs to a count of five, then exhaling slowly to a count of five, then 10, then 15 has a remarkably beneficial effect if practised regularly.

Some teachers have mellifluous, natural voices that sound like a mountain stream: clear, cool, and smooth. Other teachers sound more like an old steam engine whistle: shrill, scratchy and hard on the ears. Pity the poor children who have to listen to them day after day. Most teachers' voices lie somewhere between these extremes, but all practitioners need to improve their voice quality and technique by learning to relax when they speak, breath naturally and stand or sit comfortably. It is not necessary to have a very loud voice to deliver your lines effectively, though those teachers with quiet voices have to work hard on diction to ensure that all the children can hear what is said. Quiet speech can carry to the far corners of the room if it is well articulated, whereas muffled loud speech is difficult to absorb. If you have a strong dialect, you may need to improve the roundness of your vowels and the crispness of your consonants. In addition, it is worthwhile varying your speech pattern by occasionally slowing, accelerating or changing pitch as a means of emphasising key words, heightening interest in a phrase or adding character to the voice tone. The impact of changes in speech pattern can be increased by the use of strong eye contact and, where appropriate, adopting a fresh physical stance (see below). Variation in speech pattern is particularly important during the opening phase of a lesson when seeking to maintain the children's attention and engage their enthusiasm, and take account of their propensity to listen and academic prowess. It requires considerable skill to keep every child 'on board' and actively engaged, so it is essential to develop a repertoire of verbal delivery modes when explaining, reading aloud, questioning and responding to children's comments.

Having clear speech necessitates having relaxed face muscles and jaw, which can be achieved through regular use of a few simple exercises, such as: (a) making wide chewing motions while humming gently; and (b) carefully opening your mouth as wide as possible (as if about to yawn), while gently moving your jaw in circles and from side to side. Clarity of speech can be improved by practising tongue twisters (of the 'She sells sea-shells on the sea shore' type). Begin by repeating the words slowly and gradually building up speed until you are saying the sentence at normal conversation speed. It can also help to exaggerate the words, thereby forcing your tongue, jaw and lips to work hard. If you are an inexperienced speaker you can hone your speaking skills in front of a mirror, being careful to stay relaxed (avoid hunching your shoulders or tensing your hands). Take note of any strange faces that you pull or involuntary twitches, all of which indicate muscle tension. Some speakers chew gum regularly as a means of loosening the jaw and creating saliva. As a rule, never rush your speaking except to make a special point or gain children's attention; revert to a normal or very slightly reduced speed immediately afterwards.

In Chapter 14 of her book, Cowley (2003) suggests that caring for the voice requires that you attend to a range of issues, as follows (my comments in square brackets):

- Control the volume [Avoid getting progressively louder]

- Learn to hear yourself [The acid test is whether you would want to listen to yourself all day]

- Never shout [Speaking strongly is a different matter]

- Be quiet but deadly [Leave no doubt in pupils' minds that you mean business]

- Control the tone [Don't let it control you]

- Get their attention first [This is a basic classroom technique and reduces the likelihood that you will have to raise your voice]

- Have a calm and quiet classroom [See earlier chapters]

- You be teacher [Or better, perhaps, you be leader].

She also advocates minimising the need to raise the voice by getting physically closer to pupils when addressing them. Cowley adds that you should make it your aim to use your voice less – by employing hand signals, for instance – drink plenty of water and, if possible, receive voice training.

Good practice

Practise varying your voice tone by:

- Injecting expression during story-telling
- Speaking slowly, firmly and deliberately to emphasise points
- Showing enthusiasm when introducing a topic
- Explaining things with precise and accurate phrasing.

Head position

When addressing a group of children, it is important to keep the eyes level and speak directly ahead of you as much as possible. However, moving the position of the head slightly can be used to good effect. For example, staring down momentarily (especially with arms folded) carries the message that you are deep in thought, and may serve to increase the children's curiosity. Staring straight ahead with a serious face for a few seconds without looking at anyone in particular can be used to convey the fact that you are waiting for the children's close attention. A gentle nodding of the head, with soft eye contact and affirmative sounds, indicates that you are very interested in what children are saying and happy to be patient until the child has finished speaking. By contrast, staring up at the ceiling denotes a degree of impatience and unwillingness to tolerate the situation any longer. Of course, head position alone is not going to provide an automatic solution to the vagaries of classroom life or convince the children of your mood, but in conjunction with words and eye movement can be positively effective. It is also important to stress that the less often you have to turn your back on the class, the more direct eye contact with them is made possible and the less chance you have of injuring neck muscles as you swivel back and forth. There are three possibilities to reduce the amount of 'back-turning':

- Have resources available; for example, cards or a sheet with key words prominently displayed. If you use a series of individual cards, attach them to the board using plastic adhesive in advance of the lesson

- Invite children to come forward and write the words, draw the diagram or list the numbers. However, be aware that the involvement of children in this way tends to slow the pace of the lesson and may be practically difficult

- Use electronic means (such as an overhead projector, interactive whiteboard or PowerPoint). The employment of any electrical equipment involves space management and attention to health and safety factors.

A simple exercise to improve neck muscles and head movement is to stand still with feet apart, looking directly forward before turning the head over a count of three (say) to the left, holding for a further count of three, before returning slowly to the starting position. Repeat the exercise by moving the head to the right using the same procedure. You can also gently and slowly tip your head backwards until you are looking at the ceiling and forwards until you are staring at your toes. It is essential not to hurry or exert any strain on your body. If in doubt, take professional advice beforehand.

Eye movement

The eyes are probably the most expressive part of the body and often reveal a great deal about what someone is thinking. They betray the truth about us, and disclose whether we are sad, mad, glad or bad. Teachers in a variety of teaching situations use their eyes a great deal to bond with the children, transmit unspoken meaning and influence actions, so it is worth being aware of how you might use them. For instance, wide eyes convey your enthusiasm, amazement or incredulity, whereas narrowed eyes suggests to children that you are concentrating or mentally interrogating the facts. Many teachers develop what is often known as the 'hard stare' with fixed eyes as a method of discouraging children from unwise behaviour without having to say a word to them. On the other hand, teachers also find that a twinkling eye, a flashed smile and a simple nod of approval can transform a child's attitude and enthusiasm for learning. During interactive sessions it is important to maintain good eye contact to convey approval, amusement and affirmation.

Similarly, children should be encouraged to look into your eyes when you are speaking and when they wish to offer a comment or answer a question. If you are very inexperienced, this process of 'eyeballing' can be rather embarrassing, as you become aware that every child is looking straight at you. Over time it becomes a vital part of your teaching armoury. Since approval by touch has become more problematic in school, affirmation through the use of the eyes has assumed even greater significance and must be fully exploited if you want to communicate actively with the class.

Pauses

Although it is generally wise to maintain a steady flow of words, delivered in an interesting way (see speech patterns, earlier) there are numerous occasions when intentional pauses are useful. For instance, in the midst of speaking, you may gaze thoughtfully at the children, make a brief diversionary movement (such as stroking the chin or tapping a pencil on paper) before continuing. This technique has three benefits. First, it allows you to gain some thinking time. Second, it offers a moment of respite from talking so that the children can re-focus on the lesson. Third, the silence causes the children to gain a sense of anticipation about what follows. The impact of interrupted action is enhanced if the first few words after the pause are spoken deliberately and slowly. If the pause is part of a discipline strategy, it is often worth adding a soft but firm 'sit up and look at me please' at the same time. Although it is important not to use this strategy too often or impose an extended silence, using the opportunity to scan the class and make numerous eye contacts often provides a psychological 'cohesion'. Remember, too, that what seems to be a lengthy pause to you feels much shorter to the children. It conveys a strong sense to pupils of an adult being in command of the situation.

Stance

Maintaining a set position from which you speak to the children is useful in that it gives them a single focal point on which to concentrate and does not cause any distractions that constant movement back and forth tends to invite (the 'tennis match' syndrome, moving from one side to the other and back again). At the other extreme, a rigid pose does little to transmit a message to the children that the lesson is going to be exciting or worthy of close attention. By deliberately changing your physical position and occasionally adopting a fresh stance, however, you are encouraging the children to follow your movements closely and, if used in conjunction with some of the other strategies described in this section, will help to keep them on their toes. Thus, to sit for a short time when you have been standing, turning your back momentarily on the class before gently spinning back to face them, putting hands on hips, and even folding and unfolding your arms, can recapture children's attention. If the change of position is accompanied by a slight adjustment to another feature of the physical environment (such as straightening a chair), the impact is even more pronounced. It is important to limit the number of occasions that you adopt these fresh stances but with concomitant changes in voice tone it can have a surprisingly powerful impact on children's concentration level.

The strategies described above should be viewed as teaching skills that can be used to enhance effectiveness, and not as clever gimmicks to cover inadequacies in planning and knowledge of the subject or as showmanship. Whatever decisions you make about your use of speech, head, eye, pause and stance, it is important to constantly review and evaluate your classroom presence and the way that you engage with the children, especially when you are leading and they are listening. Exaggerated body language can lead to discipline problems if children perceive the way that you behave as whimsical. Equally, a lifeless lesson presentation results in a lack of stimulation and a dreary learning environment. Your lessons should not be like a circus act, but neither should they resemble a funeral service.

Having focused upon the significance of body language, we now consider a variety of other teaching skills commonly used in teaching, starting with forms of interaction between adults and pupils.

Interactive teaching skills

The concept and practice of 'interactive teaching' has become embedded within every teacher's vocabulary, not least because of its use in government advice about literacy teaching. Defining the term is less straightforward. Merry and Moyles (2003) distinguish between interactive teaching that is concerned with 'surface features' of classroom techniques (e.g. asking questions) and 'deep' strategies and interactions. Thus, deep interactive teaching 'appears to be a reciprocal process, genuinely taking on board the pupils' thinking as well as the teachers' objectives, and trying to encourage the children to reflect on and develop their own ideas' (2003: 29). Teachers are called upon to make dozens of small decisions every day and cope with a large number of demands, not only with respect to the activity of teaching but also ways to respond to individual children and colleagues. Although some judgements are born of wisdom and classroom experience, the development and refinement of teaching skills provides the foundation for success in learning. The following section explores a variety of those that are commonly needed by primary teachers, some of which require fine judgement, others that deal with pragmatic considerations.

Addressing the whole class

In recent years the ability to address the whole class and hold their attention has assumed increasing importance. Successful whole class teaching requires a combination of seven interrelated qualities. First, a firm grasp of the subject material so that you don't have to keep referring to notes. Second, familiarity with the lesson structure assisted, perhaps, by having a summary written in bold letters on a large sheet opposite your main teaching position. Third, use of a calm and clear voice, aided by careful articulation and a rich tone. Fourth, developing a lively (but not frenzied) manner to engage children's interest using strong eye contact and varied facial expression. Fifth, having access to relevant resources, including basic items such as board pens. Sixth, using questions effectively. Seventh, knowing when to invite, encourage and monitor children's responses. Each of these seven qualities can be improved through practice. Thus:

Grasp of the material

This ability requires dedicated study and, importantly, translating the content so that it can be presented to the children using vocabulary and concepts that are appropriate for them. If you only have a partial grasp of the material, this insufficiency will be reflected in the quality of your explanations, which are likely to be overly complex and convoluted. It is not difficult to make something simple to sound complicated. However, it takes a great deal of careful thought and study to create something straightforward and understandable from complex material.

Lesson structure

This quality is not merely a case of knowing the sequence of events, though this is clearly a fundamental requirement. It involves weaving together the lesson elements so that the total experience makes sense to the children who are on the receiving end. Each part of the lesson is referred to as a 'phase' and the move from one phase to the next is often the time when a lesson can lose momentum, so your ability to link the phases is crucial to successful learning.

Articulation

Use of a calm and clear voice is, as we have noted earlier, an essential attribute. You do not need to possess a loud voice to be effective but you must be able to speak distinctly in such a way that the children enjoy the sound of your voice. Anxiety can cause inexperienced teachers to speak too quickly or slur their words or 'drop' their consonants. It can also lead to a colourless or monotonous tone. You can improve suppleness in your facial muscles by gently rubbing your cheeks, moving your lips around in a circular motion, sticking out your tongue and opening your eyes widely for a few seconds, repeating the process several times. Momentary slowing your speed of speech and occasional bursts of speed to punctuate the regular delivery can help to add colour to your talking.

Lively manner

Some teachers can make even the dullest lesson material sound interesting by effective use of the voice (see above), raising rhetorical questions, reminding the children of what they already know, rehearsing ideas and summarising viewpoints. The use of illustrations, stories and occasional humour help to oil the wheels of an exposition, though it is important to restrict the number of these assisting strategies lest the lesson loses its direction or become trivialised.

Use of resources

Resources should not only be available but accessible. You should give plenty of thought to the practicalities of handling them while speaking to the children and interacting with them. For instance, you should take account of factors such as the time taken to distribute items, collect them in, check their condition, and so forth.

Use of questions

This skill is so important in teaching that it merits a full section to itself later in the chapter. You can begin to hone your questioning skills by clarifying in your own mind the purpose of the question, and whether it is to assess what the children already know, expand their thinking, raise issues or generate interest in a topic. Once you know the purpose for asking the question it is easier to frame it meaningfully. By mentally putting yourself in the children's place you can anticipate the sorts of responses they might provide. However, as Hargreaves *et al.* (2003) noted in their study of interactive teaching, children were rarely given 'time and space to offer extended responses, to enter into a genuine dialogue with their teachers or to ask exploratory or higher order questions of their teachers' (2003: 123). The best types of questions may raise issues that require in-depth exploration through dialogue.

Eliciting children's responses

Perhaps the most difficult aspect of whole class teaching is developing an ability to 'think on your feet' and involve the children in the lesson through verbal contributions, responses to questions, feedback and practical actions (such as writing on a whiteboard). For inexperienced trainees it is better to maintain close control over the proceedings rather than be too ambitious. Thus, to use pre-determined questions, give instructions and limit choice. Over time, you can gradually introduce greater spontaneity to the proceedings. As with all teaching skills it is sensible to practise the session in your mind and 'hear' yourself speaking to the children. In the pressure of handling the whole class it is possible to allow the lesson to 'accelerate' and find yourself carried along much faster than you intended, with the result that what was meant to be an interactive phase deteriorates into a monologue. One way to reduce the likelihood of this happening is to 'write in' deliberate pauses into your lesson plan and discipline yourself to count to five in your head from time to time.

> ### Good practice
>
> Begin whole class teaching in a situation in a straightforward way, such as reading or telling a story, giving a single piece of information or instruction, gradually increasing the tempo and complexity.

Working with children seated

The intimacy of group interaction, especially 'on the carpet', raises class management issues that are different from those when the class are seated on chairs. Some younger children in particular are inclined to call out, move around the floor and sit where they cannot see or be seen. Other children seem to have an irresistible desire to sneak up on to the nearest available chair. You have to decide whether or not to be very firm about such behaviour or accept that it is an acceptable price to pay for the increased involvement for which close physical proximity allows. During interactive sessions (teacher inviting verbal participation) watch out for less able children who do not think for themselves but merely 'cue' from more able or confident children around them. It is difficult to spot that a child is feeding off his or her more illustrious classmates but there are a number of indicators:

- They raise their hands/boards/number fans a second or two after the majority
- They sit towards the back so that they can be concealed from the teacher while having a view of other children
- They shoot their hands in the air before anyone else and feign enthusiasm for answering the question but if selected to answer offer a lame response, suddenly 'forget' or repeat a whispered answer from a more able child.

Such forms of behaviour have their origins in low confidence, an inability to cope with the conceptual demands of the questioning or (in a very few cases) unwillingness to make the necessary effort to think. To remedy such behaviour, consider whether the teaching is sufficiently targeted and differentiated. If not, it is likely that you will have to introduce some simpler questions or explain concepts using more straightforward vocabulary if you are to involve the less able and under-confident children. Second, decide whether you are placing more emphasis on speed of response than thoughtful replies. Some children need a little longer than their classmates for their brains to process the information and become despondent if quick thinkers constantly upstage them. Third, determine whether some children are cloaking their unwillingness to make a genuine effort by going through the motions of eagerness, not expending any mental energy to solve the problems that have been posed. One positive way of combating such deceit is to ask a question and insist that children work in pairs to produce a response before asking for feedback. Such a strategy does not work immediately; it requires perseverance.

When drawing attention to a significant key word, phrase or idea, use it in a sentence and encourage the children to do the same. This process of contextualising reinforces the meaning and aids children's understanding. The strategy is useful for words that are spelt the same but pronounced differently; for example 'wind' and for unfamiliar words and phrases.

Activate your thinking!

How can you involve children who think a lot but rarely volunteer answers?

Children reading in unison

When reading a passage in unison with children (during a literacy lesson, say), it is important to read much more slowly than you imagine to be necessary, or the middle range and weaker readers will soon get left behind. Whereas the whole class read the text at the start, numbers gradually drop off as the pace quickens and by the end of the passage only the teacher and the best readers (usually sitting near the front) are still reading. The other children are merely 'mouthing' the words or will have stopped trying to keep up. There are a number of strategies that you can use to maintain involvement. For example:

- You stop reading and allow the children to continue on their own for a short time
- You stress certain words (such as adjectives) and encourage the children to do the same during a second reading of the passage
- You ask the children to speak specified words in a different way (such as whispering the first word in a sentence or emphasising the last one)
- You and the children read alternate lines or sentences.

Depending upon the length of the passage, there is much to be gained from a second reading or repeating key phrases to reinforce understanding, allow children another opportunity to grapple with difficult words and spellings, and help slower learners catch up. Although bodies of text are valuable as starting points for exploring aspects of language, their vocabulary and syntax should not restrict the breadth of your questions and explanations. By asking the children if they can, for instance, suggest alternative words, provide a variation in the sentence construction, think of rhyming words, and so forth, you extend the range of their thinking beyond the immediacy of the passage and begin to enlarge thinking. Most children, regardless of age, benefit from being invited to evaluate aspects of the text, such as whether it conveys meaning clearly and if the writing excites interest. Depending on the lesson purpose and time available, more able/older children can be asked to speculate about what the author was trying to achieve and to what extent s/he succeeded or even what mood the author was in when the piece was written. Explorations of this sort that move children beyond the immediacy of print and get them to think hard about deeper meanings serve to enhance interest and excite a mood of reflection and questioning. They also make teaching more enjoyable and satisfying.

Reinforcing concepts

One way to reinforce a concept after receiving a correct answer from a child is to repeat the answer, several times if necessary, to ensure that all the children have heard. For instance:

Teacher: If I have five sweets and Jenny gives me five more sweets, put your hand up if you know how many sweets I will have altogether.

Child (selected to answer): Ten.

Teacher: That's right, Sam, well done. I'll have 10 … but 10 what?

Child: Ten sweets.

Teacher: Yes, 10 sweets, because five and five is 10, so five sweets and five sweets mean that I will end up with 10 sweets. Let's look at some pictures to prove that Sam is correct when she says that adding five sweets to five sweets gives us ten sweets.

Notice that the teacher in the example is reinforcing the concept both verbally and diagrammatically to accommodate the children's different learning preferences. Some children can grasp a concept simply by listening, other children by speaking to another and yet others by seeing it presented visually. Less able children may need some tactile (touching) experience, so if time permits, one such child can come to the front and help the teacher while s/he counts (say) two lots of five cubes into the child's hand. Most children benefit from a combination of learning modes.

The time spent in reinforcing concepts in this way is not wasted. On the contrary, coverage of the lesson content without ensuring that all the children grasp the principles leads to a flurry of questions from anxious children and disappointing outcomes when they tackle any associated tasks you put in front of them.

Responding to changing circumstances

The longer that a lesson phase continues, the less likely that the less able children and those with limited concentration will attend to what is said. There is a fine line to be drawn between persevering with a lesson – refusing to be deterred by daydreamers and restless children and insisting on full attention – and curtailing what you are presenting because the children's flagging attention indicates that they are bored or 'saturated' with content. To guide your decision bear in mind four points:

- Boredom comes because the work is irrelevant or too hard/easy to understand or you have talked too long without involving the children in something meaningful for them
- There is a difference between deliberately disruptive behaviour and restless behaviour. A useful rule of thumb is that restlessness begins to affect normally compliant children as well as the usual characters
- While it is sensible to try and keep to your intended lesson timings, they should be viewed as flexible rather than inviolable
- Your awareness of the class's general mood rather than the inappropriate behaviour of a few children should drive changes in lesson direction.

The lesson plan obviously has to accommodate various lesson circumstances and if you are inexperienced it is wise to conform to your plan and allocate the time accordingly. However, as you grow more confident you will find opportunity to make on-the-spot modifications. For example, if the children take longer over tasks than anticipated or are immersed in fruitful collaboration, you may opt to extend this phase of the lesson and reduce the end phase. Similarly, the introductory phase usually involves a lot of teacher questions and pupil answers, but the introduction of a small number of speculative questions can stimulate bursts of ideas and the generation of children's own questions. To make best use of this creative energy and maximise the learning that results, you may decide to let the discussion run for a few more minutes than you planned. This is good educational practice and should not be confused with slackness. Particularly if you are being observed it is sensible to note in your plan that spontaneous opportunities may be followed through as appropriate so that the evaluator does not think that you have 'lost control' of the circumstances.

> **Good practice**
>
> Children cannot be expected to maintain a high level of concentration throughout every moment of a lesson, especially during the middle part of the session, so try to offer some variety in teaching and learning, utilising the VAK principle: visual, auditory and kinaesthetic (hands-on).

Using whiteboards and fans

It has become common practice to make use of child-sized plastic 'whiteboards' and marker pens to promote a higher level of participation. In principle, this method has much to commend it; unfortunately, practical considerations (mess from pens, wiping boards, pens that run dry, etc.) detract from their effective use. If children are using individual whiteboards and markers, suggest from time to time that they show what they have written to a friend before showing it to you. This strategy has three advantages. First, it breaks the monotony of 'write it down and show me'. Second, it helps less able children to gain confidence from working co-operatively. Third, it gives you space to look around more carefully than is normally possible to see if any children are uncertain or mistaken. If you note that a child or some children have made an error, it may be appropriate to say something to the effect: 'Well done everyone for being so sensible. I noticed that one or two people got a bit muddled about ...' rather than drawing attention to specific individuals. A teaching assistant, suitably positioned, can send non-verbal messages to you about what is happening.

Response boards (whiteboards) and number 'fans' are often used during interactive sessions to elicit a whole class response to a question, rather than merely selecting a single child whose hand is up in the air. There are practical points to consider when using whiteboards (see also later in this chapter):

- It is essential to have a supply and reserve supply of pens

- Forbid children to elaborate what they write by drawing fancy patterns on the board

- The boards need to be properly and regularly cleaned

- Watch for less confident children that conceal their answers from you by keeping the board out of view

- Be aware that less confident children will sit so that they can see what a more able child writes, then hurriedly copy before raising the board.

There are also a number of practical points to bear in mind with use of fans:

- Small fingers may struggle to manipulate the fan

- It is difficult to scan all of the children to see how many answers are correct and if there are errors

- Younger children may reverse numbers

■ The fans need to be put to one side when finished with or they may be used as … fans.

The advantage of whiteboards and fans is that they have the potential to stimulate a higher degree of participation from a larger number of children. However, as they can generally be used only for 'closed answers' (where there is only one correct response) they encourage teachers to use fewer speculative or 'let us imagine' or propositional questions. Consequently, the session becomes dominated by questions asked by the teacher and correct/incorrect answers given by the children. This scenario can lead to an extreme situation in which the teacher is using question-and-answer to extract responses, when it would be much easier to tell the children directly. Another factor that can intrude into the dynamics of questioning is that whereas it is important to praise good responses, offering equally effusive praise to unexceptional replies demeans the commendation given for outstanding ones.

Activate your thinking!

Are you asking a question when you should be giving the answer?

Organisational skills

Organising and managing for learning is dealt with more fully in Chapter 6. Suffice it to say at this point that clarification of task, specificity about expectations, appropriate intervention, support for writing tasks and knowing how to end a session successfully are basic skills with which every teacher must grapple.

Clarifying tasks

When children say that they 'don't get it' or sit staring miserably at the page, you have to determine whether they are bored, confused or out of their depth. More often than not the child does not have the confidence or the knowledge/understanding to tackle the work, in which case you have to decide which of the two reasons (low confidence or weak knowledge) is relevant, a job made much easier when you get to know the class. Some children are academically capable but very tentative when faced with a task to complete. This category of children are doubly disadvantaged because they feel (probably correctly) that they ought to be able to do the work and hesitate to ask an adult for fear of being told so. By contrast, a less able child may feel more comfortable asking for adult support. It is best to engage the timid academic child in a cheerful manner, using a question and answer approach to reveal the nature of the learning blockage. In doing so, you should avoid giving the impression that you are surprised or disappointed with the child.

Specificity about your expectations

It is important to distinguish between instructional and invitational comments. The instructional comment anticipates compliance. The invitational comment is a recommendation rather than a command. Inexperienced teachers sometimes confuse the two and find that they have to revert to an instruction after initially using an invitation. It is possible for what is intended as a command to end up sounding like a choice or an aspiration. For example, consider the difference between:

- Can you keep your fingers away from the equipment, please? (choice)
- I'd like it if you did not touch the equipment (aspiration)
- Do not touch the equipment. Keep your hands under the table (command).

It is important to be clear in your mind which of these three types of comments (question, aspiration, command) you are employing and make it equally clear to the children. Basically, if you want something to happen, use the *command* preference; if you want children to think about their actions, use an *aspirational* statement; if you want them to make the final decision, offer a *choice* of options.

Intervening

Decisions about how much to intervene when children are working require considerable discernment (see also Chapter 7, assessment issues). Sometimes, children do not understand the concepts involved. Sometimes they have not grasped the nature of the task. Over-eagerness on your part to assist a child can mean that the child does not have sufficient opportunity to flex his or her intellectual muscle and engage with the challenge. On the other hand, reluctance to offer help may mean that the child is left floundering and becomes demoralised or demotivated as a result. As a rule, if you have explained the task carefully, clarified procedural issues and provided appropriate resources, there is every reason to assume that all the children will be able to make a reasonable effort to tackle the work that you have set them to do. Their failure or inability to engage with tasks and activities should not be taken as a signal that they cannot or that they will not. It may be the case that children lack the confidence to proceed, in which case your intervention (explaining, directing, posing questions, prescribing solutions, etc.) offers the necessary reassurance for them to move ahead assuredly. Once children are busy addressing the challenges before them, your role changes from one of manager to assessor. That is, you cease offering advice and support about how to go about doing the work and begin to make a judgement about the understanding that a child demonstrates or skill level attained.

Offering support for writing tasks

After enjoying a stimulating interactive session, children are often asked to record their ideas on paper. More able and confident children can usually make a 'running start' at such a task, but other children may spend some time in applying themselves, either because they are unsure what to write or aware of their shortcomings as writers and hesitant to commit themselves in print. Teachers differ in the extent to which they believe it appropriate to 'pump prime' the children so that they can make a more positive beginning. Some teachers feel that it is important to give the children time to mentally grapple with their ideas and learn important lessons about 'learning to learn' as a result. Other teachers foster peer support, whereby children work in pairs to share ideas before recording anything. Yet other teachers provide structured guidance in the belief that leaving less confident children to struggle on unaided invites restless behaviour and little being achieved during the lesson. All three approaches are appropriate on different occasions and rely on professional judgement as to the best course of action. The most effective teachers discern when it is best to leave children alone to grapple with their ideas, when to promote peer support and when to intervene directly and give specific guidance. You may decide that it is sensible to offer the children some 'starters' in the way of (say) opening phrases or an outline consisting of subheadings as a means of avoiding the 'blank page' syndrome that sometimes has a paralysing effect on children. For younger children, the same principles obtain, though there may be several adults to provide ideas and encourage children to think for themselves. A lot depends on what you are trying to achieve in the lesson or sessions. If you want a tailored piece of writing using a specific writing 'frame' then it is probably appropriate to offer closely structured support and guidance, such as supplying key vocabulary (written on cards, say), suggesting phrases that will enhance the quality of the writing and insisting on correct presentation. If the work is being used for formal assessment purposes, then you will need to spend much longer in explaining the task so that subsequent adult intervention is kept to the absolute minimum and the children are left to cope in the best way they can (see Table 5.1). Preparation for national tests is one such example of when the non-intervention approach is used.

TABLE 5.1 Support for tasks

TYPE OF TASK	PREPARATION	ADULT INVOLVEMENT	OUTCOME
Formally assessed	Exact instructions	Overseeing completion	Marks and grades
Specified	Task allocation	Intervention and support	Criteria-evaluated
Creative	Discussing options	Advisory role	Collaborative endeavour

Lesson ending

If you incorporate a plenary into the lesson plan, you should be clear about its purpose. For example, the following are common possibilities (with nominal times attached to each):

■ A brief time to celebrate achievement and give a few morale-boosting comments (two or three minutes)

■ A time to share a few examples of good practice; for example, reading aloud samples of written work, holding up pictures/diagrams and pinpointing their qualities (five–ten minutes)

- A longer time to 'report back' findings randomly from (say) an investigation (10–12 minutes)
- An extended time for representatives from groups to report back and demonstrate outcomes to the other groups (12–15 minutes).

Before clearing away, invoke a 20-second 'freeze' (no-one moves) while you explain that nobody leaves before the room is spick-and-span. You will need to ensure, however, that in their haste, the children don't cut corners and cram items into trays and containers. It is also right to insist that the children not only put items in the proper place but also correctly orientated. For example, that books have the main title showing, book spines are upright, uncompleted work is face up with the child's name clearly visible, and so on. These procedural niceties are not being fussy but contribute to an orderly well-run classroom that benefits you and the children.

As a general principle, it is worth inculcating basic, clean working habits into your lessons from the outset. Attention to small but important details make a large difference to classroom efficiency, such as insisting that aprons are folded before being carefully placed into a box or hooked properly onto pegs and not allowed to slide on to the cloakroom floor. Naturally, if food is involved, the strictest hygiene must be observed.

> ## Good practice
>
> Use a 'pat yourself on the knee' as an alternative to 'pat yourself on the back' when the class has done well. If you ask the children to clap for any reason, teach them how to do it using their middle three fingers on a flat palm. This technique gives a clearer, sharper tone to the clap and minimises the chances of a cacophony

Instruction

The importance of establishing learning objectives and the need to clarify learning intentions for the children in guiding lesson planning was emphasised earlier in this chapter, together with a caution that it was possible for children to spend time engaged in activities without actually learning very much. One of the direct teaching strategies that aims to combat this unsatisfactory state of affairs is through *instruction*. Despite the rather dated sound to the word, instruction is an essential part of effective teaching and a necessary skill for every teacher. Instruction takes a variety of forms but is associated with one or more of three interrelated approaches: explanation, exposition, demonstration.

Explanation

Explanation is a method by which a teacher offers information, explores situations and justifies decisions or positions in a rational, structured manner. It is a technique often used in response to the question 'why?' and frequently employs examples to illustrate key points. Explanations must pay careful attention to the age of the children by using suitable language and terminology.

As explanations rely solely on the spoken word, the information must be presented in such a way that children are given time to absorb what is said, think about the implications and ask questions of clarification. Like all good teaching, explanations should build on the children's existing knowledge and understanding.

Exposition

Exposition is a step up from explanation, involving graphic illustrations, critique or commentary on an activity or occurrence. Exposition is literally an 'exposing' or 'opening up' of a situation as viewed from a variety of perspectives. During exposition, teachers use persuasion, project their personalities into the verbal element and exhibit a little flamboyance or indulge their enthusiasms. For instance, an exposition may focus upon the harmful exploitation of indigenous populations by foreign explorers. In this case, illustrations may include statistical details of economies before and after foreign intervention, a critique of the benefits and losses which result and encouragement for the children to raise their own questions after carefully considering the issues. With younger children, an exposition may deal with issues of road safety, healthy eating or moral issues such as kindness. It is worth noting that the main feature of *expositional writing* is its explanatory purpose.

> ### Activate your thinking!
>
> But part of a teacher's skill of exposition lie in knowing when to stop talking because the pupils have stopped listening (Haydn 2006: 126)

Demonstration

Demonstration includes elements of exposition but makes use of more varied resources and equipment, together with presentations of the techniques, skills or procedures associated with the activity. For instance, a teacher may demonstrate the correct handling and techniques associated with a variety of percussion instruments or the way to access an index or thinking strategically in a games session. Demonstration depends on the teacher having a firm grasp of the processes and able to show them to an audience at the same time as talking them through the stages, so requires that the teacher possesses a firm grasp of content. A summary of the three types of instruction is shown in Table 5.2:

TABLE 5.2 Forms of instruction

TYPE	VERBAL ELEMENT	PRACTICAL ELEMENT	VISUAL ELEMENT
Explanation	Major	Minor	Minor
Exposition	Major	Minor	Major
Demonstration	Minor	Major	Major

Inexperienced teachers may be tempted to reduce the introductory phase and get children working on the set tasks quickly in the hope that lesson management will be more straightforward. However, curtailing the instructional element is often counter-productive as the lesson lacks a strong foundation and time is wasted in answering children's queries and rectifying later misunderstandings. Like any other approach used obsessively, direct instructional teaching may lose its freshness and become another tiresome teaching method so, as with other teaching skills, the guiding principle should be 'appropriateness for purpose'. Instruction can be enhanced in a number of different ways:

1. Keep the monologue succinct. Avoid droning on and on until the children lose interest. Children sometimes appear to be listening, when they have 'switched off' and are daydreaming. Making a provisional decision in your lesson planning about the amount of time you intend to spend on the instruction will act as a constraint on your excessive use of monologue.

2. Concentrate on gaining good eye contact with as wide a range of children as possible. It is tempting to select the dependable children to answer questions, respond to your points and to offer the contributors positive non-verbal reinforcement (such as nods, smiles and sitting erect) while avoiding the same level of interaction with the others. In an interactive lesson phase you should make it your aim to catch the eye of every child as often as possible. You can increase the quality of the interaction by widening your own eyes and brightening your face when you look at a child and momentarily holding their eyes with your own without making them feel uncomfortable.

3. Pause from time to time to recap, allow questions, and encourage pupils to discuss with their partners. In doing so, it is important to guide children into what precisely they should be discussing and how to go about it. You will also need to set a time limit, but don't be surprised if it is difficult to restore order. The use of a small tinkling bell to indicate a '30-second warning' works surprisingly well.

4. Distinguish between children exchanging comments during an exposition (due to boredom or uncertainty) and the excited buzz of chatter that may occur due to their enthusiasm about the ideas being presented. Inexperienced teachers become unsettled if children start to exchange comments during the presentation, assuming it to be the start of misbehaviour. It is not worth getting cross with the children concerned unless it is obviously a wilful action. Instead, try to catch their eyes while continuing with the exposition and give a little shake of the head to indicate displeasure. If normally sensible children start talking it is often the case that they are excited about an aspect of the lesson rather than bored. A simple 'hold on girls, please, you will get your chance to say something in a moment' (or similar) is normally sufficient to restore order.

5. Deal as calmly as possible with any inappropriate comments from pupils without losing the flow of ideas. Children sometimes call out because they cannot contain themselves, sometimes because they forget that they should remain silent and occasionally because they are being mischievous. You have to make a rapid decision about the reason and respond appropriately.

For instance, holding your arm outstretched, palm facing the transgressor, is often enough to put an end to comments. Meanwhile, you can continue with the instruction.

6. Ensure that resources are close at hand before the session begins. Their availability is an important factor in successful exposition and, especially, in demonstration. It pays to think through resource issues carefully beforehand. Efficient use of resources not only facilitates a smooth passage for your teaching but promotes a strong sense of security among the children as they see that you are coping confidently. Make sure that they are easily available and you have a flat surface to place them onto.

7. Use children's excitement positively. For instance you can say something like: 'I'm glad that my idea appeals to you. From your reaction, I shall expect you to come up with plenty of useful suggestions'. Although a small number of children get carried away with enthusiasm, especially when they observe a stimulating practical demonstration, console yourself with the thought that it is better for them to be excited than to be bored.

8. Avoid following a stimulating period of instruction with a mundane activity. For instance, children quickly lose enthusiasm when a stimulating visual demonstration is followed by a dull writing task. There is a time for simply savouring the moment, generating interest among the children and stimulating constructive talk (Coultas 2007).

Morgan and Saxton (1991) stress that all effective teaching depends upon recognising that effective learning takes place when pupils are active participants in what is going on. In this respect, lively exchanges and use of interesting questions from teachers and pupils has the power 'to generate ideas, spur the imagination and incite both teacher and (pupils) into a shared creative learning experience' (1991: 7). Unlike adult-driven learning that relies on extrinsic motivation (sometimes referred to by the awkward word, 'Behaviourism'), an approach that 'involves significant restructuring of existing cognitive structures' through a 'major personal investment on the part of the learner' that use 'strategies that help learners actively to assimilate and accommodate new material' (Wray 2006: 53–4) is known as 'constructivism'. Wray goes on to explain that a constructivist approach that emphasises the importance of collaboration is known as 'social constructivism', whereby pupils are required to 'develop teamwork skills and to see individual learning as essentially related to the success of group learning. This should be seen as a process of peer interaction that is mediated and structured by the teacher' (2006: 55).

Consolidation

Instruction may be followed by consolidation of children's learning using strategies such as *imitation*, whereby the children copy the teacher's technique. For instance, five year olds may copy particular letter shapes; 10 year olds may use a specific catching technique in PE. Imitation is followed by *practice*, in which children perfect the technique. For instance, five year olds use the letters in a variety of interesting contexts; 10 year olds spend time catching the ball when it is thrown to them from a variety of positions. Other reinforcement activities include *experimentation*, where children are given the opportunity to plan and execute their own ideas. For instance, five year olds make patterns with the letter shapes; 10 year olds make up their own game incorporating the catching technique. It may also be appropriate to encourage children to become innovative, where children use the ideas for a variety of purposes and outcomes. For instance, five year olds might produce paintings based on the letter shapes; ten-year-olds may develop variants on a basic technique that has been introduced to them by the teacher.

Activate your thinking!

Do you agree that the more talking you do, the less opportunity children have to think?

Questioning

Teachers ask hundreds of questions each day in their teaching, broadly categorised into two types. *Closed* questions have a single correct answer. *Open* questions require children to speculate and evaluate alternatives. Both open and closed forms of questioning are widely used in teaching, though there is a tendency for teachers to use far more closed than open ones. Teachers normally ask *closed* questions when they want to stir children's memories about previous work or to assess their knowledge and understanding of a specified content. Teachers use *open* questions as a means of stimulating interest and discussion, and extending children's thinking by making them consider possibilities that lie beyond those that are immediately obvious. Both types of question have their place in teaching, though the overuse of closed questioning can make children unsettled if they know that the teacher is looking for a specific response. The best teachers do not become irritated by wrong answers but try to probe the reasons for the incorrect responses. Medwell (2007) argues that there are two types of wrong answers, 'those due to carelessness or lack of effort, and those due to a lack of understanding or knowledge'. She suggests that an appropriate strategy for dealing with the first category of response (carelessness or lack of effort) is to move on to the next child as quickly as possible. In the second category of response, 'prompt the child by simplifying the question [perhaps breaking it into a series of small steps] or hinting' (2007: 65, author's brackets). Of course, you still have to make a judgement about which of the two categories apply before taking appropriate action; such judgement is a skill that matures with time and experience but you will still occasionally make incorrect assumptions. Sometimes, in the pressure of an intensive interactive session or in a trainee's desire to ensure that the lesson maintains pace, the opportunity to follow up children's errors during 'closed' questioning' is missed.

By contrast, *open* questions invite children to be more adventurous in their responses, though open/speculative questions require more time for answers, so fewer of them can be posed. Sotto (1994) reminds us that it is useful to follow a factual question with a more probing one:

> Teachers might first ask a question which requires the recall of information, but good teachers follow that with a question which requires a reasoned reply. No job in the world can be done by (only) remembering facts. (1994: 175)

To take a simple example of this, the closed question might be 'Which city in America is known as The Big Apple?' After receiving the correct answer, follow-up questions might include:

'Where did the name come from?' or 'Who decided the name?' or 'Why isn't New York the capital city of America?' or 'If New York changed its name, what would you call it, and why?'.

Questions can be classified as productive or unproductive with respect to pupil learning. Productive questions include those where children answer thoughtfully, those that scrutinise issues closely, those where further information or clarification is sought and those in which the children have to consider and evaluate propositions. There is also a value in posing more hypothetical questions for older children especially, by which they are encouraged to consider situations and convey opinions, values and perceptions. Unproductive questions, on the other hand, are poorly focused, require a right or wrong answer (unless teachers are using this as an assessment tool or as a source of gaining responses) and oblige the children to guess what the adult is thinking. In this last case, the teacher spends too long selecting from raised hands until a correct answer is forthcoming. The productive/ unproductive polarisation is not absolute, as your ability to put across the question, make it relevant to the children and interact with the class also contributes to the value of the question and its value in learning. The teacher's personality, zest and commitment can transform the dullest situation.

As in so many teaching situations, careful listening and affirming comments are prerequisites for successful interaction and creating a positive climate of 'yes, have a go', as opposed to 'dare not even try'. Curriculum work at the University of Southampton (2002) concluded that questioning techniques fall into five broad headings. First, it provides increasing attainment through developing wider skills associated with literacy and communication, discussion and enabling pupils to examine/question their own learning. Second, it enhances retention, such as reinforcement that can happen during the plenary. Third, it encourages participation. Fourth, it aids classroom management, such as keeping pupils actively involved in lessons. Fifth, it supports personal and social education, such as encouraging self-assessment, team-building, developing enquiring attitudes and expressing personal opinions.

Inexperienced teachers do not always take full advantage of the opportunities that questioning offer. Poor practice includes failing to acknowledge correct responses by pupils, not waiting for their attention before asking the questions and not providing the learning climate for pupils to ask their own questions. Less experienced teachers also tend to be impatient in waiting for answers from pupils, ask questions in a monotone, allow the pace of the lesson to falter and forget to praise genuine efforts as well as correct answers. Fisher (2005) claims that a common response to why teachers use questions is that they motivate, test knowledge, and promote reflection, analysis and enquiry. The practice, he argues, differs markedly from the theory. Thus: 'Questions are supposed to offer intellectual challenge, to encourage children to think. In practice, many of the questions teachers use inhibit intellectual activity and save pupils from the effort of having to think' (2005: 17). Fisher's stern warning is worth heeding.

Questioning skills do not come naturally for most teachers: they have to be practised and developed in the same way as any other teaching ability. Younger children also have to be inculcated into the process of question and answer, as some of them may be used only to answering straightforward questions spontaneously. As a result, they find rhetorical questions difficult to handle and may, in their excitement, call out answers randomly. As children get older, their attitude towards teachers' questions not only depends upon their knowledge of the area under scrutiny but also whether they feel confident to answer the particular questions. This reluctance is particularly evident if the children are anxious about the adult response that an incorrect answer might induce. Children will understandably prefer to say nothing if they feel that their responses will be trivialised or if they fear humiliation in front of their classmates. It is part of your role as teacher to encourage every child to participate in question and answer sessions and to acknowledge every opinion that is offered. You must implement a code of conduct from the start, in which mockery and tittering at someone's answer is not allowed. Kerry (1998) insists that the children must be convinced that the aim of questioning is to share knowledge and ideas within a supportive framework where each serious comment is valued. The creation of a learning environment in which children are encouraged to respond to open questions and teachers display a genuine interest in their answers is therefore essential. Harlen (2000) claims that this supportive style of teaching motivates children to answer questions without fear attached to being wrong. In this way, misunderstandings can be used constructively as a basis for formative assessment and future learning.

Activate your thinking!

How many questions do you ask in each lesson? How many are necessary? How many are productive?

Using open-ended provocative questions are less easy for trainee teachers to employ because they are difficult to think of and children's responses are harder to manage. The teacher not only has to select a child to give his or her response but also has to *evaluate* the quality and appropriateness of the reply. This process requires alertness, careful listening to what children say and sensitivity when trying to encourage responses from children.

Another important issue concerns the length of time that teachers are prepared to wait for answers to the questions. Some children think slowly and deeply, while others are more spontaneous and willing to risk making mistakes for the pleasure of being chosen by the teacher to give the answer. Owing to the emphasis on maintaining pace in lessons, a lot of teachers are nervous about silence and giving children time to consider their replies. However, allowing children to cogitate for longer improves the quality of their answers, whereas peppering questions at them in the expectation of immediate responses tends to lead to superficiality. Waiting for a little longer is likely to result in answers of a higher cognitive value and produce deep, rather than shallow forms of learning. It is, therefore, essential to be clear in your mind about the purpose that the questions are serving and adjust them accordingly. Teachers should avoid asking questions that necessitate children reading their minds. (See, for example, advice in Baumfield and Mroz 2004; Walsh and Sattes 2005.)

Good practice

To avoid marginalising the less able and less confident children, employ the following strategies occasionally:

- Offer an either/or pair of answers and ask children to wink at you with one eye if they agree with the first and both eyes if they agree with the second
- Ask a question but only allow responses from a defined group of children (such as those with birthdays in months ending with 'ber')
- Ask a question, give the children 30 seconds to whisper what they think in their neighbour's ear, reveal the answer, then ask them to raise their hands if their neighbours were correct.

Use of the board

Despite the availability of overhead projectors and other sophisticated equipment, many teachers still rely on some form of wall-mounted or free-standing board, normally a 'whiteboard', though so–called interactive (computer linked) boards are in most classrooms (see Chapter 6). There are many different ways of using (and misusing) the whiteboard, and this section provides some suggestions for more effective use. A number of basic principles should be adhered to carefully.

Ensuring that the surface of the board is in good condition

There is little point in trying to write on a greasy or scratched surface; it sets a poor example, ruins the marker and makes accurate writing or drawing a problem. A few minutes spent preparing the board each week pays dividends.

Having the proper markers available

Some boards require special markers and will be damaged by others. It is essential to replace tops firmly to prolong the life of the pen. (This also applies to children when they use miniature whiteboards.)

Checking that the board is at an appropriate height

It is easy for children to strain their eyes or adopt an uncomfortable position in order to see clearly, so be aware of this fact when organising the seating. Glare on the board reduces visibility.

Keeping the surface smooth

Although a fixed board is a tempting target for special displays, the damage inflicted by staples, pins and adhesive can be irreparable. Fitness for purpose must be the mantra.

Remembering your pupils' learning needs

Many children find it difficult to copy off the board due to the need to look up and down while transferring information to paper. If asked to write quickly, less able pupils are likely to make spelling, punctuation and letter formation errors. Furthermore, teachers' handwriting varies in quality. If children need to read something off the board, teachers must ensure that their writing is large and clear. In particular, children seated at the sides of the classroom may find it difficult to read certain words if the light creates a glare. It pays to sit with the children for a time to understand the problems they may be experiencing.

> ### Good practice
>
> To check that all children can see adequately it is worth positioning yourself before the lesson begins at different points around the room (preferably at chair height) to see whether you can see without squinting.

In direct teaching to a group or the whole class, the teacher can use the board as a memory aid by writing a list and referring to each point in turn. Sometimes the board is useful to demonstrate the correct way to set out a piece of work (in maths, say) or the heading for a letter. Similarly, it is useful to write up spellings or list words suggested by children in advance of free writing sessions. Some teachers encourage the children to use the whiteboard during a lesson for noting ideas or recording findings.

These uses are valid and can facilitate learning, but there are times when board work can lead to bored work. For instance, it is not sensible to expect a class of 30 children to strain their necks or have to keep coming up to the board to read something because it cannot be seen from the back of the room.

Using worksheets

'Worksheets' (also known as activity sheets) is a general term used to describe written material that has been produced by a teacher, downloaded from one of the many websites or taken from one of the many activity books that allow multiple copying. (*Note*: replication of copyright material without permission is an offence.) To a certain extent, information technology (especially computers) has reduced the need for worksheets and some schools have a policy that discourages or even bans them. Nevertheless, worksheets tend to fall into one or more of four broad categories:

1. *Information sheets* which children can use as a starting point for thematic or topic work. Typically, the sheets will give some background information and children will be encouraged to research further (book library or computer) to uncover fresh insights or enlarge their knowledge base.

2. *Practice sheets* that give examples for children to work through to reinforce previous learning. Computation and English grammar are commonly practised in this way. Practice sheets often require a series of single correct answers.

3. *Investigation sheets* which set out problems for children to solve using their own ideas and ingenuity. Investigative sheets are normally used by groups of children engaged on a collaborative project.

4. *Task sheets* that contain the requirements for completion of a project, areas to investigate, problems to solve or those that serve a variety of different functions. Task sheets are used in situations in which pupils are expected to demonstrate a high level of autonomy in organising their work. For instance, a task sheet might set out what the teacher expects each child to complete over the course of a day or have space for agreed pupil targets.

Worksheets can provide a useful additional tool in the teaching and learning programme. They ensure that teachers plan ahead, think through the work and, if produced by the teacher, relate closely to the work in hand. Unfortunately, there is sometimes a tendency to use worksheets obsessively and neglect other important teaching strategies. In particular, practice sheets can be over-used (with little preparation or introduction) as a means of keeping children occupied or as a substitute for proper teaching strategies such as instruction, exploration and collaborative approaches. Although the first few minutes of practice sheet work can be orderly, the lesson often degenerates into a situation in which restless and frustrated children lose heart and regularly call upon (increasingly overworked) adults for assistance.

Worksheets, if sparingly and imaginatively used, can provide children with ready information, opportunities to practise examples, a starting point for more innovative work or a reminder about key aspects of the work. However, a number of safeguards are needed:

- They should not be seen as a substitute for other teaching methods
- Limited information should be placed onto a single sheet
- The purpose of the sheet should be clearly explained to the children
- Practice sheets must allow for variations in ability, beginning with easier examples and gradually increasing the level of difficulty or using separate sheets, each one slightly more demanding than the previous one
- The teacher should try to review the key points following their completion rather than simply collect them in for marking
- Opportunities for collaboration should be exploited.

Worksheets can be very useful for a busy teacher but there are hidden time costs: preparation, reproduction and assessment. There are large numbers of worksheets available from different sources but they must always be contextualised. That is, they must serve the particular learning needs of the class. Too often, worksheets end up half completed, languishing in children's trays until the next clear-out, when they are discarded without exploiting their value. Although worksheets provide a tempting option as a holding task for one group while dealing with other children who require direct teaching or supervision, these occasions should be kept to a minimum.

Good practice

Before you spend time organising a worksheet, ask yourself the question: 'What purpose, precisely, does this worksheet serve?'.

Case study

As he had previously only worked in Key Stage 2, Bart was anxious when he heard that his school placement was with Year 1 children and, though he was reluctant to admit it, the thought of working with infants rather alarmed him. Bart's friends at the rugby club had teased him when they heard the news and his friend Ian told him to practise tying shoelaces and wiping noses. However, the female student teachers specialising in early years' education with whom he shared a house warned him that he would be in for a shock if he thought that teaching young children was easy. These conflicting comments and his own insecurity weighed heavily upon him, but he decided that he would grit his teeth and make the most of it. After all, he needed to 'pass' the school experience if he wanted to continue training to be a teacher, so it was best to be positive. The next placement would be with his favoured junior age children, hopefully in Year 6 where he could 'strut his stuff', especially in games sessions.

When he commenced the placement, Bart found that the class teacher made handling five and six year olds look simple. Perhaps teaching young children wouldn't be so bad after all. From the moment Bart was first introduced to the children, he was amazed at how small they were. In turn, they stared up at his six-foot frame with wide-eyed astonishment. One little girl asked him if he was the new head teacher. A diminutive little boy called Devon (who was to be the bane of Bart's life in school) pointed at him and screeched out that he was a giant! The class teacher, Mrs Williams, introduced him to the class as a 'new teacher who has come to help us', which made Bart feel much better. He hated being referred to as a student. The first few days came and went, and as he settled into the situation Bart realised that there was a lot more to teaching young children than he had imagined. For a start, they were much more dependent on adults than he had been used to with older primary children. Their concentration span was shorter and they lacked some of the most basic skills that he had taken for granted with 10 year olds. Procedural matters had to be explained carefully and some children still got into a muddle. On the other hand, Bart found himself enjoying the attention he received as the only male teacher in the school and quite liked the spontaneity that characterised certain parts of the day. He also noticed, and was a bit surprised by, the formality of some teaching. Bart had in his mind that little children just played. Mrs Williams explained that although she would not choose to teach so formally, it was important that the children did well in tests or the school could be marked out as a 'failing school'. Bart shuddered at the prospect.

After a few days getting to know the children by working with small groups, Bart began to teach his first whole-class lessons. He used a modified version of the plans that had been successful with older children and decided to demonstrate his interactive abilities as early as possible to impress the class teacher and establish his authority. The topic was 'Colour' and Bart had a large poster of a rainbow to use as a visual aid. He sat the children on the carpet and they waited with anticipation. Mrs Williams sat behind them, smiling encouragingly. Bart began briskly, asking the children to tell him about their favourite colours. He had not anticipated the flurry of answers that came flying at him. Some children shouted out their preferences, one little girl began telling him that her bedroom had been painted yellow, and Devon, the diminutive boy, started laughing and shaking his head from side to side. Bart was stunned and held up his hand for them to stop, urging them to sit still and be sensible. The noise subsided, but Amy stood up and tapped him on the shoulder to tell him that her bedroom was also painted yellow. Bart did not want to know. Mrs Williams uttered a few 'shush' sounds and spoke directly to Devon, who immediately sat bolt upright before shrinking and burying his face in his lap.

Bart continued and got out the picture of the rainbow from behind the table, pinning it to the board. Several children called out what it was and several claimed loudly to have seen a rainbow yesterday. One boy said that his uncle had flown through a rainbow, another pointed out that the corner of the picture was creased. Bart smiled and pretended to be pleased that the children were responding so enthusiastically. Inwardly he felt vulnerable and wanted to be stern but feared that it might be inappropriate with young children, so he commended them instead: 'Well done; well done everybody'. He then read the class a short poem about a rainbow in a slightly breathless and exaggerated way to keep their attention, a strategy that was only partially successful.

Bart decided to take a direct approach to impose some order and began talking rapidly, telling the children about features of the rainbow and how it was created. He did not venture further questions and talked 'over' the children when they tried to interrupt him. After about 10 more minutes, Bart told them to sit up and listen, which to his relief they did almost immediately. He explained that they were going to draw a picture of the rainbow and complete a work sheet (a scaled-down version of one that he had originally prepared himself for older children) in which they had to match words and provide the correct 'describing' words for blanks in sentences. The children moved to their tables and got down to work very quickly. Bart was pleased at first but soon became alarmed to see that a number of children were using the wrong colours for the rainbow; others were pressing the pastel crayons too heavily and a few were colouring the words that they were supposed to use for sentences. The TA asked him gently whether he wanted the children to work alone or together (he said he didn't mind). He heard Mrs Williams tell her group that they should try on spare paper before attempting the proper drawing. Two children told Bart that they didn't know how to draw a rainbow. A steady drift of children wandered from their seats to look more closely at the picture on the board before skipping back, adding some detail, then returning to the board again. Bart had simply not expected that such an apparently simple task would become so involved.

To Bart's credit, and with the patient assistance of the class teacher and assistant, he managed to hold the lesson together and was even able to bring the children together at the end for a useful sharing time. After the lesson he was extremely relieved to see the children leave for playtime and felt quite exhausted. Mrs Williams gave him a reassuring smile and steered him towards the staffroom for a cup of tea.

After school that night, Bart and Mrs Williams sat down and talked about the lesson. 'I know it was a disaster' Bart began, but the teacher shook her head. 'It wasn't a disaster at all. It's not at all easy working with young children and very tiring.' Bart had begun to realise the truth of what she said and when he went home that evening and was asked how the day had gone, he admitted ruefully that it had been a challenge. 'I told you it wasn't easy with younger ones,' sympathised one of the female students. Bart agreed and realised that he would need to think very hard about his teaching approach and attitude if he were to do better next time.

Evaluation of Bart's lesson

- Planning for younger children needed to take account of their experience and existing knowledge; modifying an old plan from Key Stage 2 was unsatisfactory

- It was a good idea to use a question to invite interest, but also important to clarify the ground rules for children's responses

- The use of an interesting story involving a rainbow was a useful alternative strategy for gaining interest and raising questions

- The direct transmission of information (keeping talking so that the children do not) was useful as a temporary control strategy but hopeless in terms of children's learning

- Young children need more time to absorb, reflect and explore concepts, so it was important for him to speak quite slowly and deliberately, to pause between statements and use appropriate vocabulary

- Clarification of task demands and expectations needed to be reinforced to prevent a tide of queries from children

- It was important to be aware of children with special learning and emotional needs, such as those who lacked confidence and need a lot of reassurance

- It takes time to settle down with a new class; young children have an insatiable curiosity, particularly about a new grown-up in the class.

Footnote
After qualifying, Bart was appointed as a teacher for a Year 1 class.

Further reading

Butt, G. (2006) *Lesson Planning*, London: Continuum.

    Contains a lot of advice, schedules and suggestions for effective planning.

Davies, A. (2007) *Storytelling in the Classroom*, London: Sage.

    Helps primary teachers to develop their storytelling, including how to create the plot and characters, enhance presentation techniques and use voice and expression effectively.

Galton, M. (2007) *Learning and Teaching in the Primary Classroom*, London: Sage.

    Describes how teachers can tailor their teaching methods to maximise learning, using case studies and classroom examples.

Lewis, M. and Ellis, S. (2006) *Phonics*, London: Sage.

    Offers advice on how to understand the various theories about phonics and applying the knowledge in practical teaching.

Moyles, J., Hargreaves, L., Merry, R., Paterson, F. and Esarte-Sarries, V. (2003) *Interactive Teaching in the Primary School*, Maidenhead: Open University Press.

    Provides a scholarly and rigorous interrogation of key issues for the serious student.

Otterton, M. (2004) *Teaching Techniques*, London: Continuum.

    Examines the ways in which teachers can change and improve their teaching techniques by looking at a variety of innovative approaches.

Overall, L. and Sangster, M. (2003) *Primary Teacher's Handbook*, London: Continuum.

    This book is an A to Z of guidance that includes suggestions about teaching skills that primary teachers use regularly.

Organising and Managing for Learning

Introduction

We noted in the previous chapter that learning is not a random process, so teachers need to be clear about the conditions that contribute towards a satisfactory learning environment. If organisation is the structure that facilitates effective teaching and learning, management is the means by which it is achieved. This present chapter underlines the fact that high quality organising and managing are both necessary to maximise teaching opportunities and promote sound learning and discipline.

Effective teaching

We saw in the previous chapter that successful lessons do not happen by chance, but result from a combination of careful planning, sensible organisation, skilful lesson management and enthusiastic teaching that also allows for spontaneous opportunities, creativity and the needs of pupils of all abilities. All effective teaching is enhanced by paying attention to three factors:

1. The ability to think ahead.
2. Purposeful reflection about ways to improve teaching and learning.
3. The significance of interpersonal relationships.

Thinking ahead

The ability to think ahead is crucial to success. Effective teaching is not only about coping with the immediate situation but relies on advance thought about resource provision and activities appropriate to the age and ability of the class. Inexperienced teachers tend to stare fixedly at the path beneath their feet; they must learn to look up and see the road stretching ahead. Although your priority is bound to me the next lesson, try to step back and see its place in the wider picture. Twiselton (2006: 70–1) with particular reference to literacy teaching, claims that trainee teachers tend to pass through three stages in their knowledge and understanding of teaching: (1) as *task manager* during the early stages of learning to teach, in which they view their role in terms of task completion; (2) as *curriculum deliverer*, as they see themselves as supporting learning through a scheme, curriculum or lesson plan; and (3) finally, in the later stages of development, as a *concept/skill builder*, in which they are aware of pupils' wider and deeper understanding and skill development. You must aim to reach 'stage 3' as early as possible, but also to be aware that there are no shortcuts to competence.

Purposeful reflection

Purposeful reflection to improve practice lies at the heart of improvement. Teachers are professionals for many reasons: their length of training, the significance of their job to society, the extent of their responsibilities, level of expertise and, above all, in their capacity to critically evaluate their teaching (Silcock and Brundrett 2002). The need to carry on learning applies as much to seasoned professionals as to novices.

Over recent years, there has been an increased emphasis upon establishing continuity between initial and in-service training, underlining the need for all teachers to enhance and update their professional skills, and understanding the significance of new initiatives, surveys and research findings. Standards of attainment no longer apply solely to newly qualified teachers but also to those in the induction year and beyond. Consequently, it is important that all teachers learn to evaluate their own teaching through discussion with colleagues, engagement with scholarly activities such as reading professional journals and gaining advanced professional qualifications. All of this endeavour must be grounded in regular reflection on their teaching approaches and strategies and, increasingly, keeping sources of evidence to support claims about professional attainment.

Interpersonal relationships

It is not merely in a deliberation about the mechanics of teaching that professional progress is made, but also in understanding the significance of human interaction, emotions and behaviour. Constant interrogation of the role of relationships in learning is not only important for the general classroom ethos and children's wellbeing, it also has implications for effective organisation. For instance, it is not sufficient merely to inform the children about standards of behaviour or expected procedures, but to explain why they are necessary, thereby involving pupils in decisions that influence their lives. Children are more likely to develop an affinity with a teacher who takes the time and trouble to include them in the decision-making process, if only to inform them about why something has already been decided, than with one who treats them like passive recipients of adult decisions. The teacher is, of course, ultimately responsible for what happens in the classroom, but in the meantime the children will increase in self-confidence and awareness of the issues if they develop a sense of ownership over events that directly impinge upon their lives. For very young children the decisions might involve something as simple as determining a sensible way to store wet paintings. For older infants involvement might be at the level of discussing ways to organise the fiction books. For older children the issue might relate to classroom seating arrangements. Whatever the issue, the process of teaching-and-learning is enhanced when children's views are taken into account and valued. Furthermore, children are attracted to teachers who take their views seriously and treat them civilly.

ORGANISING LEARNING

Classroom environment

Most primary teachers spend the majority of their teaching time in the same room. Despite the increase in subject specialists, advanced skills teachers, TAs and curriculum subject coordinators, the familiar pattern of one teacher taking responsibility for the learning, welfare and motivation of around 30 youngsters remains commonplace in schools. We saw in earlier chapters that teachers' job satisfaction depends principally on the success they make in shaping the lives of 'their' children. The conditions they create for learning is one factor that contributes to the extent to which this aim is achieved. One sign of a teacher's commitment to children is the appearance of the classroom, including its cleanliness, order and purposefulness (sometimes referred to as the classroom 'climate'). Despite the increasing demands made on teachers to achieve ever-higher standards in English and mathematics, primary teachers and their assistants show a determination to give sufficient time to the look of the room. Adults and children spend many hours there each day and need to feel comfortable in their surroundings (see Hastings and Wood 2002 for advice about classroom layout).

Classrooms vary in size and shape; few are ideal for every purpose. Some will suit a particular teaching approach; others will be a source of frustration to the teacher due to the room's odd shape, lack of access to resources or location (such as being at the far end of the main school building). Whatever the conditions, however, visitors will use classroom appearance as one of the measures to assess the teacher's professionalism and, perhaps, the quality of the school. Head teachers frequently show prospective parents around and make a habit of delaying in some classrooms and passing hastily through others. The reason for this behaviour is obvious.

First, it is important to examine a classroom from the pupils' perspective. What do the children see when they first enter the room? Does it look inviting, tidy, thoughtfully arranged? Is there an air of disarray and confusion, or of dowdiness? Are tables and chairs of suitable size? Are trays, books and resources clearly marked and accessible? A useful exercise is to kneel down in various parts of the room to take a 'pupil eye' view, including the doorway, and scan it for a few moments to see how things might be improved with a small amount of effort. The room can also be examined from an adult's perspective. Is there an air of efficiency due to the arrangement of furniture, tidiness and the obvious care that has been given to the overall layout? Does the classroom look cared for and the sort of place where everyone can work safely and efficiently? Is there a feeling of purpose, enriched by interactive displays, examples of good quality children's work on the walls, and well marshalled resources? A classroom like this can bring prestige and attention from the people who matter: children, parents, governors and other members of staff.

Seating arrangements

In making decisions about seating, it is important to be clear about the basis on which decisions are made. A few teachers give the children complete freedom about where they sit; others allow children to sit where they prefer for a week or two until the children's academic ability, self-discipline and inclination to work become apparent, when changes are made accordingly. In most cases, children are allocated a place for the majority of lessons and remain there unless they are moved for a specific purpose (e.g. a collaborative task or art and craft activity).

Most teachers take account of friendship patterns in making decisions. In doing so, there are a number of factors to consider. First, if children sit with their friends it can result in them chattering and disrupting proceedings; on the other hand, they are more likely to co-operate with someone they know and like. Second, if friends are separated they may be tempted to wander across the room to make contact, send hand signal messages or (worse) call out to each other. Third, although a seating arrangement made on the grounds of friendship may be popular with children, it may create problems when pupils of similar academic ability need to work together. Finally, less capable children may be tempted to copy from their more able partners, though this tendency should not be confused with genuine co-operation, when children are encouraged to provide peer support for one another.

Teachers who dictate the seating pattern will reduce some of these potential problems but generate others. For instance, many children feel more secure when sitting next to a friend and may be unhappy if separated. Teachers may inadvertently place children together who dislike each other, with the inevitable disruptive consequences. Most teachers try to strike a balance between keeping friends together in situations where grouping does not rely principally on academic ability, and separating them where this is necessary because of the differentiated requirements of tasks and activities.

In making decisions about seating arrangements, teachers need to be aware that the term 'academic ability' can be defined in different ways. The majority of teachers group according to the children's ability in English (especially reading and writing) except during timetabled maths sessions. During work outside the core subjects, pupils' expertise in areas as diverse as ball skills (in PE), computer skills (in ICT), communication skills (in discussions and collaborative problem solving) and organisational skills (in team work activities) need to be taken into account. In addition, two other factors have to be considered: the children's ages and your teaching style

The age of the children

Younger children are likely to need guidance about where to sit but are less likely to be antagonistic towards the children next to them. Nursery age children may be given considerable freedom of movement, depending upon the availability of adults to supervise their activities. Older children are much clearer about their friendship preferences and more assertive as a result. On the other hand, older primary children tend to be academically grouped and there are higher expectations about formal work outcomes.

Teaching style

If the class is taught as a whole rather than in groups, single tables with two pupils per table may be best. If collaborative tasks predominate, groups of about four are often appropriate. The structured patterns of lessons in mathematics and literacy do not leave much room for manoeuvre, as pupils are normally together at the start and conclusion of the lesson and separated into ability groups for the other parts of the lesson. If teachers use a board to illustrate what they are teaching, children must be seated in such a way that they can see clearly without getting a stiff neck or having to use a telescope.

Most teachers have a basic pattern of organisation but vary the set-up according to the circumstances. For instance, tables may be placed together for the purpose of sharing resources for a large-scale project. Children may need to move around the room if there is a 'circus' of various tasks to be completed in a given time (in science, say), each task in a different area of the room. There are also practical factors to be taken into account if children have special learning needs and, for example, require more space for wheelchair access or specially adapted working surfaces for children with limited upper-body mobility. You may tend to spend rather more time than normal on direct interactive teaching, or on group work, or on promoting individual learning; whatever your preferred approach, the room layout needs to facilitate it rather than hinder.

Health and safety

Whether a classroom is brand new or an ageing Victorian relic, the children need to be able to move around easily and use equipment safely. Every lesson should be planned with 'risk factors' in mind. If the risk factor is high, more adult supervision, discipline measures and training about the correct use of equipment is needed (see also Chapter 2). Practical and outdoor activities require particular care.

Teaching approach also has an impact upon the level of safety required, especially in respect of children's movements around the room. Generally, less pupil mobility reduces the likelihood of accidents; greater mobility necessitates more stringent safety measures. Pupils have less need to move when all the resources required for the task are readily accessible and where the teacher moves about the room to see pupils, rather than the pupils leaving their places to see the teacher. Some teachers favour bringing children from the carpet to the front to use the interactive white board or to explain what they have done; while such a strategy maintains interest and cultivates a climate of shared endeavour, it is time-consuming and can lead to accidentally crushed fingers.

Classroom climate also plays a part in health and safety. Some classrooms have a settled feel to them as pupils move about purposefully and get on with their tasks without undue fuss. Other classrooms seem like a disaster waiting to happen, as pupils mill about aimlessly, lacking motivation and arguing about resources. Most classrooms vary between a settled feel during teacher-led phases, and noise and bustle when pupils are engaged in tasks which require independent thinking and initiative. It is difficult, for instance, to imagine a time when design and technology experiments with eight year olds can be carried out in sterile, near silent conditions. There is, however, a big difference between enthusiastic application to the job by keen young minds and irresponsible behaviour from pupils who are determined to take advantage of the freer conditions. Teachers have to strike a balance between allowing children the liberty to exercise initiative and being insistent on proper codes of conduct. Nevertheless, there are at least ten health and safety rules that teachers must be alert to at all times:

1. Pathways should be clear so that pupils can walk unhindered. Tables and chairs should be set out so that children do not have to squeeze past or risk tripping over obstacles such as bags.

2. Pupils carrying out activities that require large areas should be given the appropriate spaces in which to work.

3. Equipment and resources should be stored so that they can be reached without stretching or pulling items down from the shelf, especially heavy items.

4. Wet activities should be kept to a designated area away from main walkways, and sink areas should be kept free from furniture.

5. Pupils must be taught how and when to wash their hands thoroughly, especially before meals.

6. Pupils' view of the board and other visual aids should be unhindered.

7. Pupils should not have to sit next to a draughty window, hot radiator or a tall piece of furniture with objects resting on top.

8. Pupils should only use specialist equipment with adult supervision and after proper training.

9. Pupils must not be allowed to put small objects in their mouths.

10. Pupils should walk and not run in the classroom.

Health and safety issues are particularly relevant for vulnerable pupils; for example, the very young, those with disabilities and children with allergies. However, all children should know how to use equipment correctly and should never be 'let loose' without training. In a situation where a number of different activities are taking place in the room simultaneously, teachers must ensure that sufficient adult help and supervision is available. In 'large space' activities involving heavy or hazardous equipment, all possible safety checks should be made beforehand and limits imposed upon access. It is better to use a limited range of equipment safely than to attempt too much at one time, lose control of events, and create unsafe working conditions. Even young children will, with encouragement, offer their own suggestions about improvements in safety procedures. If your instincts alert you to possible danger or hazards, take additional precautions and seek expert advice.

Large space activities also invite other potential hazards, such as children bumping into each other when running about, injuries from bats and sticks, and over-zealous physical exertion. Some children simply get carried away and don't hear your commands, so it is essential to rehearse your expectations with them and insist on immediate compliance.

Resources

The level of resources can make a considerable difference to the quality of teaching and learning, and contribute towards higher standards. Teachers are wonderfully inventive and make a little go a long way, but there is a limit to what can be accomplished. A good supply of resources, accessible and clearly labelled, makes life easier for everyone and smartens the appearance of the classroom. Pupils need to be taught how to use equipment, care for materials and, most important, return items to their correct place after use.

The type of resources will, of course, vary according to the nature of the task. A messy, creative activity (such as clay work) necessitates the availability of raw materials, tools, protective clothing and suitable working conditions such as a cleanable, flat surface located some distance from other activities. By contrast, a deskwork activity involving a single, self-contained worksheet requiring only writing implements is relatively easy to set up. Teachers need to be sensitive to the way that a shortage of resources (such as a lack of aprons) and insufficient time spent on training children to use things (such as a measuring scale) can result in arguments, unsatisfactory quality of work and avoidable accidents.

There are also financial and practical implications if resources are abused. For instance, lined paper is expensive and if used inappropriately can result in it ending up in the dustbin with just a few mis-spelt scrawled words at the top of the page. Meanwhile the child has another fresh piece and is busy making the same mistakes. In recent years there has been a move back towards the use of exercise books, which can be collected and stored with minimum effort. Even so, there are many occasions when drafts of work need to be kept safely for future use. While the use of digital cameras and computer technology has reduced problems of safe storage to some extent, procedures for use of consumable resources is still an important element of efficient classroom practice. Similarly, incorrect use of tools can lead to expensive breakages. The rule is simple: use the correct equipment for the job and monitor use of consumables to minimise waste.

As inferred above, all schools now have a range of computers and other ICT resources to support learning. Sometimes they are held in a central area, sometimes they are allocated to different classrooms; frequently both options are utilised. Each situation creates different organisational challenges. If there is a computer suite away from the classroom, supervision of children and careful timetabling is essential. If computers are located in classrooms, managing access is a priority. The use of a trained TA makes a considerable difference to the ease with which computer access is managed, but you still need to ensure that you have briefed the assistant and clarified what you hope pupils achieve through its use.

Preparing resources for a lesson can be time-consuming. Ideally, most of it should be completed during the previous evening and, where possible, left in place for easy and immediate access, especially for the first session of the day. However, it is sometimes better to wait until the morning before distributing your precious wares. For instance, if the equipment is delicate or expensive, it is preferable to wait until the last moment before setting it out immediately before the session. If an equipment cupboard key is required, allowance must be made for the time it will take to collect and return it. Some resources for the afternoon session have to be organised during the lunch break. Again, logistical considerations are important, such as whether the room is being used for (say) a lunchtime activity; or whether a sudden downpour of rain will bring the class back inside to descend on the lovingly prepared items that you carefully placed on tables when the room was empty.

Large space activities and 'design and make' tasks inevitably carry resource implications: sticky tape and adhesive pots have to be distributed in advance; clay has to be accessible; tables have to be reorganised, and so on. Similarly, equipment has to be checked in advance of PE lessons; drama 'props' have to be put in position; the floor space has to be cleared before a dance session; computers have to be switched on, programs set up and paper trays filled for printing. If arrangements are not in hand, the lesson gets off to a bad start as organising resources absorbs the time and effort that ought to have gone into active teaching, the exception being when the involvement of the children in the organisation forms an important part of the lesson. As in many complex organisational situations the support of a TA is hugely beneficial; so much so, in fact, that it is normally better to adopt a more straightforward approach until adult assistance is available.

Activate your thinking!

Well organised lessons lead to settled children and improved learning. A summary of questions helps to point up ways of increasing the likelihood that lessons will run smoothly.

- Is there sufficient time during one lesson to achieve all that you planned or are you being too ambitious?
- Have you sorted out in advance the activities that different children will be involved in doing?
- Does the TA know what is required of her?
- Are there likely interruptions to take into account during the lesson?
- Are lessons immediately before or after any events (such as assembly, singing practice or play rehearsals) that might affect the time available or pupils' concentration?

Attention to the details of organisation and daily priorities pays rich dividends. A few minutes spent reflecting systematically upon the working day is amply rewarded by the improved efficiency. It is worth developing the habit of sketching out each day's predicted pattern and needs during the previous evening, as having a well-considered framework allows unanticipated events and disruptions to the programme to be more easily accommodated.

Good practice

Before the start of each day and each session, take a moment to rehearse your programme in your mind in the form of a 'storyboard' to foresee possible hindrances and opportunities and take evasive action.

Displays

Many primary school classrooms are enlivened by displays of children's work, paintings, models and exhibits. Some corridors are festooned with colourful motifs and stimulating pictures, all of which take a lot of time and energy to produce (see Jackson 1993; Cooper *et al.* 1996; Beasley and Moberley 2000). In recent years, the increased emphasis upon the core subjects has been matched by a similar reduction in time spent on the creative subjects; as a result, many teachers find that preparation, planning, marking and target setting consumes some of the time they might formerly have spent on displaying work. Although TAs can take responsibility for organising the displays, they are often used to support the teaching of literacy and numeracy and offer specialist, targeted help to children deemed 'behind' in their academic work; as a consequence, they have less opportunity to be involved in other tasks. An additional factor to consider is that some assistants do not possess display skills or may not produce the sort of display that the teacher had in mind, so active liaison between teacher and assistant is essential.

Despite the objectives-driven nature of modern primary school life, many teachers extol the virtues of colourful and well-displayed classrooms and invest a lot of energy into ensuring that pupils' work is visible. In addition, teachers of younger children often establish different areas to stimulate the children's imagination: a *story corner* surrounded by lavishly painted pictures of characters from fairy tales; a *writing corner* separated from the rest of the room by curtains from which hang samples of completed stories and pictures; a *mystery corner* with unusual items of interest; a *home corner* full of household items. The same classroom may have a number of tables with specimens from walks, maths equipment and small scale construction materials to handle, play with and enjoy. Cards with carefully framed questions or challenges will be placed alongside the displays, prompting children to extend their thinking by handling the objects and talking about them to their friends. The pupils in these classrooms encourage their parents to come and admire their contributions. The class teacher is known throughout the school as having a 'fantastic classroom'. Even so, head teachers worry that time spent on display can mean time lost in promoting standards in the core subjects. The best schools are able to combine high academic standards with creativity.

Displaying classrooms should certainly not be a competition between teachers. Nevertheless, if displays are going to serve a useful purpose, consideration must be given to the following four factors:

Selecting work for display

Criteria are needed for selection. For instance, a teacher may want to display a single piece of work from every child, in which case some poor work will be on general view; or alternatively select the best examples, in which cases the less able children will never see their work on display. Gathering large amounts of completed work into a simply produced homemade book is sometimes preferable to pinning up the work on a board.

What displaying the work achieves

While displaying work has the benefits mentioned earlier, the quest to cover walls with work can become wasteful unless the purpose for doing so is clear. Displayed work should act as an incentive for pupils to complete work of similar quality, assist learning by offering interesting ideas, and stimulate children's imagination. Teachers can use work on display to point out high standards of attainment, commend the children who have produced it, and praise the unity of a whole-class endeavour.

Changing the displays

The fresh colours of a newly finished painting, the visual impact of a recently completed model and the charming eloquence of a poem about autumn leaves can quickly fade into an untidy collection of curled edges, cracked paint and out-of-season writing. Teachers are sometimes embarrassed to discover that the display of tessellations is more than a term old or the winter frieze is gathering dust in a revealing stream of summer sunshine. Time passes rapidly in the bustle of classroom life and displays soon become dated. A simple plan of action for changing wall displays will help to avoid the discomfiture of snowmen in June.

The destiny of old displays

Wall-mounted displays are often in a poor condition by the time they have completed their useful life and it is sometimes best to quietly dispose of them. On other occasions, the children want to take their work home, in which case it is essential that teachers have checked first that they are happy for parents to examine the work close up. Sometimes a piece of work is required for a pupil's Record of Achievement folder (see Chapter 7); if so, details of the child's name, the date of completion and a brief note about the circumstances under which it was produced are needed.

> ### Good practice
>
> Discuss your plan of action for changing displays with the TA and draw up a schedule. Check discretely that the assistant has the necessary skills to make a good job of it.

MANAGING LEARNING

Forms of management

It is unrealistic to think that because the classroom organisation has been carried out efficiently in advance of the lesson, everything will proceed without a hitch. The best teachers not only organise but also ensure that they manage classroom affairs (monitoring, intervening, guiding, assessing) so as to ensure the most favourable conditions for learning. The concept of effective management is now strongly rooted in classroom practice and poor management is likely to result in weaker teaching and pupil underachievement.

Management is derived from the root 'manage', a word we use in a variety of expressions that emphasise a successful outcome. Examples of how the word is used include:

- 'I managed to get it in on time.' That is, I succeeded in meeting the deadline

- 'She managed the final question.' That is, that she had sufficient knowledge to ensure success

- 'He managed to control the class.' That is, he had the ability to cope successfully in the situation.

The use of such expressions points to three different aspects of management that teachers need to take into account: (a) time management; (b) information management; and (c) human management. For example, in the expressions noted above, there are underlying assumptions about each of the three forms of management:

- That the person has taken responsibility to meet the deadline (time management)

- That the person needed to be sufficiently well informed to meet a requirement (information management)

- That the person coped with the challenges presented by a class of children (human management).

The significance of these three elements for teachers, who need to meet deadlines (such as finishing lessons on time), to be well informed (in particular, to have good subject knowledge) and cope with pupils (establishing and maintaining order) is considerable. A summary of the practical implications helps to underline these points.

1. *Time management.* Good time management establishes a framework for working, both within individual lessons and across a whole day. It allows for the quirks of classroom life, accommodates the unexpected and ensures that time is used appropriately. This does not mean that every moment is accounted for in the planning process or that pupils have to keep their 'noses to the grindstone' but rather that time is utilised purposefully and effectively. More information about time management can be found later in this chapter.

2. *Information management.* Good information management ensures that the teacher has a high level of subject knowledge and knows how to access additional sources as required. Teachers who are good at managing information will have the confidence to share ideas with pupils, show interest in their discoveries, monitor their understanding and encourage them to find out more by using their initiative.

3. *Human management.* This aspect involves finding ways of relating effectively to pupils and assistants, and engaging them in the teaching and learning process. Human management is facilitated by clarifying boundaries of behaviour for pupils, using stimulating teaching approaches and presenting ideas in a comprehensible form. Good human managers respect people's genuine concerns and make allowances for their failings. The learning environment

is characterised by a sense of wellbeing, mutual respect, high expectation and undisguised celebration of progress. A motto for such classroom situations might be 'all for one and one for all'.

Organisation and management are mutually dependent for successful teaching and learning. Someone who is a good organiser but poor manager promises much and delivers little. Someone who is a poor organiser but a good manager makes the most of the situation despite the low level of preparation. Someone who is both a good organiser and a good manager not only promise much in advance but make the fullest use of teaching opportunities for the benefit of every pupil.

Managing time effectively

We have seen that one characteristic of successful teachers is their ability to organise and manage their time effectively. The best teachers are normally skilful in making the best use of the available opportunities, and seem to achieve more than their colleagues and produce work of a higher standard. Brown and Ralph (1994) argue that although time itself cannot be managed, our *use* of it can. In other words, we manage the way that we manage our time. They suggest that a well ordered routine not only leads to higher standards of achievement but reduces stress levels. Brown and Ralph summarise the position as follows:

> Time is irreplaceable and has no substitute. You can't borrow or steal time or change it in any way; all you can do is to make the optimum use of the time you've got. (1994: 58)

Every teacher finds that, unless priorities are established, the hours slip past and essential things remain untouched while trivial issues or those that emerge unexpectedly take precedence. For example, imagine putting up a display during the break when the resources for the literacy session that followed were still not in place. Imagine chatting casually to a parent at the start of the day while the nursery nurses were waiting for you to discuss a particular child's needs. Imagine arriving late for the lesson because you had been doing some photocopying. Imagine spending the first 10 minutes of a lesson in sorting children into groups because you had not bothered to do it beforehand. Imagine arriving in the hall for a Movement session, only to discover that because you had been late that morning, you had left the music CD at home by mistake.

The above examples merely serve to confirm the principle that poor time management is detrimental to your work as a teacher, so it is essential to learn to 'think ahead' by deciding in advance what is *essential*, what is *necessary* and what is *non-essential*. You then decide what is *pressing* and what can wait. To avoid being overwhelmed it is useful to make a determined effort to categorise tasks under one of the following four headings:

1. NOT PRESSING and TRIVIAL

2. PRESSING but TRIVIAL

3. PRESSING and SIGNIFICANT

4. NOT PRESSING but SIGNIFICANT

It is not worth wasting time on things that are neither pressing nor significant, even if they interest you, and pressing tasks that are relatively unimportant should be dealt with as quickly as possible without trying to be a perfectionist. On the other hand, if something is pressing and significant it obviously has to be done as soon as possible. The fact that you have a hundred other things to do cannot be used as an excuse. You simply have to spend less time on other tasks and respond to the new priority. As a trainee teacher, lesson preparation will nearly always take prime position. Seek advice from your mentor if you are suddenly faced with an urgent task and feel overwhelmed. As much of a teacher's work is ongoing, use of a *planner* with interim targets is essential if you are to avoid last-minute panic.

In doing so, recognise that completing forms, filling-in lists and other mundane tasks often have a greater significance than you realise when you are training. Experienced colleagues will advise you about priorities and the categorisation listed above will help you to negotiate them. Papworth (2003) in his 'secrets of time' suggests that effective time management relies on four factors:

- Have an excellent reason
- Have an excellent plan
- Do the right thing
- Do the thing right.

Despite Papworth's useful guidance, there are always unexpected demands being made of teachers, and you need to ensure that you don't get overwhelmed through a lack of forward planning or allowing minor tasks to metamorphose into major ones because of time pressures. Obviously a job that is pressing and significant has to be tackled first; everything else can wait. However, if too many tasks fall into this category, it should act as a warning to you that you are failing to plan far enough in advance of the deadline. The majority of essential tasks should be non-urgent because you have left sufficient time for them to be dealt with. In the hurry and scurry of school life, there are occasions when unexpected events conspire to upset your carefully laid plans, but make it a rule not to be caught out too often. Effective management of time is a necessary skill for the smooth flow of lessons, administration and decision-making, but it also has more profound implications. Carlyle and Woods (2002) in their longitudinal study of stress among teachers in school found that poor time management was one of a number of factors that contributed to exhaustion and demoralisation. The intensification of work practices and increasing societal expectations of educators placed further time pressures on practitioners and exacerbated feelings of helplessness and being unable to cope. Similarly, Day *et al.* (2007) warn how work intensification 'leads to reduced time for relaxation and re-skilling, can cause chronic and persistent work overload [and] can reduce quality of service' (2007: 26). The message for all teachers that jumps out of the page is, quite simply, to ensure that they don't allow themselves to work so hard that their effectiveness is adversely affected. It is possible to *feel* that you are doing a good job because of the effort that you are making when in fact the belief is illusory.

A useful strategy to protect against unnecessary time stresses is to compile each evening a list of things that need to be done before school begins, during the lunch break and after school.

For example, whereas it is essential to have your resources marshalled in advance of the lesson, a telephone call about arrangements for an educational visit can only be made during break times. It is also important to balance the time it will take to (say) consult with a colleague with what may need to be organised for the lesson that follows. Quite simply, there may not be time to do both. Again, information may be needed from pupils at the start of the day about numbers who wish to participate in a particular event or you may have to transmit information about (say) changes in the timetable pattern to them, all of which absorbs precious moments. Similarly, if a parent has requested a brief informal discussion after school, the meeting needs to be made a priority over putting up a wall display or marking books. The balance of each day is likely to be different and unexpected events can disrupt the best-laid plans; nevertheless, the importance of looking and planning ahead is crucial to success. It is not only during lessons that you need to keep a close eye on the clock, but during every part of the day, until you act instinctively. Failure to manage your time means that events control you when you should be controlling the events.

Managing individuals, groups and the whole class

The successful management of lessons relies heavily on selecting the most suitable teaching strategy to accomplish the intended outcome. In the following section, we focus upon using teaching strategies with children in three different settings and evaluate the differing demands each makes upon the teacher's skill and expertise: one-to-one, in groups and with a whole class.

One-to-one

One-to-one opportunities exist in both the regular monitoring of progress during a lesson and in giving specific attention to a child's particular learning needs. Due to large class sizes, there are few chances to give one child exclusive attention for any length of time, but when you do so they are extremely worthwhile. A breakthrough in learning often takes place when a child has an adult's exclusive attention. There are at least four reasons for this acceleration in learning:

- The child can receive individual help without distraction
- The child can ask the teacher questions without publicly exposing his or her ignorance
- Work can be closely and accurately monitored
- A close relationship develops between teacher and child.

However, there are possible disadvantages if the individual attention is prolonged:

- The child may become over-dependent on adult help
- The child has less opportunity for collaboration with other children
- The child has little opportunity to reflect and develop solutions
- The child may miss other important teaching and learning opportunities from which classmates are benefiting.

One-to-one interaction is intensive and demanding, and can make surprisingly heavy demands upon the teacher or assistant. In addition, during regular teaching sessions, too much attention given to one child can lead to a suspicion of favouritism. Although it is often necessary to offer a struggling child extra support through coaching, the danger of teachers neglecting their responsibility to the rest of the class is always present. Younger and more timid children especially need to be helped to bridge the gap that exists between what they can do alone and what they can do with support. Shy children tend to participate less in class, hesitate to respond and often use shorter and less elaborate answers to adult's questions. The shy child's hesitation may have more to do with anxiety about being wrong than about lack of ability. If teachers have a TA, they may be able to manage priorities in such a way that one or other of them has the opportunity to spend additional time with the needy child. A large number of schools offer additional support for children who might benefit from extra tuition, though these tend to be related to those who have the potential to achieve a higher level in the national tests. Otherwise, space has to be found during assembly time, break-time, quiet reading sessions, shared class times and the like to give extra support. None of these options is ideal as they place an additional burden upon the teacher; nevertheless, certain one-to-one tasks are unavoidable and have to be accommodated somehow in the teaching programme, including:

- Hearing children read, though this process may be as part of small group work

- Conferencing (discussing the child's work in depth on a one-to-one basis)

- Discussing homework tasks, especially where the child has struggled or been lazy.

Even experienced practitioners find that hearing readers is particularly challenging and they use various means to cope with the problem of fitting them in during each week. Teachers of younger primary children utilise parents, TAs and odd occasions when the majority of the class are engaged in self-sustained play activities in order to hear readers. Teachers at Key Stage 2 find that although good readers enjoy reading to an adult, it becomes less and less useful as the children can read silently much more quickly than aloud, with the consequence that reading aloud may reduce their fluency. A balance has to be struck between hearing readers to monitor their grasp of concepts, pronunciation and intonation, and wasting valuable time working one-to-one with a child who is an independent reader and does not need to practise aloud. Many teachers, accepting that one-to-one engagement is unrealistic, utilise whole-class reading, group reading (where a number of children have the same book in front of them) or paired reading (where a more capable child assists a less capable one) as a means of coping with or enhancing the quality of reading. None of these methods are free from problems and despite the cost in time and effort, individual attention is sometimes the best option. Children who have severe problems with reading will normally receive targeted attention, though care must be taken that time spent on providing additional support does not deprive them of other learning opportunities or make them feel an oddity.

Conferencing normally takes place at least once each term and is a means of reviewing work and setting longer-term learning targets with (rather than for) the child. The teacher spends a few minutes exclusively with one child, discussing his or her work, considering the progress that has been made and, perhaps, selecting pieces of work for a Record of Achievement folder that will accompany the child through the school. These occasions need to be planned carefully and consideration has to be given to issues of privacy, confidentiality and the means of sustaining uninterrupted contact. Some schools have a policy of using a substitute teacher during the 'conferencing season' to supervise the rest of the class. Other situations are less straightforward and require the sort of imaginative strategies demanded for hearing readers. It is likely that experienced and trained TAs will also be available to undertake such a task. Some schools utilise a 'target review sheet' (TRS) to help children and teachers reflect upon the work that has taken place and what lies ahead. Typically, a TRS will contain such information as the following (child perspectives are shown in brackets):

- Name of child and the date of completion

- Past achievements (in child-speak: what I have achieved so far)

- Analysis of previous success (the reasons I have done well)

- Future plans (things I still need to persevere with to achieve)

- Analysis of struggles (reasons I have found things hard)

- Aspirations (new goals I set for myself)

- Strategies to achieve future success (how I can do better at my work)

- Celebrating success (things I can feel proud about).

The format can, of course, vary according to the age group of children and specific purpose for which the TRS is used. With young pupils it is helpful if each child shares with an adult, who writes down what is said and agreed. In many ways, the exact nature of the written evidence is less important than the conversation itself and the opportunity to reflect on individual progress. In practice, there are so many different things that could be written down that some selection is inevitable. If the child is 'driving' the agenda, then the adult has to accept that the priorities may differ from what might be expected. Encouraging children to establish their own short-term targets for learning on a more regular basis can be assimilated in to the warp and weave of regular teaching. Longer-term targets (half-termly, say) are, of course, more general in character and may be so broad that they hardly warrant special attention. Nevertheless, the principle of involving children in thinking about their learning and, to an extent, monitoring their progress is now embedded in varying degrees in the practice of nearly all schools. The ongoing assessment of individual children is addressed further in Chapter 7.

Activate your thinking!

Consider the truth of this principle: Groups can be taught but only individuals can learn.

Groups

We have already seen that the dividing of the class into groups is an important part of organising for learning. Division into groups is most often based upon the academic ability of the children for core areas (maths, science, English), friendship groups for creative activities (notably PE and art) and a mixture of friendship and ability for collaborative work in other non-core subjects. For instance, there might be three ability sets for maths, friendship groups for drama, and a mixture of children for project, thematic or topic work in the humanities (see Table 6.1).

In determining the pattern of group work, the demands made of teachers grow in proportion to the number and complexity of groups operating, so handling several groups engaged in similar tasks is easier to cope with than groups working in different areas. Dividing the class into groups must be considered alongside the challenging process of monitoring, recording of children's progress, and bringing the session to a satisfactory conclusion: the larger the number of groups, the more complex these processes become.

Many teachers are agreed that the importance attached to formal testing and national strategies for literacy and numeracy have resulted in less opportunity and time for spontaneity, thereby obliging them to become highly specific in their direction of group work. This specificity of learning objectives has sometimes resulted in less time for exploratory, enquiry-based learning.

As a general rule, teacher input is normally required before children can purposefully engage with tasks and open-ended problem-solving activities. Thus, explanation about the computer program system precedes pupils exploring its full potential; similarly, the creativity in drama emerges from a close study of the original example provided by the teacher or coach. In addition to direct teaching, teachers have a responsibility to provide the necessary structure and circumstances within which the children can subsequently explore ideas and investigate processes, a function sometimes referred to as 'scaffolding'. This procedure does not imply that children do not possess original ideas of their own; on the contrary, a well-structured approach to experiential teaching and learning will facilitate children's contributions by providing a knowledge base or equipping them with the necessary concepts or skills. The assumption is that children will find out many things for themselves and learn more thoroughly providing they are given appropriate knowledge, guidance and resources as a foundation on which to build their ideas and innovate. You create the secure learning environment and resources; the children explore the space.

As children work together they experience a range of emotions and challenges which have as much to do with learning to get along with one another as with solving problems or exploring concepts. Biott and Easen (1994) comment on the significance of friendship groups in particular:

TABLE 6.1 Group type by subject area

Subject area	Group type
CORE SUBJECTS	Based on academic ability
CREATIVE TASKS	Based on friendship patterns
PROJECT WORK	Mixed composition

Friendship groups offer opportunities for children to learn social competences in situations where they feel they can act upon shared understandings of how to be both cooperative and assertive. (1994: 65)

While there is always a danger of friends spending too much time talking about out-of-school affairs when they should be concentrating on the work in hand, the risks should be weighed against the advantages to be gained through close social interaction and mutual support in the pursuit of common aims (Street, 2004). See Figure 6.1, Social factors in collaboration and the section on learning through dialogue in Chapter 4.

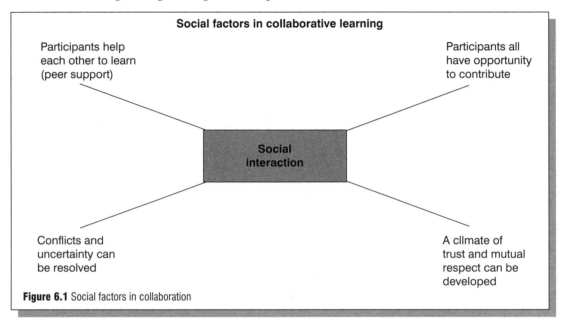

Figure 6.1 Social factors in collaboration

Teachers also have to decide whether group work is intended to enhance collaboration or used as an organisational tool. That is, whether children sit together in groups to achieve a common learning objective (collaboration) or whether they sit together and are generally co-operative while working to keep things orderly. The desirable aim to foster collaboration has to be approached wisely, for experience teaches us that although children sit together they do not necessarily work together. There are three reasons for this reluctance: (a) they have a deep-rooted concern that the interaction is a form of 'cheating'; (b) they lack the necessary skills to relate to others in a group; and (c) they prefer to work separately and resent being obliged to take account of other views and preferences. If you want foster collaboration, you need to explain the process, teach the skills and clarify the boundaries. It is important to stress that assisting a classmate is admirable and to insist that everyone has a responsibility to contribute, not merely the assertive pupils. Collaboration is typically associated with investigative, enquiry-based tasks whereas co-operation is associated with children working independently or in pairs but being mutually supportive while they do so. The relationship between these elements can be shown as follows:

Investigative task → collaborative grouping → joint outcome

Independent tasks → co-operative grouping → separate outcomes

Fisher (2005: 92) suggests that collaborative work gives children the opportunity to benefit in five ways: (1) learning from each other; (2) engaging in exploratory talk to deepen or broaden their understanding; (3) developing problem-solving skills and strategies; (4) learning to take turns, negotiate with others, see other points of view and argue for their own point of view; and (5) building relationships with a wider circle of people. He adds that it is to be expected that children working together will achieve more than working singly, but that for collaborative groups to be successful they have to be planned, monitored and supported. Collaborative tasks require the active involvement of every child to achieve the objective. Between them, pupils in a group need to offer a range of skills, principally the ability to speculate, predict, justify, evaluate and generalise (see Figure 6.2). However, even collaborative grouping can result in the exclusion of individual children from the process due to their insecurity, lack of experience as a group member or dominance by the strongest characters. Collaborative group work needs crew members; there is no room for passengers. The joint activities do not detract from the principle that each child has a personal responsibility for learning, as no one can learn for somebody else, but only help others to understand while reinforcing learning for themselves while doing so.

Activate your thinking!

Evaluate the way in which pupil groupings facilitate: (a) co-operative learning; and (b) collaborative learning. Reorganise the tables or seating arrangements to minimise unhelpful conversations and maximise learning.

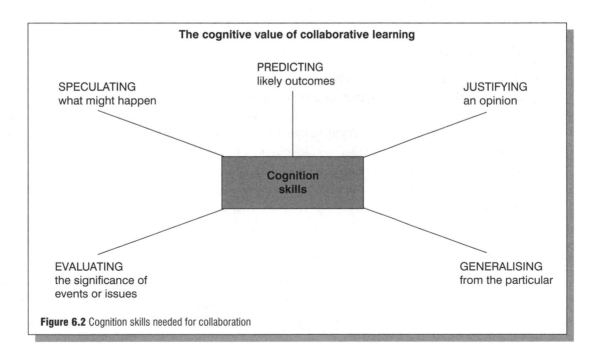

Figure 6.2 Cognition skills needed for collaboration

Close attention to a single group of children is very difficult when the whole class has to be managed. Inexperienced teachers may find themselves involved with one table of children, attempting to give them their full attention, while the remainder of the class drift along restlessly or form long queues in an endless wait for attention. You have to decide how much to permit random questions from the children at other tables and how much to insist that they persevere until you are available to assist them. Even with a TA to support you, overall class management is your responsibility. It is particularly important to recognise that control issues can soon emerge if the children are unclear about the work. Consequently, in designing tasks for groups, a number of important considerations have to be taken into account, especially with enquiry-based tasks (both practical or paper-based):

- Ensure that the children understand what is required of them, are offered some ownership of ideas and given opportunity to interpret the task

- Provide the resources and clarify the extent to which children can be autonomous in their use

- Make decisions in collaborative enterprises about who handles the resources; who takes responsibility for recording results; who reports back and how each child is to be involved

- Match task to ability and ensure that the activity lasts sufficiently long to allow children to become fully involved but not so long that they suffer from discouragement or task fatigue

- Keep noise levels suitably restrained (but avoid insisting on quiet or the whole purpose of the collaboration is stymied)

- Regulate the children's movement around the room.

Good practice

Don't be afraid to repeat activities as necessary to allow children to gain a fuller understanding of the principles and concepts involved.

Group work often makes heavy demands upon teachers who need to find the opportunity to review their classroom management, intervene where necessary and maintain a whole class perspective. The involvement of a TA is important as a means of spreading the responsibility for advising, monitoring progress and maintaining order. Opportunity for groups to share findings with the members of other groups helps to strengthen and extend learning.

Whole class

Dealing with the class as an undifferentiated whole requires additional and different skills from one-to-one and group work, and even from setting. Kutnick (1994) describes whole-class teaching as 'an efficient means of transmitting information to a large number of children simultaneously' but alerts teachers to the extent of their 'didactic control of knowledge and socialisation in the classroom' (1994: 25) as they do so. Whole-class teaching therefore demands a high level of skill and application to keep pupils attending and interested for the given period of time. There is some evidence that more frequent and regular use of whole class teaching might help to raise standards in literacy and numeracy though there are limitations attached to this approach, too, especially in the light of an emphasis on so-called individualised learning.

Many teachers find that their public performance in front of the whole class is central to successful teaching, and for inexperienced teachers it is essential that they undertake thorough practice of performance prior to the teaching session. There are few experienced teachers who can stand up and offer accurate information, demonstrate ideas and control a question-and-answer session without spending a lot of time in preparation, so you won't be any different. Some teachers write out a memory aid on a sheet of paper, which they carry around or on a large card that they pin to the back wall and glance at occasionally as a reminder of key points. As a trainee teacher, there is no shame in referring to your lesson plan, though the more that you can operate without having to stop and look down at your notes, the more in control of events you will look, feel and sound. The ideal is to have the lesson 'storyboard' clear in your mind and only refer to plans for the details (see Chapter 5).

Good practice

If you lack confidence in front of the whole class, practise on a tape recorder beforehand and write down the questions that you are going to use with them. Listen to the clarity with which you are expressing yourself. Give some thought to the types of responses your words and questions might elicit from the children and how you will use their answers to enhance learning.

Whole-class lesson procedure

Instructing is an essential element of whole-class management and if it is linked with the variety of organisation discussed earlier in this chapter, it is possible to represent this diagrammatically (see Figure 6.3).

In broad terms, Phase One links the lesson with previous work, reminding children of what went before and explaining the relevance of previous learning. In your haste to get the present lesson moving, it is essential not to overlook the importance of this phase. Without linking present knowledge to existing knowledge the process of learning becomes a detached exercise for children and is unlikely to produce the desired outcome. One way in which pupils' memories can be stirred and the new lesson introduced by the use of question and answer. The opening phase is followed by a second phase consisting of direct instruction, followed by a whole-class briefing phase. In the third phase, the class is divided up for activities using one of the options selected by the teacher. Most often, therefore, the introduction is followed by a question-and-answer phase for the purpose of task clarification or raising ideas which in turn leads to one of the teaching and learning types indicated in Figure 6.4, referring to teaching and learning types based on whole-class introduction.

Time spent on the introductory part of the lesson should be seen as an investment, ensuring that you do not have to repeat the same information and explanations to different children, still

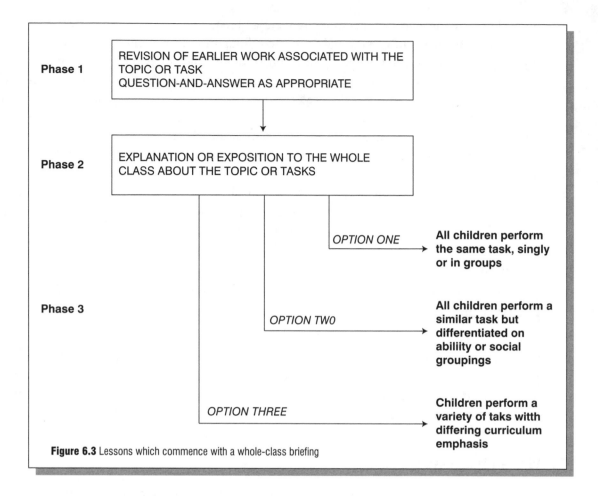

Figure 6.3 Lessons which commence with a whole-class briefing

confused about what to do. Although some children will require an adult's close direction during the lesson, the greater the independence they ultimately achieve, the greater the freedom for the teacher to monitor progress and to engage in one-to-one or group interactions.

Teaching the class together for part or all of a session is an opportunity for teachers to perfect their ability to articulate clearly, assert their authority and pace their delivery in a stimulating way that engages the children's interest. The teacher's personality is a critical factor in the prevailing mood: dictatorial or responsive, warm or aloof, humorous or sullen, encouraging or demoralising, harsh or sympathetic. There are issues of class control and discipline to consider but these should not detract from the value and sense of achievement that come about as a result of dealing with the class as a whole. Whatever the lesson structure adopted when working with the whole class, a number of issues are central to success:

- Children need to sense the teacher's enthusiasm for the subject matter in the way that the task is introduced, expectations are explained and questions are invited

- Children learn more if they are given some ownership of the task by being told the lesson purpose and why the tasks and activities are necessary to enhance learning

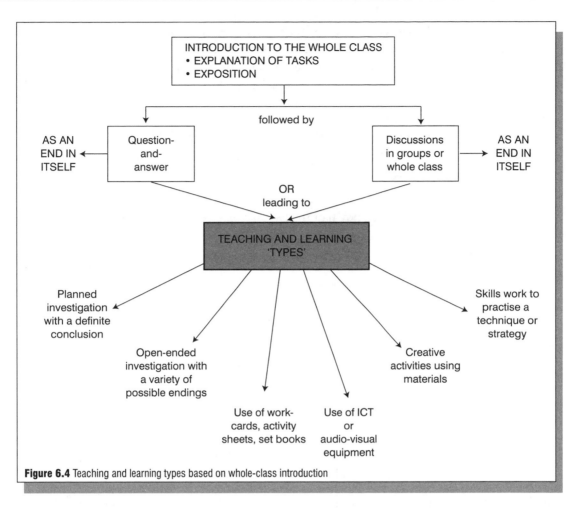

Figure 6.4 Teaching and learning types based on whole-class introduction

■ Children must be allowed some flexibility to interpret the work according to their understanding, ability and experience.

Varieties of whole-class management

Whole-class lessons are often associated with the formal structure of literacy or numeracy lessons; however there are a number of other variations in organising lessons, of which six approaches are seen in primary schools. For ease of reference, these forms of task management will be referred to as 'linear', 'circular', 'staged', 'spoked', 'single' and 'stepped'. Each approach has advantages and limitations.

Linear task management

This approach consists of a single whole-class introduction followed by tasks that gradually increase in difficulty as pupils work their way through them. All children attempt task one, some will proceed to task two, fewer still to task three and so on. The teacher monitors progress by checking that a particular task has been completed successfully before permitting children to proceed to further tasks (see Figure 6.5). Only the more able or those who work harder or faster are likely to reach the later tasks. Consequently, linear management lends itself to a straightforward form of differentiation in which a single task, progressively more difficult, is used as the lesson spine. There are a number of implications:

- The later tasks must be more challenging than the earlier ones
- There is a danger that the more able and less motivated children will linger unduly on the less demanding tasks
- If children work in mixed ability groups on a task organised within the linear approach, the more able may be slowed down or the less able may be carried along without gaining proper understanding.

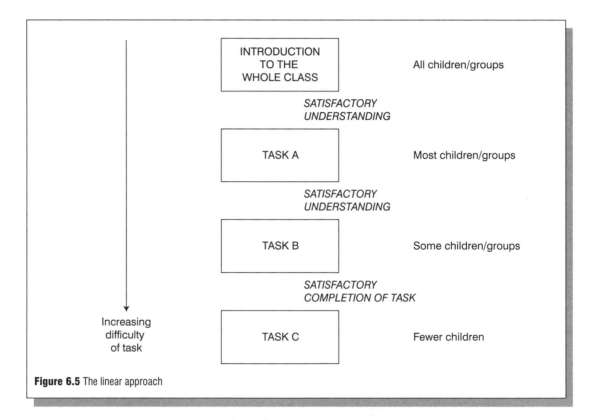

Figure 6.5 The linear approach

Another challenge for teachers is how best to pick up the threads of learning next time the class meets for that particular subject or topic as different groups and individuals will have reached a variety of end-points during the previous session, thus placing heavy demands on the quality and quantity of assessment required to ascertain progress. A good introduction in the next lesson becomes essential for the purpose of reviewing the preceding session, clarifying understanding and setting fresh targets based on progress to date. The same issue applies to the children who were, for whatever reason, absent in earlier sessions.

Linear task management is sometimes used with worksheets in subjects like mathematics in which sequential learning is more easily planned or in topic areas where there are a number of different experiences and skills to be covered sequentially over a period of time. However, there are a number of challenges for teachers adopting this approach:

- Some children view the process as a competition to see who can be furthest along the line and consequently tend to rush ahead
- Teachers can become overwhelmed by monitoring during the lesson, as they keep track of children completing different tasks at various times throughout a session
- Children may be demoralised as they compare themselves unfavourably with their more capable classmates
- Resources may become a problem if several groups reach the same task at the same time
- Subsequent lessons can deteriorate into 'Carry on with the work you left off last time' and lack any direct teacher input
- The gap between the less and more able becomes pronounced.

Teacher manuals usually stress the importance of maintaining a balance between teaching, task completion and review of work; nonetheless, it is possible for teachers to ignore the manual advice and lapse into a sedentary practice using the text as a surrogate teacher or make excessive use of activity sheets.

Activate your thinking!

All five groups in the class have completed task A, three have completed task B, one is partway through task C and one group is ready to begin the final task. How will you begin the next session?

Good practice

Make sure that you, and not the textbook, do most of the teaching.

Circular task management

A second type of task management, following a whole-class introduction, is to organise learning using a circular approach. It differs from the linear in two important respects:

- Whereas with a linear approach children can work individually, in pairs or in groups, the circular approach relies on group work
- Whereas children can proceed through the range of linear tasks at varying rates, the circular approach requires synchronised completion.

The circular approach can be used where groups are involved in working on different tasks from the same curriculum area (say, history) or tasks from different subject areas within a common theme (e.g. Festivals). It is more commonly used in science or other enquiry-based sessions. Following the introduction, each group is allocated a specific task and given a time limit within which to complete it. To ensure that groups finish at about the same time requires meticulous planning and is usually not possible within the confines of (say) a typical 55-minute session without undue haste. Teachers need to form groups so that they are of comparable size and ability, and provide sufficient resources so that each group engages with the full range of tasks. Managing resources is particularly important to the smooth flow of sessions. For instance, a lot of disruption can be caused if a group finds that some of the batteries are dead and the bulbs fade when it is their turn to try the circuit experiments. Circular tasks must be of broadly equivalent length if the system is to have any chance of operating successfully. However, despite organising the activities in such a way that they require the same time to complete, some tasks inevitably require longer than others. This fact sometimes leads to an excessive reliance on 'holding tasks' for some groups (if they finish early) and undue pressure on others to hurry and finish (if they take too long to complete).

Holding activities made available for quicker workers should, of course, serve a purpose. They are simply a device for ensuring that children who complete work earlier than expected are usefully and independently occupied before the time arrives for moving on to the next task. Groups that take longer than expected to finish will, of course, often receive additional help from the teacher or be encouraged to modify the original idea. However, it is inevitable that some slower workers will struggle to complete the task fully in the given time and accelerate in the final few minutes, with the inevitable adverse impact on quality.

Time is therefore an essential factor in the circular approach, so as to maximise resource usage and maintain control, all groups must change task simultaneously (see Figure 6.6). Once the allocated task has been completed by every group, tasks are reassigned. The children involved in the open-ended task may be given a creative task; the group practising skills may be given a planned investigation, and so on. The circular approach aims to give every child the opportunity to be involved in many different types of work over a given period, which invariably extends across several sessions or a day set aside for the purpose.

Many teachers discover that although the circular approach is challenging and difficult to organise, it is also motivating and stimulating when it works well. It is not advisable to attempt the circular approach unless you are convinced of its benefits over and above other approaches or in specialised situations with well established resources and prescribed activities (such as the whole class working on a series of designated science experiments). Trainee teachers should only attempt such complex organisation of learning with the co-operation of the host teacher and at least one other adult.

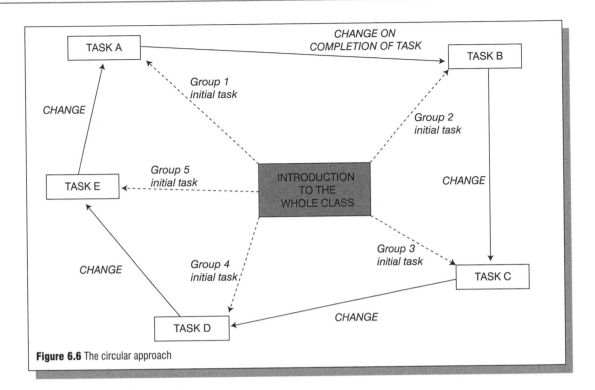

Figure 6.6 The circular approach

Staged task management

Another means of managing learning for the whole class is for children to be engaged in different subject activities (or at least different aspects of the same subject area) at the same time within the same general topic. This form of organisation is rarely used owing to the introduction of structured teaching in literacy and mathematics, but offers an exciting alternative for ambitious teachers. Groups are normally based on academic ability. One group may be working on an aspect of maths, another group employing written English, a third group on artwork. If the groups consist of children with varying academic ability, then within each of these broad groupings, differentiation takes place *within* a single group rather than across groups. For instance, group 1, consisting of 12 children, may be sub-divided into two ability sub-groups for their maths work; group 2 may be in two sub-groups working in pairs on different aspects of reported speech for English; group 3 may be working together but be found at different stages in developing a composite picture in art. Thus, the following organisation exists in the same classroom:

Maths group: two ability sub-groups.

English group: pairs work.

Art group: collaborative activities.

Sometimes the broad curriculum groupings are within the same topic or subject area. Thus, for the history unit about explorers, group 1 may be finding out about the lives of individual explorers, group 2 plotting their courses on outline maps and group 3 writing about the realities and hardships of travel:

Group 1:   Researching the lives of explorers (cross-curricular skill).

Group 2:   Plotting journeys on a map (geography).

Group 3:   Writing about the hazards of travel (literacy).

In the subject area of music, a class of Year 1 children may be developing ideas about performing and composing:

Group 1:   Creating simple musical patterns using resonators.

Group 2:   Experimenting with low notes using different shapes.

Group 3:   Making plucking instruments.

A high level of organisation and planning is necessary where a number of groups of this type are involved, not only to ensure that they are clear about the tasks but also to manage their progress. As a rule, a TA is needed to support learning and monitor progress.

Sometimes a modified version of the staged approach is used if a whole-class enterprise is intended, whereby the briefings all take place before any of the groups begin work on their specific activity. For instance, in a large space session where groups of children are working in the hall on a theme (different dance forms, say), the teacher may speak to the assembled class about each activity first so that when the groups are later drawn together, all the children are aware of what the others have been doing. If groups change activity at some point, the whole class briefing enables the transition to take place without further lengthy explanations. This approach demands that the children listen attentively throughout the teacher's explanations and understand the purpose of the final combined enterprise. This approach requires that your account of the tasks is precise, concise and clear, or when the children change activity they will need reminding of what they have to do. In this modified version of the staged task approach:

Stage 1:   All the children listen while each group is briefed.

Stage 2:   Separate groups are involved with their activities.

Stage 3:   Groups are brought together to discuss and share ideas.

Stage 4:   Activities are reassigned and the process continues.

The staged approach makes a number of demands:

■   Instructions must be explicit

■   Resources must be in place before the children are briefed

- The last group to be briefed should not be kept waiting too long

- The opening and closing minutes of a session are likely to be quite intensive.

In common with the linear and circular methods, the staged approach requires careful planning, attention to learning objectives and close monitoring of children's progress. Many teachers of younger children use a form of staged approach but only when there is a TA or another reliable adult available, as this makes this approach more manageable and less demanding on one adult. In common with the circular approach, if groups swap activities at some mid-point in the session, the staged approach requires that tasks are of similar duration, that there is account taken of more and less able children, and that early finishers are not left without a purposeful activity.

Spoked task management

Probably the most common form of managing learning is to organise children into ability groups and provide a separate but related task for each of the groups. The introductory phase of the lesson brings all the children together for the purpose of explaining and exploring the topic, raising issues, asking questions and so forth, before sending the children to their activities. The number of groups will vary according to the pupils' ability and experience. Group size is typically around eight to ten children. Thus, in a class of 30, three or four different and suitable tasks have to be provided for the session, usually in the same subject area. At the end of the task phase, children complete their work and, where relevant, reconvene as a whole class to evaluate the learning, share findings and clarify points.

The spoked approach places a heavy burden of preparation on teachers, as it requires them to design a variety of activities, monitor progress across the range of tasks and evaluate separate outcomes. It has the advantage of targeting learning and facilitating differentiation. Although you may want to concentrate on guiding one group in particular while the others work independently, in reality all children require some support and advice from an adult to make optimum progress. Without such help, pupils 'tread water' until assistance arrives, even if you encourage peer support. Ideally, the system works most effectively when the teacher is liberated from the constraints of monitoring a group and can move freely about the room, offering support as necessary.

Single task management

We have already been alerted to the importance of matching the demands of tasks with the ability and experience of the children. Poor matching leads to under-achievement (if the task is too easy) or frustration and low esteem (if the task is too hard). Alternative ways of differentiating are discussed more fully in the next two chapters.

The single task approach is used when every group is engaged on a similar task in a particular curriculum subject or area but the *teacher has different expectations* for each group, depending upon their ability and previous experience of the work. Following the introduction and explanation of the task, each group is allocated the same resources and given a similar length of time to complete the problem, investigation, experiment or research. As part of this process, children write up the work in different ways. For instance, a low ability group may use more diagrammatic representations than the extended written forms used by a more able group. Towards the end of the time, the groups report and compare findings. The teacher is able to draw the various strands together, acknowledge the diversity of outcomes and weave them into a comprehensible set of conclusions (see Figure 6.7). The single task approach offers a number of advantages:

- A single set of learning objectives can be established which apply to all pupils
- The process is relatively easily managed
- All the children are involved throughout the lesson
- Groups of children do not have to wait around to receive instructions before commencing their task
- The teacher is able to make reference during the lesson to the progress of other groups working on the same or similar task.

There are also disadvantages, as follows:

- The single task has to be carefully planned and appropriate to every child
- There have to be sufficient resources for everyone to do the same activity at the same time
- Group composition has to be appropriate to avoid children becoming marginalised (unless the children are working individually)
- The teacher requires a high level of skill to draw out all the learning points in a way that can be understood by all the children.

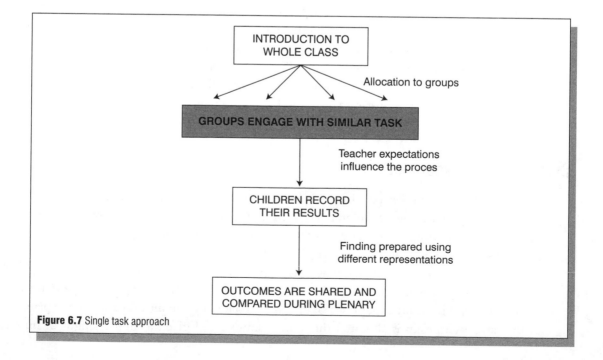

Figure 6.7 Single task approach

The single task approach, like any other, is better under certain circumstances than others. In particular, it has value in investigative, open-ended tasks in which collaboration and whole-class sharing are significant. However, the principle is also embodied in literacy and numeracy sessions in which lesson objectives are common for the whole class and the children tend to be allocated similar group tasks to reinforce and extend their learning. Owing to the fact that the single task approach is relatively easy to manage compared with others referred to above, it dominates much of formal primary education.

Stepped task management

The stepped approach is most commonly used in organising and managing large space lessons (PE, gymnastics, games and drama) and requires specific and detailed explanations/demonstrations by the teacher, followed by more independent activities undertaken by pupils. In the stepped approach, all the children are introduced to an elementary task, which they then explore or practise for a given length of time, followed by introductions to increasingly complex tasks, each of which the children engage with as individuals, pairs or small groups. Thus:

TASK ONE (elementary) leads on to

TASK TWO (more involved) leads on to

TASK THREE (most complex).

It is often the case that the teacher encourages children to try a form of the activity on their own initially, then (say) in pairs, then as a small group. Depending on the theme and subject, it may even be appropriate to bring the whole class together to demonstrate progress, asking each group to report in turn. The overall whole-class management for each task may look like this, beginning with the elementary task:

- The teacher introduces the activity and explains/demonstrates what the children have to do
- The children practise the skills individually or in pairs
- Individuals or pairs combine to create small groups, who work together
- Each group takes a turn to show what it has done to the rest of the class.

Once the teacher is happy that the first task is successfully completed, the class is brought together and the second task is explained or demonstrated. Depending on the nature of the task, children repeat the sequence noted above or work in small groups immediately. The pattern is repeated for the third task, and so on.

One advantage of the stepped approach is that it enables you to explore each step fully until you are satisfied with the product. If the children are not progressing as you hoped they would, you can spend longer on enhancing the skills or techniques required, rehearse the ideas and repeat the activities. If they make more rapid progress, it is relatively simple to move on to the next task with minimum delay or offer the children the opportunity to explore the theme to promote initiative and creativity. An example will help to illustrate the approach. Example: *The impact of heat on life forms (movement and drama)*:

1. Year 4 children have been working with their teacher on the cross–curricular topic of 'heat', noting the variations in climate in different countries and the effects of extreme temperatures on human habitation, fauna and flora. The teacher wants to employ some of the concepts in drama and, as it is November, decides to use the familiar phenomenon of melting ice (as the weather is getting colder) and burning branches (after Bonfire Night celebrations).

2. In the hall, the children warm up 'on the spot' individually by stretching and moving different parts of their bodies, to raise awareness of the movement possibilities and limitations, guided through each step by the teacher. Children with limited mobility are encouraged to contribute at their own level of physical comfort. The teacher concentrates the children's attention on fine motor skills and less obvious body movements, such as use of fingers, facial muscles, shoulders, hips and toes. Children are asked to 'melt down like a snowman in the heat' as a task that will enable them to practise the movements. Initially, the children just collapse in a heap, but the teacher uses a tambourine to sound out first 10, then 15, then 20 beats as the time frame for the action.

3. After a minute or two of individual effort, the teacher then asks the children to work in pairs and rehearse the 'melt down' while facing each other, again using a 20 beat time frame, trying to co–ordinate their actions so that they finish simultaneously (as puddles on the floor).

4. The teacher asks for volunteer pairs to demonstrate their actions to the rest of the class and selects three of them, commending and pointing out features of their actions.

5. While the children sit and listen, the teacher plays some music from the film *The Snowman* to remind them about the dance of the snowmen scene and the melting that happens to the main snowman character at the end of the film. (The TA is responsible for controlling the CD player so that the teacher can concentrate on class management.)

6. The children individually explore larger movements associated with the dancing, each child in a separate area of the hall to avoid accidentally hitting one another. The teacher moves about commenting on the actions, suggesting alternatives and offering advice.

7. The teacher asks the children to explore in pairs, then in double pairs to create a foursome.

8. The teacher asks for volunteers as before to demonstrate their ideas to the rest of the class.

9. Finally, the teacher asks the children to combine their dance and the 'melting down to a puddle' movements, first individually, then in pairs, then in groups, using the music as before.

10. Realising that there is insufficient time to explore the burning tree activity, the teacher decides to postpone it until the following lesson rather than force it into the small amount of remaining time. Consequently, the children stay in their prostrate positions while the teacher moves quietly around the room, sprinkling some 'magic dust' on them as a signal that they are to 'come alive' and sit up straight.

11. Before returning to the classroom, the teacher spends the last two minutes raising some of the issues from the movement and drama, praising their hard work, inviting comment about the impact of heat and cold on life forms, and linking the comments to work being undertaken for the topic.

12. The children return to the classroom as silently as snowmen.

During the next movement lesson, the teacher spends a short time reminding the children about the previous work, practising some of the movements associated with melting, and introducing the 'burning trees' theme. She stresses the importance of fire safety issues and the devastation that can occur when people are careless, but also explains that burning can destroy pests and reinvigorate growth. The lesson follows a similar pattern to the one described above but concentrates on the effects of wood as it turns to charcoal/ash 'from the tips of fingers (twigs) to the end of toes (roots)'. In the later stages of the lesson, the teacher puts the children into groups to explore fire spreading across a forest, tree by tree, until all the children have become piles of charred and smoking charcoal/ash. The process is then reversed as the 'new growth' eventually creates young saplings that bend and sway in the breeze as they reach for the sky. Finally, the process is brought together in an extended performance, with appropriate supporting music, from the first burning to the final resurrection.

There are many teaching skills employed in this example but for the purpose of this section on managing the whole class, it may be seen that although the basic format was straightforward, it required a lot of thought and preparation to ensure the best outcome. In practice, the lesson did not progress in the smooth way that the above description might portray (it seldom does) but the stepped principle of exploring thoroughly a relatively easily-controlled task before moving on to a slightly more complex one is clear to see.

Activate your thinking!

How would teaching be different if clocks and watches were not allowed in the classroom?

Managing the learning of young children

There are numerous basic and essential teaching strategies for the effective management of young children: clarity of explanation, use of repetition, employment of visual aids, setting a number of short-term goals, active use of TAs, and the development of reading skills. The Foundation Stage was the name given to the first part of the National Curriculum (NC), focusing on children from the age of three years to the end of reception year (aged five years), though use of the term 'foundation' in government documentation is a controversial one (Fisher 2002), implying as it does that early learning provides the necessary bedrock for further learning and is not valuable in its own right. The philosophy underpinning the foundation stage was that learning should be planned and structured with an emphasis on fun, relevant and relevant activities that motivate them. From 2008 the Birth To Three Matters Framework and the Foundation Stage merged to form a single Early Years Foundation Stage (EYFS) covering care, learning and development in all early years settings from birth to the August after their fifth birthday. In effect, the EYFS is separate from the NC, though there is meant to be a synergy between the two. The EYFS welfare requirements are intended to safeguard and promote children's welfare in four key areas:

- The suitability of the adults that look after them
- Safe and suitable premises, environment and equipment
- Every child receiving an enjoyable and challenging learning experience
- The records, policies and procedures for the safe and efficient management of settings and meeting the needs of the children.

The principle underpinning the EYFS is that every child is an individual with unique needs and entitled to have the opportunity to learn at his or her own pace and preference; consequently, all children should be able to work and play in a safe and secure environment to explore and investigate the world. Personal, social and emotional development involving children's emotional wellbeing, developing respect for others, and building social skills and a positive disposition to learn is viewed as being of central importance. It is important to remember that young children have already had a number of years of education in the care of parents and family, so continued partnership and discussion with parents is essential when formulating policy and practice (Feinstein at al. 2008) Implementing the EYFS curriculum requires thorough preparation but also sufficient flexibility to allow children to initiate some activities themselves. However, a vital aspect of the adult role is to intervene and assist children when they are frustrated with their inability to complete a task or are thwarted in their enthusiasm to perform an activity, where possible offering them alternative activities and the support to complete them successfully. As in all areas of school life, reinforcement of positive behaviour, acknowledgement of effort and praise for achievements should form an integral part of daily practice (see also Chapter 8). Regular monitoring and evaluation can take place using observation checklists, child development profiles and, crucially, regular meetings between groups of staff.

The EYFS guidance promotes the importance of outdoor opportunities as being crucial to a child's growth and development, and the expectation that, wherever possible, there should be access to an outdoor play area for every child. In practice, this facility may not be immediately accessible, but it is hoped that other arrangements can be safely made.

There is also a lot of emphasis on the use of systematic and discrete phonics, as the prime approach taught to all children to help them to recognise key words. The phonics teaching should use familiar and well-known stories, characters and situations to engage the children's interest; it should also be multi-sensory: visual, aural and tactile. All four interdependent strands of language: speaking, listening, reading and writing are significant but it is particularly important to foster speaking and listening skills, as these lay the foundation for later reading and writing and help to develop the full range of children's communication skills.

Good practice

The emphasis on speaking and listening in early years' education should be continued into Key Stages 1 and 2.

The early learning goals include six areas of learning and (non-statutory) 'stepping stones' of progress towards the goals. The guidance clarifies strategies by which teachers and other adults working in educational settings (not only schools) can help children to make optimum progress. The six areas of learning are organised as follows:

- Personal, social and emotional development

- Communication, language and literacy

- Mathematical development

- Knowledge and understanding of the world

- Physical development

- Creative development.

Curriculum guidance contains examples to help teachers and support staffs identify the progress that children are making and suggest how the practitioner can use this information to support and consolidate learning and help children to make progress. The guidance is intended to help practitioners ensure that each child is given the opportunity to make good progress towards the early learning goals and in a few cases to exceed them. The sections entitled 'communication, language and literacy' and 'mathematical development' cover the stage for children aged three to the end of the reception year. In theory, the early learning goals synchronise with the objectives in the frameworks for teaching literacy and mathematics throughout the reception year, facilitating ease of planning. Reception teachers have a choice about whether to cover daily literacy and mathematics lessons across the day or in a single unit of time. In order to ensure a smooth transition to the literacy hour and daily mathematics lesson during Year 1 (children aged five to six years), both are intended to be in place by the end of the reception year.

The curriculum guidance stresses that the six areas of learning are intended to help practitioners plan the learning environment, activities and experiences for children, and provide a framework for the early years' curriculum. However, this does not mean that young children's learning needs to be divided into separate and distinct areas, but rather that the document assists teachers in *organising* the curriculum. Thus, one 'unit' of experience may provide a child with opportunities to develop a number of competencies, skills and concepts across several areas of knowledge. For instance, creating a 'shop' area may help children to develop social skills, communicate their ideas to others, handle elementary money exchanges and use their experiences from shopping as a guide to appropriate behaviour when dealing with people. Thus, children can develop language, mathematical, physical, personal and social skills through a single activity, though it is far from easy for a teacher to monitor progress and development in each area for every child when using this 'mixed economy' approach. The EYFS uses practitioners' observational assessment of children's progress in everyday activities on an ongoing basis to inform how they can best plan further learning and development activities appropriate to the stage that each child has reached. Assessment results also allow the staff to provide parents and other professionals with more accurate information about the children's progress.

Thus, the early learning goals establish expectations that most children are likely to reach by the end of the stage, but are not intended to provide a rigid curriculum but rather provide a structure for planning to be built on for future learning. By the end of the stage, it is likely that some children will have exceeded the goals, whereas other children will be working towards some or all of them. Those who are still 'working towards' normally include younger children (summer born), those without much or any previous early years' experience (nursery education), those with special educational needs and those learning English as an additional language (EAL).

The guidance identifies 'stepping stones' of progress towards the early learning goals and so helps practitioners to understand and interpret what the goals mean for young children throughout this stage. The stepping stones identify the sorts of knowledge, skills, understanding and attitudes that children need if they are to 'achieve' these early learning goals by the end of the stage. Progression is shown by the use of yellow, then blue and then green bands that are not intended to be age-related goals, and the number of steps varies between and within areas of learning. In some cases the stepping stones relate to an individual aspect of an early learning goal, while in others a group of closely linked aspects are brought together.

Although the stepping stones are not age-related, it is anticipated that most three-year-old children will be better described by the steps described through the yellow band, while the green band will usually reflect the attainment of five-year-old children. Although the stepping stones tend to be presented in a hierarchical order, not all children conform to this sequence of learning. For example, some children will attain confidence in some of the later stepping stones but struggle with some of the earlier ones. Again, some stepping stones will be achieved quickly, whereas others will take a lot longer. However, if all goes well, as children move from one stone to another, they should take with them what they have already learned and continue to practise, refine and use their previous learning.

Once children reach the reception class, the teacher in charge has a major responsibility in monitoring and assessing children's competence and progress. Completion of the full schedule is onerous. Many versions of this 'baseline assessment' have been employed. The final observational assessment – or Early Years Foundation Stage profile – is recorded at the end of the reception year.

Primary Framework for literacy and mathematics

The changes contained in the renewed Primary Framework for literacy and mathematics (DfES 2006a) compared with the original national strategies for literacy and numeracy (now referred to as mathematics) are said to build upon research and evaluation undertaken since the introduction of the strategies at the end of the 1990s. The structured approaches to literacy and mathematics lessons as promoted in the original Frameworks continue to be recommended as a useful model for lesson planning, but the new guidance promotes greater flexibility. In particular, links between mathematics, literacy and other subjects are promoted, along with a range of different lesson structures and mini plenary sessions (as opposed to a single slot at the end of the lesson). The Framework is organised into 'strands' (12 for literacy and seven for mathematics) relating directly to the Early Learning Goals and to English and mathematics at Key Stage 1 and Key Stage 2. The construction of the frameworks around strands helps teachers to highlight some of the specific aspects of literacy and mathematics that some children find difficult to learn.

The slimmed-down learning objectives from Foundation Stage to Year 6 are presented in two ways: (a) by year or stage; and (b) learning objectives presented across the strands showing the specific progression in learning through each strand. Foundation Stage elements mirror the relevant sections in the EYFS (see earlier) and the objectives are referenced to the Early Learning Goals. Objectives also show Year 6 progression into Year 7. The main changes relevant to the primary phase of education include:

- Creating a clearer set of outcomes to support teachers and practitioners in planning for progression in literacy and mathematics

- Helping raise the attainment of all children, personalise learning and secure intervention for those children who need it

- Bringing an increased sense of drive and momentum to literacy and mathematics through the primary phase, involving some scaling up of expectations and a greater focus upon planning for progression

- Supporting schools and settings in implementing high-quality teaching of phonics and early reading

- Introducing a new, electronic format that allows for customised planning, teaching and assessment, linking to a wide range of teaching and learning resources.

Literacy Strategy

The original National Literacy Strategy (NLS) was launched in 1998 as part of the government's attempts to raise standards in schools. Basic literacy involves the ability to read and write, speak and listen; however, fuller details were included in the framework document and required that literate primary pupils should be able to:

- Read and write with confidence, fluency and understanding
- Use reading cues to monitor their reading and correct mistakes
- Use the phonic system to read accurately
- Use the spelling system to spell accurately
- Have fluent and legible handwriting
- Have interest in developing a fuller vocabulary
- Write using a range of genres
- Be familiar with narrative structures
- Use and understand non-fiction texts

- Plan, draft, revise and edit their own writing
- Use a suitable technical vocabulary to discuss their reading and writing
- Be interested in books and evaluate their content
- Develop powers of imagination, inventiveness and critical awareness through reading and writing.

The structure for teaching literacy focuses on reading and writing objectives linked to designated texts. Except in the case of reception age children, the objectives are sub-divided for each term. Key Stage 2 objectives assume that pupils will have attained a basic level of reading fluency, so that by Year 3 the majority of children should be able to:

- Read simple narrative and information texts with confidence
- Read aloud accurately and silently with understanding.

Consolidation and development of these skills are expected to take place over Years 3 and 4 and beyond. Three 'strands' to literacy work were identified for all children:

- Word level: emphasising phonics, spelling and vocabulary
- Sentence level: emphasising grammar and punctuation
- Text level: emphasising comprehension and composition.

Details about curriculum content were contained within the closely prescribed framework and teachers were only given a small amount of flexibility in the way they planned and taught literacy, as the structure of the literacy hour itself was tightly defined. The literacy hour framework was meant to introduce common practices and routines across the school in order that the quality of teaching and its impact upon pupils' achievements could be easily monitored. It did, however, require a considerable amount of effort on the part of teachers and pupils to maintain the approach from day to day. As such, it was essential to avoid any sense of 'here we go again' but rather to use the time as a stimulating opportunity to interact with children and establish a sound basis for other curriculum work.

The Primary National Strategy Framework (PNS) for literacy was introduced in 2006 and incorporates recommendations from a review about effective strategies for the teaching of reading, and replaced the NLS. The PNS places much stronger emphasis on drama and speaking and listening and on assessment for learning (AFL). Four seminal principles operated in developing the framework:

- To ensure the best teaching of early reading
- To build on high quality speaking and listening
- Systematic high quality phonics teaching as main first strategy
- The use of so-called synthetic phonics in building words; for example, c–a–t = cat.

In addition, children should experience a rich literacy experience, including drama, stories, speaking and listening around this. Communication skills, depend on children being competent in a number of key skills, together with having the confidence, opportunity, encouragement, support and disposition to use them. There is a greater focus upon teachers and practitioners using their assessment to personalise learning than in the NLS. The PNS framework for literacy has 12 strands, with learning objectives listed as follows:

1. Speaking
2. Listening and responding
3. Group discussion/interaction
4. Drama
5. Word recognition
6. Word structure and spelling
7. Understanding and interpreting texts
8. Engaging with and responding to texts
9. Creating and shaping texts
10. Text structure and organisation
11. Sentence structure and punctuation
12. Presentation.

Objectives from each strand are united within coherent units of work that may last three to five weeks. Through these units, speaking and listening, reading and writing are developed. The objectives are presented by year group from Foundation Year (reception) to Year 6. They are not split into terms as in the NLS. They are not under headings of word, sentence and text. Objectives are also presented by strand, e.g. strand 1 (speaking) contains objectives from Foundation to Year 6, so that a model of progression is included. Online resources on the PNS literacy site exemplify how to plan and include units for teachers to work from. The EYFS (see earlier) is intended to feed seamlessly into the PNS framework for literacy.

The *Searchlights* model of reading has been subsumed into *The simple view of reading* based on the idea that children need to develop word recognition and language comprehension skills. These are presented as two complementary processes. All the NLS documents that support planning and teaching (grammar for writing, etc.) are available via the site as links from planning units. Attention to children with EAL remains high and to the progress of boys in general. The introduction of more screen-based texts is evident through the objectives and there is an emphasis on creating cross-curricular links where possible, a practice not promoted in the original strategy.

Activate your thinking!

Towards the end of the group time the children are still engrossed in their work. What factors would you take account of in deciding whether to allow them additional time or move to the next phase of the lesson?

> ## Good practice
>
> Never assume that a so-called 'independent' group can be fully independent. Spend extra time explaining the task to avoid a situation in which the children are struggling to cope. At the same time, always introduce a straightforward open-ended element to engage their interest, should they conclude the main activity sooner than anticipated.

It is worth noting that Hardman, Smith and Wall (2003) noted that during literacy lessons, even teachers that used a strongly interactive style tended to focus on question and answer that required low cognition and asked only a small number of genuinely challenging questions that caused pupils to think hard. Teachers were also inclined to accept brief answers from children instead of probing what they had said and encouraging them to think more deeply. The teachers who were willing to dwell on a topic of interest for a little longer generally elicited more thoughtful and extensive responses. Teachers of younger children were especially prone to accepting superficial answers and opportunities for sustained and extended dialogue were rare. Westwood (2004) refers to the importance of 'metacognition' in promoting pupil thinking and addressing learning difficulties, which 'often involves inner verbal self-instruction and self-questioning – talking to one's self in order to focus, reflect, control or review' (2004: 29). Studies suggest that these objectives are not pursued with sufficient rigour by many teachers, and not only in literacy teaching. For further information about questioning, see the section devoted to this subject in Chapter 5 and Moyles *et al.* (2003).

Mathematics Strategy

The first National Numeracy Strategy (NNS) was implemented in September 1999 in an attempt to raise teachers' expectations and improve standards in mathematics. Numeracy was broadly defined as knowing about numbers and number operations and required an ability and inclination to solve numerical problems, including those involving money or measures. It also demanded that pupils became familiar with the ways in which numerical information is gathered by counting and measuring, and presented in the form of graphs, charts and tables.

Every teacher had to teach maths daily for between 45 minutes and an hour, and lessons incorporating the following elements:

- Regular oral and mental work
- Good quality questioning to the whole class
- A variety of whole–class teaching and group work
- Instruction, demonstration and explanation
- Formal and informal assessment of pupils' progress
- Identifying and correcting pupils' misconceptions.

The original strategy encouraged teaching approaches that gave more emphasis to oral and mental work before written methods were introduced. As calculation skills require that pupils must learn some things by heart, daily practice to reinforce their grasp of the facts was (and still is) seen essential, supported by the use of correct vocabulary and notation. Numeracy was to be used in subject areas outside the immediate maths lesson.

Effective teaching that involved using whole-class teaching was at the core of lessons, supposedly as a vehicle for pupils to respond to questions, ask their own questions, learn from one another and explain where they are unsure about mathematical concepts or techniques. Teachers had to be ready to listen closely to what children are saying and offer comment which helps them think 'beyond' the immediate problem and consider the way that maths influences real-life situations.

Group work had to be differentiated with respect to pupils' attainment, though teachers found that creating too many groups could be counter-productive as classroom management becomes difficult due to the spread of demands upon the teacher's time. Paired work is a helpful strategy, with activities such as number games where pupils can probe one another's thinking and interact purposefully. Individual work also has its place in teaching maths; again, too much individual work may lead to teachers spending too much time 'troubleshooting' when pupils were 'stuck' and insufficient time on teaching strategies for solving problems.

The renewed Framework (introduced in 2006) is different from the 1999 Framework by referring specifically to 'mathematics' and not to the unsatisfactory overarching term 'numeracy', and in three other ways:

- It is an electronic version linked to a range of teaching and learning resources, intended to help teachers to plan, teach and assess more easily with regard to their own pupils
- Only seven strands of learning in mathematics are identified to give a broad overview of the mathematics curriculum in the primary phase.
- Objectives have been slimmed down to give sharpen attention on the important aspects of mathematics that need to be taught.

The seven strands are as follows:

1. Using and applying mathematics.
2. Counting and understanding number.
3. Knowing and using number facts.
4. Calculating.
5. Understanding shape.
6. Measuring.
7. Handling data.

Of particular interest in the new Framework is the place of problem-solving, reasoning and the newly defined numeracy, which is located within processes such as seeking patterns, making connections, recognising relationships, working with numbers, shapes, space and measures, and counting, sorting and matching. Children are to be encouraged to use their knowledge and skills in these areas to solve problems, generate new questions and make connections across other areas.

Furthermore, for younger pupils in particular, mathematical understanding should be developed and enhanced through teaching strategies that incorporate stories, songs, games and imaginative play. In practice, this diversity of options allows you to be creative in your approach and not to feel locked into narrowly focused and formal teaching, but to be more adventurous in allowing children to explore ways in which mathematics has relevance to many different contexts. Thus, you can promote an understanding of maths indoors (such as wallpaper patterns) and outdoors (such as product use); in everyday activities (such as volume of water used for different activities) and financial transactions (such as monthly payments).

Finally, parents are important in promoting positive attitudes towards maths and supporting their children's learning. As such, regular homework and close liaison between parents and schools is essential to consolidate learning in school. Nevertheless, you have to bear in mind that some parents have a negative attitude to maths and others do not possess more than a basic level of understanding of the subject. Children from weak academic backgrounds may be further disadvantaged if parents respond negatively to a school's request for their help. Similarly, account needs to be taken of children with SEN and English as an additional language in determining the most effective teaching approaches and extended learning requirements. In addition, you cannot assume that every child has access to a computer at home.

Activate your thinking!

How much mental agility do the children require to respond to your questions? How much opportunity do you give them to ponder problems at length?

The use of ICT

We have, over recent years, seen a significant change in the status of Information and Communications Technology (ICT) in primary schools, leading to a situation in which it is now considered to be one of the 'core' areas of the curriculum, alongside English, mathematics and science. The Government has also shown itself to be committed to supporting the development of ICT in education. It is true to say that ICT has permeated every area of society and schools have received large investments to provide computers and software to support learning, with concomitant training of teacher and TAs. It is not unusual to find a TA taking considerable responsibility for the management of a school's computer suite and even carrying out minor maintenance.

The Standards for the award of qualified teacher status state that ICT has an important role to play in most aspects of teachers' work in schools: in the act of teaching itself and also promoting learning for individuals, small groups and whole classes. ICT has become increasingly influential in the processes of planning, assessment, evaluation, administration and management. ICT has become especially significant in compiling statistics of children's test performances and producing detailed facts for parents about their children's progress. Two of the Q-Standards for Qualified Teacher Status (QTS) in England and Wales state that trainee teachers should: (a) know how to use skills in literacy, numeracy and ICT to support their teaching and wider professional activities (Q17); and (b) be able to design opportunities for learners to develop their literacy, numeracy and ICT skills (Q23). Not only should you be able to use ICT in your teaching but also to complete pupils' records of progress, prepare resources for pupils and reduce the time you spend on administrative tasks.

In supporting good practice in teaching, ICT can, for example, enable a teacher to respond to a pupil's piece of writing at different stages of the process due to the fact that the text can be saved and progressively modified over a period of time. Within the context of mathematics, a child can be encouraged to develop logical thinking from an activity that involves instructing a programmable robot to follow a particular path, and then to modify these instructions in the light of the robot's movement.

A further point is associated with teachers' ability to use ICT in a way that supports their own professional role. Commonly, teachers download the latest guidance for aspects of teaching such as 'support for early years' from a website, or using a word-processor to prepare a standardised template for lesson planning, and to find the desired teaching post. However, it is worth noting the warning from Allen *at al*. (2007) who suggest that, 'Even in areas where there is rich provision of equipment and/or Internet connections, it is possible to find evidence that the computer is not always fully or usefully integrated into the curriculum' (2007: 14). Indeed, you may discover that your knowledge and expertise exceeds that of the host teacher.

Activate your thinking!

If you are a younger trainee, it is more than likely that you will be more comfortable with the use of ICT than the majority of older teachers in the school.

The National Curriculum for ICT

The statutory statement on the use of information and communication technology across the curriculum within the NC states that pupils should be given opportunities to apply and develop their ICT capability through the use of ICT tools to support their learning in all subjects with the exception of physical education throughout Key Stages 1 and 2. Pupils should be able to use ICT tools appropriately to help them to find, explore, analyse, exchange and present information clearly and creatively after considered thought and selection. You can teach pupils how to employ ICT for rapid access to ideas and experiences from a wide range of people, communities and cultures. For instance, you may be able to 'twin' with a school in another part of the world to exchange ideas and learn about one another's cultures. Increased capability in the use of ICT promotes initiative and independent learning, with pupils being sufficiently knowledgeable to make informed judgements about when and where to use technology to best effect. In other words, random use of ICT, however skilful, is unsatisfactory; discrimination over its use is as important as the technical abilities that children employ.

Organisation of ICT resources

Schools will organise their ICT resources in different ways, according to the number of computers for use and the space that is available to house them. Decisions about organisation may also be influenced by a teacher's preferences with regard to teaching and learning style. Many schools will have at least one computer suite that is used to accommodate large groups or even a whole class of children such that they can all work at the computers at the same time. The suite will normally consist of a room that can either be booked in advance by the teacher or will be timetabled for each class throughout the week. Most teachers like to have one or more computers in their own classroom, enabling the children to make use of it throughout the day to access the Internet or print out completed work.

Over recent years nearly all schools have purchased *interactive whiteboards* (IWB) for use in the classroom and is not uncommon for an IWB to be seen in every room. These resources have proved to be particularly effective in whole-class teaching situations; for example, as part of a literacy or numeracy lesson. Another way that schools have chosen to deploy their ICT resources is by setting up clusters of computers in, for example, the library or other open-access areas around the building so that groups can work with (say) a TA to explore or revise an area of learning. A much more flexible solution to the problem of providing access to ICT for the pupils is to employ portable computers that can be moved to wherever the children happen to be working, which may be outside the classroom (or even outside the school). However, cost constraints and concerns about damage to the machines generally restrict such ambition. A few schools have created electronic links between school and home to facilitate (for instance) homework submission.

Management of self

Enthusiasm in teaching is important and can sometimes compensate for other shortcomings. However, as noted in Chapter 2, even the greatest enthusiasm fades in the fierce glare of regular classroom commitments and other school responsibilities, which can exhaust even the fittest teacher. All too easily, the early gush of commitment to the job can be replaced by the heaviness of fatigue, so it is important to keep things in perspective and take note of the fact that:

- Teachers are only one of the children's educators
- Children suffer if teachers work so hard that they become exhausted
- Every teacher has poor lessons from time to time
- Mistakes are inevitable and should be viewed constructively rather than as a cause for despair.

Teaching is both exhilarating and tiring. Exhilarating because of the engagement in an exciting and stimulating process; tiring because of the constant expenditure of effort to ensure that the children are learning and on-task. The personal satisfaction gained as a result of a good lesson can keep a teacher fresh and in good spirits long after it is finished. Tiredness, on the other hand, can lead to listlessness and a distorted sense of priorities. Minor problems expand and fill the horizon. A tutor's constructive advice feels like a major reprimand. A lively group of children comes across as an untamed rabble.

In addition, sensible pacing of your efforts throughout each lesson and pausing from time to time to enable body and mind to relax are essential for combating the danger of exhaustion, which tends to creep up on you unawares. However, it is possible to retain a relaxed yet purposeful approach during lessons if you:

(a) Feel in control of the situation.

(b) Provide appropriate learning opportunities for the children so that they are happily occupied.

(c) Do not attempt to achieve too much in a single lesson.

(d) Ensure that the children work as hard as you.

The third point is often overlooked. Inexperienced teachers tend to squeeze as much as they can into a session in the mistaken belief that it somehow demonstrates their commitment and determination to promote learning. In fact, when you have a class of your own you will soon discover that although you achieve curriculum coverage, there is little deep learning involved.

If every lesson is spent hauling the class along, like a mule pulling a cart through a swamp, then it is little wonder that teachers tire quickly. If you flit from one child to another in an effort to respond to everyone's questions, behaviour and demands, you will soon feel exhausted and dispirited. If you spend most of the lesson on direct teaching, leaving yourself little time to recover between sessions, your energy level will drop rapidly. Good teachers do not exhibit manic behaviour but pace themselves in such a way that over the weeks and months of the term they can maintain the consistency necessary for effectiveness. This stable state is not easily attained and you must make sure that you don't confuse thoroughness with saturation. Teachers should not, therefore:

■ Spend too much time talking during a session

■ Rush around doing things for the children that they can do for themselves

■ Feel guilty that they are not 'actively on task' for every moment of a session.

Teachers should make sure, however, that they:

■ Leave opportunity for moving around the class to monitor and praise the children in their work

■ Encourage children to be independent and try to resolve their own problems, with peer support as appropriate

■ Step back from the flurry of activity and review the success of their classroom management and calmly assess pupil progress.

Activate your thinking!

It is generally agreed that an on-task work rate of about 75 per cent is reasonable. How do the children and you compare with this figure? How do you know?

Good practice

O'Flynn and Kennedy (2003: 140–5) suggest a number of strategies for surviving in the job, including: (a) build regular physical activity into your routine; (b) plan some quiet relaxation time each day; (c) seek support and help others who need it; (d) conserve energy during the day be remaining calm and pacing yourself; and (e) aim for good enough, not perfect.

Management of self can be compared to an aeroplane pilot who sometimes has to grip the controls and steer the plane in a predetermined flightpath, sometimes has to manoeuvre and change course if the conditions demand it and sometimes puts the plane on automatic pilot to chat with crew and passengers. For the pilot, different amounts of concentration are required at different stages of the journey. The take-off and landing present the most hazardous and stressful stages, whereas the main part of the journey allows for moments of relaxation and flexibility. There would be a sharp decrease in air travel if passengers believed that the pilot was continuously under pressure. Similarly, those teachers who never use the 'auto-pilot' during a session have either failed to plan their lessons appropriately or fear that if they take their hands off the controls for two minutes the enterprise will crash.

Unless teachers find some time for stepping back and gaining an overall impression of the children's progress and the direction of the lesson, they will be swept along from start to finish and feel more tired than the children by the end of it. Unfortunately, some teachers feel guilty about separating themselves from the main action for a time, either because they think that they will be failing in their job or because they fear disruptive behaviour. These emotions are particularly acute among trainees, who also fear being 'marked down' by a tutor if they draw breath for an instant. These concerns are understandable but unnecessary since:

- The well-organised lesson does not require constant teacher intervention and interaction with pupils. It should be possible to stand still for a few moments and scan the class without the lesson falling apart

- Stepping back actually enhances the teacher's ability to monitor and assess the situation and take appropriate action or make suitable responses.

Activate your thinking!

Who is most tired at the end of the session, you or the children?

Good practice

Find a way to isolate yourself from the class for a minute or two each lesson whenever possible by standing at a particular spot in the room with your arms folded to observe what is happening without being disturbed. If you let the children know what you are doing they will soon stop bothering you because they know this is your 'time-out'.

Case study

A group of six Year 2 children, mixed ability and academically weak, were working with a trainee teacher, Mia, in an art area adjacent to the main classroom. The area had two tables, a sink, a workbench and various science and technology resources. Mia planned to introduce the lesson by reference to previous work and explain what the children were to do. She was going to instruct them to pour lukewarm water into glass bottles and wrap them in different materials (secured with elastic bands) to insulate them. The children's task would then be to measure the temperature immediately and then after a ten-minute interval. Mia hoped that in doing so they would come to realise that the temperature loss was different depending on the material used and thereby reinforce the concept of insulation.

During the 10-minute 'cooling time' interval, Mia decided to engage the children in a series of questions and answers so that they would not become restless. After that time she would let them measure the water temperature a second time, feel the outside of the bottle and make statements about the insulation properties of the materials. Finally, she thought that it would be a good idea for the children to share their experiences in a plenary, in which she would record their answers on a large sheet of paper under three main headings: *What we did/ What happened/What this means.*

The problems

The lesson idea was sound and the practical work had the potential to take learning forward and engage the children's enthusiastic participation. However, by the end of the session Mia was weary, frustrated and a bit depressed about the children's fractious behaviour and way the lesson had deteriorated. The reasons for this disappointing outcome can be explained as follows.

First, Mia did not clarify the significance of the current work for the children or explain what she hoped they would learn. Consequently, it seemed to the children as if they were being taken on a 'mystery tour' rather than having a reasonably clear idea about their ultimate destination. Second, there were a variety of organisational and management problems that Mia had failed to foresee:

- The bottles were made of glass and potentially hazardous
- Water spilt over the table and soaked some of the photocopied sheets

- The scissors were not sharp enough to cut the material properly, which meant that the children became reliant on adult help and the process was slowed
- The thermometers were too closely calibrated and difficult for children to read
- Children held the thermometers in the water so that they touched the bottom of the bottle, thereby giving a false reading
- The slowness of the wrapping meant that considerable temperature losses occurred before the insulation material could be placed around the bottle
- Children fiddled with the bottles and fabrics during the question-and-answer time, annoying the trainee and souring the atmosphere
- The process of writing down children's responses onto the sheet of paper was ponderous for the teacher and difficult for them to read due to her hurried scrawl

Most worryingly, Mia had not grasped the basic scientific principle for herself. When the children felt the warmth coming through to the outside of the bottles, they ignored the data from the temperature measurements (though in fact they were generally inaccurate) and assumed that the warmest bottle was the best insulated when, in fact, it was the other way around. Far from explaining the true situation, Mia brightly confirmed their comments and commended them for getting things correct.

Activate your thinking!

How could some or all of these problems have been avoided? See below.

Possible lesson modifications

As well as taking a few moments to tell the children why they were about to perform the experiment and giving them opportunities to ask questions, clarify their concerns, chat to a friend or offer suggestions, Mia could have taken a number of simple steps to ensure that the organisation and management of the lesson was more effective. Thus:

- Use plastic bottles instead of glass
- Use funnels for pouring the water
- Pre-cut the material
- Use larger calibration thermometers
- Train the children to hold the thermometers correctly before commencing the practical work
- Place bottles out of reach on the shelf while the question-and-answer session takes place
- Give more time to explaining the insulation concept

- Supply children with activity sheets with boxes to tick or colour as a means of self-recording.

Comment

As a lot of time was spent coping with practicalities, not enough time was left to give a sufficiently rigorous explanation about the key concepts. The lesson was highly teacher-directed, which meant that the children did not have the opportunity to explore ideas or modify the proceedings. A more successful outcome could have been gained by thinking more carefully in advance about the organisational implications. In the prevailing circumstances, there was little sense of enthusiasm among the children.

Further reading

Allen, J., Potter, J., Sharp, J. and Turvey, K. (2007) *Primary ICT: Knowledge, Understanding and Practice*, Exeter: Learning Matters.
Written to familiarise trainees and newly qualified teachers with ICT and its use in the primary classroom.

Barber, D., Cooper, L. and Meeson, G. (2007) *Learning and Teaching with Interactive Whiteboards: Primary and Early Years*, Exeter: Learning Matters.
Takes a thematic approach, examining key issues required to gain greatest benefit from this technology.

Casey, T. (2005) *Inclusive Play*, London: Paul Chapman.
Contains numerous practical suggestions and insights, as the title suggests.

Drake, J. (2003) *Organising Play in the Early Years*, London: David Fulton.
Full of interesting ideas and activities that provide plenty of useful material for teachers of younger children.

Joliffe, W. (2007) *Cooperative Learning in the Classroom*, London: Sage.
Promotes structuring lesson activities to encourage pupils to work collaboratively in pairs or small groups to support each other's learning.

Packard, N. and Higgins, S. (2007) *The Really Useful ICT Book*, London: Routledge.
Helps teachers and assistants understand how and why ICT can enhance their teaching and open up learning opportunities for pupils.

Prendiville, F. and Toye, N. (2007) *Speaking and Listening through Drama*, London: Sage.
For teachers who want to use drama to promote speaking and listening for pupils, including children with learning difficulties.

Assessment, Recording and Reporting

Introduction

In this chapter we explore the many facets of the assessment process, ways in which information about children's academic, physical and social progress can be recorded, and some techniques for reporting to parents and colleagues. The balance of the chapter deals with an exploration of assessment for learning (AFL, formative assessment) and assessment of learning (AOL, summative assessment), the importance of monitoring and intervention, and the factors influencing a teacher's judgements about a child's attainment.

ASSESSMENT

Forms of assessment

The close relationship between effective planning, monitoring of progress and assessment that informs further planning has been a theme throughout this book. The importance of clarifying learning objectives and appropriately differentiating work to take account of children of varying abilities has been placed firmly at the heart of the teaching and learning process though, as we have often noted, it is important to avoid making pupil learning intentions so rigid that spontaneous opportunities are neglected. In particular, any assessment of children's progress has to be considered within the teaching programme as a whole, for pupil progress is not only an indicator of children's ability, but of the appropriateness of the curriculum provision and the skill of the teacher to motivate and inspire. Assessment should not be viewed in isolation but as part of a broader picture that is built up over time by teachers' evaluation of pupils' progress and, where appropriate, results from formal tests. The teacher's role in the process is crucial as children are observed daily and a picture of their understanding and attainment is acquired through regular verbal and social interaction in the classroom setting. As Stierer *et al.* (1993) rightly comment:

> ... the assessment of young children can only be valid and authentic when it is achieved through the gradual building up of a picture of the child based upon evidence collected over time in a range of everyday contexts. (1993: 9)

Lloyd and Beard (1995) argue that assessment opportunities exist whenever children are working alone, in a group, on problem-solving activities, in fantasy play and in the playground, as well as in the structured classroom environment. Drummond (2003) similarly argues that assessment involves far more than pragmatic procedural conformity or a means of social control. Rather, assessment makes 'moral and philosophical demands on our thinking ... The practice of effective assessment requires a thorough understanding and acceptance of the concept of rights, responsibility and power, lying at the heart of our work as teachers' (2003: 11). Drummond offers numerous examples from classroom practice to unravel the complexity of children's learning. She insists that whatever the external requirements of product-focused assessment, teachers must be aware of the sense of personal failure that assessments can engender. Drummond suggests that all educators are alert to three fundamental questions in respect of learning: (1) What is there to see? (2) How best can we understand what we see? (3) How can we put our understanding to good use? However, as explored in Chapter 4, it is often a challenge for teachers to know what children know. Indeed, the notion that a teacher can look into the head of each and every child to ascertain precisely what the child understands about every aspect of every subject is clearly impossible. And even if it *were* possible to do so, devising a programme of work and teaching approach to fully respond to all the vagaries of children's knowledge and understanding would make equally impossible demands of practitioners. In reality, assessment helps teachers to understand better where children are placed with regard to key concepts and the acquisition of facts. It is only the children who can make sense of things and establish meaning for themselves. Assessment, therefore, is a process to assist teachers in facilitating learning but not a guarantee of it.

Assessment takes many different forms, some of which are carried out formally in response to specific criteria and others that are rooted in regular classroom interactions. However, with regard to assessment criteria, it is important to focus on concepts and skills, and not on superficial knowledge. For instance, a design and technology experiment that involves children creating a wheeled vehicle to ascertain (say) factors influencing movement down a slope, assessment criteria should relate to the conceptual principles underpinning the lesson rather than just the ability to handle materials. Thus, criteria might include: (a) understanding that there is a causal relationship between incline and speed; (b) the ability to make comparisons between the performances of varied types of moving object, and so forth. The criteria that focus on learning are different in kind, and more important, than those of a functional nature, such as being able to construct a moving object or use materials appropriately. Assessment has a number of implications for teaching, as follows.

All assessment should help teachers to plan more effectively

Assessment is of little value in its own right unless teachers use the results to modify their practice, teaching approach and curriculum content. The collation of formal test results is an important element of publicly demonstrating pupil progress but is an end result and not the core of a teacher's work. The quality of children's learning, their ability to co-operate and collaborate, and the continuity of experience all contribute to the evidence upon which teachers can base amendments to the teaching programme.

Assessments can have important consequences for a child's future

If assessments are used as a basis for decisions about pupil competence, allocation to groups and (when they transfer to secondary education) future school placements, there needs to be confirmatory evidence which can be used for verification. Some schools maintain records that consist of photocopied samples of children's work taken (say) once per term to illustrate the sort of progress that they are making over time. However, results in national tests (so-called SATs) and end-of-year tests have become increasingly significant.

Assessments have implications for the school and its staff

The results of national assessments are used as a measure of a school's effectiveness and have funding, as well as professional implications. A lot of time is spent by teachers of Year 2 and Year 6 children (in particular) in preparing them for the end-of-key-stage tests. The results of the Key Stage 2 tests are collated and published. League tables of school performance have now become an annual event, and the figures are pored over by parents and politicians.

For all teachers, assessment involves a great deal of informal data gathered throughout the day as pupils work with set tasks. This informal assessment is carried out by listening to what children say, watching the mistakes they make, reflecting on the reasons for errors and misconceptions and asking questions to clarify the extent of their understanding. Interestingly, in their study of effective primary teaching Gipps *et al.* (1999) found that 'Over half the teachers explained that they used listening as an assessment technique' (1999:81). Similarly, Broadhead (2006) emphasises the importance of careful observation, interaction and reflection about the work and progress of younger children in particular. In doing so, teachers have to recognise that children's mistakes can be due to misunderstanding about what is required rather than the inability to grasp the concept. A poorly produced piece of work may say more about motivation, misunderstanding or uncertainty about the task than a lack of conceptual understanding.

Teachers often find it helpful to use *elicitation* techniques to gain a clearer picture about the things that children know, understand and have experienced. In addition to information gleaned through discussion and question-and-answer, three elicitation methods are helpful:

1. Divide the children into pairs or small groups with a blank sheet of paper and ask them to write down as many words associated with the topic that they can think of. Groups of younger children require direct adult assistance with the task.

2. As in point 1 above but give the children a number of key words or phrases (five, say) to use as starting points for a 'bike wheel' diagram, with spokes from the centre and other associated words written at the end of each spoke.

3. As in point 2 above but incorporating pictures, diagrams and other visual representations.

Following this opportunity to record their ideas, the information on the sheets can be shared with the rest of the class and, perhaps, placed around the room on temporary display. Discussion with pupils about the content of the sheets will not only assist in clarifying children's familiarity with the curriculum area but also, crucially, the depth of understanding they possess.

Assessment based on the Early Years Foundation Stage (EYFS) curriculum helps teachers to develop a richer and more diverse perspective on the attributes that children should be encouraged to develop, using the following 10 headings:

1. Personal, social and emotional wellbeing of children.
2. Attitude and disposition to learning.
3. Social skills.
4. Attention skills and persistence.
5. Language and communication skills.
6. Reading and writing skills.
7. Mathematical ability.
8. Knowledge and understanding of the world.
9. Physical development.
10. Creative development.

The *Foundation Stage Profile* is a way of summing up a child's progress and learning across the six areas of learning at the end of the Foundation Stage (see also Chapter 6). Thus: Personal, social and emotional development; Communication, language and literacy; Mathematical development; Knowledge and understanding of the world; Physical development; Creative development.

The Foundation Stage Profile is made up of 13 scales based on the early learning goals and stepping stones set out in curriculum guidance for the Foundation Stage. The Department for Children, Schools and Families (DCSF) has published a Foundation Stage Profile handbook and advice about observing children as guidance for practitioners on how to make assessments on the basis of their observations and knowledge of the whole child.

When considering the development of 'the whole child' these assessment points remind us that while academic prowess is important, educational progress involves the heart and mind, as well as the head. There are some key qualities (such as creativity), which, though they defy quantitative measurement, are nevertheless prized attributes if children are to attain their potential and eventually become thinking, responsible adults. See Doddington and Hilton, 2007, Chapter 4 for an exploration of the concept of child-centred education and the 'whole child' as a person.

Taking account of circumstances

Carrying out effective assessment for every child in the class is a demanding and difficult skill and requires teachers and their assistants to be alert and closely engaged with children's understanding of the work. Wragg (1997) reminds us that in the classroom environment, where so much is happening so quickly, 'teachers have to think on their feet and are denied the luxury of hours of reflection over each of their pedagogical choices' so that 'assessment has to be carried out on the move' (1997: 5). Accurate assessments therefore require a combination of these rapid skills during lessons (for immediate purposes) and creating a composite picture over the longer term. Every decision about the quality of children's work also needs to be made with reference to a number of factors, including:

- The child's age
- The child's work habits
- The child's past accomplishments
- The learning climate
- The quality of the teaching.

The child's age

Assessment approaches will vary according to the age of the child. Older primary school pupils tend to produce a great deal of written and other 'visual' forms of work that can be used for formative assessment purposes and designated a numerical figure as measured against standardised attainment level descriptions. However, since younger pupils produce relatively little written output, teachers have to rely more on their observations of children and listen attentively to the things that they say about their work that reveal the depth of knowledge and understanding. The younger the child, the less the evidence of learning is tangible and the more the teacher has to rely on observation and discussion with the child about the work.

The child's work habits

Children may be slow workers or deep thinkers or both. They may struggle with particular aspects of the work but excel in other, related parts. There will be gaps in their knowledge due to a failure to grasp ideas initially through a lack of motivation, immaturity or poor teaching. Some children hesitate to tackle unfamiliar or demanding tasks; others relish the challenge. Many children operate more effectively when working with a partner. These factors should be taken into account when work is assessed if you are to gain a true picture of the child's progress. A slow worker may produce a high quality final product if allowed extra time. A faster worker may be capable of a better end product if the first attempt is treated as a draft. Children working in pairs may accomplish more if together or (perhaps) separated or placed with someone different. With the advent of lessons in which specific time allocation for different phases is considered to be critical (especially in literacy sessions), there has been less flexibility to allow for such individual differences. The greater flexibility introduced through the Primary National Strategy Framework (PNS) for literacy and mathematics (formerly 'numeracy') and emphasis on individual learning offers opportunity to be more imaginative about ways of organising for learning (see Chapter 6). You are constantly faced with challenges about determining the quality of attainment that might have been possible for a child under different circumstances. Although you can only use 'hard' evidence to assess progress, an awareness of pupils' work habits assist you in evaluating what they are capable of achieving, raising expectations and establishing realistic learning targets.

The child's past accomplishments

The longer the teachers spend with a group of children, the more effective they are in assessing their achievements and potential. A child may have made considerable strides to accomplish something, which, for other more capable children, would be unacceptably poor. Over time, it becomes evident whether children are progressing satisfactorily with reference to past achievements or whether their present work-rate and performance indicate that they are being lazy, indifferent or unmotivated. Although formal assessments such as national tests and tasks may provide a grade or figure, they do not take account of these distinctive factors. Although it is part of your responsibility to help children to develop less secure areas of their knowledge and understanding, it is patently obvious that expectations must be reasonable and informed by earlier achievements. A lot of a teacher's work is taken up with rehearsing knowledge and reinforcing understanding that has been introduced at an earlier stage.

The learning climate

Lessons take place under varying circumstances: some teachers and children enjoy undisturbed tranquillity; others endure the loud noises from local building work. Some lessons take place within the regular rhythm of daily lessons; others are wedged between getting changed after swimming and going home at the end of the day. Some lessons are uninterrupted; others stop and start as children go out for music lessons, extra tuition and so forth. The quality of resources can also affect achievement, particularly when children are engaging with experiential tasks in which practical investigations form the heart of the lesson. Similarly, the behaviour of peers and numbers of pupils in the room can all have an effect on learning outcomes, notably in the personal attention that an adult can give a child. Teachers need to be wise when selecting work that is 'typical' of a child's ability to ensure that adverse contextual factors did not appreciably influence the outcome. As a trainee teacher you have probably been asked to collect samples of work to inform you assessments; in all cases, take note of the circumstances that pertained to the task completion, as the 'raw' evidence doesn't always tell the whole story.

The quality of teaching

Teachers sometimes blame a child for underachieving or producing a poor piece of work when they bear some of the responsibility. If an explanation of the task is poor, expectations are not clarified or organisation is clumsy, it should be no surprise if the results are disappointing. Regular evaluations of your practice are ultimately for the children's benefit.

> ## Good practice
>
> Never use a single piece of work, taken at random, to draw significant conclusions about a child's attainment and ability. Always use a range of evidence unless you are using a standardised test (and even then be aware that some children under-perform in formal settings).

Formative assessment (assessment for learning)

The type of assessment that is ongoing and helps children to improve the quality of their work is referred to as *formative assessment* and is found in the warp and weave of classroom life (e.g. Torrance and Pryor 1998; Drummond 2003; Lord and Slinn 2007). In recent years the process of formative assessment has been 're-branded' as 'assessment for learning' (AFL), with an emphasis on the word 'for'. Bates and Munday (2005: based on 58–9) suggest that the key features of AFL include:

- Learning objectives are made clear to pupils and success criteria are established
- Learning (as opposed to task outcome) is reviewed at the end of the lesson or lessons
- Oral and written feedback enables pupils to understand what they have achieved and how to move forward in their learning
- Pupils are involved through peer and self-assessment
- Pupils are encouraged (with adult support) to set achievable personal targets
- Teachers and pupils work together to create a climate of success in the classroom.

Kirton *et al.* (2007) report from a study about formative assessment in 16 Scottish primary schools and two junior high schools. They conclude that there is some evidence that use of formative assessment 'led to pupils taking more responsibility for their learning, contributing to improved motivation, confidence and classroom achievement, especially for lower attainers' (2007: 605). The authors warn, however, that the tension between constructive formative assessment and summative ('end product') assessment (see later) is an uneasy one, for the simple reason that formal assessments through testing assume such significance for teachers and pupils. 'Such a tension between summative and formative assessment needs to be resolved so that the dominance of assessment for accountability does not drive out assessment for learning' (2007: 624). They quote one pupil who, when asked about formal assessment, replied: 'If you got it wrong in a National Test it would be the end – to me it would be the end of your life'. From both an academic and social perspective, the stakes are high.

Good relationships and a relaxed atmosphere allow this process to take place constructively and unthreateningly. The use of question-and-answer sessions, child–teacher dialogue and the teacher's professional judgement are important elements of formative assessment. The teacher's informal records (both written and remembered) will be full of perceptive observations about individuals:

'Emma benefited from the extra help in spelling.'

'John still struggles to grasp the concept of area.'

'Ranjit is showing a talent for expressive painting.'

'Briony works well with her friend Eileen but seems lost when asked to work alone.'

'Ziad is a good reader but struggles at number work.'

'Darren seems to be tone deaf.'

And a thousand other insights that help to build up a picture of an individual child and guide future planning and appropriate work. These perceptions are not gained, of course, through detached observation and evaluation of children's work, but rather through active involvement in their learning. An integral element of this involvement is *monitoring* (close awareness of what children are doing and what they are thinking about their work) and *intervening* (an adult offering direct and indirect support to children while they are engaged in work). Unless you sit with your eyes and ears closed during a lesson, it is impossible to avoid monitoring progress; however, to become proficient and enhance your professional skills requires more than a casual acquaintance with such complex judgements. Children will normally let a teacher know if they have concerns or questions about tasks, but it is also important to develop the skill of scanning the class to pick up clues about the level of adult support that is needed by a child. As explained in earlier chapters, the relationship between monitoring and intervening is not an exact science. Sometimes you may be aware that a child is struggling but decide to delay your intervention to allow opportunity for the child to think and engage with the problem. On other occasions you may decide to be highly specific and tell the child precisely what must be done. Suffice it to say that the formative assessment of children's progress provides numerous insights into at least five components:

(a) The clarity of the task (your responsibility).

(b) The child's conceptual grasp of the task.

(c) The child's willingness to persevere with the task.

(d) The child's self-confidence.

(e) The extent of the child's ultimate success in accomplishing the task.

Unless the clarity of the task (a) is explicit, everything else will be distorted. If the child lacks understanding (b), it may be that you have assumed too much or failed to explain adequately. If the child is unwilling to persevere (c), it may signal a poor attitude or a weak aptitude towards learning. If the child lacks self-confidence (d), you have a major part to play in helping to build self-esteem using confirming strategies. If the end result is disappointing (e), points (a) to (d) need to be reviewed and appropriate remedies put in place. For example:

(a) Spend more time explaining what has to be done, where it fits with previous learning and directions about how to go about it.

(b) Revise basic knowledge, offer explanations in a different way from those used originally; invite the children to repeat and rehearse ideas; use story, familiar settings and diagrams.

(c) Set short-term targets (making the target time as low as a few minutes initially and gradually increasing it) and offer close adult support and encouragement.

(d) Praise effort as much as result; offer reassurance; quietly celebrate minor progress.

As you become more familiar with the class and the evidence accumulates, the general observations noted earlier can be sharpened:

'Emma can now learn a list of words and get them correct in a spelling test but cannot use them successfully in a piece of open written work.'

'John understands that units of measurement are needed to measure area but cannot understand why using smaller units produces a larger total.'

'Ranjit has an excellent sense of perspective in drawing but lacks imagination.'

'Briony has a good brain and grasps ideas quickly but is afraid of making a mistake.'

'Ziad can read aloud accurately but without any great understanding.'

'Darren is fine in the lower ranges but gets lost as the notes rise.'

It is not difficult to see that formative assessments are of little value unless action is taken to remedy a situation or encourage greater achievement. The process may be considered as comprising five stages:

Stage 1:   A general impression is gained from children's work and comments.

Stage 2:   Over time, a more exact judgement is made of the child's aptitude and ability.

Stage 3:   Action is taken to improve or enhance the situation.

Stage 4:   A further 'fine-grained' assessment is made on the basis of the revised work programme.

Stage 5:   Individual needs are more adequately catered for, especially children with particular learning difficulties.

Two important points need to be understood. First, the best formative assessments are also *diagnostic*; that is, not merely descriptive but providing evidence to assist in the formulation of appropriate teaching and learning strategies. Second, there is a limit to the amount of informal formative assessment that a teacher can record or remember. A system has to be established whereby the evidence from children's work and their responses to questions and so forth can be confirmed and, in some cases, quantified. Thus:

By how much has Emma's spelling improved and in which areas?

Does John have similar difficulty with other aspects of measurement?

Can Ranjit transfer his skills to planning in DT?

What is Briony capable of achieving when given plenty of reassurance?

Would Ziad benefit from focusing on specific aspects of textual interpretation?

Is Darren's problem one of confidence or competence or physical limitation?

Answers to these detailed questions allow teachers to modify work for an individual child or for a group of children, in order to improve their chances of grasping the skills and concepts in the area of weakness or enhancing their experience in areas of strength. The process of formative assessment should be located in the overall framework of planning, practice, assessment and recording, in the following way:

- Planning for teaching and learning: based on the school's agreed curriculum programme
- Teacher assessment for learning (formative assessment): daily observation and professional judgements based on the quality of work that children are producing
- Modified practice: adjustment of work patterns on the basis of the formative assessment
- Evaluative assessment (assessment of learning): focused judgements with reference to National Curriculum (NC) documents
- Recorded findings: using recording sheets
- Reporting findings: to parents and colleagues, in person or in writing.

Despite the helpful information accrued through assessment, it is important to be reminded that the simplistic notion of a procedure whereby teachers introduce a topic, sets tasks, assess children's progress and adjust their teaching accordingly is an idealised version of the reality. Ultimately, children must make sense of learning for themselves, aided by informed adults and peers.

Monitoring

As referred to in the previous section, monitoring progress is an essential skill for every teacher to develop and is concerned with two aspects of classroom life: effective learning and effective discipline. The two elements are often closely related; well-behaved and motivated children have a much better chance of doing well than restless, bored ones. The following five factors need to be considered as part of the ongoing process of assessing pupils' progress through monitoring.

The clarity of the task

Whether there are specific areas of the work causing concern to one or more pupils that need your attention.

The task demands

Whether the demands made by the task are enthusing and motivating pupils.

The availability and distribution of resources

Whether every pupil is receiving a fair share of resources and gaining access to the equipment.

The level of co-operation/collaboration

Whether children are working together responsibly.

The standard of work

Whether pupils' achievements align with their potential.

Teacher assessment of pupil attainment relies largely upon monitoring their progress during the lesson and examining the results of their endeavours by looking at their written and recorded work. Monitoring progress during the lesson requires a number of sophisticated skills including the following.

Seeing what needs to be seen

Monitoring demands focused and deliberate observation of a given situation.

Drawing the correct conclusions about what is seen

For instance, whether particular forms of pupil behaviour contribute to or detract from effective learning or whether the work is inappropriate or the child is demoralised.

Deciding what action should be taken

That is, determining the appropriate form of intervention based on decisions above.

Considering that the monitoring process has to take place spontaneously on numerous occasions during each session, it is hardly surprising that inexperienced teachers sometimes find it difficult to be aware of what is happening throughout the classroom. Before teachers can make decisions about suitable intervention strategies, they have to synthesise factors that arise from the monitoring process and make a number of judgements as a consequence. For instance.

General class order

Are pupils concentrating satisfactorily on their work? Is the noise level too high? Are groups collaborating or chattering? Is the movement around the room purposeful?

The behaviour of individuals

Is the child sufficiently compliant, bearing in mind his or her previous history? How many minor infringements should be ignored (if any)? How often should verbal reprimands be used? (See also Chapter 8.)

Health and safety

Are the pupils' actions potentially dangerous? What is 'reasonable risk'? How long should the situation be left? Will pupils' common sense prevail?

During monitoring of pupils' work, teachers confirm the acceptability of children's effort and progress by their responses (or lack of them). Every time you tick a page, express pleasure about a pupil's efforts or commend an approach, you are providing a confirmation of their validity. Of course, the opposite is true, in that every time you express doubt or suggest alternatives or offer guarded praise, the children become insecure unless you make it clear that there is an easy way to remedy the position (work harder, be more careful, do it this way, concentrate, and so forth). Indeed, offering immediate endorsement of a child's work provides valuable incentive and is preferable to the familiar and rather uninspiring process of: work is set/children do the work/the work is handed in/the teacher assesses the work/the work is handed back. The appropriateness of your responses based on the above considerations will not only influence the learning climate but will determine how and when you intervene. As a rule, the more feedback you can give 'on the spot', the more the child benefits. See also below.

Intervention

Children need adult and peer support in their endeavour to master new skills and concepts. The concept of 'scaffolding' learning by providing advice and guidance to steer children towards deeper understanding and extending their knowledge is well established. Teacher intervention is a crucial element of the scaffolding process and can be required for any one of at least five reasons:

- The teacher's poor initial lesson introduction, resourcing or organisation means that further explanation is required
- Poor matching between child/group and task leading to confusion or uncertainty
- The child's lack of confidence (as opposed to ability) leading to tentativeness
- The child's lack of ability leading to not knowing how to do the task
- The child's lack of concentration leading to the need for regular reminders.

Regardless of the subject matter or area of learning, every teaching-and-learning situation requires a variety of intervention skills and judgements that can make the difference between an active, progressive atmosphere and an oppressive, anxious one. Thus:

Knowing when to intervene

Part of knowing when to intervene is discerning when to leave things alone. Experienced teachers seem to develop an aptitude for spotting the events, comments and behaviours that require immediate attention, those that can be left for a time and those which are best ignored. It is important to weigh up the situation, remain calm and avoid saying too much before the child has had time to speak and the facts become clear. Once the position has been clarified, appropriate action can follow, though its precise nature has to be determined immediately; if you are inexperienced, you won't always get it right.

Allowing time for pupils' self-correction

As noted above, it is sometimes useful to allow time for the pupil to self-correct or take advice from a friend rather than rushing in straight away, particularly if the lesson purpose is principally about allowing pupils to grapple with difficulties rather than providing immediate solutions (e.g. in enquiry-based/problem-solving activities). Children need to be taught self-sufficiency rather than unintentionally promoting their over-reliance on a teacher, but there is little point in leaving a child to flounder for too long without offering help. (See later in this section.)

Knowing how to say what has to be said

Two teachers monitor children's work and offer suggestions for improvement: the first teacher depresses the pupil by being heavily critical; the second brings about the desired change by the use of carefully chosen words, precise guidance and suitable target setting. It is obvious which of the two approaches is going to bring about enhanced learning.

Unless the occasion is a formal test, in which assistance is not permitted, every teacher has to balance the importance of offering encouragement and guidance to children against intervening to such an extent that the child loses ownership of the task. Many children are happy to be told instead of putting their minds to the problem and as most pupils want to please the teacher, there is always the danger that your suggestions will be accepted uncritically. Consequently, a pattern of behaviour emerges:

1. Child engages with task.
2. Child encounters difficulty.
3. Child asks for assistance and advice.
4. Teacher obliges.

However, it is useful to introduce a 'delayed intervention' by employing phrases such as 'Have a try for yourself first and I'll come back in a moment if you are still stuck' or 'Ask a friend first before you ask me again'. You can also use a three-step procedure that children must always follow, namely: (1) think for yourself; (2) ask a classmate; and (3) ask an adult. Consequently, the behaviour pattern is gradually changed, as follows:

1. Child engages with task.
2. Child encounters difficulty.
3. Child thinks about solutions for one minute.
4. Child seeks advice from a friend.
5. Child seeks advice from an adult.

A lot depends on the nature of the lesson as to how flexibly the steps need to be followed; for instance you may want the children to work independently and not liaise with classmates. Nevertheless, the principle of encouraging children to think for themselves before seeking help allows you to evaluate children's ability to solve problems and persevere, rather than their ability to prise information from the teacher. Much formative assessment is based upon this interplay between intervention and giving children time and freedom to explore, evaluate, experiment, argue and so forth.

Good practice

Make it clear at the start of the session or activity the extent to which you want the children to: (a) work unaided; (b) actively collaborate with classmates; and (c) actively seek advice from an adult.

Assessments must, therefore, take into account the extent of teacher intervention and perhaps, peer involvement, in evaluating work quality and alerting you to possible pupil misconceptions or misunderstandings. Teachers have to weigh the benefits of co-operation and shared learning experiences with the possible disadvantage that one child may do most of the thinking and planning, while the other has minimal involvement.

Teachers also have to make allowances for particular times of the day and circumstances in judging how and when to intervene. Experienced teachers allow children time to settle after a 'wet' playtime rather than raise tension by being unduly assertive and may be more lenient with the work standards of a pupil who has come to school burdened with emotional cares than with a pupil who is being wilfully casual. Over time, all teachers tend to fall into particular patterns of monitoring and intervention that have consequences in promoting sound learning and discipline. As a result, it is essential to think carefully whether your intervention strategies are the most effective ones in the circumstances or whether different actions might result in more successful learning outcomes. Making such judgements comes as a result of time spent engaged in active classroom teaching, reflection on children's responses and evaluation of work quality. Your TA is also a valuable source of advice; so don't be afraid to seek it.

Activate your thinking!

Consider the truth of the following statement: Every intervention is preceded by an assessment based on careful monitoring of a child's progress.

> **Good practice**
>
> Categorise the types of active intervention you commonly use under the following headings: (a) those that result from a child's question; (b) those that result from your awareness of a problem; and (c) those that enhance work that is already of good quality.

Summative assessment

By contrast with ongoing formative assessments, those that take place at the end of a definable period of time such as the end of a day or half term or year or at the conclusion of a Key Stage are referred to as *summative* or the now favoured expression, 'assessment of learning' (AOL). The outcomes from summative assessments are intended to confirm the teacher's opinion of what children have learned and what progress has been made. Summative assessment is more systematic than formative assessment and may take the form of a written or verbal test carried out under specified conditions or a series of small tasks with which children have to engage in order to show their level of competence. The most significant type of summative assessment is through the national tasks and tests that relate to the core subjects of the NC, the results of which must be made available to the parents of each child. Some schools provide parents with the teacher's assessment of the child's progress in all the curriculum subjects once a year. Reports on art, music and PE only refer to end of Key Stage descriptions rather than the level descriptions used for the other non-core subjects. A summative assessment is not required for religious education. The use of ICT is now firmly established in schools, and pupils' ability needs to be monitored closely and their progress noted in reports to parents. ICT is sometimes referred to as the 'fourth core subject' to highlight its significance.

Summative assessments also have to take account of short-term target setting (see later in this chapter) whereby pupils are given specific learning targets to achieve by a given time. Although the targets do not form part of the formal assessment process, they help teachers to keep close track of pupil achievement. Through target setting, summative and formative assessment become two sides of the same coin: the formative element influences children's progress that is ultimately identified through the summative assessment. In turn, the summative element provides information for teachers to become more alert to the suitability of their formative assessment, and so on.

The process of assessment and recording and reporting children's progress is a crucial element of the teacher's work. A number of booklets have been produced by the Qualifications and Curriculum Authority (QCA) to help teachers in England and Wales understand the requirements of national testing; these are essential reading for a fuller understanding of the assessment process.

Although summative assessment forms an integral part of every teacher's agenda, there are some important considerations of which to take account. For instance, studies suggest that summative assessment has an adverse effect on low-achieving pupils' self-esteem compared with the impact it has on higher-achievers and the frequent use of practice tests in advance of 'the real thing' reinforces less able pupils' negative self-image. Similarly, major test events can cause considerable anxiety, especially among vulnerable pupils generally and girls in particular. On the other hand, some children thrive on tests, notably academically and confident pupils who view them as an opportunity to demonstrate their prowess and compete against children of similar ability. The overall effect is therefore to increase the gap between the motivation levels of high- and low-achievers. Some teachers also argue that summative assessment relies too heavily on extrinsic forms of motivation, whereby pupils respond to the promise of some kind of reward (high marks, accolades, merits, adult pleasure), rather than intrinsic motivation in which they perform because they are interested in the subject area and want to do the work for their own satisfaction.

There is also ample evidence that 'teaching to the test' unhelpfully narrows the curriculum, by placing an undue emphasis on literacy and mathematics at the expense of the non-core subjects. One result of curriculum 'narrowing' is a distortion of teaching approaches, such that teachers adopt a more didactic (transmission) style of teaching and stop employing more exploratory, enquiry-based methods. Teachers justify this change of technique for the following reasons:

A pragmatic reason: they are anxious to ensure that the children do well in the tests, regardless of the temporary loss of pupil autonomy.

A philosophical reason: they believe that repetition and reinforcement will almost certainly increase test success.

A professional reason: they don't want to be the teacher responsible for a class of children viewed as 'failing'.

A personal reason: they want to feel that they have done their best for the children and their parents.

In practice, teachers can spend a lot of time on preparing for, and conducting assessments of pupils' learning, which may reduce their motivation and create restless behaviour, especially if 'practice' tests and 'cramming' (now referred to more eloquently as 'coaching') dominates curriculum time and pupils feel constrained and/or deprived of other, more enjoyable experiences. If you are placed with a Year 6 class in the Spring Term, these challenges will be particularly acute, but an increasing number of schools have non-statutory end-of-year tests for years other than Year 2 and Year 6, so the issues are widespread.

Testing does not only take place as end-of-year events; there are numerous occasions when a formal, measurable assessment of ability is used to indicate pupil progress. It might be argued that summative assessment is being carried out every time (say) a child reads to an adult and a record is made of progress, or a spelling test is given to the whole class. Teachers have a responsibility to ensure that children (especially in Key Stage 2) approach tests seriously, while reassuring anxious pupils that they can only do their best and that weak results do not reflect badly on their characters unless, of course, they have been lazy or indifferent.

Activate your thinking!

Consider the validity of this statement: 'It is impossible to carry out an assessment *for* learning without also doing an assessment *of* learning'.

Feedback to children

One of the principal ways in which a positive learning environment can be achieved is through effective and sensitive feedback to children about the quality of their work. It is essential to ensure that the process of marking/grading work not only provides information for the teacher but also for pupils, offering useful data to them about the quality of their endeavours and their overall progress. Sometimes the feedback will be verbal and sometimes in the form of a grade, mark, smiley face or another symbol, remembering that the child who has persevered to achieve something worthwhile deserves the same level of commendation as the more capable pupil. Clarke (2001) suggests that teachers carry out as much marking as possible with children present, rather than marking away from the child, though this is not easy in practice. It is also important for teachers to avoid falling into the 'yes, but' habit, whereby children never receive unconditional praise because the imperfections of the work are highlighted at the same time as the approval. Although it is part of your role to help children improve their work, this should not be done at the expense of them feeling that absolutely *nothing* will ever satisfy their finicky teacher. The following principles will help to ensure that feedback is beneficial:

1. Mark as much as possible with the child present and celebrate achievement spontaneously.

2. Consider the *effort* made as well as the outcome, being careful not to foster excessive competitiveness.

3. Take account of circumstances in making judgements. For example:
   - the difficulty of the work
   - the time available for task completion
   - whether the child was trying to be innovative
   - whether the task was individual, in pairs or group.

4. Avoid the impression that the only reason the children are doing the work is to please the teacher.

5. Keep your eye on the long-term intentions for children's attitude to learning:
   - enthusiastic and motivated
   - self-sufficient and independent
   - confident at his/her own level of ability.

Activate your thinking!

Part of the teacher's role is to raise children's self-esteem by promoting a culture of success and encouraging children to tackle problems without fearing the consequences of failure. How do you rate yourself in this regard?

The need for accurate formative assessment also places a responsibility upon teachers to ensure that they use the most appropriate descriptors. For instance, when describing a child's work, teachers frequently make use of a general term such as 'good'. In doing so, they can be making a number of different statements:

- It is good compared with the last piece of similar work the child completed

- It is good compared with other children's work in the group or class

- It is good because the child has made a considerable effort to do well, despite the relatively poor quality of the end result

- It is good compared with other children of the same age in neighbouring schools (far more difficult to ascertain).

A similar list can be made about why the work is described as 'poor'. Even if a piece of work is judged as poor, teachers have then to determine what should be done about it. Simply telling children that their work is poor or giving them a low mark/grade is probably only confirming what they already know, so teachers need to employ strategies to assist children to do better next time or to improve the current piece of work. Strategies may involve spending time with an individual privately, asking for the attention of the group and making a general statement about the issue, or providing direct teaching to the whole class in the form of explanations, demonstrations or exposition as a means of revising or reinforcing the concept or procedure. A number of individuals may not have grasped what the teacher intended them to do and may need a few minutes of intensive tuition before they can respond adequately. The task may expect too much of the children and to redress the mismatch between task and ability, remedial work or a modification of what is required may be needed before further progress is possible.

Positive remarks about a child's progress may be useful as a means of encouragement but unhelpful in diagnosis. A 'Good, well done' indicates the teacher's pleasure but may have limited value for ensuring that the child has thoroughly grasped the intended concept, skill or knowledge. A 'Good, well done, I can see that you have really tried hard' indicates that the teacher is pleased with the effort made despite the outcome. However, a 'Good, well done in (these particular ways)' is better still. The distinction between the different expressions is significant for children who may subconsciously perceive that the only way to earn favour with the teacher is to 'do good work'. More open relationships result in a fuller discourse between you and the child and pave the way for more focused attention on specific areas of work. Most children try hard for most of the time, but it is worth reminding yourself that everyone, including adults, has off-days, so don't get tense about pupils under-achievement; they may just be bored or feeling unwell or distracted. Simply remind them of what you expect and what you believe they are capable of achieving.

Activate your thinking!

Whatever forms assessment takes, three factors are always relevant:

- Knowing where a child 'started from' before trying to assess progress
- Ensuring the form of measurement of ability is valid (i.e. it measures what it is supposed to measure)
- Establishing a close link between assessment, planning and record-keeping.

Good practice

As you give feedback, put yourself in the children's place and imagine the impact of your words upon their determination to do better and to their self-esteem.

Assessments and learning objectives

It is important in assessing children's progress to bear in mind the learning objectives and continuity, expressed through building conceptual understanding in a systematic (though not inflexible) way. Many tasks and activities involve several stages before completion. For example, a full painting will probably require time to be spent on colour mixing, painting a backwash, use of different paint textures and addition of fine detail that may not be achievable in the space of a single session owing to practical factors of paint drying, available space and maintaining children's concentration levels. Similarly, a drama production normally involves preparation through role-play, improvisation and numerous rehearsals prior to the final performance. In English, draft versions of a piece of writing usually contain mis-spellings and grammatical errors that may need to be corrected before the final version is produced. It would be unreasonable to treat these early stages as if they were the completed task and base judgements upon them, though teachers pick up many clues by observing how a child approaches the work and the kinds of errors they exhibit. The establishment of clear learning objectives and sufficient time spent explaining the nature of the tasks to the children is essential if they are to make efficient use of their opportunities. Children may panic and rush to complete a piece of work for fear that time constraints make such haste necessary, when a more considered and thorough job would have been possible had you made the position clearer and, perhaps, tried to achieve less coverage of the curriculum and greater depth of understanding.

For instance, consider how planning a number of maths lessons on naming and using common coinage with reception age children might link with assessment criteria. The teacher may design a series of sessions consisting of four broad phases:

Phase 1: Understanding the use of pennies to pay for goods up to the value of 5p.

Phase 2: Understanding the use of pennies to pay for goods up to the value of 10p.

Phase 3: Establishing the exchange relationship between 1p, 2p and 10p coins.

Phase 4: Establishing the exchange relationship between 1p, 2p, 5p and 10p coins.

Of course, each phase will not necessarily correspond to a single lesson. The concepts associated with each phase may have to be revised and rehearsed a number of times before learning is secure. The problem for a teacher is to determine when such certainty has been accomplished. Using assessment criteria provides a means by which pupils' confidence about the concepts can be confirmed. In the above example, each set of objectives is accompanied by a corresponding set of criteria that are used to assess the children's progress. Thus:

Phase 1 assessment criteria

The children can:

- Identify and name pennies
- Count out the coins up to 5p
- Exchange the coins for items costing up to 5p.

Phase 2 assessment criteria
The children can:

- Count out the pennies up to 10p
- Count the cost of buying more than one item up to 10p.

Phase 3 assessment criteria
The children can:

- Identify and name the 2p coin
- Exchange pennies for 2p coins
- Count the amounts of money using 1p and 2p coins up to a maximum of 10p.

Phase 4 assessment criteria
The children can:

- Identify and name 5p coins
- Exchange 1p and 2p coins for 5p coins
- Exchange 1p, 2p and 5p coins for one or more items costing up to 10p.

There may be disagreement among teachers about the precise ordering of the criteria and the way that they are arranged, but the principle of linking lesson objectives and the assessment of pupil attainment across a period of time is one which underpins planning. Although children do not learn in the smooth, uninterrupted fashion that the above criteria may suggest, the concept of employing assessments that are closely linked to learning objectives is valid for all subject areas.

The above comments and insights should have convinced you that keeping track of children's progress requires careful judgement about the evidence to use in forming an opinion about children's progress. It is one of the key skills for teachers and well worth persevering to master. The issue of recording pupil attainment is addressed later in the chapter.

Target setting

In recent years, the need to identify and reach targets has become rooted in work at every level of society and schools are no exception. Willick (2006) argues: 'Developing and setting clear goals is a critical aspect of motivation and this involves being able to conceptualise the gains involved in reaching that goal' (2006: 46). Wyse (2001) refers to the complexity of setting targets and subsequent assessment, notably the amount of interaction time with pupils that was required to plan future targets in literacy. He suggests that for the process to be purposeful, 'high levels of skills and understanding were required to be coupled with the ability to develop strategies to improve management of the process' (2001: 16). From his study of final year trainee teachers, Wyse noted the following (paraphrased and amended):

- Accurate target setting has to be based on a clear understanding of previous development and attainment

- It is important to recognise that children reach the same targets at different rates

- Targets should not be too numerous or difficult

- Frequent reference to targets is necessary, supported by maintaining target sheets, cards or notices for each child

- Targets need to be discussed orally to support understanding and to assess progress

- It is important to identify the nature of what the target is related to (level descriptions, SAT, Framework for Teaching, etc.)

- A lot of marking can be replaced by oral discussion with children

- Specific marking is more productive than making general summary comments

- Formative assessment (feedback and intervention during lessons) is particularly useful for the purpose of setting and monitoring targets

- Self-assessment is a useful tool to enhance pupil participation

- Extra adult support is often necessary to enhance target setting

- Unachievable targets are demotivating for children and result in slower progress.

Clarke (2001) suggests that there are three broad types of targets:

- Quantitative targets using numerical data (such as a percentage of children to reach a particular pass rate)

- Qualitative targets based principally on written evidence (such as children's ability to spell certain words correctly in different contexts)

■ Non-recorded targets based on children's self-evaluation of their progress (such as those resulting from informal conversations between teacher and taught).

The principles of target setting (based on those suggested by Clarke 2001: 86) are that targets should be at three levels: school, class and child. They must be realistic, manageable and challenging and based on an analysis of data from children's achievements, including regular summative assessments. Targets should be expressed in appropriate language that children can understand, and shared with children (in the short term) and with parents (in the long term). Children should participate in establishing and meeting targets, which should be regularly reviewed. It is important that targets are supported and met by effective teaching, learning and assessment, and not allowed to become free-standing entities, detached from the regular classwork and homework. Target setting has, therefore, become significant for every teacher and is important at three levels:

(a) Immediate targets for individual children in different subject areas.

(b) Longer-term targets for children over (say) half a term.

(c) Targets for year groups of children in national tests (Year 2 and, especially, Year 6).

Immediate targets for individual children

These targets are based upon children's ongoing classroom work. As teachers evaluate pupils' progress, particular aspects of their work are identified as needing special attention and improvement. Recognition of pupils' achievements inevitably involves seeing how the present work can be improved or built upon, and responding accordingly. The process of 'recognition and response' has, of course, been at the heart of teaching for generations; however, today such issues are very much at the forefront of education debate and political priority. Older pupils can take more responsibility for monitoring their own progress and establishing reasonable targets; younger ones will need the strong support of teachers to identify specific ways in which improvements can be identified and addressed. With or without active teacher involvement, target setting for individual children needs to take place with respect to a number of key factors

First, target setting must be specific. Broad targets such as 'I must get better at reading' are inadequate. Instead a target such as 'I must learn to pause at full stops when reading out loud' or 'I must select non-fiction books for personal reading' should be identified. Similarly, in maths there is little point in setting a target such as 'I must learn my multiplication tables' but rather 'I must use my calculator to check my work, not to carry out the calculation' or 'I must work out multiplications without adding up all the numbers'. Target setting can also include specific aspects of improving presentation of work, learning to work as a member of a group and mastering techniques.

Second, target setting must be realistic. Learning does not follow clearly defined pathways. It is gradual and, in some cases, wholly unpredictable. If targets are too ambitious, children will lose heart. If they are undemanding, children will not take them seriously. Learning will not necessarily come more quickly simply because targets have been set. Nevertheless, a sensible target can act as a prompt or encouragement for children to focus their energies constructively.

Third, target setting must take account of time factors. Most concepts and skills cannot be mastered overnight; it takes a lot of trial and error, perseverance and determination before understanding comes and abilities are honed. Although it is easy to monitor the setting of a few spellings to be learned at home, targets which involve a lot of library or internet research (for instance) will take longer to achieve than those which can be done on the spot.

Finally, target setting must be manageable. There is little point in having a system that is so unwieldy that it demands an unreasonable amount of effort. Sophisticated systems are fine in theory but usually crumble on the sharp edge of reality. Manageable strategies include giving children small 'Targets' notebooks to write down their targets (or, where appropriate, have them written by the teacher). Some teachers use a system of marking work in different coloured pens or markers to indicate that the area of work requires improvement or needs to be more thoroughly mastered. Whatever system is adopted, it is important to minimise your workload and not distract from the main purpose of promoting successful learning by creating a lot of additional and unnecessary paperwork.

Longer-term targets for individual children

Most schools encourage the children to 'look ahead' and discuss with the teacher and/or their classmates the things that they are keen to improve and attain over (say) the next half-term. It is impossible and undesirable for children to become submerged in minutiae, such that they become obsessed by the need to 'hit' a large number of disparate targets, but a sensible discussion about key learning needs can help to focus attention on desirable outcomes. For instance, a child may be struggling in changing from printing letters to a cursive script and require guidance, constant practice and opportunities to use the skill in extended writing. Again, a child may be perplexed by the concept of division of whole numbers in mathematics, necessitating a considerable amount of concentration and wrestling with the principles that support the operation, perhaps supported by a TA.

By contrast to the more immediate targets that can be achieved through pupils' self-motivation and resoluteness, longer-term targets necessitate a need for expert advice and support from an informed adult (who can see further ahead the pupil learning curve). In other words, the mere agreement about a target serves limited purpose unless there is a strategy to help the child achieve it and some way of monitoring it.

Identifying when a target has been 'achieved' or 'met' can also be problematic, as even the most carefully defined outcomes are subject to personal opinion and interpretation. For example, it is difficult to determine whether a child is writing more creatively or is able to participate more constructively in a discussion than was previously the case. Nevertheless, it is important to review targets periodically and help children to take some ownership of their learning instead of relying wholly on an adult's direction and approval.

Targets for year groups of children

National tests have become increasingly important for all schools as a failure to improve year upon year can bring about additional inspections or intervention by the local authority. The establishment of targets has created a considerable amount of activity in schools as they have responded to the considerable challenge in raising standards of literacy and mathematics in the national tests (SATs). Part of the process of reaching and maintaining these standards involves a process known as Agreement Trialling, in which teachers responsible for children of the same age in a district (or, in the case of large schools, within the school) meet to consider their assessments of work to ensure that there is a degree of comparability.

On the other hand, it is possible that pupils may be burdened with the weight of teacher expectations, especially if they fail to achieve at least level 2 (at Key Stage 1) or at least level 4 (at Key Stage 2) in the tests. Many schools give 'booster classes' to underachieving pupils at Key Stage 2, which, though they may have a positive impact upon attainment, can be deleterious to children's self-esteem and confidence if they perceive themselves to be failures. It is therefore essential for teachers to keep target setting in proportion and not allow it to completely dominate the educational agenda. Many schools use end-of-year (non-statutory) tests to monitor pupil progress and identify weaknesses. A few schools test children every half term. With the advent of 'value-added' league tables that rely on the *progress* that children have made from the previously established benchmark, even schools with a large number of children attaining level 4 in the end-of-key-stage tests are being obliged to aim for an increase in the number attaining level 5. Schools compile impressive sets of statistics to demonstrate results in national tests for literacy, mathematics and science at the end of Key Stages 1 and 2; predicted results for children currently in Years 4 and 5; and a Foundation Stage Profile.

Targets also play a role in teacher appraisal ('performance management'), adding to their significance for practitioners at all levels of experience. Not only do teachers have to take increasing responsibility for their own development by setting themselves professional targets, the attainment of the children in their classes is a key factor in determining their suitability for in-school advancement or promotion. While it is reasonable to expect teachers to deliver on standards, there is an increasing understanding on the part of policy-makers that the one-size-fits-all philosophy pervading the education system has to be more sensitive to local factors. The group of children in front of you will never be identical to another group, yet the same expectations apply to all.

Limitations of targets

Setting targets depends on teachers being clear about what children know and planning lessons accordingly. However, there are strict limits on how detailed these insights can be. While it is relatively simple to ascertain whether children possess certain forms of knowledge, such as being able to recite the alphabet, count to 20 or know historical dates, it is almost impossible to discern precisely what every child understands about (say) human behaviour or the morality of historical events. These limitations have two consequences. First, it is tempting to concentrate your attention exclusively on aspects of knowledge that are measurable. Second, the concept of matching teaching to 'gaps in children's knowledge' is something of a fallacy. Setting targets is a useful strategy for maintaining a well-controlled teaching system but to be truly effective it must also acknowledge that not everything worth knowing falls neatly into the teach/assess/ amend teaching formula. Teachers are understandably reluctant to improve test results for the sole purpose of complying with political ambitions or advancing their own career prospects but in the prevailing climate it is difficult to resist.

Activate your thinking!

What do you understand by the expression 'raising standards'? Does it only mean 'raising test scores'?

Assessing collaborative activities

Assessment of individual children is more difficult when children are involved in collaborative work. Although enhancing pupil skills in collaborating is a valuable dimension of learning, it can also mask the progress in learning made by individuals in the group. The sight of children explaining to and assisting one another to complete tasks is rightly viewed as worthwhile by most teachers; however, this is different from one child acting as a surrogate teacher and continually intervening in another child's work. For example, if four groups of children are engaged in doing the same task, there will be different levels of task interpretation and outcome depending upon the ability and expertise within the group. The teacher will need to be aware of the group's academic potential and previous learning when determining what constitutes a satisfactory learning outcome, as reflected in the quality of the group's recording of findings or presentations to other pupils.

From Figure 7.1 we can see that the least able group (A) is likely follow the procedures without deviating from the teacher's instructions. Group B may follow the procedures but interpret them more imaginatively. It can be anticipated that Group C will amend the procedures significantly and introduce their own ideas and modifications. Group D (the most able) may reinterpret the task and develop a wholly innovative approach that answers slightly different questions and involves other pathways from those envisaged by the teacher. Although teachers will expect all children to use their intellects and make the best contribution possible, they will also take into account the children's potential and limitations. Thus, Group A will be commended for accurately following the set procedure while Group D's accomplishments will be assessed using a different set of criteria. If, on the other hand, Group C operated only at the level expected from Group A, then the task was too tedious, the group were under-performing or the teacher's original expectations were unrealistic. Differentiating through outcome provides the teacher with a means of acknowledging a group's particular contribution and effort without directly comparing group with group. Pupils in the less able group may achieve a lot within the limits of their capability and the teacher's expectations.

Figure 7.1 Assessment of groups through outcomes

Confirmation of progress in learning will rely upon the individual's contribution to the group effort as perceived by the teacher, subsequent work in the same area of learning, ability to explain things coherently and the quality of the write-up or other representation of the work such as diagrams, maps, pictures or models.

Sometimes a teacher's assessment will be based on factors other than the final work outcome. For instance, you may want to evaluate pupils' willingness to co-operate, creative thought, enthusiasm or commitment to completing the task; these are important assessments which relate more closely to social behaviour, personal growth and attitude than to measurable academic performance but are essential in helping to create a fully 'educated' person.

Activate your thinking!

As it is not possible for one teacher to know about each child's work and progress in detail for every curriculum area, judgements often have to be based largely upon the outcome of the group's combined efforts.

Good practice

Select a 'key' child from each group each week for careful observation and assessment. Choose a new target child from each group every week until you have worked your way through each one.

Assessing children for whom English is an additional language

In 2007 the latest standards for qualified teacher status in England (those for Wales and Scotland are very similar but are described and presented differently) were produced by the Training and Development Agency (TDA) include the requirement that newly qualified teachers should:

> Know how to make effective personalised provision for those they teach, including those for whom English is an additional language or who have special educational needs or disabilities, and how to take practical account of diversity and promote equality and inclusion in their teaching (Q19).

In particular, there is a need to assess pupils' competence in English through their ability to comprehend through listening, speaking, reading and writing. Pupils' responsiveness when hearing English spoken can be assessed with reference to the 'extended scale for listening' (QCA 2000). Their ability to speak and use spoken English can be assessed with reference to the 'extended scale for speaking'. Their familiarity with the conventions of print and understanding written English can be assessed with reference to the 'extended scale for reading'. Their ability to write for different purposes can be assessed with reference to the 'extended scale for writing'. Broadly, it should be possible to make judgements for listening, speaking, reading and writing using the descriptions below. Thus:

Listening

You can distinguish between children who respond to spoken English in specific circumstances (e.g. a regular instruction such as 'please sit down'), those who can understand what is said but do not respond, and those children who can talk to others as a result of their understanding.

Speaking

You can distinguish between children who are able to say a few words, those who can sustain a conversation, and those who can modify their speech according to context and circumstances.

Reading

You can distinguish between children who are able to grasp basic written conventions those who can read with support, and those who can read with a large degree of independence.

Writing

You can distinguish between children who are able to write English letters and their name, those who can use letter patterns, and those who can write recognisable letters, words and phrases.

Formal assessment of English as an additional language are described with reference to a scale consisting of four stages for those who have yet to reach NC attainment target 1, namely:

- Step 1… for the least competent users

- Step 2

- Level 1, 'threshold'

- Level 1, 'secure'.

Characteristics of each stage are described closely in QCA (2000: 12–15). The scale for speaking and listening is separately listed for the four stages but combined for level 2 and above. There are separate scales for reading and for writing. As with all assessments, however, the purpose of placing a child at a particular stage is not for the sake of completing a record sheet and satisfying external requirements, but to assist the child's learning. Subsequent planning of an appropriate curriculum programme for children with EAL will depend upon a variety of factors, not least whether there are other children in the class with the same first language and the availability of a TA. It is also important to take account of the disorientation that a child experiences when suddenly thrust into a confusing new situation, with unfamiliar language, cultural norms and procedures. Every new child takes time to adjust to the pattern of working, and this problem is magnified for a child who speaks little or no English. Your assessment record might consist of a summary paragraph about the child's abilities in speaking and listening, samples of written work as evidence for writing, and regular reading records for progress in reading. Assessment profiles of this kind should allow you to trace the child's curriculum experience in school and provide diagnostic information that allows you to discuss the child's progress with other staff and parents. As a trainee teacher you will need to take advice from experienced colleagues and, in particular, from the teacher in the school charged with such matters (e.g. SENCO, leader for literacy).

Policy with regard to bilingual children (those who speak two or more languages, though not necessarily fluently) has developed considerably in recent years due to the sharp increase in immigration. The PNS document *Learning and teaching for bilingual children in the primary years* (DfES 2006a) was introduced into schools during 2007–8 and provides guidance on EAL pedagogy, planning and assessment, as well containing practical materials and examples that cover most aspects of teaching bilingual pupils in mainstream primary classrooms (DCSF 2006).

Activate your thinking!

The assessment of children's work can tell teachers as much about the effectiveness of their own teaching as it does about the child's learning.

Good practice

Use assessment as a forum for celebrating success.

RECORDING AND REPORTING

Forms of records

The emphasis throughout this book has been upon the inter-relationship between planning, assessment, record-keeping and reporting children's progress to parents, both informally and formally. Few practitioners enjoy keeping records, but they are a necessary part of professional responsibility. They can provide information about curriculum coverage, pupil progress and issues that arise from teaching and learning. Following any block of teaching and learning, teachers are confronted with a number of questions with respect to pupils' attainment:

- How much did the children learn from the lesson or lessons?
- What evidence is there of individual progress?
- What evidence is there of group (collaborative) progress?
- How will this information affect future lesson planning?
- How will the evidence be recorded?

Although teachers hold a lot of information about children in their heads, there is a need to keep written records that assist with the twin requirements of assisting with future lesson plans and reporting to parents. One of the principal difficulties for teachers is deciding what to record and what to omit. It is no exaggeration to claim that teachers could spend more time recording than they do in teaching if they attempted to write down everything. In addition to influencing their planning, both trainee teachers and qualified ones have to ensure that their records are up-to-date, though for rather different reasons. Trainee teachers need to show to their tutors that they are engaging with the process of evaluating pupils' work, assessing their progress and noting outcomes (summative in character). Qualified teachers need to provide evidence for their teacher-assessments; to have forms of evidence to support their decisions; and to supply information required in respect of performance management (salary increases and promotion to senior posts). Consequently, the precise forms of records that are maintained depend upon their purpose. Records take a variety of forms and are kept for a number of different purposes, including the following.

Organisational planning

This type of record is based on curriculum coverage. For example, noting which group has covered which topic and modifying the content of future lessons as a result.

Strategy for managing

This type of record is purely organisational and acts as a reminder for teachers and assistants about the children's level of engagement with work. For example, checking who has read to the teacher during the week, noting who has used the computer, and so on.

Information relating to National Curriculum demands

This type of record offers evidence of children's progress that helps to inform formal teacher assessments; in particular, evidence for end-of-key-stage assessments.

Information for parents

This type of record is a summary of key facts for easy transmission to a third party; for example, informal notes in preparation for parents' evening.

Recognition of children's efforts

This type of record consists of representative samples of children's work for inclusion in a Record of Achievement folder, class books, wall displays, etc.

The most immediate records for teachers to maintain are those that show areas of work covered (curriculum coverage) and those that show children's progress (individual records). It is important to distinguish between the two types of records for, as noted earlier, mere completion of a task or activity does not necessarily show the extent of understanding or mastery, as the following makes clear.

Curriculum coverage

Records of curriculum coverage take many forms. The best are straightforward to use and easy to modify. A rigid, over-detailed format is time-consuming, rarely justifies the effort and should not be confused with the detail required for end of Key Stage national tests and tasks. Many schools plan in half-termly blocks in which the main topic, theme or subject is identified and NC and links established, particularly with literacy and mathematics, but also with other subject areas. A weekly overview is then drawn up by staff teams that teach the same age group or by individual teachers; lesson planning emerges from this common structure. The subsequent records of curriculum coverage reflect the nature of the planning and are likely to take one of two forms: records that state curriculum coverage based primarily on Programmes of Study (PoS); and records based primarily on concepts, skills and knowledge.

Much depends on the way in which a particular school organises its learning programme: the more subject-centred the programme, the more likely that PoS predominates. The more process-centred or thematic the programme, the more likely that concepts and skills are emphasised. Two simple examples of *pro formas* are shown in Figures 7.2 and 7.3.

Record of activities for the whole class

Figure 7.2 can be used when the activities (or tasks) are appropriate to the whole class. For example, the children might all be doing some observational drawing. The record sheet will help the teacher to see who has completed the task and who has not. The names of the children

TOPIC/THEME

Names of children

Activities

Figure 7.2 Record of activities (for the whole class)

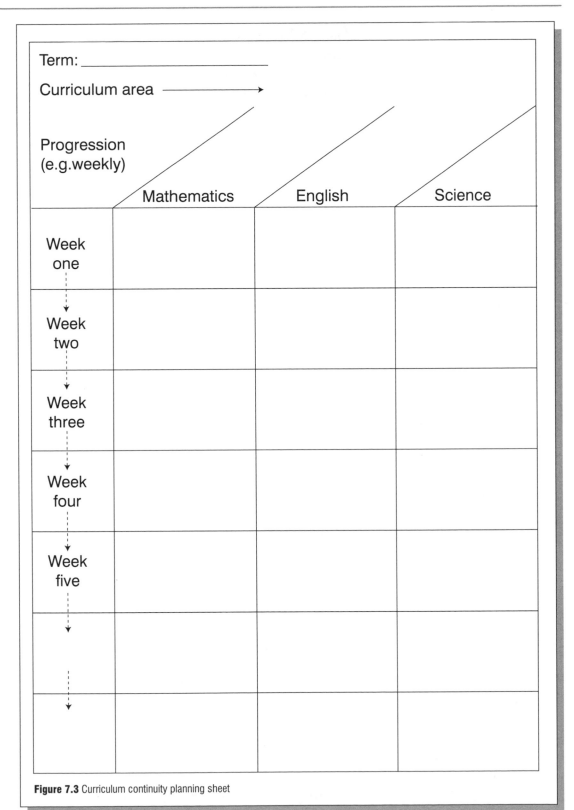

Figure 7.3 Curriculum continuity planning sheet

are written in the left hand column. The activity is written in the skewed box near the top of the page. The appropriate box is ticked or shaded when the child has completed the activity or task. A simpler version with fewer names can be adopted to record the work of a single group. If several groups are involved with different curriculum areas, the need for maintaining careful records is even greater.

A curriculum continuity planning sheet

Figure 7.3 indicates the sort of record that can easily be made of coverage in core subjects and provides an overview of the planning process. The numbers on the left hand side refer to the weeks of the topic, theme or project. A note of the specific teaching area covered or the NC reference can be made in the subject columns. The sheet can be modified in imaginative and useful ways; a similar format can be used for other subjects.

> ### Good practice
>
> It is useful for inexperienced teachers to see samples of previous end-of-year reports from across the age range spectrum as a means of identifying the overall curriculum and school learning priorities.

Individual progress

This area of recording is probably of most interest and concern to new teachers. Since it is not possible to assess a child's thought processes directly, teachers have to collect evidence relating to the product of those thought processes. The most usual product is a piece of written work, but observations help the teacher by providing information from ongoing interactions while the child is working (see, for instance, Nilsen 2004).

Records of activities covered with a group or class are important but do not tell you anything about the assessment of individual pupil progress. Use of NC documents such as the PoS assist in planning and monitoring curriculum coverage but are less helpful for charting individual progress. Ideally, it is desirable to plan every intended learning outcome for each child, monitor progress, assess the extent of the learning and record it in a manageable form. In practice, this is impossible unless the class is exceptionally small. Teachers may suffer agonies of conscience over the fact that their files are not full of pages of information plotting the progress of every child in every aspect of learning in every subject area, but such self-recrimination is unnecessary. We have seen that learning is rarely smooth and uninterrupted but rather that in the ongoing process of formative assessment, most children can be deemed to have a broad grasp of the intended outcome if they complete the set work to the teacher's satisfaction. Careful monitoring of the ongoing work, together with individual notes made about each child's perceived difficulties, is preferable to endlessly listing the things that the child knows and understands. Put simply; spend more time noting the things that a child does *not* know than the things the child *does* know. The information in records can then be used diagnostically to improve future teaching and learning rather than as a list of content coverage.

Records of every individual's progress in detail

Careful records have to be kept for core subjects, especially in the areas of literacy and mathematics. Information can be gained from in-class tests, completed exercises as part of the regular class work and pupils' verbal contributions. However, it is not necessary, sensible or realistic to maintain detailed records for all children of every step they take in their learning. If you are uncertain about whether or not to record an aspect of children's progress, use the following three criteria in helping to make a decision: (a) Will you need to share the information with the child or another adult (e.g. a special needs' teacher or a parent)? (b) Will details be required to support a judgement about grade allocation (e.g. for the purpose of allocation to a 'set' or teacher assessment at the end of a key stage)? (c) Will the information help you to plan future lessons to accommodate individual pupil learning requirements? Unless you have a very small class, several assistants or exceptionally fast handwriting, there is little point in recording too much information, other than that which might be requested by your training provider.

> ### Activate your thinking!
> The more information children are given about what they are meant to achieve, the more they can be involved in monitoring their own progress.

> ### Good practice
> In maintaining records, assume that if children complete the tasks and activities without excessive adult support, they have at least a reasonable grasp of content and understand the associated concepts.

As a first step in assessing and recording individual's progress during tasks and activities that you have allocated for children to complete as part of the regular lesson structure, it is helpful to use a 'Goldilocks and the Three Bears' approach in monitoring the way that children progress and cope with the work. A small number of children may struggle because the content of lessons is 'too hot'. A small number may sail through because the content is 'too cold'. The majority will cope comfortably because the content is just the right temperature. By placing children in one of the three categories, it soon becomes obvious where the problems lie and what sort of help is needed. For example:

Too hot: Malichaba, Esmie, Tallis.

Too cold: Damien, Chris, Becks, Amanda.

Just right: The rest of the class.

Consequently, pupils in the 'too hot' category require less demanding challenges, whereas those in the 'too cold' category need more demanding work. Equally, you need to be careful not to ignore the potential of middle-of-the-road children, who may not excel or struggle but still deserve as much attention as those at the extremes. The process is more manageable and representative of true ability if records show the extent of individual progress across a series of lessons rather than a single one. Although this unsophisticated approach cannot be used for formal records, it is useful as a memory aid for busy teachers.

In an attempt to balance reality with aspiration, some schools have more sophisticated records relating to the core subjects only, one sheet per child. These usually contain details about the content and learning relating to particular attainment targets in a subject; these are ticked or blocked according to an agreed system and kept with the child's records, sometimes together with a sample of work for evidence. Schools will often have an agreed marking policy to support the monitoring process so that there is consistency across and within year groups. As a trainee teacher, you may have to use an existing school record system or complete sample records on *pro formas* supplied by the Faculty/College. Typically, inexperienced trainees are asked to identify a small number of children and track their progress; more experienced trainees, especially those in their final placement, should be looking ahead to the time when they will have responsibility for a full class of children and thinking in terms of tracking each child – though far from easy to achieve.

Activate your thinking!

After three weeks with your class, a parent comes into the room and approaches you. 'Hello', she smiles, 'I'm Delia's mum. I wondered how she was getting on in her work.' Where would you begin? What would you say?

Good practice

Consider how you would explain the way in which you record children's progress to an interested friend who does not work in education.

Earlier in this chapter, it was emphasised that records of children's progress and attainment serve two principal purposes. First, so that you have access to data that can influence lesson planning; second, to provide information in formal records for other audiences, notably colleagues and parents. The two reports set out below are genuine, though some details have been altered to ensure anonymity. As a trainee teacher, you will not be required to write such a report, but as soon as you qualify and take responsibility for your won class, you will be. In studying the examples, bear in mind that parts of the text for Key Stage 2 in particular are generated by computer software, but that the teacher still needs to know individual children well enough to provide specific insights into their progress. No report can say everything about a child, so a selection of key issues and learning outcomes is inevitable. Making this selection provides one of the key challenges for a teacher, who may be writing up to 30 reports for infants and even more for juniors. Note that the Year 3 report contains a lot more information about the curriculum content. In addition, the new responsibilities of TAs may include the administration (but not the writing) of reports, though how this works in practice will depend upon school circumstances.

Case study: sample reports for parents

1. Saleha, Foundation Stage

Personal, social and emotional development: Saleha has been eager to learn and is confident about speaking in whole-class situations. She has improved in learning to wait her turn to speak. Saleha has become more independent but still needs reassurance from adults at times. She enjoys looking after visitors to the classroom and is very caring towards children that are hurt or upset.

Communication, language and literacy: our class work has covered a variety of traditional tales, modern fiction books and humorous poems. We have used illustrations to help us predict stories and used initial letters to help us work out unfamiliar words. Saleha enjoyed writing notes to the imaginary creatures in the garden and has been involved in preparing and presenting short plays in front of the other children. Saleha's reading is progressing very well and she can read a wide range of words appropriate to her age. Her writing has also developed well and she takes a pride in being neat. Saleha is now listening more carefully to aduls and is working much better as a member of a group. She loves to hear stories, songs, music, rhymes and poems. Saleha's literacy work has developed well and I am extremely pleased with her overall progress. She is now ready to tackle the greater demands of Year 1 work.

Mathematical development: key objectives for this year have been to become familiar with numbers from one to ten, using them in songs and rhymes, counting situations and simple quizzes. We have also introduced the numbers 11 to 20. Salha handled 1p, 2p and 5p coins. She used and described basic 2D and 3D shapes and also used non-standard but uniform units (such as hands, feet, bricks) to estimate and measure lengths, masses and capacities. Saleha continues to learn quickly and has exceeded the minimum expectations for the year.

Knowledge and understanding of the world: the reception group took part in a 'forces and motion' science topic by bringing in wheeled vehicles and observing the result of pushing and pulling them along. We also had races between toy cars and discussed why some toy vehicles are faster than others are. During our 'sounds and hearing' topic the children described sounds that they heard around them, both in the school building and grounds. We observed what happens when we move away from the source of a sound. Saleha took part in these sessions and was very interested all that happened. In the ICT suite, she learned mouse control and became familiar with a range of computer programs. She also used a 'floor turtle' to estimate distances. In RE, Saleha listened with interest to stories and was willing to discuss what they meant.

Creative development: Saleha has represented her creative ideas in a variety of ways and has grown in confidence. She has worked happily on group projects, such as building large models that are later played with, and individual projects when she did painting and collage. Saleha has learned to use a range of tools and materials, and particularly likes colouring on her own. She recognises that instruments can be played in a variety of ways and has developed group pieces based on different moods and places.

Physical development: Saleha has become more independent and now responds well to instructions. Her co-ordination continues to improve and she is becoming more spatially aware. Saleha has had PE lessons using the climbing apparatus and is learning to move carefully around others and handle small equipment. She especially likes PE outside, when we play whole-class games and team sports.

Personal comments: Saleha is enthusiastic about all that we do in school. She picks up new ideas very quickly and has made excellent progress overall. I am sure that she will do well in Year 1.

Head teacher's comments: Saleha's good humour and determination to do well, even when she has been a little uncertain, has been delightful to see. Well done, Saleha.

Targets for next year: Saleha must build on her good progress this year and continue enjoying learning.

2. Marshall, Year 3

VISITS
Autumn Term: Museum, local Priory, Woodland walk.
Spring Term: Cathedral.
Summer Term: Local Mosque, local Christian Centre.
ENGLISH
Reading curriculum:

- Range of fiction genre, including play scripts and poetry
- Library skills and use of the Dewey system
- Research skills, scanning, skimming, note-taking
- Phonics and spelling.

Writing curriculum:

- Writing for a variety of purposes (creative, narrative, persuasive, research, expressive, instructional)
- Sentence grammar and punctuation

Reading: Marshall has made good overall progress. His expression is developing well and he is noticing punctuation in the text. He is able to talk about his reading and make inferences from the text. Marshall receives extra literacy support and is able to apply skills learnt to his own reading. He has begun to scan text to find information.

Writing: Marshall has made steady progress. He has lovely ideas for story-writing and is remembering to use adjectives to create a picture for the reader. Sometimes his enthusiasm to write sometimes means that Marshall misses out words and forgets to use punctuation, making it difficult to follow the story plot. He can use a simple dictionary but does not always check his spellings. In handwriting, Marshall still needs to make tall and short letters more clearly distinguishable. He can join up his letters but does not always do so.

Speaking and listening: Marshall is able to listen and ask questions to help his understanding. He has an intermittent stammer that can cause him difficulty in expressing himself.

Next steps in English: Marshall needs to make inferences from the text when reading. In writing, he needs to check his work more carefully to make sure that sentences make sense. He needs to think more carefully before speaking during discussions.

MATHEMATICS

Mini-topic curriculum:

- 2D and 3D Shape
- Symmetry
- Weight and length as forms of measurement
- Data-handling
- Angles and movement
- Volume and capacity
- Time

Marshall has worked hard and made steady progress. At the start of the year he found mental/oral subtraction problems difficult but is now much more confident. He is able to find the inverse for addition and subtraction sentences and is being encouraged to use more than one strategy to solve problems.

Next steps in mathematics: Marshall needs to look carefully at a number sequence to find pattern and use this to predict the next number.

SCIENCE

Curriculum:

- Shadows and reflections
- Earth in Space
- Materials and their uses
- Changing materials
- Teeth and healthy eating
- Living things and their environment
- Green plants as organisms.

Marshall is able to talk about the properties of materials and sort them into groups according to their properties. He can describe differences between living and non-living things and has begun to think about factors that cause change.

Next steps in science: to plan a fair investigation where only one factor will change, other factors remaining constant.

HISTORY
Curriculum:

- Romans as an in-depth study
- Anglo-Saxons (outline study)
- Vikings (outline study).

Marshall thoroughly enjoyed the visit to see the Roman exhibits at the museum and the old Roman wall. His hands-on experience brought history to life for him. He has developed a growing awareness of chronology and can give some reasons why people leave their homelands and settle in another country.

GEOGRAPHY
Curriculum:

- Locality studies: the local woodland walk
- Settlements: the country of Zambia
- Mapping skills and co-ordinates.

Marshall can compare different localities, noticing similarities and differences in land use and physical features such as valleys and wooded areas. He is aware of how some land use has changed and can make suggestions as to how it might be improved.

ART
Curriculum:

- Colour-mixing and combinations
- Powder paints portraits
- Observational drawings of plants and flowers
- Batik flowers and weavings.

Marshall has worked hard to create texture in his artwork with paints, drawings and textiles. Following the educational visit, he produced a weaving that reflects the colours and feelings of the landscape. He includes a lot of fine detail in all his drawings.

MUSIC
Curriculum:

- Structure and pitch
- Duration and dynamics

- Timbre and texture
- Listening and appraising
- Composing own music.

Marshall is now able to recognise notes of differing pitch (high, low, the same). He has created repeated sound patterns and has begun to work with others to fit patterns together. He has also started to understand that layering sounds creates musical texture.

PHYSICAL EDUCATION

Curriculum:

- Games – sending and receiving ball-skills, racket-skills, team games
- Gym – pathways and levels using floor and apparatus
- Dance – linking movements, responding to narratives, rhythm and tempo.

Marshall shows good control when planning a sequence of actions, both on the floor and on benches. In games he has learned the skills of attack and defence, as well as developing accurate overarm and underarm throws.

RELIGIOUS EDUCATION

Curriculum:

- Exploring what is meant by faith and the difference it can make to people's lives
- The place of worship and prayer
- Signs and symbols
- The significance of Christmas and Easter
- Basics of Christianity and Islam.

Marshall is able to think about his own experiences, commitments and values, and contrast them with those of other people. He can explain how some aspects of religious belief are practised. He can retell the Easter story in his own words.

DESIGN TECHNOLOGY

Curriculum:

- Making permanent joins
- Investigating different temporary joins
- Making picture frames
- Moving toys
- Linkages and levers
- Problem-solving 3D construction challenges.

Marshall knows how to join a range of different materials to create permanent and temporary fixtures. He can talk about the uses for different joins. He has used his skills to create a picture frame.

INFORMATION TECHNOLOGY

Curriculum:

- Word-processing and text handling
- Textease
- Graphics
- Data-handling
- Control and programming using Roamer
- Creating and sending emails.

Marshall has used computer software to recreate part of an artist's picture and used the full range of tools to create texture. He has used a simulation program, involving mathematical problems and logical thinking. He has input data for data-handling and used word-processing. Marshall has a reasonable grasp of the function and purpose of emails.

PERSONAL, SOCIAL, CITIZENSHIP AND HEALTH EDUCATION

Curriculum:

- Friends and relationships
- Healthy living
- Keeping safe.

Marshall is now able to express his opinions and give reasons for doing so. With adult support, he is able to contribute towards setting termly targets for his development. He is also able to identify things he has achieved. Marshall understands why rules are needed and begun to exercise a level of responsibility in the classroom.

SUMMARY

Marshall has been a lovely member of the class. He has grown up a lot during the year and is taking more responsibility for his own learning. He still struggles to concentrate for any length of time and is sometimes easily distracted. Marshall tends to be careless with his work and needs to check more carefully before being satisfied. He loves to play with other children but does not have a close or special friend.

Attendance:

- Number of sessions attended since last September 292
- Total possible sessions since last September 308
- Percentage attendance 95 per cent
- Number of unauthorised absences 0.

Activate your thinking!

Imagine you are the parent. How easily would you interpret the information provided? Which information would interest you the most/the least?

Further reading

Briggs, M., Woodfield, A., Martin, C. and Swatton, P. (2003) *Assessment for Learning and Teaching in Primary Schools*, Exeter: Learning Matters.

Written for trainee teachers and newly qualified teachers teaching in Key Stages 1 and 2 who wish to develop their understanding and practice of assessment.

Drummond, M. J. (2003) *Assessing Children's Learning*, London: David Fulton.

Provides a balance of theoretical perspective and practical examples, written by an author with considerable experience in this field.

Lord, L. and Slinn, K. (2007) *Curriculum Planning and Assessment for the Foundation Stage*, London: Sage.

Provides guidance about assessing learning and how to help children in an early years' setting achieve high standards. Includes a CD-ROM.

Trodd, L. and Goodliff, G. (2007) *Achieving EYPS: Success in your Assessment*, Exeter: Learning Matters.

Structured around the three skills areas of communication, decision-making and leadership, with reference to the Early Years' Standards.

Behaviour Management

Introduction

Trainee teachers whose greatest concern is exercising class discipline should be reassured that most children enjoy school, behave sensibly for the majority of the time and want to have a positive relationship with adults and other pupils. This chapter explores a range of issues associated with children's behaviour and the strategies available for ensuring that the teaching and learning process is not hindered by the struggle to maintain order. A variety of discipline strategies are offered for consideration but these are underpinned by an acknowledgement that behind every settled classroom is a lot of hard work by the teacher in establishing and maintaining positive relationships, generating work that motivates the children and enforcing an agreed behaviour policy.

Creating a positive learning environment

It takes a visitor only a few minutes in a classroom to detect whether or not a teacher has managed to establish and maintain a positive learning environment. In the best-run classrooms, the children are lively but not silly, speak naturally to adults, treat one another kindly and do their best to succeed. Teachers use a positive tone, employ humour without losing control and rarely raise their voices. The children respond to instructions, and even to being chastened, without rancour or discord. The prevailing mood is 'all for one and one for all', rather than 'first one to the top gets the prize'. Trainee teachers often say of such situations: 'That is how I want my own classroom to be.'

The terminology used for class control issues varies but the word 'behaviour' tends to be used with respect to the child's actions and 'control' and 'discipline' with respect to the teacher's actions. That is, the teacher attempts to influence the child's behaviour through effective discipline in the belief that this is the most effective way of exercising control. However, the imposition of external constraints has limited value in as much as children ultimately need to exercise self-control rather than have it imposed on them. As Wright (2006) reminds us, a situation can arise in which a teacher 'seems to be naturally popular or charismatic', with the result that pupils want to please her or him; in doing so, however, the children may 'not assume responsibility for their own behaviour' (2006: 53). Consequently, when a different teacher is in charge, pupils who were well behaved with the first teacher fail to do so for the next.

Furthermore, it is important to remember that the term 'behaviour' does not simply encompass a child being good or naughty; it also includes other manifestations such as exhibiting shyness, withdrawal from mainstream activities and idleness. These, too, are behaviours seen in classrooms with which teachers have to cope and, hopefully, change for the better.

Teachers quickly discover that children's willingness to comply and conform to established norms of behaviour varies considerably. Some children do not have the strategies, willpower or grasp of conventions to know what 'behaving' means or the self-control to change it. As a result, the unacceptable behaviour continues and inexperienced teachers in particular may become increasingly exasperated, berating the child by fruitlessly repeating the demand to 'behave'. In addition, a small number of pupils understand the conventions but wilfully disregard them. Children therefore need to be provided with an enforceable rule framework, sensibly but consistently applied, within which they can gradually strengthen their own self-control. Dreikurs *et al.* (1998) stress the importance of helping children to take responsibility for their own actions. They cite an example of a boy who kept calling out in class. The teacher despaired of finding a solution until she asked the boy himself for his suggestions. He imposed a sanction on himself (loss of two minutes free time for each transgression) and the problem was cured within a week. Newell and Jeffery (2002: 43–8) emphasise that teachers should model good behaviour to children. Strategies include being prepared to say sorry, explain that teachers as well as children have rights, taking a keen interest in learning, demonstrating a strong sense of purpose in teaching and showing that even difficult behaviour can be overcome. Teachers have to take into account the age and experience of the children, as well as school behaviour policies, but the twin principles of consistency and fairness must apply whatever the circumstances. As Chaplain (2006) notes, 'Rules alone do not guarantee good behaviour. They need to be linked to consequences – which means *consistently* rewarding pupils who follow the rules and applying sanctions as a deterrent to those who do not' (2006: 110, author's emphasis).

Good practice

Seize the initiative early on. Don't allow yourself to be quizzed by the children, however sincerely interested in you they may appear to be. Just be politely friendly during the early encounters.

Unacceptable behaviour

Unacceptable behaviour takes many forms. Some children constantly push the boundaries and their names are upon every teacher's lips. Some children cause trouble for certain teachers but act sensibly for others. Whereas children who actively resist conforming and often behave unreasonably may require special help and intervention policies, the majority can be dealt with using basic classroom rules and procedures. Learning to cope with the vagaries of children's behaviour is helped when teachers admit that unacceptable behaviour is sometimes due to an uncertainty in children's minds about where the boundaries lie. McPhillimy (1996) issues a warning about the need for teachers to examine the *cause* of problems rather than their symptoms:

> Misbehaviour in itself is therefore mainly a symptom of a problem rather than the problem itself. If the underlying problems are dealt with, then the symptom is likely to disappear. (1996: 61)

It is also important for teachers to recognise the difference between two types of inappropriate behaviour, namely, children who misbehave and children who fail to conform.

Children who *misbehave* often do so out of choice. They understand the rules but make a decision to disregard them; they are also aware of the likely consequences but hope that they won't get caught or are insufficiently impressed by the sanction to worry if it is applied. Younger children are more likely to misbehave due to a lack of understanding of the rules and school conventions or confusion about adult expectations or an inbuilt naughtiness (not a popular word but very apt in some cases).

Some children *fail to conform*, either because they do not see the need to do so or lack the maturity to comply. In most cases, the situation can be remedied by patient, persistent explanation and use of peer pressure. Children new to school may simply lack awareness of what is required; older ones may be egocentric or come from a family/cultural background that fosters single-mindedness. Typically, the behaviour of non-conformists varies little inside and outside school. Such children seem puzzled when confronted by an insistent adult who explains to them that a particular action is not acceptable. Parents, when asked about their non-conformist children, will often sigh and admit that they cannot do anything much with them either. Children who fail to conform may be highly motivated or sluggish, popular or aloof, pleasant or miserable, but they have in common their persistent refusal or inability to act in a conventional manner. Non-conformists wander when they are meant to be seated, approach their work differently from others, insist on working alone instead of collaboratively and show an attitude towards the teacher which varies from disdain to wild enthusiasm. Repeated day after day the irregular behaviour can, understandably, cause teachers to become irritated and frustrated with the child.

It is desirable but far from easy to channel the energies of non-conformist children into productive activities. Teachers are keen to curb the unacceptable behaviour but fear that if they are too insistent the child concerned may suffer a loss of confidence or start to rebel and turn into a persistent offender. Regular calm explanations and consistent teacher direction help to regulate the situation but the children's inability to grasp conventions makes the process protracted. Inappropriate behaviour of all types may not arise due to pupils' inability to understand what is expected of them but from a teacher's failure to gain pupils' respect due to a timid personality, mundane teaching approach or lacklustre content to lessons. In such cases, efforts to gain control are likely to fail.

Activate your thinking!

Consider the children in your class who exhibit inappropriate behaviour. Try to categorise as follows:

- Those who are regularly mischievous but generally harmless.
- Those who misbehave wilfully.
- Those who are non-conformists.

Consider how you might react to the same sort of inappropriate behaviour from a child in each of the categories.

Factors influencing behaviour

Terminology is important when considering issues of control and discipline. *Bad behaviour* involves making a judgement about someone's actions and intent. In school, the person evaluating the behaviour is usually the teacher and the one being judged, the pupil. Bad behaviour may be wilful (deliberate) or unintended. Similarly, all children (and adults, for that matter) are capable of *irresponsible* behaviour when, for a short period of time, common sense and rational thought seem to disappear. Such moments are different from the concept of indiscipline which occurs when children know what they should do but choose not to do it.

When teachers have to deal with unsatisfactory behaviour, it is a signal that something has already gone wrong, so it is important for them to give serious thought as to why it has happened and whether it can be prevented in the future. If a framework of rules is established early on, discussed with the children and frequently reviewed, it provides a yardstick against which to judge behaviour and determine sanctions (where appropriate). However, it is important to distinguish between 'order' in the classroom and an 'orderly' classroom. Order can be achieved by insisting that the children adhere to a rigid set of requirements of the 'do this but do not do that' type, reminiscent of military commands. Children have only to step slightly out of line to invoke a sanction, placing a considerable strain on the purposeful classroom environment that you are trying to achieve. Orderliness, on the other hand, stresses the fact that the classroom functions smoothly because everyone is clear about the boundaries, involved in reviewing them and invited to talk sensibly about infringements. In an orderly classroom, teachers and other adults are uncompromising about deliberate improper behaviour, but more concerned with achieving satisfactory outcomes than inflexibly applying sanctions. Indeed, Willick (2006) warns against the 'over-reliance on sanctions that can create an atmosphere of distrust, fear and resentment, as well as having a negative effect on relationships' (2006: 72). Punishments should be reserved for deliberate offending against the rules. Unintended infringements and silliness can normally be resolved through dialogue with the child and establishing a target for rectifying the situation.

Adult–child relationships

We have already noted that the majority of pupils of all ages want to do well and please their teacher. Effective working relationships develop gradually through regular interaction between adult and child, relevant work and interesting lessons. Teachers who are harsh, unreasonable, condescending or insincere are inviting problems of indiscipline as children react negatively towards such attitudes or lose confidence and thereby underachieve. A positive classroom climate is assisted by being firm, fair and tolerant of genuine mistakes. Teachers who have a natural manner and develop a sincere approach to their teaching, aided by a cheerful disposition, are unlikely to suffer unduly from misbehaving pupils. Good relationships are not built overnight; they require perseverance, application and a genuine desire to help children succeed.

Developing a philosophy

Establishing and maintaining high standards of behaviour depend, in part, upon a teacher's philosophy of education. As noted elsewhere in this book, teachers will use teaching strategies and approaches that reflect their own beliefs about the ways that children learn best. Teachers who are willing to persevere in order to achieve their educational aims, yet who are ready to accept advice and modify their practices accordingly, are usually at ease with themselves about their work, and transmit this confidence to their pupils. Teachers that have no clear idea about the direction of their teaching, and meander from one extreme to another, are almost certain to produce an unstable learning environment. Trainee teachers are, to a large extent, bound by the host teacher's preferences and ideals. However, over the period of the placement you should be able to gently influence the situation, such that your developing beliefs about teaching and learning can be tested, refined and implemented during your interaction with the pupils.

Activate your thinking!

Consider how much these three wise sayings reflect your own views:

> The main part of intellectual education is not the acquisition of facts but learning how to make facts live.
>
> Attributed to Oliver Wendell Holmes

> I cannot teach anybody anything, I can only make them think.
>
> Attributed to Socrates, Greek philosopher

> An educational system isn't worth a great deal if it teaches young people how to make a living but doesn't teach them how to make a life.
>
> Source unknown

What would your 'wise saying' be?

Cementing the bond

Children react adversely against autocratic teachers, those who try to lord it over them and those who demand too much, too soon, without offering patient help and advice in the completion of tasks. It is essential for teachers to win pupils' co-operation and show that they like them, but in such a way that the separate adult and child identities are maintained. To win co-operation necessitates teachers taking a real interest in the children, listening to their comments and requests, and responding with positive suggestions, praise, encouragement and trust. All teachers have times when they struggle to make headway with their class; the bank of goodwill that is stored up during the 'plentiful' times needs to be there to draw on in the hard times.

True freedom

It should be evident that blatant contravention of rules has to be dealt with firmly, yet some inexperienced teachers seem to imagine that if things are ignored they will fade away naturally. However, offering pupils 'freedom in learning' is not the same as giving them 'freedom to behave in any way they choose'. Children need to know what is judged to be acceptable and appropriate behaviour, including the way they address one another and the teacher, their application to the task in hand and the extent of their co-operation. The occasional unsettling incident in which children say, in effect, that they are free to do what they want, how they want, provides a stark reminder (if any were needed) that selfish behaviour leads to unhappiness and insecurity. While you will doubtless be striving to involve children in decisions about their lives in school, your position as the experienced adult, plus your knowledge of whole-school policies (about which pupils may have little knowledge) entitles you to be the final arbiter.

Emphasising the positive

Most unsatisfactory behaviour can be resolved without causing humiliation or loss of face to either child or adult. This is not the same as saying that children should get away with things, as they need to realise that every action has a consequence. Some children are unaware of the impact their behaviour has on others and it needs to be pointed out to them that they have responsibilities as well as rights. The majority of children respond positively to genuine praise and encouragement, and even the most mischievous tyke prefers specific guidance and the opportunity to master skills and to learn something new to aimlessly causing disruption. Kohn (2004) warns, however, that teachers need to be careful not to create what he describes as 'praise junkies', as a calculated tactic to control children's behaviour rather than as a genuine expression of admiration. Although class control and discipline require the application of appropriate techniques and strategies to curb inappropriate behaviour and ensure that potential troublemakers are kept in check, the most effective learning environment grows in the soil of high motivation and a desire to learn. Children will not want to misbehave if, in doing so, they reduce the thrill and adventure that happy learning experiences bring.

The teacher's role

Although it is not popular to say so, teachers can sometimes contribute to the causes of bad behaviour. Unfairness, impatience and poor lesson preparation can create the conditions for resentment and discontent to occur. The end result is a deterioration of the atmosphere, control problems and a negative impact on learning. Jacques (2007) comments that trainees and some experienced teachers tend to blame the children when behaviour difficulties arise. Jacques emphasises the point that different circumstances simply mean that different discipline strategies have to be employed. While in the normal run-of-the-mill times, a teacher can rely on the existing good relationship that exists with pupils to allow simple tactics such as a shake of the head to diffuse the situation, on other occasions some tight control strategies have to be employed. Nevertheless, if children are regularly proving to be a headache, it is important to take a step back and consider reasons other than placing the blame *wholly* on them.

There are many ways in which poor behaviour may be, at least in part, a reflection of the teacher's failings; for example, it might come about through a lack of dialogue with the children that lead to misunderstandings, intolerance, inappropriate lessons, harsh sanctions or petty fault-finding. However, as Haydn (2006) notes, most pupils behave better when the teacher comes into the session equipped with a well-prepared lesson. Haydn cannily points out that pupils as well as teachers differentiate, but whereas teachers focus on the tasks, pupils focus on the teachers.

Conflict in the classroom is not inevitable and can usually be avoided by following the advice offered elsewhere in this chapter and implementing appropriate strategies. In addition, by using the strategies listed below, your classroom has a good chance of becoming the positive and industrious working environment you want it to be, and your lessons will be a joy instead of a chore.

Demonstrate genuine caring

Although teachers care about their pupils, it probably does not occur to most pupils that this is so. Teachers have, therefore, to demonstrate a caring attitude through the way they address children, the interest they show in their welfare and the action they take to ensure that justice is done and that no child is disadvantaged. Caring is also shown by insisting that rules are followed and by giving vulnerable children a secure framework within which to develop good patterns of behaviour.

Stay calm and alert

Teachers have little chance of improving a situation of potential conflict if they lose their self-control. When problems appear to be developing, it is important to reassure pupils that things are in hand. You will be better equipped to cope by breathing deeply, speaking a little more slowly than usual, smiling gently when speaking and keeping wide-open eyes. Potentially difficult situations can often be defused if teachers simply refuse to be rattled by them. Even if an unwanted incident occurs, make sure that you are decisive but not explosive.

Do not jump to conclusions

Situations are not always what they may seem. Taking time to discover the facts before making a judgement or accusation and issuing sanctions is essential in settling disputes. It is better to spend a little time sorting out a *real* problem than acting decisively in dealing with an imagined one. Pupils become exasperated and annoyed when teachers blunder in and make matters worse by jumping to unwarranted conclusions. On the other hand, when the position is clearer, do not hesitate to make tough decisions in cases of serious misconduct.

Concentrate on what children are saying

The only way for adults to discover the truth is to listen carefully to what children have to say. Some teachers try to listen but due to the pressure of the moment do not properly hear what is being said. Wise (2000) argues that the most effective teacher–pupil relationships are built by teachers listening attentively to their pupils and hearing their voices.

Enter a constructive dialogue

Although children normally begin by defending their actions, accusing others or reacting angrily, it is important to introduce a positive element to the conversation as soon as possible. Skilled teachers ask distracting questions which focus attention away from the problem. For example: 'Whose class are you in?' or 'Have you told Mrs Osman about your concerns yet?' rather than 'Who started hitting first?'. Once the children become less animated and begin to speak in a natural tone, the main issues can usually be discussed without undue rancour.

Avoid banal questions

Some questions that teachers ask are not really questions at all, but rather a poor attempt to exercise control. For example:

The unanswerable question: For goodness sake, what's the matter with you today?

The threatening question: Are you going to finish that work or do you want to stay in at playtime?

The self-evident question: Do you mean to say that you weren't you listening when I told everyone?

The banal question: Would you behave like that at home?

Such pointless questions are likely to irritate children and may invite ridicule and sarcasm from older pupils. Far better to say something like this:

'You seem very unsettled today. Is there any reason for the fact that you are saying silly things? (Pause) Well, please keep quiet and don't talk to anyone for the next five minutes.'

'Do you know how to do your work? (Pause) Well, we only have 10 minutes until we clear up before playtime, so you'll have to work extra hard to finish.'

'Graham, please whisper to Jack what I said to everyone a few moments ago.'

'Sara, we don't allow rude words in school. Please do not say it again.' (But don't be surprised if Sara innocently asks you why it is rude.)

Facilitate agreement about the way ahead

In situations of potential conflict, it is possible for teachers to deal with the immediate circumstances but fail to offer pupils a strategy for the future. Once a satisfactory dialogue has been established, children must be given clearly defined steps to follow so that improvements can be monitored and approved, both by the teacher and the child. If you don't offer such strategies, you will probably be dealing repeatedly with the same issue.

Silly behaviour

It is important to be reminded of the basic truth that children are just that, children. Most of them enjoy life and have fun; they want to do well at school and be happy with their friends. In the average class, the vast majority are likeable and a pleasure to teach. Very few children are deviant, though some are regular rule-breakers and persistent offenders. It is likely that such children have had poor parenting or may suffer from a poor attitude that creates in them a tendency to defy authority or to be self-centred. However, most unacceptable behaviour is due to silliness rather than deviance and takes a number of different forms:

Uncontrolled behaviour: shouting out an answer to a question without permission.

Arrogant: calling out a 'clever' remark.

Distractive: showing off by doing something daring.

Detached: deliberately working very slowly.

Spiteful: teasing another child.

Insolent: asking pointless questions or making crude remarks.

Deceptive: pretending not to understand.

These instances are common in some classrooms and are associated with inappropriate work, boredom or general lack of respect for adults. Silly behaviour may signal that it is time to change content, terminate a teaching approach or re-evaluate lesson management. On such occasions it is important that teachers try to understand the behaviour and respond constructively rather than unthinkingly. Thus, with respect to the above seven categories:

Uncontrolled behaviour: children who call out without permission lack self-discipline or do not understand the rules. The most appropriate response is to ask the child to tell you the rule; if an answer is not forthcoming, ask another child to state it.

Arrogant behaviour: children who call out a silly remark may be signalling a lack of respect for the teacher or simply showing off to impress friends. If you ask the child to stand up and, after getting the other children quiet, ask him or her to repeat the comment. This may well trigger raucous laughter, but ignore it and insist that the child repeats the comment once again. After three or four repeats the humour will dry up and it will be obvious to everyone that arrogant remarks are simply not worth making. After the lesson talk to the child individually and sternly, in sight of another adult.

Distractive behaviour: children who show off are probably doing so because it is more enjoyable than concentrating on tedious work. Apart from making the work more interesting, the most effective strategy is to set short time-related targets and monitor them closely.

Detached behaviour: children who work very slowly may be showing that they are not prepared to engage with uninteresting or unduly demanding activities. Some children suffer from diagnosable attention-deficit, which may require specialist advice; on the other hand the child may be lazy or indifferent. Such problems usually take a considerable amount of time to resolve, so trainee teachers can only keep the class teacher informed of developments and persevere.

Spiteful behaviour: children who deliberately tease another child are enjoying the power that accompanies ridicule. Immediate action is required. Follow the school's guidelines and keep a record of incidents.

Insolent behaviour: children who ask pointless questions are wasting time but avoiding confrontation with the teacher by giving the appearance of interest. Don't play this game. One useful strategy is to be dismissive of the question and turn your attention immediately to another matter. Insolent children thrive on the oxygen of publicity, so make sure you deprive them of it.

Deceptive behaviour: children who pretend not to understand may be trying to undermine the teacher's authority and create a distraction from the main point of the lesson. There are occasions when it is worth following children's genuine and spontaneous interests. However, as you become aware of deceptive behaviour it is a relatively simply matter to tell the child to see you after the lesson to discuss the matter. The chances are that he or she will be first out of the door.

These and similar strategies are used by the very small number of children who have decided that messing about is preferable to concentrating on the work; their actions are deliberate but not necessarily serious if attended to appropriately from an early stage. Although teachers rightly feel annoyed by the disruptions, they also act as a warning signal about the need to review the lesson's effectiveness and relevance. It is difficult to make every lesson stimulating and relevant for all children, but persistent boredom not only affects the quality of the children's work but also influences their attitudes (see Figure 8.1).

Faced with silly behaviour, inexperienced teachers may be tempted to ignore it or hope that by sounding fierce they can minimise the disruption. In fact, ignoring the behaviour is rarely effective (though there are exceptions to this rule, see later) and may indicate to the class that the teacher is not in control of events. Similarly, severe comments often make matters worse in the long term and lead to teacher exhaustion and distress. The problem with harsh reactions is that they deal only with the symptoms and not the underlying causes such as boredom, bravado,

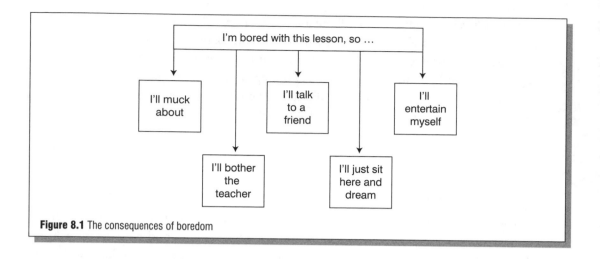

Figure 8.1 The consequences of boredom

inappropriate lessons, inadequate lesson management, and so on. Quite often, these underlying causes take time to diagnose and remedy, so a teacher may have to resort to *holding measures* as a temporary means of counteracting the silly behaviour. Examples of holding methods for each of the above categories of behaviour include the following set of reactions:

Uncontrolled behaviour. 'Olive, you forgot our count to three before you speak rule. Please remember in future.' (The response is merely a statement of fact and avoids attributing blame.)

Arrogant behaviour. 'John. Remember to put your hand up first and take your turn if you've anything to say.' (The response strengthens the teacher's authority, reminds everyone of the rules and avoids confrontation with John.)

Distractive behaviour. 'Please sit still on your chair, Rhoda, we don't want anyone injured, thank you.' (The response focuses upon Rhoda's welfare rather than her inappropriate behaviour.)

Detached behaviour. 'Are you finding this difficult, Ellie? Perhaps I can help you along a bit.' (The response allows the teacher to set short-term targets for Ellie.)

Spiteful behaviour. 'If you've got anything to say, Ben, say something kind; otherwise keep quiet. Let's see how helpful you can be for the remainder of the lesson; I'll ask you about it after everyone has gone out.' (The response indicates the teacher's displeasure, sets boundaries upon Ben's behaviour and offers him the chance to redeem himself.)

Insolent behaviour. 'Put your hand up if you think you know the answer to Gordon's question.' (The response focuses upon Gordon's 'ignorance' and allows other children to gain satisfaction from offering the correct answer. An ironic afterthought is also useful: 'It looks as if everybody knew the answer except you, Gordon. You will need to work harder if you want to keep up with the others.')

Deceptive behaviour. 'If you don't understand by now, Julie, you'd better stay behind after the lesson and I'll explain it to you then.' (The response calls Julie's bluff and puts the onus upon her to complete the work.)

Good practice

Don't just remind the children of the agreed procedure; *rehearse* it with them.

These holding responses do not solve the underlying problem but allow a teacher to continue the lesson without undue disruption, losing face or causing damage to relationships. If the behaviour is repeated or is serious, the teacher will certainly want to see the child after the session and express disapproval in an uncharged atmosphere or in the presence of a senior teacher. Children who misbehave through silliness rather than deviance are corrected through a combination of firmness, fairness and attention to future lesson content and delivery. However, teachers who rely on the holding strategy without looking more deeply into the situation are likely to experience a recurrence of the unwanted behaviour and further struggles to gain control.

Whenever possible, speak to a child directly after the session about the unacceptable behaviour. Make sure that other children nearby do not interrupt you. Tell the child how you feel. Express your disappointment. Ask for an explanation. Listen carefully to the reply. Don't patronise or ridicule. Stay calm and serious but speak naturally. Look the child in the eye and try to show that you are interested in what she or he has to say. If appropriate, ask the child what he or she suggests can be done to improve the situation. End the conversation positively and indicate that you are expecting something better in future. Over the next few sessions, do not pay the child unnatural attention but if possible find opportunity to commend work without fuss. Don't expect miracles. Keep things in proportion. React but don't over-react to silly behaviour.

Good practice

Try treating silly pupils with a greater level of seriousness than their behaviour deserves. Pretend that they are sensible children and trust them with some responsibility. Speak to them in a more 'grown-up' manner. Evaluate over a period of a few days whether the way you treat them affects the way they begin to behave.

Deviant behaviour

In contrast to silliness, deviant forms of behaviour can be intimidating to the teacher and threaten the wellbeing of the other children. Deviant behaviour is typified by one or more of the following: belligerent answering back, fierce anger, agitated protest and shouting, and refusal to do any work. Every school has a policy for dealing with this type of indiscipline and the agreed procedures have to be consistently followed if progress is to be made. If the child exhibits worrying traits of the sort described, it is certain that the head teacher is already well aware of the problem and parents have been contacted; however, you must still ensure that you keep senior staff informed about developments. In situations where there are repeated instances of wilful behaviour, write a brief note of each incident (what happened and when) for future reference.

Deviant behaviour in which pupils are wilfully disobedient or defiant is thankfully rare but can be unnerving for teachers, who then agonise over ways in which they might contain a situation that will certainly not correct itself without intervention. While action is being taken with the assistance of more experienced colleagues, you will have to be sternly insistent and openly state to the child the things that will not be tolerated. Setting realistic and enforceable short-term goals is essential, but in reality you may have to accommodate minor points of behaviour when addressing the central misdemeanour. For example, if a boy is behaving wildly in a games' session, the fact that he is using bad language is not of prime importance and can be dealt with when the situation is calm. Similarly, a young girl throwing a tantrum can tie her flapping shoelaces later. These 'secondary' matters *should* eventually be dealt with but not in the heat of battle, unless they provide a useful distraction.

Inducements to more acceptable behaviour have to be used within a strictly defined code, explained to the child and, if possible agreed verbally by him or her. More serious situations will involve the SENCO and, perhaps, a school–home agreement involving parents. Progress with pupils showing deviant tendencies is likely to be slow and in a tiny minority of cases a trainee teacher on placement may only see marginal improvement during his or her time in school. If the indiscipline becomes very serious and other children's learning is deemed to be suffering, the head teacher may decide to remove the transgressor from the classroom or, in the most extreme cases, exclude the child from school. Unfortunately, children who exhibit deviant behaviour often come from homes in which such behaviour is condoned or parents are grappling with similar challenges themselves. Trainee teachers should never be, and rarely are, left to struggle unassisted with devious children. When the behaviour is deemed to be sufficiently serious, a learning support assistant may be allocated to work with the child for part of the day.

Finally, it is important to distinguish children who are behaving in a deviant manner from those who are struggling with a diagnosable condition, such as attention deficit and hyperactivity disorder, ADHD (see, for example, Kewley 2001; Lougy *et al.* 2007). ADHD is a common behavioural disorder that affects an estimated eight per cent to 10 per cent of school-age children. Boys are about three times more likely than girls to be diagnosed with the problem, though it's not yet clear about the reasons. Children with ADHD act without thinking, are excessively active, and have trouble focusing on a task. They may understand what's expected of them but have trouble following through because they can't sit still, pay attention, or attend to details. Although there is still active debate about the concept of ADHD, the principle for every teacher should be to deal with the causes of the behaviour as well as the consequences. In doing so, it is generally accepted that the disorder takes one of three forms: (a) inattentiveness; (b) hyperactive-impulsiveness; and (c) a combination of types (a) and (b). It is obvious that the most challenging behaviour occurs in type (c). The condition of *inattentiveness* is characterised by some or all of the following:

- Lack of attention to detail; a tendency to make careless errors

- Short concentration span (for example, when playing)

- Poor organisational skills; messy; random

- Inconsistent listening skills

- Avoidance of tasks or activities that require prolonged mental effort

- Easily distracted

- Forgetful

- Tendency to mislay or lose items.

Type (b), *hyperactivity-impulsiveness*, is characterised by:

- Difficulty in sitting still; fidgeting, squirming in the seat

- Unpredictable tendency to run, sprint or dash about

- Excessively talking and moving about

- Calling out random answers to questions

- Reluctance to take turns or queue up

- Constantly interrupting, imposing on and annoying classmates.

It is important to remember that children genuinely suffering from ADHD are not 'being naughty' in the commonly accepted sense of the term; they may be suffering from an undetectable brain disorder or have been affected by (say) difficulties during the mother's pregnancy or environmental factors (e.g. a chaotic lifestyle at home or even too much exposure to TV/video games). You can, however, assist these children – indeed, *all* children – by using a variety of strategies, including:

- Ensuring a regular routine, e.g. using a specific peg to hang coats; sitting on the same chair in the same place; always occupying the same position in a line of children

- Providing specific assistance in organising belongings, trays, books, and so forth

- Minimising the chances of distraction by careful positioning of the child's seating, insisting that other children do not become bothersome and allowing extra time to complete an absorbing task

- Using brief and clear instructions

- Limiting choices to two or three rather than having many choices

- Employing an easily comprehended reward system, with smaller, short-term rewards (e.g. having first choice of toys; allowed to use the computer during a wet playtime) as well as major long-term ones (such as a certificate or special mention in assembly)

- Using loss of privilege as the main discipline tactic

- Finding and promoting any interest or talent that the child may possess.

As a trainee teacher you will find it hard to distinguish between pupils who deliberately 'play you up' because they choose to do so, and pupils who suffer from a hyperactivity disorder that creates inattentiveness (e.g. 'daydreaming') or impulsive behaviour. Seek advice from more experienced colleagues (including TAs) and avoid becoming unduly frustrated with the child. Look for redeeming features in the child, such as simplicity of character, enthusiasm and spontaneity, rather than dwelling endlessly on the flaws.

Responding to unacceptable behaviour

Taking suitable action when faced with poor behaviour is one of the challenges that teachers face as they seek to establish a well controlled yet inspiring classroom environment. Tolerance of minor instances of unacceptable behaviour will be counter-productive if it leads to a worsening situation in the long run. On the other hand, early intervention can also be unhelpful if it disrupts the flow of a lesson, sours the atmosphere or creates unease among more timid children. Some trainee teachers regret that they were 'too soft' early on in their teaching and insufficiently firm in the opening encounters with a new class. Others employ unnecessarily heavy-handed tactics when a lighter touch would be enough, thereby causing ill-feeling and dismay among the children. There is always a danger of developing an impulsive response to every slight breach of the rules that result in stress for both teacher and children.

Circumstances need to be taken into account when deciding how to respond to misbehaviour. For instance, the child who is normally sensible but on one occasion excitedly throws a rubber across the room is unlikely to repeat the action if chastened; it would be foolish to over-react by using fierce remarks or invoking a sanction. On the other hand, a persistently troublesome child is unlikely to respond to a gentle approach or to sanctions that have been used repeatedly without effect. In this case, a much firmer response is required (in accordance with school policy). Similarly, common sense suggests that end-of-term bravado or wet playtime excitement induces unnatural behaviour and should be treated understandingly. At the other extreme, a single act of bullying needs to be dealt with firmly, regardless of the circumstances.

If teachers show agitation every time a child is perceived as behaving unacceptably, it is the child who is controlling the situation and not the teacher. Unless the boundaries of acceptable behaviour are clear, the action–reaction process continues, both teacher and child become edgy, and nothing is improved. During succeeding days, the pattern is repeated:

Step 1: Child behaves unacceptably > Teacher responds agitatedly.

Step 2: Child repeats the behaviour > Teacher responds sternly.

Step 3: Child repeats the behaviour once again > Teacher imposes sanction.

And so on.

The problem with this action–reaction process is not only that the child is dictating the pattern of teacher response but also that the causes of the unacceptable behaviour are not being addressed. In particular, a characteristic of effective behaviour management is that it *acts to prevent*, deter or reduce the undesirable actions, rather than remedying them once they have occurred.

Understanding the distinction between 'prevention' and 'cure' is important for every practitioner. Put bluntly, poor behaviour is often an indication of the behaviour management's failure.

Whether unacceptable behaviour is an occasional wilful act or a persistent trend, teachers understandably interpret it as a challenge or threat to their authority and a reflection upon their ability to cope. However, if these feelings result in a series of instinctive, defensive reactions, little is gained and the situation will probably worsen. Teachers rightly argue that 'something has to be done' but it is not merely a case of 'doing something' but of doing the right thing. In deciding upon the most appropriate strategy to use, a number of factors need to be considered:

A teacher may not recognise the message that the behaviour carries

As noted earlier, poor behaviour sometimes indicates that there is something wrong with the lesson, the teacher's attitude or the teaching approach. It is easy to blame the children or refer to a class as 'difficult' without examining teaching factors that may be contributing to the problem. Inappropriate work, over-reliance on a single teaching method or poor organisation can create or foster a restless climate.

Differences between the teacher's and the children's perceptions

Although there are obvious instances of unacceptable behaviour, adults may find themselves attaching far more significance to an act than was intended by the pupil. Even wilful behaviour is not necessarily directed at the teacher but may be a consequence of youthful exuberance or high spirits. Learning to distinguish between silliness and wilfulness is a skill that every practitioner needs to sharpen.

Children may be experiencing hardship outside school

Uncertainty or anguish about personal circumstances can make it almost impossible for a pupil to behave rationally. Children, like all of us, react differently when home life or relationships are unsteady. Allowance needs to be made for irrational behaviour from a normally compliant child. It is often sufficient to have a quiet word after the session to ascertain the source of the problem.

Responding to unacceptable behaviour is a challenge for every teacher. It requires patient, determined application, particularly in new situations. Strategies that appear to work with one group of pupils may be less successful with a different set of pupils, even in an almost identical situation. The challenges are particularly acute when starting to teach in a new school, where codes of conduct and accepted procedures are taken for granted by the existing staff and pupils but have yet to be learned by the new teacher. Trainee teachers on placement are, of course, regularly experiencing this impediment, but Neill and Caswell (1993) describe how this situation faces all new teachers, even experienced ones:

> Experienced teachers who move to a new school are sometimes surprised by the sudden need to put effort into controlling their classes. They are not always aware how much they previously relied on

their thorough, but subliminal, knowledge of the formal and informal procedures of their old school and their reputation among the children. (1993: 4)

Consequently, if you are a trainee teacher on school experience, it is hardly surprising if the first few weeks with a new class prove to be challenging. In every placement there is a 'tipping point', after which the situation settles and the conditions improve, or they remain as unsatisfactory but you learn to cope, howbeit miserably. The trainees whose circumstances improve are those who resolve early behavioural challenges and strive to create a relaxed but purposeful learning climate, where mutual respect and the desire to succeed are normal. Trainees who merely survive are those who never manage to resolve the challenges; instead, they adjust their teaching approach – usually becoming more formal and austere – to contain the worst of the behaviour. It is obvious which of the two situations is preferable. Killick (2006) reminds us that being relaxed is important for thinking in a more creative way, and adds that if people are feeling as if they are being evaluated this is likely to lead to increased arousal. He summarises his argument with reference to Stallard (2002) in a simple sub-heading: 'Think good – feel good; feel good – learn good'.

Activate your thinking!

Consider the extent to which pupils' behaviour patterns have been determined by: (a) their uncertainty about the rules; (b) their wilfulness; and (c) your own lack of dynamism and resourcefulness.

One way or another it is essential that you do not exacerbate control and discipline problems by your ignorance of the way things are done in the school/classroom or pupils' expectations about what is required of them. If children sense that you are allowing them liberties that their other teachers forbid, they are likely to take advantage of you. The following offers a summary of key strategies that should result in harmonious teaching and learning.

Speak naturally

Shouting rarely works and damages the classroom climate as well as your voice. Developing a strong voice takes practice but is more effective than a shrill or strained one. Ideally, your voice should be natural and carry authority for, as Rogers (1998) puts it, 'the adult tongue is a powerful weapon' (1998: 223). See also Rogers, 2006.

Distinguish between enthusiasm and disobedience

Some children get so absorbed in their work that they are reluctant to stop. Avoid being irritated; instead say something like 'I'm pleased that you are so keen on your work, Jack, but everyone is waiting for you'. Younger children's voices become high-pitched if they get carried away with enthusiasm for what they are doing. Persevere with gentle, personal (rather than public) reminders to individual children to speak normally. It is worth modelling the different voices to a child and encouraging him or her to practise using an appropriate tone along with you.

Make your instructions direct and specific

A comment like: 'Douglas, please concentrate on what Rachel is saying' is preferable to 'Douglas, stop messing about with Wayne'. Again, it is better to say 'Put your pencils down after finishing the next sentence and look this way' than to say 'Everybody pay attention to me'. Many teachers give out too many general statements such as 'Settle down' or 'Get on with your work quietly' or the ubiquitous 'Sh-hh' rather than giving specific commands.

Relax your voice when asking for children's attention

If possible, lower the pitch rather than raising it. Give pupils time to respond. If they are slow in responding, use a technique such as 'fingers on lips' (or the agreed signal to pay attention) or say 'If the person next to you is not yet paying attention, please whisper in his ear that we are waiting'. Do not 'wait for ever' but avoid getting frantic and, crucially, do not allow other children to say 'shh' or rebuke classmates on your behalf, which over time undermines your authority.

Decide when it is right to get angry

Some trainee teachers feel awkward about expressing anger. Instead, they hold their feelings in and pretend to be sweet and sugary with the children. In fact, anger is neither right nor wrong. It depends on the circumstances under which it is used. In the general run of classroom life, a teacher who frequently got angry would either be a nervous wreck or be terrorising the children. Anger should be expressed calmly but assertively through voice tone and body language. The best teachers do not have to shout but have the ability to speak with such precision that even the worst offender is chastened.

Do not confuse anger with rage

Most adults can, if they wish, frighten children by their rage and temper. This form of conduct is professionally unacceptable and may even be interpreted as bullying. If you feel yourself 'coming to the boil' it is better to stop the lesson and stare through the window for a few seconds, hands loosely at your side and breathing deeply. Slowing the voice, deepening the tone and moving a little closer to the children will convey your feelings and may save you from saying something in the heat of the moment that you later regret. It is particularly galling when you sense that the children are being wilfully mischievous, but focus on the basic advice given in this chapter and don't be a helpless victim of your own emotions.

Commend appropriate behaviour

When pupils respond appropriately, thank them and continue immediately. Do not begin a speech to the effect that you are not prepared to be kept waiting like this in future, etc. When a class is settling or coming to order, commend the children who are doing well rather than spending all your time criticising the unco-operative types. When the class is settled you can spend a moment saying 'Well done. I was very pleased that so many of you tidied up so quickly. Thank you. A few of you were leaving it to the others. I've made a note of who you are and next time I shall expect you to make a special effort.' Even in your commendations, be fairly brisk and sound as if you expected good behaviour.

Motivate pupils to secure best results

It is important to remind yourself of the cardinal truth that motivated children rarely misbehave. If pupils are under-stimulated, unclear about standards of work and get away with a final product of mediocre quality, then it is little wonder that their behaviour deteriorates and their respect for you diminishes. Make your classroom buzz with interest and be a place where children can learn about the world, themselves and one another. Reassure them that getting something wrong or misunderstanding an idea is an integral part of the learning process; celebrate achievements cheerfully; share humorous moments; be serious when necessary; have fun; be the sort of teacher they will one day tell their grandchildren about.

Learning to cope with every eventuality

First encounters

Throughout their student life, trainee teachers dream of the time when they will have their own classes, free from the constraints of fitting in with someone else's routines and preferences, and liberated from being assessed by class teachers, mentors and college tutors. In reality, to have your own class is both delightful and daunting: delightful because it is the culmination of years of study and provides the opportunity to exercise your own judgement; daunting because you quickly become aware of the enormous responsibility lying before you.

To paraphrase comments from many newly qualified teachers as they reflect upon their first day with a class: 'When you walk into that classroom, shut the door and look at the class of children in front of you, you suddenly realise that you are on your own. You don't know whether to cry from fear or elation'. This mixture of emotions that wells up when newly qualified teachers first face their class is a powerful one. Trainee teachers, standing in front of a new class for the first time, experience similar feelings.

Over the coming days and weeks, nervous new teachers discover that they are not alone, that education is a joint endeavour involving colleagues, parents and numerous unseen members of the community. Nevertheless, those first few days are important in respect of maintaining and establishing order. More experienced teachers have the advantage of knowing the ropes and having had opportunities to establish their relationships and school–wide reputation; new teachers have not. More experienced teachers are described by the children in various ways:

'Miss Chapman's really nice and reads us funny poems.'

'Mr Howard plays his guitar and does singing with you.'

'Mrs Ballam brings in animals from home.'

'Mr Fielding'll *do* you if you muck about.'

And so on. After teaching for a year or so, the reputation of teachers (for better or worse) goes before them and provides a platform for establishing a satisfactory learning environment. The new teacher and trainee teacher, entering the classroom for the first time, do not have this advantage, and need to work hard to ensure that things run smoothly. In doing so, a number of assumptions can be made:

- The children will be as excited and expectant as you are

- Many children will test the boundaries of behaviour and note your reactions

- No matter how much planning is done, it will take time before lessons and sessions settle into a routine

- There will be some misunderstandings as the settling process takes place

- Relationships lie at the heart of successful teaching and learning.

Even experienced teachers find that it can take several weeks before the classroom rhythm becomes established. In particular, the first few days are crucial. Younger children require specific guidance about basic procedures; older ones need to know how the new person's expectations and ideas differ from those of previous teachers. Even if you feel insecure and uncertain about what to expect, you need to give a strong impression of decisiveness and confidence to convince the class that you are in control and intend to be taken seriously. As part of the settling procedures, certain times of the day and certain events provide opportunities for unacceptable behaviour. Teachers sometimes refer to these occasions as the 'sticky spots' and the following are typical.

The start of a session

This is an important phase of every lesson. Simple strategies such as counting down from five to one, encouraging children to chant a simple rhyme as they settle or subtracting the time you are kept waiting from their playtime assists a smooth start. Eventually you will want the children to settle without direction, though very young children may need guidance about where to sit. If the children have been in assembly just beforehand, it is sensible to use a few physical stretching exercises or give them a minor desk-task for a few minutes (such as copying some spellings or drawing a diagram) before commencing the formal session.

After a wet playtime

A wet playtime means that the children will have been inside with little chance to expend their energy. The classroom may be hot and airless and the children restless. Consequently, except in the worst weather, it is worth opening the windows for a few minutes and (again) spending a short time in a simple but orderly whole-class activity. For example, using a 'do this, do that' game or write-draw five creatures that wriggle to move (or a similar straightforward task that helps them to concentrate). Although the settling activity absorbs a few minutes of the lesson, it is preferable to making an attempt to begin the main session with a class full of unsettled children who have little inclination to learn.

Moving out of the classroom

Children who tend to misbehave usually find some opportunity to do so when moving to a new location. Consistent routines and clearly rehearsed expectations will reduce the likelihood of silliness, but the prankster or mischief-maker will sometimes take delight in disrupting proceedings by showing off, making strange noises, stepping out of line and squabbling over who should be first/last in the queue. Until the situation is under control, you need to be firmly insistent and rigorous in approach, involving TAs wherever possible. Later on, when things have settled, a more relaxed approach will be possible. Strategies such as standing at the front of the queue, facing the children, asking them to stand upright and still, and choosing who should go first and last (with a promise that it will be someone different next time) all help to maintain an orderly atmosphere. Hopefully, by the time the children are approaching the top end of the junior phase, they will have sufficient self-control to be allowed more autonomy; but you may be shocked how unco-operative even Year 5 and Year 6 pupils are capable of being.

Special occasions

Children would not be children if they did not get excited during special occasions. Changes of routine, greater freedom of movement around the school, teacher activity and the arrival of visitors all combine to create an atmosphere in which conventional procedures fluctuate from normal. Even sensible children can exhibit a surprising side to their natures; passive children become active and active children become hyperactive. At such times, teachers need to remain exceptionally calm themselves; it is easy for adults to get caught up in the frenzy and worsen the situation by over-reacting. A cool, purposeful attitude and firmness mixed with understanding can help to keep matters under control.

As with all aspects of school life, there is no substitute for thinking ahead. Most problems can be avoided through sensible preparation and recognising that there will always be situations in which some children try to take advantage and others simply get carried away with the elation of the moment. Nevertheless, a failure to come to grips with the sticky moments can jeopardise the rest of the teaching programme as bad habits spread to other areas of classroom life, so don't be caught out.

Strategies for improving classroom behaviour

Every teacher wants to have a well-ordered classroom in which children are learning, teaching is taking place effectively and there is a sense of purpose and endeavour. No teacher wants to waste time in dealing with squabbles, confrontation or pettiness that result in an unsatisfactory lesson and a reduction in pupils' appetite for learning, even those with a positive attitude. Chapman (1995) summarises the position succinctly:

> If I cannot manage a class sufficiently well, the most invigorating and original lesson will fail. If I cannot control children using positive means wherever possible, then their self-esteem and motivation will be damaged. (1995: 36)

Haydn (2006) has even produced a 10-point scale to identify the working atmosphere in the classroom (2006: 3–4) ranging from Level 10 in which teacher and pupils are working together, enjoying the experiences involved, to Level 1 in which the teacher's entry into the room is greeted by jeers and abuse. Haydn explains the scale was 'originally devised to encourage trainee teachers to think about the degree to which teachers are in relaxed and assured control of their classrooms and can enjoy their teaching, and also, the extent to which there is a "right to learn" for pupils, free from the noise and disruption of others' (2007: 2). The scale is not for the purpose of judging teachers but as a means of helping them to evaluate the factors affecting classroom climate and its impact on teaching and learning. Dockrell and Shield (2006) concluded from their research that general 'babble' in the classroom was particularly disadvantageous to pupils with special educational needs.

It was noted earlier in the chapter that there is no substitute for having effective working relationships with children, interesting and relevant work for them to do, and clarity of purpose. We have seen that the key to dealing successfully with misbehaviour is to try and prevent it from happening in the first place. Most experienced teachers seem to deal successfully with incidents as they occur but this instinctive response is due to years of coping with similar circumstances and having an armoury of available strategies. The correct action comes so naturally that they rarely reflect on why they act as they do. However, it is worth remembering that every experienced teacher has worked hard to reach this point of competence and almost as hard to maintain it. New teachers soon find out are no quick-fix solutions to gaining and maintaining control in the classroom.

Some trainees may be deceived into thinking that if they could only discover the right strategy to use with children, then all their discipline problems would be solved. They imagine that there if they look hard enough, they will discover a method to combat all ills. Consequently, slogans are employed to reassure anxious students. For instance:

'Begin by being fierce and ease-off later'

'Let them know who is the boss'

'Don't smile for quite a while'

'Keep their heads down and don't give them a moment to breathe'.

While there may be some truth in each of these and similar statements, they offer a distorted perspective about the centrality of adult–child relationships in maintaining a healthy learning environment. In fact, as noted earlier, the best teachers rarely need to employ such stern, and ultimately unsustainable, tactics. Nevertheless, it is useful to have a bank of tried-and-tested strategies from which you can select one to use as appropriate.

Helpful strategies

Helpful strategies include the following:

- Gazing hard at the transgressor and acknowledging the pupil's appropriate response
- Going across and speaking quietly but firmly to the individual concerned
- Signalling the child to come across to you and explaining your dissatisfaction
- Chivvying and gently chiding ('Come on Andrew, more work and less chatter please. I'll give you until half-past to finish')
- Giving a specific command to clarify work expectations ('Sam, I want you to have finished that page by ten o'clock please').

Unhelpful strategies

Unhelpful strategies include the following:

- Shouting (other than in cases of health and safety)
- Calling out an individual's name across the room in a fierce voice (as it distracts everyone else and draws attention to the transgressor)
- Using a pseudo-question as part of a generalised command to no one in particular such as 'Can everybody get on quietly please' (as this is usually obeyed by those who conform and ignored by those who do not)
- Using the same child's name in a non-specific rebuke such as 'Daniel, get on with your work' (Daniel needs to be given a clearer instruction).

However, it takes time and experience to know which approach to use on which occasion and with which child. Sometimes it is difficult to achieve a satisfactory balance and there is bound to be a time of adjustment with a new class. Grossman (2003) reminds us that different children respond differently when adults speak to them, especially about aspects of inappropriate behaviour. For instance, it is normal to expect a child to look at the adult when being spoken to; however, Grossman explains how children from certain cultures are taught that it is discourteous to look at an adult when being addressed. Other children come from backgrounds where a more formal adult–child relationship is normal. Consequently, some pupils may appear to be insolent by refusing to look the teacher in the eye, when in fact they are displaying good manners. Again, pupils who appear to resist your friendly overtones may simply be reflecting a cultural norm by maintaining a suitable 'distance'. With such a multiplicity of combinations, even after some weeks of regular contact, it is not possible to get your reaction right every time; this is a fact that you will have to live with.

Whatever strategy you use to improve pupils' behaviour, it is important to resist lapsing into an artificial pattern of responses in the hope of gaining popularity or creating a false climate of enthusiasm for learning. McPhillimy (1996) views the matter like this: 'Mechanical, calculated smiles and praise, as well as being morally repellent are very unlikely to be effective as a reward' (1996: 80). We noted in Chapter 2 a warning by Wright (2006) about the danger of becoming a 'passive' teacher and trying to become popular as a mask for an inability to act decisively and show classroom leadership. Do not allow your self to lapse into such a defensive state of mind and action.

To avoid the risk of confrontation, it is tempting to take the easy route and pander to the small number of disruptive children at the expense of the others. For instance, a teacher may decide not to tackle an adventurous lesson for fear that the unusual circumstances or increased opportunities for naughtiness will prove irresistible to the disrupters and the whole lesson purpose will be undermined. Instead, they opt for a heads-down, individual paper and pencil approach, resulting in a far less engaging teaching and learning environment. While a heads-down approach has advantages in reducing noise level and leaving the teacher available to monitor the classroom more easily, it is difficult to maintain such an approach without stagnation and alienating the children who wish to benefit from exciting opportunities. Any containing strategy must, like most control techniques, be used sparingly, for in the longer term the innovative and interesting lesson will provide the foundation for strengthening the bonds between teacher and children and enhancing the learning environment. It is axiomatic that the few do not dictate your agenda or unduly influence the teaching approach at the expense of the majority.

Body language

Body language can be a powerful strategy for maintaining effective discipline. Neill and Caswell (1993) claim that teachers' verbal communication strategies can account for up to 80 per cent of the impression they convey to pupils and have at least four important functions:

- Gaining pupils' attention
- Conveying the teacher's enthusiasm to the class
- Dealing with confrontations and other control issues
- Relating to individuals during lessons.

Neill and Caswell argue that non-verbal signals send messages to pupils that identify teachers' feelings (both positive and negative) and support their spoken word. Thus, as well as teachers preparing lessons thoroughly and developing effective speech, they also need to cultivate appropriate body language.

Positive body language

Positive body language should include the following;

- Good eye contact with children

- Affirmative nods (expressing interest and approval of child)

- Expressive and reassuring facial tones

- Open body position (indicating trust)

- Facing a child directly when speaking one-to-one

- Squatting or sitting at children's eye level when speaking one-to-one

- Smiling and laughing at genuinely humorous situations.

Less helpful body language

Less helpful body language includes the following:

- Minimal eye contact

- Sighs and distracted facial movements, suggesting boredom or limited interest

- Stony-faced responses, indicating a lack of warmth

- Compressed body position (arms crossed or elbows squeezed into the ribs), conveying unease

- Side-on position when speaking to individuals, indicating adult superiority

- Scowling, accompanying loud verbal rebukes

- Maintaining a rigid stance when speaking one-to-one

- 'Never smile until Christmas' attitude.

However, 'less helpful' body language, if used occasionally, can be a powerful device for showing disapproval. If teachers are respected and liked by the children, such action can reinforce their authority. On the other hand, without children's respect, the use of negative body language can lead to a further breakdown in relationships.

Activate your thinking!

Read the accompanying extract from Canter (1998) about assertive discipline. Think especially about: (a) principles that apply to every teaching situation; (b) modifications to practice depending on the age and maturity of the child; and (c) the impact it might have on children exercising self-control:

> This [assertive discipline] approach is based on the idea that pupils and teachers have rights as well as responsibilities. Pupils need and respond to limits set by teachers, and teachers therefore should ensure those limits are established … A positive classroom atmosphere is established through meeting pupils' needs, planning and implementing classroom rules, teaching pupils how to behave appropriately, providing positive attention and engaging in productive dialogue with disruptive pupils. Teachers are described as assertive if they effectively communicate the behaviour required of their pupils and the actions by which they intend to achieve this behaviour. Appropriate actions must follow words, otherwise responses are non-assertive and therefore ineffective. Teachers must respond positively to pupils who display appropriate classroom behaviour, thus recognising their efforts to achieve the teachers' goals. It is important that teachers are sincere when recognising pupils' attempts to meet their expectations. (1998: 44)

Coping with insolent behaviour

It is unusual to encounter a lot of insolent behaviour in primary schools, though it would be foolish to imagine that it can never happen, even in the most settled circumstances. Despite following the strategies suggested earlier in the chapter, you may discover that you are faced with some difficult and unsettling situations from time to time, especially if you are a trainee teacher working with a demanding group of older children. Interesting lessons of the type described elsewhere in this book go a long way towards moderating the worst excesses of insolent behaviour but if it does happen it is likely to emerge in one of the following forms.

Pupils ignore you

If you are addressing a large group or class and some pupils ignore what you are saying, it is reasonable to stop, wait and make a comment such as 'Please look this way and watch my lips'. It may be, of course, that the very children you are concerned about will not respond because they are not listening in the first place. In such a situation, it is often helpful to put the person's name in front of the statement; thus: 'Patty, please look this way and watch my lips. Thank you', though avoid attaching the same child's name to a reprimand too often or the name itself gains a 'naughty' connotation. If you are speaking to a small group of pupils and one or more begin to look around at their friends or stare away while you are speaking, it may be that you have not yet established your authority in the class or that the children are nervous about the close encounter with you or that they do not accept your authority. It is essential to remain unruffled, ask for their attention, and to say what needs to be said clearly and unambiguously (without threats). Whenever possible, end the conversation on a positive note, even if it's only: 'Do you understand what I have said to you?' and if they affirm it: 'Well done. Off you go'. If you feel that there are deeper issues at stake it is not worth trying to resolve them through a single conversation. However, you can begin the process of establishing your presence as a teacher by being clear, definite and showing that you won't stand any nonsense.

Pupils talk when you are talking

It is irritating when you are addressing the class and a few children start to giggle among themselves or exchange whispers. On such occasions it is perfectly in order to stop what you are saying abruptly and coldly stare at the miscreants until they come to order. When you recommence, keep you eyes fixed on them for the next few seconds and then, as you relax into your theme, make a deliberate point of looking at them from time to time. If the behaviour continues, stop again and, using hand signals only (not speaking) indicate that one of the children should sit elsewhere out of direct eye line with the others. The next time you reach a suitable point, praise the children for their attention and also remind them about the courtesy rule that it is rude to interrupt when someone else is speaking. If you feel strongly enough, you can ask the perpetrators to see you at the end of the session. Note that it is unwise and counter-productive to create a fuss during the lesson if avoidable; but don't let the matter rest.

Good practice

If you are uncertain about tackling calling out, ask the main perpetrators for their idea. You may be surprised how effective their suggestions are. At the very least, it will put it at the top of the agenda.

Pupils answer back

Children answer back for a variety of reasons. They may find what you say unsatisfactory or unhelpful or confusing. They may just want to show off in front of their friends. A small number of children answer back because they do not have the social skills to cope with the social situation. You have to determine which of these reasons is the most likely. It is usually fairly plain when a child is showing off and a simple response such as: 'Please don't show off, Eric,' before continuing with what you were saying is surprisingly effective. If the behaviour continues, you must exert your authority quickly and calmly to prevent the situation getting out of hand. There are a number of possible approaches:

- Use an indirect strategy such as: 'Stephen, please sit up straight, keep your hands and tongue still, and look at me.' This approach has the advantage of diverting attention from the original behaviour but needs to be followed up at a later stage (perhaps after the class has gone out) when you can warn the child that you will not tolerate such rudeness

- Respond with a sense of outrage, such as saying quietly (in a cold tone of amazed incredulity): 'What did you say?' If the child refuses to respond, then add: 'Don't let me hear you calling out in class like that again. If you want to say something put your hand up like everybody else', before continuing

- Align yourself with another teacher, such as saying: 'Alexis, you would not speak to Mrs Archer like that, so please don't do it with me'. If the child persists or argues back then say to the rest of the children 'Please put your hand up if you know what Alexis should have done', wait for correct responses, then remind Alexis that, as everybody else seems to know the rule, you would be grateful if she would kindly do the same

- Use an abrupt approach, such as 'Stop. No. You know the rule, Chang, so please don't interrupt me or call out'. A palm held out towards the child adds weight to your comments. If possible (but not threateningly) take a pace or two forward and lean forward while speaking to emphasise the fact that the child is not going to 'hide' behind the space between you

- Ask the child to stand up and repeat the remark. There are dangers attached to this strategy as the child may gain further publicity for the clever comment. If, however, the child declines, it is worth pretending to make light of the matter momentarily by saying in a gentle tone with a hint of menace: 'No, we would all love to hear what you said, then you can go and explain to Mrs Archer why you have been so rude'. If the child refuses to respond, carry on immediately with what you were saying before being interrupted, glancing sternly across at the child from time to time.

Whatever response seems appropriate, keep the lesson flowing but do not ignore rude or 'smart' remarks that other children have obviously heard, as if they had never been made. It also goes without saying that you should make quite sure that the child really *was* answering back and not merely struggling to find the right form of words to add a useful comment. Clearly stated rules for classroom talk, understood by all the children, make your task of maintaining order much simpler. Obviously, calling-out is more prevalent during adult–pupil interactive sessions, especially when a variety of viewpoints are being sought; in the light of this fact, it is often better to use less interactive methods until you are more confident about maintaining order.

Pupils treat your commands as optional

Very young children may not always realise that what an adult says, an adult means. They set their minds on doing something and the fact that you have told them to do something else seems to make little impact. In such cases, a lot of patient perseverance is required, taking into account that some of the children may have come from a home, nursery or play-school situation where they could make many more of their own decisions and may therefore perceive a teacher's insistence as unreasonable. With the majority of children, loving firmness and persuasion (such as mentioning the exciting things that are possible *when* they have completed the task you have set them) usually does the trick. Older pupils may be more mischievous and pretend that they do not understand in the hope that the teacher will give up trying to explain. A group of children may decide not to obey what you have said, either because they do not want to do it or because they genuinely think that there is a better option. When children ignore your request, it is normally best to ask them what they are doing and why they are doing it. If they give a reasonable response, you may wish to allow them to carry on (at least for a time) while reminding them that in future they should consult you first before making decisions. If you are not happy that they should continue, ask them what they *ought* to be doing and do not let them off the hook until they tell you. You can then insist that they do what they are told and offer full support while they do so, including approximate time allocation, such as: 'You should manage to finish this part by half past 11.' Pupils treat a teacher's instructions as optional for many reasons, not least that they have misunderstood what has been said to them; your clarity of speech and careful lesson management is therefore essential in minimising the risk. Deliberate avoidance is an entirely different matter.

Pupils respond with ribald comments

This behaviour normally applies to older primary pupils and happens for one of four reasons: (a) the children are over-excited and need to calm down before lesson progress can be made; (b) they have got away with it before and are trying their luck again; (c) they are bored and distracted by the lesson content or the teacher's lacklustre delivery; and (d) they lack motivation generally and have become disaffected with school. Your response depends upon the reason for the behaviour:

If the children are over-excited and calling out silly things you have a choice over whether to change course for a few minutes and give the whole class a straightforward task until they are more composed (during which time you can quietly single out the culprits and speak sternly to them).

If they are trying their luck, use one of the tactics suggested above for when children call out.

If they are bored, you need to increase the lesson's tempo, ask some interesting questions or get the class working on group activities fairly quickly. Your low expectations can also trigger restlessness as it induces a 'why bother?' attitude.

Disaffection has deeper roots and you cannot hope to solve the situation by yourself. It is worth noting, however, that Kinder *et al.* (1996) claimed that disaffection is normally the result of boredom, anger or even fear. They suggested that improvement will come gradually as lessons are made more relevant, teachers are perceived as fair, pupils are treated with respect rather than disdain and (in some cases) parents are involved in working out solutions (Crozier and Reay 2005). Such improvement does not take place overnight.

Flickers of such behaviour need not spell disaster if the warning signs are heeded and appropriate action is taken quickly. Such action involves teachers in making the correct responses but also, more importantly, examining their lesson content, delivery, organisation and management to see if negative pupil behaviour results from one or more weaknesses in these areas. Insolent behaviour is always unsettling, sometimes worrying and occasionally frightening for teachers. If handled badly it can result in confrontations and angry scenes. If handled correctly it is an opportunity to learn about effective classroom strategies for dealing with disruptive youngsters. Trainee teachers should never hesitate to seek advice and assistance from a tutor or host teacher. Don't be tempted to imagine that matters will somehow resolve themselves if you keep silent. They won't. Denial is delusory.

Activate your thinking!

Consider the truth of the statement: Insolent behaviour has its roots in disaffection.

Good practice

Aim to be friendly towards children but not friends with them.

Special cases

All children are special to their parents, friends and family. Somebody treasures even the children who cause a teacher anguish and frustration. Trainee teachers who imagine that the mother or father of the class troublemaker feel the same resentment towards the child as they do have a nasty shock in store. Although parents may acknowledge their son's or daughter's shortcomings, such an admission does not diminish their love and they will quickly defend their offspring if they think that the teacher is unfairly critical. A few parents will defend their children even when it is blatantly obvious to everyone else where the blame lies.

All teachers experience children who cause particular problems through being unco-operative, unwilling or unsettled. A minority of unco-operative children will resist offers of help, disturb others in the class and generally upset the classroom atmosphere. Particularly difficult children act as a distressing reminder that sometimes, despite a teacher's best efforts, there appears to be little that can be done in the short-term to remedy the situation. A child who struggles with academic work may react to his or her difficulties by behaving erratically. A disturbed child may be academically capable but fall behind due to having a poor attitude or personality defect. The reverse is also true: a child who begins to succeed will probably behave in a more settled manner; the child whose circumstances become more secure will begin to gain success in schoolwork. It is important to be aware of these links as the special needs of children are evaluated. By adopting a positive attitude, taking an interest in the children's out-of-school interests and enthusing about their achievements, you have more chance of eliciting the very best from every child, but occasional reversals of fortune are inevitable.

Older primary boys

Children at every stage present their own challenges and joys; as such, there is no 'easy' age group. Different teachers like working with different year groups and it is interesting to reflect upon the similarities and variations in emphasis between teachers of nursery, Key Stage 1 and Key Stage 2. In previous chapters, we saw how some young children find adjustment to school routines challenging. Teachers of Key Stage 1 children spend a lot of time and effort encouraging good learning habits, independence and basic skills. Teachers of seven to nine year olds cope with classes of very mixed ability (socially and academically), in which some children still display immature behaviour, while others display surprising sophistication and make heavy demands upon the teacher's resourcefulness. During the transition between Key Stages 1 and 2, dominant children emerge and children with learning difficulties are identified more readily than earlier, when maturity factors made evaluations of need more problematic. Some groups of older children provide particular challenges to a teacher's ability to maintain control and ingenuity, requiring courage and tenacity. Although all children exhibit inappropriate behaviour at times, it is often with the oldest children that control issues become sharply focused. Such pupils can be simultaneously a delight and infuriatingly troublesome. In recent years, more emphasis has been placed on early diagnosis of emotional and learning shortcomings, in the sensible belief that early identification is far preferable to later attempts to rescue lost causes. Teachers of younger and older pupils are therefore all working towards the same end goal, namely, well-adjusted young people and future citizens.

Older boys are often enthused by sport (especially football), swapping collected cards, displaying their latest fashion fads and, in some cases, showing off to the girls. These characteristics are not true of every older boy, of course, but even the most enthusiastic teacher can feel exhausted after handling their loud demands, excited responses, intensity of feelings and the rapid movement from protective comradeship to antagonistic dispute. The expression that 'boys will be boys' may invite criticisms of stereotyping but does indicate the impact that groups of older boys, who have been together in school since they were very small, can prove a handful (as well as a source of fulfilment) for any teacher.

It is important to recognise that high spirits rather than wilfulness are at the heart of much banter and conceited behaviour exhibited by older boys. Things really matter to them and often lead to expressions of indignation and highly charged reactions as they attempt to justify their behaviour or criticise others. Although not every older boy behaves in this manner, many do, and with this in mind teachers must ensure the following three things.

That they are firm but not unreasonable

For instance, to punish an older boy who loves to play a sport by denying him the chance to do so because of his overzealous behaviour in a lesson can be counter-productive, resulting in grievance, frustration and resentment (though such a course of action may be necessary if the non-co-operation persists). Usually the mild threat of such a sanction will cause a sporty boy to try to mend his ways, so give credit for effort, even if the behaviour remains less than perfect.

That they don't allow dominant boys to suppress or exclude less assertive children

So-called 'macho' behaviour by a small number of boys should not be allowed to frighten other children or undermine their self-esteem. The non-sporty boys sometimes have a difficult job to compete and find their place in the social hierarchy; it is the teacher's responsibility to ensure that they have opportunities to succeed and gain status in other ways, such as encouraging them to bring in photographs or certificates or other status-enhancing items to share with the class. In doing so, make sure that the items are not perceived as 'babyish' by the other children, or more harm than good will be done. Your sensitivity and wisdom in monitoring the situation is crucially important.

That they make it clear that the high standards the boys set themselves in sporting activities are equally necessary in academic work

Some boys who throw themselves into outdoor activities are loath to apply the same rigour to their class work. It is useful to face this inconsistency openly with them and attempt to feed their enthusiasm into the academic rather than suppress their love of physical activities.

Garnett (2006) argues that school is too content-driven for many boys and has little relevance for them. He notes that boys tend to be characterised by eight tendencies:

- More competitive
- Rush to finish their written work
- Unconcerned about presentation
- Inconsistent spelling and grammar
- Sometimes make inaccurate verbal comments
- Indulge in aggressive or physical 'horseplay'
- More outgoing and friendly
- Show off and take centre stage.

Whereas girls tend to show seven characteristics:

- Willingly collaborate
- Willing to persevere with tasks
- Take care over presentation of work
- More accurate with spelling, grammar and content
- Quieter than boys and happy with a small group of friends
- Rarely indulge in 'horseplay'
- More self-conscious. (adapted from Garnett, 2006: 80)

These characteristics are, of course, only generalisations. There are plenty of exceptions, However, his summary of typical behaviours may assist you to keep matters in perspective when boys behave as they often do. Some purists may sneer at the claim that 'boys will be boys' but there is some substance to the assertion, as every teacher will agree. Garnett recommends that improving attainment among boys require that teachers pay attention to nine factors: (1) promoting active learning; (2) developing high order skills; (3) creating effective learning zones (emphasising boys' need to feel comfortable in their immediate learning environment); (4) promoting success; (5) providing effective feedback, with an emphasis on skills and content rather than on presentation; (6) recognising and creating learning windows, when pupils are at their most attentive; (7) developing good relationships; (8) developing productive pedagogy, with a high degree of pupil involvement; and (9) incorporating their perspectives. There is a sense in which Garnett's advice applies to all children, girls as well as boys, but the practices he recommends particularly resonate with the needs of older boys, some of whom may appear confident and a little cocky, but are inwardly insecure and anxious. There is little point in trying to win children's co-operation by being rigid, criticising the appearance of work, emphasising the end-product at the expense of the process and even humiliating them; in the case of many boys, such an approach will only increase antagonism and inflame resentment.

Older boys are an exhausting but exciting group to work with. If teachers can win their hearts by exuding energy, fairness and enthusiasm they will secure undying loyalty and receive commitment and wholehearted zest for learning; however, troughs as well as peaks in the process should be expected.

Older primary girls

Most girls are enthusiastic about schoolwork and determined to do well. Every survey shows that the majority of girls make more rapid progress, both academically and socially, than boys of the same age. You must bear this fact in mind in addressing the needs of the class; though resist making it an excuse for low achievement. After all, nurture (upbringing) also plays a part in determining behaviour, as do 'natural' tendencies and character traits. A small number of mature older girls find it hard to feel part of a primary school culture and may express this by separating themselves from other children or showing disdain for academic work and sport. Girls normally mature earlier than boys and precocious older children may find that they are emotionally and physically advanced compared with their classmates. They have to cope with adolescence and rapid growth at a time when they are still in the primary school environment. This can be difficult for them to accept and can result in phases of intensity, exaggerated behaviour and an explosion of boy-related imagery, conversation and action. It is important to remember that these girls are grappling with a rapid series of changes in their lives and bodies, and need to be treated with courtesy and consistency, while insisting on basic standards of behaviour from them.

It is sensible to avoid heavy-handed approaches that threaten to humiliate older girls or, at the other extreme, being patronising to them. Younger male teachers, in particular, need to be discreet: thus, although gentle teasing and pleasantries are part of the interactive process and can lead to a healthy relationship, men should think carefully about words and body language which may be misconstrued by older girls. Dominant older girls can also be bossy and unkind to their less mature peers and, in some cases, may try to lure passive girls into a closely-knit group whose membership is open only to those who will espouse their particular, closely defined attitudes. In dealing with older dominant girls, a number of factors need to be considered, as follows.

Those who mature early do not do so out of choice

It is easy for a teacher to resent these hormonal intrusion into the otherwise child-like environment. A tolerant understanding of the emotions at work is essential.

Mature older girls are still primary school pupils and come under the same general rules of conduct

Although sensible discretion needs to be exercised, it would be a mistake for teachers to allow any non-conformist behaviour to dominate classroom or school life.

Unkind words and vindictive attitudes from mature girls towards weaker children is as serious as physical bullying

Such behaviour should be dealt with according to the school's agreed policy. For trainee teachers, unsure about how to cope with regular minor instances of gossip or unkindness, the best course of action is to seek advice from senior colleagues. It is helpful for you to introduce an easily remembered rule of the kind, 'If you must say something about someone, say something helpful'. The same rule applies to adults, too, of course.

Firm control needs to be exercised over mature girls who endeavour to draw less mature, wide-eyed boys into silly or disruptive behaviour

The boys are often thankful to be saved.

Although some older girls can disturb a class through their casual approach and restless behaviour, they usually respond well to teachers who offer them the opportunity to behave maturely within clearly defined limits. Despite their unpredictable behaviour, they often prove to be among the most loyal and supportive class members during times of crisis. Maturity cuts both ways. On the one hand it may serve to upset and unsettle. On the other hand, it can produce remarkable examples of loyalty, sensitivity and enthusiasm to delight and encourage weary teachers. As with every age group, your own positive attitude, high expectations and good humour will combat most unsavoury elements of behaviour and bring out the best in every child (see, for example, Burgess *et al.* 2000; Loomans and Kolberg 2002).

Demoralised children

Occasionally, teachers come across children who, for various reasons, seem to have given up on school (Makins 1997; Ravet 2007). They may not be persistent troublemakers and may even plod along with the work, albeit unenthusiastically, but it is evident that they have lost heart and are simply passing the time as comfortably as possible before leaving. Typically, such children will be found at the upper end of the school, though younger children can show the same attitude.

Although the reasons (such as home circumstances) may lie outside the teacher's immediate control there are a number of positive strategies that are worth considering which help the children to regain their zest for school and learning in general.

Find regular opportunities to interact on a one-to-one basis

In the busyness of the day it is difficult to find opportunities to interact on an individual basis with every pupil other than during formal sessions, when the adult–child relationship is influenced by epistemology rather than empathy. However, a deliberate attempt to exchange a private word with key individuals each day helps to build understanding and convince the children that the teacher's interest in them goes beyond merely improving their academic results. Although TAs can play a significant role in pursuit of this goal, your involvement is crucial.

Avoid making a fuss

Unless they are displaying their disillusionment by wilful misbehaviour, children often shun the limelight and do not want to be the public centre of a teacher's attention. Attempts to grant them a form of 'celebrity status' by making an undue fuss of their endeavours will often backfire and cause them to become more inhibited. By giving individuals deliberate, regular and low-key attention, teachers can gradually enhance their feelings of self-worth and raise their self-esteem.

Take an interest in their out-of-school activities

Children who lack academic motivation will sometimes spark into life when a teacher shows an interest in their hobbies or pastimes. The occasional enquiry about how they are getting on in a sports tournament, competition or in collecting items of interest can sometimes initiate a trust in the teacher, which in turn, increases the child's determination to succeed in school work, too.

Enthuse gently about their successes

Depressed or unmotivated children not only believe that they have failed in the past but convince themselves that they are incapable of improving their situation. Teachers can contribute to the confidence-building process by making specific comments about positive achievements. Although it takes time to convince demoralised children that they can succeed, they need help in being able to recognise where progress has been made and (like every other pupil) how to improve their existing achievements. Your initial attempts to praise their achievements may be rebuffed, but perseverance brings its own reward.

Request their assistance

Asking children who seem to have given up to assist another child or to take responsibility for a small but important task is a useful means of building self-confidence. Children who have become used to a cycle of failure and defeatism may take some persuading that they have the capability to undertake the task, but small victories accumulate and create an archive of success to which you can refer as a sign of what can be done.

Persevere

Confidence and self-belief are not developed overnight. However, teachers who are willing to persevere and establish an open, positive approach with pupils to celebrate modest achievements and offer specific support when progress is slow, will help children to rediscover their zest for learning. When you are tempted to be discouraged, remind yourself of how much that child will benefit from your caring approach, which Liston and Garrison (2004) courageously and correctly refer to as 'loving'.

One of the reasons that many people become teachers is because they enjoy working with and supporting children. Helping children who are finding life difficult to cope with is an excellent opportunity to gain that kind of fulfilment.

Activate your thinking!

Children are asking one question above all others: 'How much are you interested in me as a person?'.

Good practice

Use the above strategies over a period of two weeks to evaluate the improvement in the attitude towards and aptitude for work of any disaffected children.

Confidence and judgement

Establishing and maintaining class discipline is a difficult and demanding task for every teacher, especially for trainee teachers and inexperienced practitioners. However, we have noted the axiom that all teachers can improve the situation by ensuring that lessons are interesting and relevant, instructions are clear and specific and responses to unacceptable behaviour are appropriate. In fact, all teachers who successfully maintain order possess two essential qualities: *confidence* and *wise judgement*.

Your *confidence* emerges gradually. It grows when you know what you are doing and why. It is a delicate flower and can easily be crushed by a poor lesson, an unthinking comment from a colleague or a seemingly intractable situation involving a recalcitrant pupil. A positive attitude, firm but natural speech; strong, enthusiastic personality; and appropriate body language, all contribute towards building your confidence. It is helpful to remember that you are a capable adult who possesses the knowledge and skills to teach effectively. Consequently, nothing (and certainly not a naughty child or unthinking adult) is going to deter you from achieving your goals. In addition, however, it is equally important to recognise that some problems (including discipline) will be the result of your own inexperience; be encouraged to know, however, that acting upon advice from others, and your own thoughtful deliberations will combine, over time, to improve the situation gradually.

Wise judgement is more difficult to define or recognise. Some teachers seem to possess an instinct for handling situations; many have to learn the hard way. However, the following 10-point strategy will help you to improve your success rate:

- Have a big 'presence' around the room (but not brash)
- Practise your diction and speak at a speed that allows pupils time to absorb what you are saying
- Maintain a steady pace to the lesson
- Vary your tone and communicate your enthusiasm through firm statements of approval
- Avoid confrontation wherever possible, but if it is not possible try to ensure that the outcome leaves your authority and the pupil's dignity intact
- Use a variety of good quality questions (closed and open) and show a keen interest in pupils' replies
- Organise thoroughly and anticipate sticky spots
- Do not introduce activities or interactive forms of teaching that might excite too much fervour until you are sure that you have sufficient class control
- When unacceptable behaviour occurs, concentrate on the act rather than the perpetrator
- Think positive. Be positive
- Convince yourself and your children that they have got a teacher in a million.

Activate your thinking!

How would you act wisely in the following circumstances?

1. The more assertive children are dominating the use of equipment during collaborative activities.

2. Freda, aged nine, tells you that she does not have to do what you say because you are 'only a student'.

3. The same two children are always last to be chosen for games' activities.

4. You are told a racist joke by a child in the class.

5. You are asked to make sure that the books on the classroom shelves are suitable for children.

6. Meena, aged eight, comes to you in tears because no one wants to play with her.

7. A child confides in you that his parents are separating.

8. Some children in your class complain that a new girl to the school who is new to the school had been swearing openly at other children. [Note: Would it make a difference if you knew that the girl was from a very unsettled background?]

9. A parent tells you that she did not want her five-year-old sitting next to a particular child because the child smells.

10. A parent tells you that she does not want her able 10 year old sitting by a less able child because the child is always asking questions about the work.

Case study

It is Wednesday morning in a Year 4 class. Tim and Ali, firm friends, sit together pondering the work in front of them. The trainee teacher is still finding her feet and determined to clamp down on inappropriate behaviour.

Trainee: Okay, get on with your work.

Tim: (speaking to Ali) What are we meant to be doing?

Ali: I dunno. (Tim gazes around hoping to gain a clue from what the other children are doing.)

Tim: We're supposed to write something down about the things we saw on our walk, I think.

Ali: I dunno. I'm just gonna write something. It doesn't matter. (Ali begins to write studiously, bent over his paper, hoping that the trainee doesn't look too closely.)

Tim: I'll ask Angie. (He gets up and wanders over to Angie.)

Trainee: (crossly) Sit down Tim and get on with your work.

Tim: I was just asking Angie something.

Angie: (a conscientious girl, anxious that she might be getting in trouble, glances nervously at the trainee) Go away, Tim. You're bothering me.

Trainee: (assuming that Tim is being troublesome) Sit … down … and … get on.

Tim: (slumps back into his seat, chin on hand) This is useless.

Fifteen minutes later Ali has written half a page of low-level work but in bold handwriting. Tim has scrawled a few indecipherable words on the sheet and sits staring vacantly into space. The trainee is praising Angie and others for their efforts. She walks across to Ali and Tim.

Ali: (glancing up) Look, Miss, what I done.

Trainee: (without reading it closely but noticing the tidiness and length and relieved that he has made an effort) Well done, Ali, that's excellent (turns to Tim, looks at his paper and scowls) What on earth do you call that? (Tim says nothing). Right. You can stay in at playtime and finish it off.

Tim: (urgently) But Miss, I've got to see Mr Ward about playing in the team and …

Trainee: You can forget about that. I'm sick of you messing about and not doing your work and if you say another word you can come with me and see Mr Pretiman. (Tim visibly shrinks; Ali glances across sympathetically; a few children in the corner snigger quietly).

The trainee's perception of the boys' behaviour was affected by her initial belief that Tim was causing trouble. From this point, the relationship between adult and child became tense. Dialogue was limited due to the trainee's unwillingness to ensure that Tim was clear about the task and to offer some ongoing 'scaffolding' to his learning through appropriate monitoring and intervention. Her failure to explain the task adequately and her apparent reluctance to attend to Tim's individual learning needs meant that at the end of the allotted time his progress was minimal and she felt obliged to invoke sanctions. The end result was an unhappy child and a strained trainee. Tim was far from being a model pupil and his unwillingness to consult the trainee teacher may have been a contributing factor, but the trainee made the situation worse by her ill-judged comments and hasty reactions.

Activate your thinking!

Activate your thinking!

- What steps might have been taken to ensure that the boys were clear about the task?
- What are the prospects for settled relationships and effective teaching and learning if these conditions persist?
- What is the trainee likely to say to Ali's and Tim's parents during the parent interviews?

Good practice

Examine your class list and sub-divide the children into three broad categories:

1. The majority who endeavour to work hard and do their best.
2. The small number who will get away with doing the bare minimum.
3. The minority who cause regular problems.

Reflect upon appropriate strategies for moving children from group 2 to group 1, and from group 3 to group 2. Now celebrate that there are so many names in the first group.

Further reading

Cipani, E. (2007) *Class Management for all Teachers*, New York: Prentice Hall.
Based on the idea that a behaviour management plan can be as effective in preventing problematic classroom behaviour as in managing it and addresses problems relating to on-task time/assignment completion and disruption/rule violation.

Haydn, T. (2006) *Managing Pupil Behaviour*, London: Routledge.
Draws on case-study material and recent research to develop insights into a range of factors impinging on a teacher's ability to manage the class.

Porter, L. (2000) *Theory and Practice for Teachers*, Maidenhead: Open University Press.
Provides a comprehensive overview of the major theories of behaviour, illustrated with numerous case studies. It covers the secondary as well as primary phase.

Rogers, B. (2006) *Classroom Behaviour*, London: Paul Chapman.
Offers a wide repertoire of relational management skills and guidance for putting professional integrity and emotional literacy into practice from an early stage.

Tileston, D. W. (2004) *What Every Teacher Should Know About Classroom Management and Discipline*, Thousand Oaks, CA: Corwin Press.
A book that is easy to dip in and out of. It has a strong US flavour in the way it is written but approaches issues from an engaging perspective.

Inclusion and Special Educational Needs

Introduction

Over the past 25 years or so the education of children with Special Educational Needs (SEN) has assumed an increasingly high profile in schools. Once seen as a specialist area, it is now the responsibility of every teacher. This chapter starts by reviewing background information about relevant legislation and giving a historical perspective on the subject. An understanding of the terms 'special educational needs' and 'inclusion' is then explored, with reference to the Code of Practice. Finally, advice is offered about successfully dealing with SEN in the classroom, including writing an individual education plan (IEP) and working with other professionals.

Legislation

Until 1971 about one per cent of the population was deemed uneducable, and did not attend school at all. When this population became the responsibility of the Department of Education and Science (as it was then known), a committee was set up under Baroness Warnock to report on the education of 'handicapped' children (the *Warnock Report*). The committee widened its brief, abandoning the notion of handicaps and establishing instead the notion of Special Educational Needs; it moved beyond the two per cent who were then educated in special schools to an estimated 20 per cent of children who were likely to experience a type of SEN at some time in their school career. This larger group had formerly been referred to as 'remedial' or slow learners.

The report *Children with Special Educational Needs* was published in 1978 and paved the way for the far-reaching legislation of the Education Act 1981. The Act stated that, in principle, children with SEN should be educated alongside their non-disabled peers, that their resource needs should be safeguarded by a 'statement of need' that would be binding on the local authority and abolished the pre-existing categories of handicap to replace them with a single notion of special educational need. However, a set of descriptive categories was still deemed necessary (e.g. descriptors such as moderate learning difficulties, hearing impaired, etc.). The Act came into force on 1 April 1983 and the period since then can best be seen as the attempt by the teaching profession to move from a *segregated* form of provision (where pupils with identifiable needs were separately educated) to an *inclusive* one. To understand the difficulties in so doing it is worth looking briefly at some of the historical background.

Historical background

The system we have inherited grew up piecemeal over a considerable period of time and has embedded in it periods of inertia in which little thought was given to appropriate forms of education for all children. Some countries, such as Italy and the Scandinavian countries were, for historical and geographical reasons, able to build education systems based on more inclusive assumptions at an earlier stage. Britain, in 1983, already had a fully entrenched segregated system, and undoing the precedent is proving to be a difficult task. British teachers were used to a system that spared them from having to deal with directly with needy pupils, as the children were in other specialist institutions. Furthermore, there were specialist schools and a variety of qualified and experienced professionals who rightly prided themselves on their ability to deal with the children's needs in specialised, separate accommodation, and it was difficult for them to give up the status of being the experts in a certain field. In recent years there has been a tacit acknowledgement by Government that the abolition of all specialist schools on moral or educational grounds is unwise.

Barton and Tomlinson (1984) trace the changes in statutory categories for special provision until the 1981 Act. Thus, in 1886 there was statutory provision for those diagnosed as Idiots and Imbeciles. These seemingly insulting words were at the time clearly defined clinical categories, comprising those that we would now describe as having profound or severe learning difficulties. By the end of the century categories of schools for the blind and deaf had also been established. Schools were founded for the indigent blind, the word 'indigent' meaning needy or impoverished; stereotyping expressions such as 'the blind beggar' is one such example. These institutions taught crafts and trades that would facilitate some sort of financial independence for pupils when they had completed the course (e.g. as piano tuners for the blind and partially sighted), and were seen as a philanthropic act of kindness and charity. These institutions were normally founded by charitable or religious bodies, and helped to rectify the shortcomings of the state system. Similarly, separate institutions were set up for the 'physically defective', again focusing on learning a trade that would offer future employment and security. After the First World War came the development of separate schools and classes for the 'feeble minded', who were judged incapable of following the normal curriculum. The growth of educational psychology under Cyril Burt saw the widespread use of Intelligence Quotient (IQ) tests to identify those in need of special education (an IQ of 70 or below being the cut-off point).

Thus, a range of separate provision grew up in piecemeal fashion, seen at the time as appropriate and additional to the norm. When the 1944 Act secured universal free education, including secondary education, it was deemed necessary to extend this right to all 'educable handicapped children.' Consequently, until the 1981 Act, special educational provision was premised on categories of handicap (e.g. malfunctioning limbs), rather than educational need and access to a common school experience and curriculum. Numerous problems emerged as educationists attempted to make a success of the system which tended to take account of the 'handicap' as the prime consideration and educational need as the second. These and many other related issues led to the questioning of the then existing forms of provision and the categories and labels that were in use, and to focusing instead on the actual educational needs of children. This bold move engendered the current debate, including the use of language in labelling, and issues about segregation, integration and inclusion.

Activate your thinking!

What do you 'see' first, the person of the child or the child's disability?

The language of special education

Prior to the 1981 Act labels were used to describe the features that led to educational difficulty, e.g. an educationally sub-normal child, a blind child. The *Warnock Report* sought to move away from this and focus on the needs of the child in the particular context of provision they found themselves in. As early as 1984 Lady Warnock herself admitted regret about coining the term 'special educational needs' and wondered how long it would be before the word 'special' accrued pejorative connotations. We can now see that in the intervening period the term has indeed come to function as a label for children, rather than focusing on their needs. In every staffroom it is possible to hear talk of 'SEN children' or 'statemented children', neither of which is accurate. A statement of special educational needs is about provision, and not about the child.

There is a considerable variability in the use of statements across the country. The possession of a statement often says more about the *situation* the child is in than anything intrinsic to the child, yet labels that focus on the child are still in common use. As more and more money is devolved to schools there are signs that the use of the statement will decline; indeed, the use of the terms 'learning needs' and 'learning difficulties' are now in vogue. Additionally, the universal acceptance that all children have strengths and weaknesses in specific subject areas – as opposed to being viewed as either 'generally able' or 'generally not able' – has paved the way for a re-evaluation of individual learning needs ('individualisation') and ways in which weaker areas can be addressed, and stronger areas enhanced (so-called 'personalisation'). These various terms may, in turn, become labels rather than educational principles, but the concept of meeting each child at the point of his or her need across the curriculum has become accepted practice (though in reality, the vast majority of resources are directed towards literacy and mathematics). One way and another, it is important to see children as individuals with different needs that change over time rather than members of a group, all assumed to have the same characteristics requiring identical treatment.

The problems attached to seeing pupils in terms of labels rather than as individuals are well documented. For instance, two groups of trainee teachers are shown the same piece of videotaped classroom activity. One group is asked to record what they saw without further guidance; the other group is told that some members of the class in the tape exhibit features of learning and behavioural difficulties. The first group sees only the normal classroom interaction, whereas the second group is able to identify a range of special needs, in line with its expectations. Such studies demonstrate that we tend to see what we believe or are told is present, rather than assessing the situation professionally. It points up the danger of attaching negative labels to aspects of behaviour in such a way that practitioners have preconceived ideas, and subsequently convince themselves that what they are led to believe is there, is genuinely so.

Using language accurately and appropriately is something to which every teacher should aspire, and it is important to avoid unintentionally giving offence or being insulting by the inaccurate use of terms. This issue is given a thorough airing in Corbett's thought-provoking book, provocatively entitled *Bad-Mouthing, The Language of Special Needs* (Corbett 1995). Basically, the situation can be greatly improved if we abide by three simple precepts:

1. Avoid language that is clearly insulting or inaccurate, e.g. mongol, spastic, cripple.

2. Avoid patronising euphemisms, e.g. vertically challenged, differently enabled, etc.

3. Use the preferred terminology of the group in question, e.g. Down's Syndrome, deaf, etc. This usage will change over time, but it is a real sign of respect when talking to children and their families that you have bothered to adopt non-offensive terminology or, if uncertain, have taken the trouble to ask their preference.

Most of the categories of learning difficulties listed earlier are typically of low incidence. For instance, you may never teach a child with Down (or Down's) Syndrome or Autistic Spectrum Disorder. However, it is important for you to develop an inclusive philosophy, being willing to support a range of learning difficulties where necessary, and knowing where to go for additional knowledge and support at the appropriate time. The SEN Code of Practice gives useful outlines, there is a plethora of practical guides and texts available, and the Internet is a wonderful source of information if used with discrimination.

Not all disabilities are chronic (persistent) ones; for instance, all teachers, need to be aware of the common condition known as 'glue ear'. Many young children experience heavy catarrh, which leads to an intermittent hearing loss that can have an effect on language development. The condition eases as the child grows older, but the gaps in learning remain, and the effects on further development are cumulative and need to be addressed. Decongestants and the fitting of grommets (by means of a small operation) can alleviate the symptoms and allow the child full access to language, especially at the vital stage when sound symbol correspondence is being achieved. Nevertheless, you should be on the lookout for children suffering intermittent hearing loss, urge parents to take medical action and ensure that the child, who may appear distant or confused, is able to understand the teaching that he or she is experiencing, especially in the field of language development. It is tempting to label a child as a 'daydreamer' or even as having symptoms of 'attention deficit' when the problem has a more straightforward explanation.

Activate your thinking!

What labels have you heard used to describe children with SEN? Consider whether labels tell us more about those using them, rather than those they purport to describe.

Segregation, integration or inclusive education?

Segregation

Perhaps the major determinant of our success in educating children with SEN is our view about what should be done to enhance their learning, and whereabouts particular forms of intervention should be placed in the schooling process. The ideology behind segregation is that we are only responsible for children of 'normal' abilities and that specialist teachers should take the residue (i.e. children deemed 'not normal') elsewhere, so (the argument goes) teachers don't need to change their practice to be more inclusive. The flaws in this argument hardly require exploring, not least because defining the concept of 'normal' is highly problematic.

The term 'segregation' not only applies to separate special schools, but also to a form of educational partitioning that can take place in mainstream schools, by means of special classes for the least able, groups permanently composed on ability lines, and (notably) withdrawal from class for extra help on an ongoing basis through 'coaching' – often from a TA. However, there is a less visible form of segregation that takes place when an assistant is allocated to one pupil who is considered to need close tuition and sits with him/her, thereby accentuating the child's difference and progressively disempowering the child from becoming an independent learner. There are, and have been shown to be, all sorts of practical problems with this sort of segregated education, which can be summarised thus:

- Because a group of children share some difficulties, it does not follow that they require the same kind of education provision

- Children who are separated from classmates have limited exposure to a model of classroom behaviour experienced by their peers

- When children are extracted from class they are falling further behind in the normal class work and may miss out on access to the full curriculum

- The work children do under segregated conditions may not be related to the curriculum or the skills they need to access it; rather, it may be practice in basic elements or an excessive concentration on the use of worksheets

- There is plenty of evidence to support the principle that children learn most effectively in group interaction, so the efficacy of 'one to one instruction' is questionable.

All children have varying abilities in different areas, so even if they benefit from individual instruction in one area it does not mean that they should be excluded from the other wider class and social activities. Even where children value and benefit from separate treatment, there are stigmas attached to being seen as different by other members of the class, many of which are subliminal. The practice of removal may give unhelpful messages to the child about their perceived low standing, with the resulting damage to their self-esteem and confidence. Because of the above factors and the staffing costs involved, there has been a move towards more integrative and inclusive practices, as described below.

Activate your thinking!

Try to imagine what it must feel like to be treated differently from most other children and lose touch with aspects of mainstream classroom life.

Now imagine what it feels like to have special and exclusive attention from an adult, whose sole aim is to help you improve academically.

Integration

Integration is the name given to the process whereby formerly excluded pupils were to be brought back into regular schooling, either moving from special to mainstream schooling, or by adopting class or group-based activities rather than individual 'remediation' in isolation. Pupils with special needs were to be integrated, or re-integrated into the heart of regular school life, but the nature of the school system remained largely unchanged. In other words, the basic assumptions behind the curriculum, assessment methods and teaching remained unaltered, and the underlying objective was seen as fitting the child to the existing provision, not adjusting the provision according to the needs of the child. As the school system had not been designed on the principles of inclusive assumptions, i.e. that it should be open to all members of the community, the practices it had developed over the period characterised by segregation were not based on the needs of individuals. For instance, the buildings were often inaccessible to anyone who had mobility problems; the curriculum was not necessarily relevant to all; and the practices of grading made it inevitable that a certain percentage of children would experience stigmatising failure. It was probably optimistic to believe that the ills of segregation could be alleviated by easing a few more disabled people into a system that was not designed with them in mind. From this point, educational policy started to move towards the principle of an inclusive system to meet all needs, though in some cases the practices that were used for integration have continued, and merely changed their name to inclusion.

Activate your thinking!

Should schools exist to promote success for all or to reinforce failure?

Inclusive education

Inclusive education is best understood as an aim, aspiration or even a philosophy, rather than as a set of techniques that can be applied to a situation (such as in school). The school community is charged with offering education to all members of the community that it serves by modifying the way that all those involved work so that all needs are considered, such that practices that tended to exclude pupils are replaced by more inclusive practices (Hayward, 2006). Moving in an inclusive direction entails a problem-solving exercise on behalf of all those involved. Jacklin.

Griffiths and Robinson (2006) stress that the entitlement for all children to receive a rich and relevant education involves 'differentiated teaching, supporting and extending the least and most able pupils, and above all, setting high expectations and standards for all, irrespective of gender, ethnicity, race, disability or social background, are all part of the day to day role of a primary teacher' (2006: 78). They admit that such demands are likely to overwhelm beginner teachers and recommend six strategies (see 2006: 89–90 for the comprehensive list):

- Remember the needs of all pupils, rather than a few individuals or groups
- Be aware of your own bias and preconceptions and do not allow them to interfere with your professional responsibilities
- Talk to and observe experienced teachers
- Draw on the expertise of specialist units or teachers in the school, as well as outside experts
- Work alongside TAs to help support learning
- Use your ongoing evaluations and assessment of children's learning to support your planning and teaching. (Modified list)

The role of the teacher in addressing Special Educational Needs

The duties of schools and teachers are clearly laid out in the Code of Practice and the Special Needs and Disability Act. All schools should have copies of relevant documents, as well as a set of practical pamphlets on implementing the Code of Practice. The Code outlines the framework for identifying, assessing and making provision for children's special educational needs, though the actual assessment and teaching measures used are left for individual teachers and schools to develop. Whenever and wherever you work in a school it is essential to be aware of the identity and role of the Special Educational Needs Co-ordinator (SENCO), though note that school governors have statutory roles in constructing policy for special educational needs.

The SEN Code sets out a graduated approach to the identification and assessment of special needs and also the provision of suitable resources (including personnel). It makes clear that the Code is only concerned with interventions that are additional to or different from those provided as part of the school's usual differentiated curriculum and strategies. In other words, it should normally be possible to accommodate the range of pupil learning needs within the format of the regular lesson structure without triggering a request for additional intervention via the Code. Specifically focused and planned teaching, together with consistent discipline, will help to prevent unmanageable difficulties in learning from arising. Despite teachers' best efforts, however, it is likely that some children will experience difficulties that require extra or different kinds of support for learning. The Code describes two stages at which this more focused assessment and provision operate, these are known as *School Action* and *School Action Plus*.

At the level of *School Action*, the teacher decides that the child may need additional support to help his or her progress (statistically, the child is likely to be a boy), following consultation with parents. The SENCO is then involved, and short-term support from outside agencies may be involved (see section on working with other professionals later under *Every Child Matters*).

Information about the child's academic progress is gathered, and evidence collected about the interventions that have been previously tried. The information is recorded on the child's individual record, and an Individual Education Plan (IEP) is produced laying out the plans for the next stage of the pupil's education.

School Action Plus involves a request for help from external services, and will normally follow a decision made by the SENCO and colleagues, in consultation with parents, after the evidence from a review of the IEP indicates that there is a need to consult specialists. A range of specialists may be approached, depending on the nature of the need, and a new IEP produced. As the IEP is reviewed and monitored, the school may request a statutory assessment from the local education authority if the pupil has demonstrated a significant cause for concern. This assessment process may lead to a formal statement of special educational needs that will specify the additional support required or, in some cases, a move to specialist provision from outside the school. At this stage it is necessary to define more specifically the nature of the child's special need. Note that, unlike previous forms of labelling (see earlier), the categories below focus on learning needs or a description of the physical limitation, and not an implied 'deficiency' in the person of the child. The suggested categories are as follows:

Cognition and learning needs

- Specific Learning Difficulty (SpLD)
- Moderate Learning Difficulty (MLD)
- Severe Learning Difficulty (SLD)
- Profound and Multiple Learning Difficulty (PMLD)
- Behaviour, Emotional and Social Difficulty (BESD).

Behaviour, emotional and social development needs
Communication and interaction needs

- Speech, Language and Communication Needs (SLCN)
- Autistic Spectrum Disorder (ASD).

Sensory and/or physical needs

- Visual Impairment (VI)
- Hearing Impairment (HI)
- Multi-Sensory Impairment (MSI)
- Physical Disability (PD).

Other (OTH)

Chapter Seven of the Code of Practice goes into more detail on these categories and the resultant needs of the children.

Assessment

There was a time when specialist teachers were equipped with a battery of tests and associated remedial programmes, which were designed to identify and 'remediate' weaknesses in child's abilities through a diagnostic approach. The emphasis has now changed to looking at all children in terms of access to the curriculum, which is already assumed to be differentiated for a range of needs, and open to the schools normal assessment procedures.

Importantly, teachers now look for strengths as well as weaknesses in pupils' work and attitude, pay close attention to different ways in which learning can be strengthened, monitor and celebrate progress at all levels. They search for alternative learning strategies that are appropriate for the child, rather than trying to remedy the child's perceived shortcomings by a 'quick-fix' solution. If the general assessment policy is adequate, then the regular pattern of teaching and learning provides the information that teachers require in assessing the pupil's needs, rather than employing a test. Subsequently, assessment linked to pupils' learning needs is used to generate individual learning targets for each child. This broad process provides a sound basis for the more fine grained assessment needed to support a range of specific needs (see Figure 9.1).

GOOD PRACTICE provides assessment information
ASSESSMENT INFORMATION generates learning targets
LEARNING TARGETS are monitored by the teacher
MONITORING provides finer-grained assessment information
FINER-GRAINED ASSESSMENTS facilitate support for a range of particular learning needs

Figure 9.1 Teaching, assessment, targets and individual needs

For children with special needs, therefore, you should monitor closely any strategies that have been tried by the host teachers and assistants, learning from them and giving careful consideration to the implications for your own practice. As a picture of the pupil's favoured learning styles and areas of particular difficulty is slowly constructed, you will begin to understand better what works for each child. Many children learn best through a visual or a kinaesthetic ('hands-on') mode; others benefit from diagrams; yet others enjoy the medium of stories; of course, many pupils learn best from a combination of approaches. All teachers need first to take account of the preferred learning style or styles of the pupil, then to devise strategies that capitalise on their strengths. However, despite the apparent simplicity of this explanation, the reality is rarely as straightforward, not least because a proportion of children with learning needs also struggle with emotional disquiet, expressed as poor behaviour, inability to concentrate or low self-opinion.

Good practice

As far as possible, assessment should be part of the normal classroom experience. Children with a history of failure are more likely to be put off and under-perform if they are aware that they are being tested and treated differently from everyone else.

Targets and the Individual Education Plan

The Individual Education Plan (IEP) is an important tool in meeting a child's learning needs. The form of the paperwork varies from one local authority or school to another, but contains the following information:

- The short-term targets established for the child
- The most appropriate teaching strategies to be used
- The provision to be put in place (level of adult support, additional resources, etc.)
- When the plan is to be reviewed
- Success and or/exit criteria (i.e. ways in which the project is evaluated)
- Outcomes recorded when the IEP is reviewed.

The IEP should only record that which is additional to or different from the school's differentiated curriculum plan for all children. It should be crisply written and focus on three or four individual targets, chosen from those relating to the key areas of communication, literacy, mathematics and behaviour and social skills that match the child's needs. Crucially, the IEP must be discussed with the child and the parents. As with all learning, the more the child is involved in understanding and monitoring his own targets, the likelier it is that they will be reached.

It is important to realise that while the targets are individual in that they relate to a child's specific needs, this fact does not imply that they involve only individual, solitary tasks (such as completing work sheets). Many effective targets outline strategies for including the pupil in collaborative or whole-class activities where this has been a problem in the past.

At this stage it is not necessary to categorise the pupil's special need, but to concentrate on their particular learning needs, realised as workable targets, in much the same way as with any other child. These should be as precise as possible, such that the particular elements that the child has to concentrate on are capable of being defined, monitored and assessed. For example, if concentrating on spelling is identified as a target, there is little point in giving spellings for a test without offering advice about strategies for mastering them. When vague language is used to define targets, such as 'improve spelling' or 'behave appropriately', there is little clue as to what the child should actually do and it is extremely difficult to show that progress is being made. Under such conditions, target-setting becomes a pointless ritual and makes little contribution to learning.

There is very good reason for restricting the number of targets to three or four. Remember how disheartening it is for a child to have a page of work returned with only suggestions for improvement written on it, and no verbal positive feedback. It is too easy for teachers to give the message that the child is a failure and despair about cause them to despair about how to address all their weaknesses. Many children are tempted to give up if they perceive that the task of meeting an adult's aspirations is beyond their capability. If, however, children's attention is directed to specific, achievable targets, they can, with adult support and assistance, find succeed and become more optimistic about their future chances of doing well. Too many children expend great energy, and no little ingenuity in avoiding tasks because the fear of failure is too great. The secret is for you to engage them in progressively demanding experiences through which they feel that they can succeed, given appropriate support, and create a history of achievement, rather than compounding failure. At the same time it is essential to encourage a risk-taking climate and engender a belief that it is better to have made the effort and fallen short, than never to have made the effort at all.

Teaching approaches

Teaching children with SEN should be seen as a subset of good teaching for all pupils, not as a different kind of practice. It is helpful to remember that everyone finds difficulty in learning certain things at some level, but we can all make progress when the conditions are favourable and supportive. By the time children start school they have already shown themselves to be expert at learning, having absorbed more in their first five years than they will ever learn again. Furthermore, they will continue to learn things that are important and useful to them outside their school education. It is therefore more positive to view the child as a teaching challenge or potential success, rather than as someone with a 'learning difficulty'.

Flexibility is a key factor in teaching. If a child is finding difficulty in learning then it is wise to try a different approach, rather than repeating the same teaching more slowly (like a tourist attempting to order food in a foreign restaurant). Keys to flexibility include:

- A concentration on oral work
- Sustained meaningful talk through discussion
- Use of group and peer support (collaborative exercises)
- Use of a range of sources in providing evidence of learning (not merely written)
- A concentration on the processes of learning as they vary across subjects.

Most importantly it is always necessary to try to discern what meaning children are trying to make or express, rather than discounting their efforts as incorrect understandings. Pupils' miscues can be very revealing and provide a starting point for building on their ideas rather than demolishing them and starting again. For instance, when setting out subtraction sums such as 45 – 27 then some children always subtract the smaller from the larger number and will come up with the answer as 22 (by subtracting the smaller digits from the larger ones, 4 – 2 and 7 – 5). The children concerned are clearly capable of subtracting digits, but have either misunderstood the algorithm or have not developed a sense of place value. The perceptive teacher sees the incorrect answer as providing an opportunity to explore the child's lack of full understanding and not simply as something wrong that must be done again. Some seemingly bizarre answers or contributions in class discussion often make perfect sense if you are willing to explore the meaning that the child is intending and identify gaps in knowledge or conceptual understanding that can be used as a basis for the next stage in the pupil's learning. Too often, however, a teacher already has the correct response in mind, and quickly moves on to a child who is more likely to give the approved answer, thereby overlooking the opportunity that the original misconception has provided.

Activate your thinking!

Some children give wildly inaccurate responses as a method of deflecting attention, as the teacher often dismisses the inadequate answer and moves quickly on to another pupil. How can this situation be resisted?

The importance of oral work for children with special educational needs in a group or paired context cannot be overstated. McNamara and Moreton (2001) give a very useful rationale, and many examples of good practice, arguing that the best way to learn something is to have to teach it. For example, how many teachers knew much about the Aztecs before they had to plan lessons about the topic? Whenever possible, you should provide the children with the experience of being 'the expert' in at least one small area of the curriculum, as this is a powerfully affirming experience for a child used to being labelled a 'slow learner'. The most appropriate place to begin is with an area that interests the individual and to allow him or her to share informally with the group.

Evidence of learning

Some children do not become disenchanted with school because they find the curriculum uninteresting, but because they are daunted by the demand to write everything down, when writing for them is a slow, exacting process. Of course teachers must help every child to be more literate, but not at the expense of engagement with the curriculum and loss of motivation. There are many ways to evidence learning other than by individual children recording outcomes in written form without adult support. For example, evidence of children's learning can be provided through oral presentations, drawing, singing, drama, by contributing to group posters or presentations, or by having another child doing the writing task. (See also the use of story explored by Leicester and Johnson 2004.) With writing especially, it is important to remember that it is something activated in the mind. The process of physically writing things down, or scribing, is a separate (though related) activity. Thus, many famous authors have exciting ideas in their heads and choose to use audio technology and secretarial services, rather than writing manually to express what they want to say. Similarly, pupils with special educational needs can be encouraged to be writers if someone else (e.g. learning support assistant or classmate) assists with the act of writing. Drafting and editing discussions, where an adult or more capable pupil discusses with the individual ways to improve and enhance what has been accomplished so far, can be used to help the child shape and refine the writing. The process also gradually gives him or her more responsibility for the surface features of the work – such as punctuation and sentence construction – as well as content.

Maintaining the integrity and complexity of the subject matter is also important. We noted earlier that it is depressing to witness children with SEN effectively being excluded from more stimulating elements of the work by being given repetitive, low level tasks that do not engage the mind in the distinctive processes of the subject. For instance, investigative science is an area of the curriculum that fascinates children, in which they enjoy the chance to observe, categorise, hypothesise and experiment. None of these processes necessarily involve writing, though recording in some form (e.g. completing a pre-designed chart) is an important element of the process. Unfortunately, it is sometimes the case that children with SEN are denied involvement in these exciting opportunities, and are offered instead simplified worksheets, filling in gaps so that vocabulary can be learnt and similar tedious tasks. In such cases, they are really only receiving extra English tuition, with the main subject providing the backdrop. The same issue can be applied to other subjects such as history and geography, where the pupil needs first to be engaged with the processes and vocabulary of the subject. Only then should close attention then be given to refining their recording skills. Crucially, it is vital to avoid subjecting children to a plethora of worksheets (for instance) before they are offered the opportunity to do anything interesting; neither should they be sent off just to 'draw a picture of it' while their peers are engaged in genuine problem solving activity.

Activate your thinking!

Consider the truth of the statement: Children with special educational needs require stimulation, not stagnation.

Good practice

Always ensure that children with special learning needs have access to as many exciting opportunities as every other member of the class.

Every child matters

A 'joined up' provision for children and young people up to the age of nineteen years has its roots in the initiative, *Every Child Matters: Change for Children* (DfES 2005), the aim of which is for all children, regardless of their background or circumstances, to be supported in staying healthy and safe, achieving success, making a positive contribution to society and (rather oddly for primary age pupils) striving to achieve economic wellbeing. As a result, the organisations involved with providing services to children (hospitals, schools, police, voluntary groups and so on) are organised to share information and work together to protect and empower children and young people. The first Children's Commissioner for England was appointed in March 2005 to pay particular attention to gathering and promoting the views of those children and young people considered to be most vulnerable. Thus, *Every Child Matters* establishes five outcomes that matter most to children and young people:

1. Being healthy: enjoying good physical and mental health and living a healthy lifestyle.

2. Staying safe: being protected from harm and neglect.

3. Enjoying and achieving: getting the most out of life and developing the skills for adulthood.

4. Making a positive contribution: being involved with the community and not engaging in anti-social or offending behaviour.

5. Economic wellbeing: not being prevented by economic disadvantage from achieving their full potential in life.

While the vast majority of practitioners will view these aspirations as unexceptional and a reflection of what comes naturally, the ECM agenda is making the implicit (what practitioners believe) more explicit (their beliefs reflected in practice). All teachers need to demonstrate that they are taking these issues seriously in at least three ways:

■ Through the formal curriculum (what is taught)

■ The way that they relate to pupils and encourage pupils to relate to other people

■ Their active engagement with other (non-education) services.

Activate your thinking!

The ECM is frequently referred to as the 'ECM agenda'. Whose agenda is it?

The third bullet point is especially significant, in that in supporting children, and particularly those with special educational needs, you will inevitably work with a range of other professionals. Learning to work co-operatively, and take and give direction appropriately are essential skills that need to be developed. The key colleague is likely to be the SENCO, so it is vital that you talk to the SENCO about the additional help for children and practitioners (Cheminais 2005). Some schools have appointed a person with special responsibility for implementing the ECM requirements.

Most local authorities have a range of advisory teachers that are available for help and advice. These include specialists in teaching the hearing impaired, visually impaired and other areas of learning difficulty, behaviour support teams, a range of para-professionals such as speech therapists and physiotherapists, social workers, educational welfare officers, and medical services. As more multi-agency work is being encouraged, teachers have to be aware of the range of available services in the area. Trainee teachers are unlikely to have direct dealings with these service providers, but it is your responsibility to be alert to their existence and identify ways in which they are able to help you.

Working as a team member to improve the learning environment for all children, rather than sitting an adult alongside the 'problem child' to keep him or her occupied, needs careful planning and liaison. Outside the immediate professional domain you will also work with parents (perhaps in as well as out of school time) and members of the community who volunteer their services. Recruiting and managing these sources of additional support has to be fully thought out and integrated into a school-wide plan. If you are new to the school it is essential to find out how the system operates and to be clear about what specific support you would like parents to give. Parents' evenings are a useful occasion to make suggestions about helpful and unhelpful methods of supporting a child, though it is better to concentrate on straightforward strategies to support learning (such as reading aloud to the child) than to make suggestions about discipline strategies. Nevertheless, as Knowles (2006) rightly argues:

> If ECM is going to have a positive impact on children's lives, the key to its success is the realisation of the duty on children's services' agents to co-operate and work constructively with families … [and] … acknowledge the importance of seeing the child and his/her family in a holistic manner and work within a framework of joint understanding. (2006: 45)

See Chapter 3 for more information about working with other adults.

It is possible and desirable for all teachers to develop their teaching so that it is more accessible and inclusive. Perhaps the pupils who find the greatest difficulty in learning can be teachers' best critics, indicating the areas in which they need to be clearer or more flexible in approach. If you make learning easier for those experiencing the greatest difficulty, there is a strong likelihood that you will improve it for every child in your class.

Case study

Vijay, aged nine years, had a troublesome speech impediment. Owing to a jaw deformity, he spoke slowly and occasionally slurred his words. Worse still, his poor muscle tone would sometimes result in traces of saliva trickling from one side of his mouth. As a result, Vijay experienced severe embarrassment that affected his self-esteem and confidence. The teacher tried hard to include Vijay, encourage him in his work and involve him in whole-class activities, but he remained subdued and deliberately curbed a lot of his natural spontaneity and enthusiasm. After several discussions with parents and with advice from the SENCO, they agreed that to raise Vijay's self-esteem, they would offer him a responsible and privileged task as one of the six school librarians. This post gave him some genuine responsibility that did not require too much speaking but allowed him to interact with a wider range of children. The teacher also mastered and began to use some simple sign language with the whole class from which Vijay (especially) gained considerable benefit. The strategy also had the unexpected consequence of reducing noise levels generally. Finally, during choir practice, a TA noticed that Vijay had quite a good voice and his singing did not appear to be affected significantly by his impediment. The teacher gently encouraged Vijay to take a supporting role in the school concert, which was very successful. At a subsequent meeting with Vijay's parents to discuss his progress, they commented that he had never been happier at school.

Further reading

Carpenter, B., Ashdown, R. and Bovair, K. (eds) (1996) *Enabling Access: Effective teaching and learning for pupils with learning difficulties*, London: David Fulton.

Deals with the implications for different curriculum areas and contains good practical suggestions.

Cheminais, R. (2001) *Developing Inclusive School Practice: A practical guide*, London: David Fulton.

An easy-to follow guide, clearly presented and imaginatively structured.

Connolly, P. (2004) *Boys and Schooling in the Early Years*, London: Routledge.

Includes detailed and contemporary analyses of national evidence about gender differences in educational achievement.

Crosse, K. (2007) *Introducing English as an Additional Language to Young Children*, London: Sage.

Helps teachers to develop the confidence in meeting the individual needs of young children with English as an additional language.

Thomas, G. and Vaughan, M. (eds) (2004) *Inclusive Education: Readings and Reflections*, Maidenhead: Open University Press.

Brings together the key ideas and perspectives that have led education in an increasingly inclusive direction.

PART

3

Qualified Status

The Induction Year

Introduction

You've made it! Congratulations! All the hard work has paid off and now you are a qualified teacher, ready to take charge of your own class. All newly qualified teachers are required to serve an induction year, which was introduced to provide a solid basis for professional and career development. At its best, induction helps new teachers to show their potential, make steady progress in becoming effective practitioners and make a positive impact on the school's overall development and, in particular, the education of the children for whom you have responsibility. This chapter contains advice about achieving these goals.

Background

You saw the job advertised and made your application. When the governors received your form, they probably knew nothing about you unless you taught there during a school experience placement, so the form was initially their only source of evidence. They were persuaded that you were someone worth considering further, so they followed up one or more of your referees. Eventually they decided to put you on a 'short list' and invite you for a more formal interview (though the degree of formality varies considerably from school to school). In doing so, the head teacher and governors were asking four basic questions about the candidates:

- Can this person handle a class from top to bottom? (That is, can this person not only teach well but also maintain class order?)

- Will this person fit into our staff? (Is s/he reasonable, pleasant, honest, sympathetic etc?)

- How will parents react to this person? (Is s/he approachable, a good communicator, understanding of parental concerns, etc.?)

- Will this person help to raise standards of academic achievement, especially in core subjects? (Will s/he prepare children for their national tests, while retaining a vital spark of creativity?)

They saw from your initial application that you were someone who might fit the bill. You were invited to look around the school and sensibly kept a low profile, while staying alert and picking up clues about the school's priorities. Before the formal interview, you may have written down some likely questions that the panel might ask you and recorded your answers on to a tape. You were horrified how hesitant you sounded (everyone has a similar reaction to the sound of their own voice) but it gave you time to think through and clarify your beliefs beforehand, so that you had your answers reasonably well formulated.

During interview the panel expected you to be passionate about your desire to teach in *their* school (not just any old school). Your letter of application was further scrutinised, your references studied closely, and your response to a series of probing questions satisfied them that you were the person for the job. Perhaps you were asked questions such as:

- How will you organise for learning in literacy to differentiate for the ability range and personalise learning?

- How will you organise your room and what will it tell us about your teaching?

- What sort of things will you do to promote children's thinking skills?

- How will you ensure that gifted and talented children achieve their potential?

- Give us some examples of how you use assessment for learning

- Can you describe for us the sorts of contributions that you can make to the school's work in your specialist curriculum area?

- What sort of things will you do to promote an effective working relationship with parents?

- How will you know that you are succeeding in raising standards?

You were not confident with every answer and did not try to pretend that you knew something if you were uncertain. However, you did your best to be honest, upbeat, cheery but not unnatural, relaxed but alert. You listened carefully to the questions and thought briefly before you responded. You were positive, but tempered it by stressing that you wanted to continue learning throughout your career and do well for the children. You did not raise dilemmas or problematic issues or admit to misgivings about aspects of the job that you secretly held. Finally, despite your nerves and uncertainty about some of the tougher questions put to you, a combination of your bright personality and confident responses convinced the head and governors that you were the best person for the job. Well done! Now the fun begins!

Activate your thinking!

How would you respond to the following interview questions?

Professional requirements
What sort of learning climate will you promote and how will you go about it?

Teaching and learning
How will you go about setting high, but not unreasonable, expectations for the full range of ability?

Adult relationships
How might you employ the skills of a 0.5 TA?
What practical steps will you take to involve parents in their children's learning?

Self-development
How will you know if you are succeeding as a teacher?

Preparation and planning
How will you organise your literacy lessons?

Purposeful teaching
What strategies might you use to motivate children who find learning difficult?

Special needs
How do you envisage an 'inclusion' policy operating in your classroom?

Organising and managing
Teachers are busy people. How will you prioritise your time and workload?

Behaviour and discipline
Describe the way that you will ensure that children are well-disciplined without being crushed in spirit?

Extended professionalism
Tell us something about the duties of a teacher other than teaching.

Assessment
How will you use assessment to improve teaching and learning?

Equal opportunities
What steps will you take to ensure that all children have a fair chance?

Making the transition

It takes time to adjust from being a student to being a 'real' teacher. Newcomers have to adjust quickly to a new community, getting to know people, routines and facts, appreciating the ethos of the school and understanding protocol. Breaking into the professional circle can be forbidding and requires a subtle blend of tact and assertion. You have been a trainee teacher for at least a year, possibly three or four years, and suddenly, like a chrysalis turning into a butterfly, you grow your wings and become a fully-fledged teacher. If you don't feel like one and wonder if it can really be true, don't be alarmed. Most NQTs wonder how they are ever going to survive and if they have got what it takes to make a success of the job. It is not uncommon to experience a sharp decline in confidence following the end of your training course and, though you wonder at yourself for feeling this way, to half-wish that you could be a student again with all the protection it afforded. When you were training, the children in your teaching experience schools sometimes asked you the same question at the start of every new placement: 'Are you a real teacher?' and you hardly knew what to say. You probably ended up by sounding a little indignant and replying that *of course* you were a real teacher (but not feeling like one at all). You longed for the day when you could answer the question honestly, but now that the day has arrived you still find yourself wondering if it is true.

Other anxieties may begin to emerge: What if a parent asks if this is your first class? What if colleagues begin to probe your subject knowledge, classroom management expertise and understanding of assessment and reporting procedures? In fact, what if someone begins to expose all the sorts of things that troubled you as a student, but that you successfully concealed from the tutor? In short, what if you are found out? Panic may set in as you realise that you know absolutely *nothing* about teaching, you don't know why on earth it ever occurred to you to do the job, and you wonder why you didn't take your friend's advice and backpack around the globe. 'Too late now!' you lament. Jacklin, Griffiths and Robinson (2006) refer to the study they conducted, in which newly qualified teachers all admitted to the swing of emotions they experienced during the first term in particular. Thus:

> At times they felt confident, excited, enthusiastic and part of a team within the school. At other times they felt anxious, isolated and worried about their own and their pupils' progress ... They told us that often they felt as if they should know the answers and were concerned that others would see their questions as trivial. (2006: 29)

It is worth noting from the Jacklin, Griffiths and Robinson research that the swinging emotions were present in N-+QTs regardless of the level of support they were receiving in the school; so you are not alone. If you are feeling this way, you can be reassured that the anxieties will gradually subside. Although some parents may ask if this is your first class, and colleagues will chat about aspects of school life and how to cope with it, they rarely do so with ill intent. In fact, parents often like their children to have new teachers in the belief that they will introduce fresh ideas and sparkle to the teaching and learning environment. Many colleagues are hoping to get some useful suggestions from you to use in their own lessons. The arrival of this talented young star (you) is eagerly awaited, so make sure you don't do or say too much at the start that reveals your insecurities and damages your image. On the other hand, it is instructive that research by Day *et al.* (2007) suggests that 'teachers do not necessarily become more effective as they grow older ... teachers in their early professional life phases ... are more likely to be effective than their counterparts in the middle and later professional life phases' (2007: 256). Although these conclusions must be treated with a degree of caution, they should provide reassurance that 'inexperience' does not equate to 'ineffective'.

To a certain extent, the nervous tension that rises from the pit of your stomach towards the end of the holiday period will be a feature throughout your career. If you ask experienced teachers about the few days leading up to the start of a new term, they will confess that it is a miserable time as doubts about their own ability to cope with the demands of the job surface, and uncertainty hangs over them like a damp fog. Once they are back in school and the new term begins, the tension evaporates in the fever pitch of meeting the children, organising lessons, relating to colleagues and parents, re-establishing their credentials as a teacher to be reckoned with, and reminding themselves that they have not, after all, lost their ability to thrive and prosper in teaching. So don't be surprised if you have similar sorts of worries before the start of every term and equally powerful feelings of reassurance once you have begun.

New challenges

Being a qualified teacher carries many advantages over being a trainee teacher. For a start, you will not have a tutor observing your lessons, though you will not be spared this ordeal entirely as there will be occasions when a senior colleague comes to watch you teach (probably once or twice per term; peer observation is also common in schools among members of the experienced staff). However, you will be able to discuss issues on an equal footing rather than feeling at the mercy of the college assessment system. Second, in the earlier stages of the school year there will be far fewer forms to complete, though as the year unfolds there will be a lot of recording and report-writing to do. Third, there will not be any need to write screeds of self-analysis about how you might have improved your lesson or what went wrong during the session (although it is worth keeping a diary about important issues that emerge throughout the year). The most notable advantage about leaving student days behind is being able to relish the freedom you gain from knowing that you are no longer dealing with somebody else's class and will not, after a period of some weeks, have to hand the children over to the class teacher again and trudge wearily back to college for more lectures. Now you have an opportunity to show what you are made of.

Gradually, however, other aspects of the job will emerge that you may or may not be expecting. The rest of this chapter is designed to assist you anticipate some of those challenges, deal with them effectively and play your part in providing the sort of education that you would want for your own children, were they in your class.

Requirements

As part of teachers' continued professional development, each is allocated a fellow staff member to be a mentor (induction tutor) who will help the NQT to negotiate his/her first year. The induction tutor offers advice about many aspects of school life, such as time management, handling paperwork, dealing with troublesome children, relating to parents and maintaining a reasonable work/leisure balance. By the end of their induction year, all new teachers must have demonstrated their mastery of the Qualified Teacher Status (QTS) standards on a consistent and sustained basis, while teaching continuously in a school, with the direct and personal responsibility and accountability for pupil performance that accompanies it. They must also have shown that they have built on, and progressed beyond, the QTS standards in key areas such as managing pupil behaviour and contributing to pupils' learning, and to the planning and achievement of their school's performance targets.

The most recent set of Induction Standards for newly qualified teachers came into force in 2006 and consist of six categories that are intended to build on the standards for QTS and must be 'achieved' by the *end* of your induction, with the emphasis on 'end'. Thus:

Induction standard a: Professional values and practice

Seek and use opportunities to work collaboratively with colleagues to raise standards by sharing effective practice in the school.

Induction standard b: Knowledge and understanding

Show a commitment to their professional development by:

- Identifying areas in which they need to improve their professional knowledge, understanding and practice in order to teach more effectively in their current post, and
- Taking steps to address these needs (with support).

Induction standard c: Teaching: special educational needs

Plan effectively to meet the needs of pupils in their classes with special educational needs, with or without statements, and in consultation with the SENCO contribute to the preparation, implementation, monitoring and review of individual education plans (IEPs) or the equivalent.

Induction standard d: Teaching: liaising with parents and carers

Liaise effectively with parents or carers on pupils' progress and achievements.

Induction standard e: Teaching: working as part of a team

Work effectively as part of a team and, as appropriate to the post in which they are completing induction, liaise with, deploy, and guide the work of other adults who support pupils' learning.

Induction standard f: Teaching: securing appropriate behaviour

Secure a standard of behaviour that enables pupils to learn, and act to pre-empt and deal with inappropriate behaviour in the context of the behaviour policy of the school.

The Training & Development Agency (TDA) specifies that schools are expected to provide new teachers with the support they need in order to demonstrate that they are meeting the standards. NQTs need to take account of the induction standards when they meet with their induction tutors as they establish objectives and plan professional development opportunities. The TDA also advises that NQTs should not simply 'tick off' standards as achieved too early in the induction year but rather to see each standard or part of a standard well established over a period of time before recording its success. In fact, a careful look at the Induction Standards (above) shows that it is far more difficult to fail to reach them than to achieve them. In practice, the vast majority of new teachers are successful; in the extremely rare case where there are problems (unless it is inappropriate professional conduct) there is normally opportunity to redeem the situation. It is, of course, important to view the induction year as an exciting opportunity to build upon your existing professional expertise with the help and support of more experienced colleagues, and not a depressing re-run of the fearsome pressures that you felt during your training. Jacklin, Griffiths and Robinson (2006) offer wise advice in this regard. Thus:

> Remember that the purpose of engaging in professional development is to improve your understanding, knowledge and skills, to develop your practice and its impact on pupil learning. Think small, be focused, work with colleagues and enjoy it. (2006: 167)

Activate your thinking!

There are now standards attached to professional development beyond the induction year. Thus:

- For teachers on the main scale (Core, C)
- For teachers on the upper pay scale (Post Threshold Teachers, P)
- Excellent Teachers (E)
- Advanced Skills Teachers (ASTs, A).

Do you know the status of the teachers in your school?

The induction year can be served in any maintained school, with certain exceptions:

- Pupil referral units
- Secure training-centres
- Schools requiring special measures, unless one of Her Majesty's Inspectors certifies in writing that the school is suitable for providing induction
- Independent schools that do not meet specified criteria
- Further Education Colleges, unless a sixth-form college
- Independent nursery schools and other early years' settings that do not meet the criteria described in the section on independent schools above
- British Schools abroad, apart from those described in the section on independent schools above.

If you are interested in working in an independent school, it is essential to check that the school is approved to run an induction programme.

As described above, NQTs are entitled to receive support from the head teacher, induction tutor and colleagues, and must reach clearly defined standards in their classroom practice and wider professional conduct as staff members (Cole 2002). Normally, NQTs will start their induction year as soon as they leave training college and commence their first permanent teaching post. Those who only manage to acquire a temporary post lasting less than one year can build up to a total of one year in different schools. For instance, an NQT might find employment in three separate schools, each lasting one term, or work for two terms in one school and a term in a second school. In unusual circumstances such as lengthy sick leave or maternity leave, the induction process can be extended beyond the one year until the equivalent amount of time has been served.

If an NQT has been absent from work for 30 school days or more during the induction period, the induction period is extended by the aggregate total of absences. For example, if they are absent for a total of 35 days, the extension will be for that length of time. If a female NQT has a break in the induction which includes statutory maternity leave, she may choose whether or not to have the induction extended by the equivalent of the part of her absence which was statutory maternity leave. A final decision is normally made by the NQT when she returns to work and has given the matter careful thought, but any such request has to be considered by school governors. However, if an NQT chooses not to extend her induction period following an absence of maternity leave she is still assessed on the same basis as any other NQT. Note that conditions vary slightly between England and other parts of the UK.

Conditions of service

The induction year is intended to provide NQTs with a bridge from initial teacher training to effective professional practice. Conditions of service include the provision of well-targeted monitoring and support, a reduced timetable (even taking account of planning, preparation and assessment time), and to help nurture an ethos of continuing professional development (CPD) and career development. NQTs will not normally be expected to cope with excessive demands by (say) having responsibility for a very large class or a group of particularly difficult pupils. They should only teach for only about 90 per cent of the time to give them opportunity to gain wider experience by working alongside a colleague, visiting other classes and local schools, and attending in-service courses.

The induction tutor may be a senior teacher (in a larger school) and the deputy head or experienced teacher (in a smaller school). In addition to providing regular advice about aspects of the teacher role, the tutor will encourage you to contribute to curriculum working parties, act as a guide in visiting other local schools (including a special school) to enhance your knowledge and experience of education, and facilitate your initial liaison with the SENCO. Establishing and maintaining contact with other new teachers in the area is also essential, as it is easy for NQTs to become isolated in their first post and imagine that they are the only teacher in the world struggling with discipline and keeping pace with the relentless demands that teaching sometimes imposes. As Cockburn (1996) realistically acknowledges:

> Whether you are an experienced teacher or new to the profession, starting a new job is often an exhilarating, challenging and daunting experience rolled into one (1996: 27)

Part of your development as a teacher is learning to work closely with and alongside colleagues, accept majority decisions and strive to operate within the agreed guidelines and policies. You will not agree with everything that is taking place when you arrive at the school or all the subsequent decisions. Some aspects of school life will irritate you. Some colleagues will disappoint you. Some procedures will appear unnecessary or irksome. Although you are entitled to ask for explanations about why things are done in certain ways, it is important to understand that every new teacher has to learn to fit in to the school situation as it exists and accommodate its vagaries. This is not to say that with the help of your influence certain aspects may not change or be modified over time, but the best forms of change come slowly and, however convinced you may be that you know best, it is wise to listen, watch and wait before passing judgement. Your contributions to debate will be valued and respected if you express them with humility and a genuine willingness to learn. As the old saying goes, fools rush in where angels fear to tread.

As a qualified teacher you are expected to contribute towards the whole school endeavour and make an effort to lend your expertise to improving standards of learning, behaviour and social awareness. Just as happy children work more enthusiastically than unsettled ones, so a contented staff will achieve more than a discontented one. As a newly qualified person, you may not believe that you have much to offer your colleagues, but this is untrue. Other teachers and ancillary staff, while anxious that you settle in quickly and do well in your job, also hope that you will play your part in being an effective team member. Head teachers want teachers that help to raise morale, work well with colleagues and parents, and provide a positive role model.

Succeeding in your induction year

You will have worked very hard to gain QTS and been looking forward with excited anticipation to the day when you have responsibility for your own class. In the light of all the effort you have made to reach this point, the induction year may give the appearance of being yet another hurdle. However, it is important to view the year as part of the support mechanism available to new teachers, without which you would be less equipped to deal with the rigours of teaching. As you may have noted above, the induction year standards are not dissimilar to those for qualified teacher status. Basically, you need to be able to demonstrate your competence in planning, teaching, class management, monitoring, assessing, recording and reporting, though there is greater emphasis for you take account of the needs of individual children and ensure that all children are included (see Chapter 9). There are also expectations with respect to deploying and working with other adults (including parents), implementing school policies (such as dealing with bullying and racial harassment) and taking responsibility for your professional development.

Success in the induction year is much less a case of whether or not you will pass (as almost everyone does) but of how much progress you make as a teacher during that time. If you end the year feeling more confident about the job and your ability to thrive, then the year has been a success. Remember that the induction year is only the first of many years that you will spend as a teacher (Bubb 2004; Holmes 2004), so see your progress in the longer term, rather than 'surviving' to the end of next term.

Positive attitudes

Active and enthusiastic collaboration is at the heart of effective schools, so make it your aim to get on well with everyone in school, including non-teaching staff, and maintain a positive attitude towards life. You do not have to go around the school with a permanent grin on your face, of course. A pleasant smile and responsive manner is quite sufficient to convince those around you that you are worth all the effort they expend on your behalf. Similarly, the respect that you display towards other adults working in the school will help to seal your reputation as a person of integrity. As we noted earlier in this book, positive attitudes are contagious; they not only affect the quality of interpersonal relationships with colleagues but upon the classroom teaching-and-learning environment.

Effective schools are places where teamwork and staff loyalty are embedded into the fabric of the place. Being a teacher, like most other jobs, is as much about corporate endeavour and teamwork as the technical ability to teach. Once you enter a school, you have a responsibility to a range of different groups: children, parents, governors, members of the community and your colleagues. Even if you are a novice teacher, you must still demonstrate a willingness to support other teachers and trainee teachers in their efforts to improve their practice and contribute to the children's education. Genuine comments to staff expressing your appreciation for their help and the way that you value their guidance will greatly encourage them. Similarly, the caring way in which you react to colleagues, especially when they need someone to talk to about important issues, will create enormous goodwill and strong feelings of camaraderie that are essential for effective teamwork. Commitment to fellow workers goes beyond sitting and listening while they sound off their complaints; it involves being willing to act for your colleagues in practical and active ways whenever possible. Strive to become the sort of teacher that *you* would hope to see in a colleague.

Getting on well with the head teacher

You will probably have quite a lot of contact with the head teacher during your early days in school as a qualified teacher. Most head teachers make a special point of nursing new members of staff through their first few weeks in the job rather than leaving it all to the induction tutor. Others believe that it is better to stay at a distance and allow new teachers to make their mistakes in private. Although head teachers tend to be extremely busy at the start of term and may seem a bit distracted, you should not misinterpret this as unfriendliness. Over time, you will discover that heads are under a lot of pressure to achieve high standards of education in the school, though many of their struggles take place behind closed doors. It may appear to you that a head is a free agent, who can make autonomous decisions without regard to what others think; in fact, nothing could be further from the truth, for heads are obliged to seek the views of parents and discuss with governors any significant changes they are hoping to make in the school.

Head teachers have spent many years in school and cannot be fooled by a jaunty remark and artificial smile, but they appreciate teachers and other adults who have the courtesy and maturity to make good eye contact and speak out clearly. If at some point in the future you apply for a post in another school, you will need to put the head teacher as one of your referees, and as heads talk to one another regularly, there is a strong chance that your reputation will reach the ears of other local head teachers. You can be sure that whether the head is highly personable or somewhat aloof, you are rarely off his or her mind when you first arrive in school.

Activate your thinking!

How true are the following?: (a) I am displaying a willing, enthusiastic approach to the job; (b) I am doing my best to value those around me; and (c) I am making the best of those things that irritate me.

Contributing expertise

Every teacher has some special skill or ability that may be useful for the common good and benefit colleagues and children. Learning to learn from one another is something that every school has recognised as important and taking responsibility for your own professional development is an important element of your role. NQTs are sometimes appointed on the understanding that they will try to contribute curriculum strengths as a co-ordinator, leader or curriculum manager throughout the school. However, this additional responsibility can be difficult even for experienced teachers and places heavy demands upon an already busy practitioner (Farmery 2004). There is always so much to do and think about that finding the time and opportunity to work alongside colleagues, advise them about possibilities for developing a curriculum area or taking their class as a subject specialist is difficult. All schools have a development programme in which subjects and topics are examined systematically, which gives teachers responsible for that area the opportunity to share and to exercise leadership during the discussions. In some cases, the teacher concerned may be asked to provide a draft policy statement, guidelines or a review of the existing situation. The extra responsibility for curriculum development or an aspect of learning (such as assessment and recording) has to be fitted alongside other teaching duties. Few schools have the resources to give teachers the time to pursue these responsibilities during the school day, though as noted earlier, with the restructuring of the workforce it may be possible to free some time through use of experienced TAs to oversee the class for a time.

As part of team membership, teachers have to attend staff meetings. Full meetings are normally held once a week, though additional team planning meetings and age-phase meetings commonly occur on a fortnightly basis. Attendance at meetings can become burdensome and all teachers have to make allowance for the time and energy they consume. It can be a bit galling to attend a meeting when you are desperate to mark books, organise equipment or complete some records, but you simply have to accept the fact and organise your day differently.

When decisions have to be made, some schools make them on a strictly democratic basis in which a vote is taken; more commonly, curriculum leaders and senior staff draw up papers for discussion and present suggestions about future programme modifications. These are subsequently discussed and revised until a suitable format is agreed across the staff. In a small number of schools, the curriculum leader and the head teacher determine the strategies beforehand; these are presented to the staff for implementation rather than acceptance, modification or rejection. In such cases, debate is concerned with the detail rather than the substance of the issue. Most teachers welcome clearly presented ideas that will help their teaching and supervisory responsibilities but are suspicious of innovations which they perceive as reducing their autonomy. Finally, all head teachers are subject to Government demands and requirements. Local authorities (LAs) also put pressure on schools to adjust what are perceived as weaker areas as indicated through test results; they are generally less concerned about non-core subjects. A coming inspection sends shivers down the spine of every practitioner and school governor, and numerous preparation meetings are held beforehand, though schools deemed successful in a full inspection may then receive a 'short' inspection with only a few days notice.

From time to time, the school governors decide that the school's budget allows them to give teachers an extra allowance for their contribution as curriculum leaders. Additional increments are offered to the teacher directly or, more usually, the post is advertised internally and any member of staff can apply. The requirements of the post may vary: 'language co-ordinator' or 'assessment at Key Stage 1' or 'curriculum leader in science'. Some teachers may be have passed through the 'threshold' and be on an upper pay scale; others are designated 'excellent teachers' (ETs) and yet others, 'advanced skills teachers' (AST), a position gained after passing a national assessment. ETs have a distinctive role in helping other teachers improve their effectiveness and are intended to have a major impact on improving pupil attainment across the whole school. ASTs are given additional payment and increased non-contact time in order to share their skills and experience with other teachers, within their own school and from other schools.

Although certain teachers have formal responsibilities for areas of school life, there are a number of teachers in every school who, by dint of personality, length of service at the school or experience are the 'unofficial leaders' of the staffroom. To the newcomer, unofficial leaders may not appear initially to be influential but behind the scenes they are affecting the course of staff opinion and attitudes towards options and decisions. You may find yourself benefiting greatly from their informal advice and counsel.

Older, experienced teachers can offer leadership through their calm presence during turbulent times. Younger staff can lead through their infectious enthusiasm, willingness to embrace change and introduction of new ideas. The secret of effective informal leadership is to support the official leadership wholeheartedly, while using every opportunity to encourage others, empathise with the downhearted, sympathise with the broken-hearted and provide practical support and advice to colleagues in need. The best informal leaders do not seek adulation or power for its own sake; instead, they gain satisfaction from being positively influential and genuinely admired by staff and parents. You may be a new teacher but you can quickly become influential if you demonstrate these qualities.

Activate your thinking!

What percentage of your time should be spent throughout a week on classroom teaching, other supervisory duties, attendance at meetings and general preparation and maintenance tasks? How might this balance of activities vary at certain times of the year?

Good practice

Make a firm decision that you will gain a reputation as a positive and caring person.

Growth and development

During your induction year you will need to secure and enhance the competencies that you acquired during your initial training. It is worth bearing in mind that however well you performed as a trainee teacher, there will always be areas of your teaching requiring close attention. Even some of the basic skills, such as class control, can prove difficult during your first post. It takes time to settle in and find your feet, so you will have to persevere and use every strategy at your disposal to avoid feeling overwhelmed. You will also need to take account of the standards in the professional codes for the General Teaching Councils in England, Wales and Scotland. Thus, the GTC for England refers to young people and pupils, teacher colleagues, other professionals, parents and carers, school in context and learning and development. Wales GTC includes details relating to teaching and learning, pupils, colleagues, parents/guardians, other professionals, and professional development. Scotland GTC (by far the longest established of the three) focuses on expertise, collegiality, equal opportunities, responsibility, legal framework, responding to individual needs, professional relationships and professional integrity. (See Arthur, Davison and Lewis 2005) As you increase in confidence and find your way through the initial challenges, allow the following principles to act as a guide:

- Learn to trust your own judgement
- Share your concerns and joys with colleagues and friends
- Pace yourself so that you don't attempt too much, too soon
- Use every possible resource available, including published material such as textbooks and electronic sources
- Take regular rest and holidays.

Your Career Entry and Development Profile (CEDP) provides a useful starting point for future career development and should be used alongside the issues arising from the regular review meetings with your tutor to shape and refine your skills. For instance, your CEDP may show that you have had little opportunity to master aspects of ICT or gained limited experience of teaching PE while you were a trainee teacher. Whatever the specific area for enhancement, you will be encouraged to learn from other colleagues with more expertise and attend appropriate courses to extend your knowledge. Do not be embarrassed that you have areas that require further development, as even qualified teachers need to update and refine their knowledge and understanding, regardless of the years they have been teaching.

Whatever your particular subject expertise may be, you need to concentrate on the following aspects of your role during the induction year, and persevere with those aspects that you find difficult. The following list, based on guidelines for the induction of new teachers offers a useful means of monitoring your progress:

Classroom climate

Every teacher is instrumental in helping to create socially responsible attitudes among pupils by encouraging co-operation and collaboration rather than animosity and selfish forms of competition. Your teaching will be sensitive to the ethnic and cultural diversity in your class and valuing every child as a unique and special individual.

Classroom order

Securing good classroom order by establishing effective relationships with pupils and clarifying with your pupils what you are, and are not, prepared to tolerate resides at the heart of successful teaching and learning. Frankly, if you cannot maintain good order and establish a positive ethos, you are not going to enjoy other aspects of your role. In this regard, Dixie (2007) offers a stark warning about the significance of what he calls 'the establishment phase' by stressing that it is important for teachers of all ages and experience to be clear about exactly who they are, what they believe in and what they expect from their pupils. In other words, start as you mean to go on.

Lesson planning

Planning lessons thoroughly is essential, but with awareness that teaching is not an exact science. That is, to be willing to deviate from the plan if, during teaching, it becomes clear that a different approach is called for. One of the major differences between your time as a trainee and a qualified teacher is that you are responsible for continuous sessions, so planning tends to be with blocks of lessons in mind, rather than individual and discrete ones. In other words, your focus becomes much longer term than previously.

Individual differences

In conjunction with assessment (below) your role in identifying and supporting low achievers, either through appropriate tasks, support from peers through collaborative activities, or help from a TA forms an integral element of your teaching. You must liaise with the SENCO or senior teacher for pupils who provide exceptional challenges and try to involve parents from an early stage.

Assessment

Assessing pupils against tests and targets has dominated educational practice over the past decade. This practice involves taking account of pupils' previous achievements from reports, notes and conversations with other teachers and (in some cases) parents, and talking to the children themselves. It is also monitoring daily progress, identifying children who might be under-achieving in literacy and mathematics, and providing additional resources to remedy perceived pupil shortcomings.

Target setting

Monitoring pupils' progress and setting appropriate learning targets for groups of children and individuals have become key features of teaching in recent times. For instance, a group of children may need more opportunity to work co-operatively; an individual may be set specific time limits to complete work or given a longer term goal such as mastering a family of spellings or learning how to access information sources. It is important to discuss targets with children and help them to monitor their own progress wherever realistic to do so.

Home–school

You need to take every opportunity through formal and informal liaison with parents to express your enthusiasm for their children's progress and communicate your pleasure (and occasional concerns) by word of mouth and letter (see Chapter 3). This contact is particularly important for new school entrants in the Foundation Stage of their education; parents of older children are just as interested in their children's progress and happiness, but may be less available for regular informal discussions.

Other adults

Ensuring that TAs are clear about their role and your expectations of them has become increasingly significant in recent years. It is worth remembering that assistants now have the opportunity to gain formal qualifications and regularly update their skills, and there is a possibility that the TA is a qualified teacher who, for a variety of possible reasons, decided to become an assistant. Experienced TAs or higher level teaching assistants (HLTAs) may be capable of supervising a group or even the whole class during your absence from the room, which makes it doubly important that you have fully briefed them.

Staff membership

As noted on a number of occasions throughout this book, playing your part as a team member by offering support and encouragement to those with whom you work is vitally important. You also have a professional responsibility to implement school policies as fully as possible, and inform senior staff where you experience difficulties in so doing. As part of your wider role you should contribute to extra-curricular activities where appropriate, though not at the expense of your regular teaching. Helping to maintain and enhance the school's reputation in the community by your positive attitude, creative teaching and personable manner also forms part of being a staff member.

If the above list looks daunting, remember that you have already demonstrated your capability during pre-service training and have a whole year to improve weaker areas. Some requirements will naturally fall into place; others will need perseverance over a period of time. Mistakes and occasional instances of poor judgement are inevitable; try to take it in your stride and not become dispirited if things go wrong. The induction year may well prove to be the most demanding, worthwhile and exciting time of your life so far.

Doing your best

You want to do well in your new job, of course, but beware of trying to do everything at once. It is true that you are to some extent under scrutiny, but most teachers are too busy with their own affairs to worry overly about what you are getting up to. It is important to recognise that you will tire very quickly during the first term, so it is essential to pace yourself and not to develop a whirlwind mentality, flitting from one thing to another like a performer keeping plates spinning on the end of a dozen canes. You will want to be determined but not frantic; conscientious but not a perfectionist; idealistic but also keeping your feet firmly anchored to the ground. Contrary to how it might be expressed in the media and by some politicians, the future educational success of the kingdom does not rest solely at your feet! You are neither responsible for every bit of learning that children experience nor the only contributor to the aspirations of every parent. You have an important role in ensuring that your class makes good progress in learning, and there would be something strange about teachers who were not interested in ensuring that their pupils attained the highest standards, but you are not the only interested party or influential factor. Some children are motivated by caring and thoughtful parents; others are not. Some children have material advantages that benefit their progress; others lack the basics. Some children are emotionally secure; others are vulnerable or even frightened. As the teacher, you have to provide the best education for them that it is reasonable to expect, but you are not a miracle worker and should not attempt to be so.

The truth about being a teacher is that even if you worked 24 hours every day and performed heroic deeds, it would not satisfy all the demands that are made of you. Regardless of the time you arrive at school and leave for home; despite the countless hours you commit to preparation, marking and sorting out individual needs, it will never be enough. It may sound trite, but the old adage that you can only do your best applies to teaching as much as to any other job. Some teachers allow the job to dominate their lives and seem to spend every waking hour in tasks associated with it. Although it can be difficult to stop yourself from becoming obsessed with your new role, it is important to resist the relentless demands that might be made of you by the many different people associated with the school. Like the waves of the sea, additional work and commitments will keep rolling up to your feet, and though you may sometimes feel like King Canute in trying to repel the tide, it is worth persevering to develop a lifestyle that allows for recreation and separation from the job's requirements. This will not be easy. Most NQTs acknowledge that the first year is difficult, demanding, stimulating and a bit scary; yours will not be any different. The advice contained within this book should help you to keep things under control but one thing is for sure: if you don't look after yourself, nobody else will.

Another important thing to remember is that although you are new and feel vulnerable, the children and parents see you as 'the teacher' (albeit young looking, perhaps) and do not distinguish you from any other teacher in the school. So you do not have to prove yourself in the same way as when you were a student. You can move into the realms of super-teacher and being the focus for hero-worship when you have got a few years of teaching under your belt. Concentrate on your classroom work, make an effort to be a supportive colleague and a good team member, and don't use your inexperience as an excuse for a poor quality performance.

Health issues

Illness is an unfortunate fact of life. Trainee teachers and qualified teachers alike are prone to succumb to it at some time or another. As a student, it was possible to miss a couple of lectures if you felt ill or, if it was during a teaching experience, to grit your teeth and struggle on for a couple of weeks until the end of the placement. As a qualified teacher the battle to retain good health is complicated by two facts. First, that the daily contact with children increases the likelihood that you will pick up infections. Second, that as you are now the responsible person for your class, you will be reluctant to take time off and disadvantage the children. You may also be anxious lest your absence is perceived by colleagues or the head teacher as a sign of weakness. Worries about comments such as 'They don't make them like they used to' and 'The slightest little thing and these new teachers take a day off' may unduly influence what you decide to do and tempt you to struggle in when you should have stayed at home. There is little point in crawling in to school when you should be resting in bed. As O'Flynn and Kennedy (2003) state emphatically, should teachers fall ill and need time off, they are likely to be horrified by how easily they have been replaced and by how little the system cares for them.

It is important that you protect your health to minimise the possibility of picking up every nasty bug that is floating around the school, so it is essential to do regular exercise and maintain a balanced lifestyle. On the other hand, even the fittest person suffers from ill health occasionally, so you should not view time off work as a crime. In fact, if you go in to school when you are unwell, you may cause one of four unpleasant effects:

1. You are unable to teach properly, so the children do not learn much.

2. The illness tends to make you less tolerant and more grumpy than usual, adversely affecting your relationship with the class.

3. Others on the staff may catch your germs, causing more staff and child absences.

4. You further damage your health by working when you should be resting.

In short, if you are unfit for work you should not agonise about it, but accept the fact and let the school know as soon as possible. If you feel unwell during the previous evening, inform the appropriate person straight away; tell them that you are coming down with something and will probably need to take time off. If, by the following morning, you have made a miraculous recovery, inform them immediately to prevent any unnecessary arrangements being made. The chances are that if you feel really unwell in the evening, you will not have recovered sufficiently by the next day.

If possible, try to indicate how long you expect to be off work. This helps the head teacher to plan whether there is a need for substitute teachers or, if necessary, whether to farm out groups of children from your class to other teachers. If it is not possible to say how long you expect to be off school, keep the secretary/administrator or head teacher informed of your progress. One of the most exacting aspects of a head teacher's role (or the person to whom the responsibility is delegated) is covering for absent staff.

Activate your thinking!

Teachers who take care of themselves are in a better condition to take care of the children in their care.

When you do return to work, it will be assumed that you are fit and well. Do not expect too much sympathy or any allowance for the fact that you are still struggling. This attitude is not callousness, but simply a reflection of the fact that it is not normally practical to nurse along a half-fit colleague; either you are well enough to do the job or you are not. If you go in to school when you should still be off sick, you can antagonise other staff, who may perceive your courage as foolhardiness.

Dealing with your emotions

One of the unexpected elements of being a teacher is the emotional strain it brings. All NQTs know that the job will be demanding and consume a lot of time and energy. They may be less prepared for the inner turmoil that can sometimes threaten to undermine the good work they are doing. You know from your student days that concerns about whether you were good enough to reach the standard and cope with the numerous demands that were placed on you, while working as a guest in someone else's classroom threatened to overwhelm you on occasions. You know how a single wretched lesson could undermine your confidence; and why was it that the tutor was always there to observe when things went wrong and never present when you had a wonderful session. But even when you are qualified there are questions that can disturb and unsettle you, including:

- Am I coping with my responsibilities or are people secretly saying that I'm not up to the job?

- Am I placing my efforts where they are most needed?

- How do the support staff feel about me?

- Did I do/say the right thing when I dealt with the incidence of misbehaviour?

- Will the child be encouraged or upset after I spoke to him about his ability to improve with more effort?

- How will parents react when they hear that I kept their daughter in during break-time to finish her work?

- Is the child all right after sustaining that small bump on the head during PE?

- Did I speak out of turn during the staff meeting when I expressed my frustration with the present break time arrangement?

- Can I ever hope to motivate that difficult child?

And so forth. There are no easy ways to deal with emotional pressures, but it is important to remind yourself regularly that you have been appointed on merit. Other candidates applied for the job, but only you were successful. Nevertheless, you have to accept that in the rush and tumble of school life you will make minor errors of judgement. These occasions do not, however, spell the end of your teaching career. In trying to maintain a sensible perspective on events, it may be helpful to remember that every NQT has had to tread the same path as you have. Some new teachers have a fairly smooth passage; others struggle to accommodate the demands of the job or work with colleagues who have a different view of life and education from their own. However, it may be the case that those who have fewer problems are the less ambitious teachers, preferring to 'play safe' and maintain a strictly controlled environment based on closely regulated lessons and rigidly enforced behaviour management. More ambitious new teachers may encounter more problems initially because they want to 'light a fire' and passion for learning in children through creative teaching and innovative activities. As a result, children become more animated, noisier and self-confident, with the discipline challenges that such behaviour evokes and the inevitable sidelong looks from colleagues. On the other hand, the ambitious teacher might become more accomplished than his or her cautious peer.

O'Flynn and Kennedy (2003), quoted earlier in this chapter, warn against becoming a perfectionist. They describe an occupational hazard of teaching as being 'stuck in a correcting, improving, self-righteous mode of being, which is too narrow to allow for human frailties'. They explain that some teachers 'work themselves to the bone, even to the extent that they break themselves physically or mentally' due to the fact that 'their need to prove themselves takes precedence over everything else' (2003: 142–3). Make sure that you don't fall into this trap by resisting the tendency to confuse your inexperience with incompetence. The former is true of every new teacher, whereas the latter is rarely true of *any* teacher. Try to focus your attention on your positive attributes and successes and, if problems begin to emerge, seek advice earlier rather than later. In addition to the induction tutor, it can also be useful to confide in a friendly, older colleague who understands what you are going through and will help you to be more objective in your view of your progress.

Most teachers encourage children to keep a profile of their achievements but fail to do the same for themselves. Your emotional stability is likely to ebb and flow throughout the term. Fatigue, over-commitment and a defensive attitude all conspire to drain your energy, reduce your confidence and open you to fears and doubts which would not normally bother you. Give your emotions as much attention as you do to every other part of your mind and body; and look forward to half term.

Checklist

At the end of your first half term as an NQT, divide the following list into three groups: those things you are doing well; those you are doing satisfactorily; and those you are doing badly. It is likely that nearly all will fall into the first two categories:

- I am taking an interest in the welfare of individual pupils
- I am preparing my lessons thoroughly
- I am taking account of differences in pupils' ability
- I am teaching consistently
- I am maintaining an industrious classroom climate
- I am getting on with my colleagues
- I am making contact with parents
- I am keeping up with my marking
- I am setting suitable homework tasks
- I am keeping my room in reasonable order
- I am attending the required staff and team meetings
- I am motivating and inspiring the children.

Activate your thinking!

During your induction year you should take account of the following targets:

By the end of term 1: to consistently fulfil the requirements for QTS and make inroads into the induction year standards.

By the end of term 2: tc make good progress towards fulfilling the induction year standards.

By the end of term 3: to meet fully the induction year requirements.

Case study

When Carmen was appointed to a post in a large infant school as a teacher for reception aged children, a male teacher who was just completing his induction year gave her the following advice. First, he suggested that it was useful to sort out certain details before the term began, even though in the normal way a TA might do some of the tasks:

- The names, ages, dates of birth and any major details of children's ability and aptitude
- Reports and records, school policies, schemes of work, long-term plans
- Special needs children and their support
- Samples of children's previous work
- The names of other teachers, assistants, administrative staff, caretaker and cleaners
- The School Prospectus
- Staff handouts on health and safety (including fire alarm procedures)
- The person you can contact out of school hours for help/advice
- Timetables, school starting and finishing times, breaks, lunch times
- Procedures for attendance registers and dinner registers
- Times of assemblies and if/when your class may be involved (though don't volunteer too quickly)
- Regular weekly meetings and events, such as staff meetings, team meetings
- Important dates during the first term that you need to know in advance, such as Parents' Evenings, staff training days
- The system for setting and monitoring homework
- The school's dress code, including expectations for PE and games
- How tea and coffee are provided; how to pay for it; whether you need your own cup
- Whether you will be required to do any additional duties, such as bus duty.

He also recommended:

- Put names on drawers and pegs, and make sure resources are clearly labelled
- Plan the furniture layout, including where to site computers to suit your way of working (you're in charge now)
- Check that you have sufficient stock for the first couple of weeks, including paper of various kinds, exercise books, paper, pencils, markers, scissors …
- Set up a book display and have some tried and tested storybooks for reading to the class
- Ensure that you are familiar with the IT provision, including software
- Make a simple, bold but interesting display, perhaps including some artefacts with a few questions

- Check the whereabouts of the equipment for PE and games. If possible, make an inventory
- Have paper cut to a variety of sizes, ready at hand
- Have a good supply of easy-to-do work sheets and handouts to give you a breathing space during the first few intensive days.

Within the first week:

- Establish your ground rules immediately but don't expect miracles. Learn to persevere
- Explain to the children your expectations about behaviour and standards of work and regularly remind them
- Be firm about the need to share, your dislike of bullying and your insistence on a harmonious working environment
- Establish a clear system for leaving and entering the classroom
- Make sure that you have informal contact with parents at the start and end of the day
- Ensure that all your children achieve success in some aspect of their work as early as possible
- Praise and commend genuine effort at every opportunity.

Be realistic:

- Do not to try to 'make a big impression'. Be yourself. Don't get exhausted. Work steadily
- You may get the feeling that you are being watched. You are. Use it to show what you are made of
- Parents will be asking what you are like. Consider what the children might be saying about you at home but don't agonise?
- Fabulous lessons can wait for a while until you have settled and established your routines
- Don't be too upset when you make mistakes; learn from them quickly and move on. Children have short memories
- However successful you were on final TP, the first half-term of your first post is likely to be quite demanding. Try to stay cheerful but don't be afraid to seek advice if you are struggling.

The common experience of new teachers is that sorting out the classroom often takes much longer than they expected. Although colleagues are as helpful as possible, everyone is so busy at the start of the term that they cannot spare much time to help you. Even if you are not able to fulfil all of the above action points, things fall into place very quickly once the term begins. The more that has been dealt with beforehand, however, the easier the start to the new term becomes.

Further reading

Bubb, S., Heilbron, R., Jones, C., Totterdell, M. and Bailey, M. (2002) *Improving Induction*, London: RoutledgeFalmer.

A comprehensive and scholarly review of key issues relating to induction.

Holmes, E. (2003) T*he Newly Qualified Teacher's Handbook*, London: Kogan Page.

The book provides an extensive treatment of relevant issues, packed full of information.

Jacklin, A., Griffiths, V. and Robinson, C. (2006) *Beginning Primary Teaching*, Maidenhead: Open University Press.

Draws on the experiences of new teachers and provides authentic accounts of their early encounters, challenges and achievements.

Wallace, W. (2005) *Oranges and Lemons: Life in an Inner-city Primary School*, London: Routledge.

Focuses on the progress of individual children from their time as new entrants, and illuminates contemporary urban school life, including the way that teachers and support staff cope with the demands and pressures.

Conclusion: The Way Ahead

Professional learning

Although you are rightly concerned with the successful completion of your training course and acquisition of QTS, your development does not stop there, as there is always more professional learning to do. The induction year means that you will have to continue extending your expertise throughout the first year of teaching, but beyond that point your future progress will depend upon your enthusiasm, commitment and ambition. After the initial settling period is over, it is surprisingly easy to lapse into a self-satisfied mode and imagine that somehow you have 'arrived' in teaching. In fact, the best teachers are those who are never fully satisfied with their performance and consider themselves to be life-long achievers (see Chappell 2003). Teachers who grow complacent are in danger of atrophying, depending too heavily on past experiences and growing stale without realising it. Despite all the emphasis on standards for going through the 'threshold', and becoming an expert or advanced skills teacher, it is actually possible to get worse at teaching as well as better at it because you learn how to give the right appearances without actually being different and effectively 'tread water'.

Once qualified, you will probably find that all your attention is focused on your classroom teaching and learning to prosper as a member of the staff team. There are publications to consult that summarise recent education research findings, but many teachers admit that they never read a journal unless they are taking an advanced course or degree. This is understandable but regrettable. There are a number of publications specifically designed to help busy teachers keep abreast of key findings and it is worth consulting one with summaries of findings from a broad range of education interests – rather than those issued by the Government, which are inevitably rather self-congratulatory and general.

In addition to ensuring that their staff have good teaching skills, enjoy a good working relationship with children and knowledge of the curriculum, head teachers and governors value particular characteristics in their teachers. See how you shape up as someone who is willing to:

- Continue learning and persevering
- Assume a fair share of the responsibilities
- Take a positive approach to the job
- Relate well to colleagues, ancillary staff and parents

- See the funny side of life
- Contribute positively to the full breadth of school life
- Encourage others whenever a suitable opportunity arises.

Heads and governors are not well disposed towards teachers who think they know it all, who constantly complain, put minimal effort into their work and walk around with a glum face as if the world owed them a living. They will celebrate the positive difference that you make to the atmosphere of the staffroom and school by your presence.

Relish the joys of teaching

Regardless of the difficulties and challenges that your first year of teaching brings, it is good to remind yourself that this is the way that you want to spend your life. It is probably true to say that with the exception of parents, teachers are the most influential figures for most pupils, and the effect of their teaching will far outlive the whims of Government, policymakers and educationists. Eaude (2006) reflects on the role as follows: 'As a teacher, you are important. Part of the excitement of teaching is to create a world of opportunities, with power to transform and create' (2006: 110).

You will not always succeed. Some days you will feel, and will be, uninspiring. On other days your most carefully laid plans will fall apart at the seams. Despite the occasional setback, however, there are many privileges attached to being in the job, not least the thought that the impact of your words, actions and ideas will play a significant part in shaping and developing young lives. Nothing can take that entitlement and responsibility away from you.

When next you are shopping locally and you hear a small voice proudly declaring from the next aisle to anyone who cares to listen, 'That's my teacher' your heart will glow with pride as if it could burst.

Activate your thinking!

Think of ways to bring joy into the classroom. Smile and laugh at children's innocent antics and remarks. Be willing to dance, sing, cheer, celebrate, empathise and love. Look for ways to make even mundane learning interesting. Think of the thousands of children you will influence as a teacher. Never lose sight of your calling.

Good practice

Write down this list of statements. Pin them up somewhere. Read and inwardly digest them each day:

- I contribute to the development of good relationships in the school
- I have a reputation for being a pleasant, warm and caring person
- Children in my class are making good progress with me
- I keep events in proportion and do not become too intense or too indifferent
- The school would be a poorer place without me.

   Now start believing them!

Case study

A true story ... Ken had retired from teaching some years before and was wandering down the High Street when he heard his name being called loudly and urgently. He looked up to see an enormous shape of a man descending a ladder on an adjacent building site, muscles rippling, tattoos dancing across skin hardened by constant outdoor work. To his consternation, Ken recognised him as the grown-up version of one of the most difficult children he had ever taught and with whom he had had numerous confrontations. Ken waited tentatively to receive the full blast of long-suppressed anger; instead the man smiled warmly, told Ken who he was (though Ken already knew; despite the passage of time, it was a face he was unlikely to forget) and reminded him of the good times they had together in school. (Ken had markedly different memories but thought it wiser to hold his peace.) They parted like old friends and life continued. As he reflected on the incident, Ken told me that he never ceased to be amazed about how influential teachers were and how time mellows even the toughest experiences in school. Ken, a modest and generous-hearted man, concluded by saying, 'It made me feel that my life had really been well spent'.

   I couldn't have put it better myself!

References

Brighouse, T. and Woods, D. (2006) *The Joy of Teaching*, London: RoutledgeFalmer.
   The book celebrates the importance of teachers, reminds current teachers why they joined the profession, encourages others to join and reflects on the craft and artistry of teaching.

Hayes, D. (ed.) (2007) *Joyful Teaching and Learning in the Primary School*, Exeter: Learning Matters.
   Uses a practical, subject-based approach in promoting creativity, innovativeness and enthusiasm as integral to effective teaching and enhancing attainment.

References

Acker, S. (1999) *The Realities of Teachers' Work*, London: Cassell.

Adams, J. C. (2002) *Local Delivery of a National Agenda: Citizenship, rights and the changing role of school governors in England and Wales*, Hertfordshire: University of Hertfordshire.

Adamson, S. (2007) *Start Here: What new school governors need to know*, Norwich: Adamson Publishing.

Alderson, P. (1999) *Young Children's Rights: Beliefs, principles and practice*, London: Save the Children/Jessica Kingsley.

Allen, J., Potter, J., Sharp, J. and Turvey, K. (2007) *Primary ICT: Knowledge, Understanding and Practice*, Exeter: Learning Matters.

Alloway, T.P. and Gathercole, S.E. (2007) *Memory and Learning*, London: Sage.

Apter, M. and Kerr, J.H. (1991) *Adult Play*, Amsterdam: Swets and Zeitlinger.

Arthur, J., Davison, J. and Lewis, M. (2005) *Professional Values and Practice: Achieving the Standards for QTS*, London: RoutledgeFalmer.

Arthur, J., Grainger, T. and Wray, D. (eds) (2006) *Learning to Teach in the Primary School*, London: Routledge.

Balding, J. (1996) *Bully Off: Young people that fear going to school*, Exeter: Schools Health Education Unit, Exeter University.

Balshaw, M.H. (1999) *Help in the Classroom*, 2nd edn, London: David Fulton.

Barber, D., Cooper, L. and Meeson, G. (2007) *Learning and Teaching with Interactive Whiteboards: Primary and Early Years*, Exeter: Learning Matters.

Barton, E.A. (2006) *Bully Prevention*, 2nd edn, London: Corwin Press.

Barton, L. and Tomlinson, S. (1984) 'The politics of integration in England', in Barton, L. and Tomlinson, S. (eds) *Special Education and Social Interests*, London: Crook Helm.

Bates, J. and Munday, S. (2005) *Able, Gifted and Talented*, London: Continuum.

Baumfield, V. and Mroz, M. (2004) 'Investigating pupils' questions in the primary school', in E.C. Wragg (ed.) *Teaching and Learning*, London: Routledge.

Beaudoin, M.N. and Taylor, M. (2004) *Creating a Positive School Climate*. London: Sage.

Beardsley, G. and Harnett, P. (1998) *Exploring Play in the Primary Classroom*, London: David Fulton Publications.

Beasley, G. and Moberley, A. (2000) *Seasonal Displays*, Pittsburgh, PA: Scholastic.

Bentham, S. (2005) *Teaching Assistants' Guide to Managing Classroom Behaviour*, London: Routledge.

Best, B. and Thomas, W. (2007) *The Creative Teaching and Learning Toolkit*, London: Continuum.

Beveridge, S. (2004) *Children, Families and Schools: Developing partnerships for inclusive education*, London: RoutledgeFalmer.

Biott, C. and Easen, P. (1994) *Collaborative Learning in Staffrooms and Classrooms*, London: David Fulton.

Bird, R. (2006) 'Personalisation: what does it mean?', *Secondary Headship*, 49, November, pp. 4–5.

Bowkett, S. (2005) *100 Ideas for Teaching Creativity*, London: Continuum.

Brandling, R. (1982) *A Year in the Primary School*, London: Ward Lock.

Briggs, M., Woodfield, A., Martin, C. and Swatton, P. (2003) *Assessment for Learning and Teaching in Primary Schools*, Exeter: Learning Matters.

Brighouse, T. and Woods, D. (2006) *The Joy of Teaching*, London: RoutledgeFalmer.

Broadhead, P. (2006) 'Developing an understanding of young children's learning through play', *British Educational Research Journal*, 32(2), pp. 191–207.

Brooker, L. (2002) *Starting School: Young children learning cultures*, Maidenhead: Open University Press.

Brown, B. (1998) *Unlearning Discrimination in the Early Years*, Stoke-on-Trent: Trentham Books.

Brown, M. and Ralph, S. (1994) *Managing Stress in Schools*, Plymouth: Northcote House.

Bruce, T. (2001) *Learning through Play*, London: Hodder & Stoughton.

Bubb, S. (2004) *The Insider's Guide to Early Professional Development*, London: RoutledgeFalmer.

Bubb, S. and Earley, P. (2004) *Managing Teacher Workload: Work–life Balance and Wellbeing*, London: Paul Chapman.

Bubb, S., Heilbron, R., Jones, C., Totterdell, M. and Bailey, M. (2002) *Improving Induction*, London: RoutledgeFalmer.

Burgess, R., Nelson, C. and Dreyer, D. (2000) *Laughing Lessons*, Minneapolis, MN: Free Spirit Publishing.

Burnett, G. and Jarvis, K. (2004) *Parents First*, Carmarthen: Crown House.

Burnham, L. (2006) *101 Essential Lists for Teaching Assistants*, London: Continuum.

Butt, G. (2006) *Lesson Planning*, London: Continuum.

Byre, B. (1993) *Coping with Bullying at School*, London: Cassell.

Campbell, A. and Fairbairn, G. (eds) (2005) *Working with Support in the Classroom*, London: Paul Chapman.

Canter, L. (1998) 'The assertive discipline approach', in Ayers, H. and Gray, F (eds) *Classroom Management*, London: David Fulton.

Carpenter, B., Ashdown, R. and Bovair, K. (eds) (1996) *Enabling access: Effective teaching and learning for pupils with learning difficulties*, London: David Fulton.

Carlyle, D. and Woods, P. (2002) *Emotions of Teacher Stress*, Stoke-on-Trent: Trentham Books.

Carter, J. (2002) *Just Imagine: Creative ideas for creative writing*, London: David Fulton.

Casey, T. (2005) *Inclusive Play*, London: Paul Chapman.

Casey, T. (2007) *Environments for Outdoor Play*, London: Sage.

Chaplain, R. (2006) 'Managing classroom behaviour', in J. Arthur, T. Grainger and D. Wray (eds) *Learning to Teach in the Primary School*, London: Routledge.

Chapman, R. (1995) 'New to teaching', in J. Bell (ed.) *Teachers Talk About Teaching*, Maidenhead: Open University Press.

Chappell, C. (2003) *Reconstructing the Lifelong Learner*, London: Routledge.

Charlton, T., Jones, K. and Flores-Hole, H. (1996) 'The effects of teacher behaviour upon pupil behaviour', in Charlton, T. Jones, K. and Cummings, M. (eds) *Pupil Needs and Classroom Practices*, Cheltenham: Park Published Papers.

Cheminais, R. (2005) *Every Child Matters: A new role for SENCOS*, London: David Fulton.

Cipani, E. (2007) *Class Management for all Teachers*, New York, NY: Prentice Hall.

Clark, C.M. (1995) *Thoughtful Teaching*, London: Cassell.

Clarke, S. (2001) *Unlocking Formative Assessment*, London: Hodder & Stoughton.

Claxton, G. (2004) *Burning Issues in Primary Education Teaching*, 11, Birmingham: National Primary Trust.

Cockburn, A.D. (1996) *Teaching Under Pressure*, London: Falmer Press.

Cohen, D. (2006) *Social Skills for Primary Pupils*, Birmingham: Questions Publishing.

Cohen, D. (2006) *The Development of Play*, 3rd edn, London: Routledge.

Cole, M. (ed.) (2002) *Professional Issues for Teachers and Student Teachers*, 2nd edn, London: David Fulton.

Collins, M. (2001) *Because We're Worth It: Enhancing self-esteem in young children*, Bristol: Lucky Duck Publishing.

Collins, M. (2007) *Circle Time for the Very Young*, 2nd edn, London: Sage.

Connolly, P. (2004) *Boys and Schooling in the Early Years*, London: Routledge.

Cooper, H., Hegarty, P. and Simco, N. (1996) *Display in the Classroom: Principles, practice and learning theory*, London: David Fulton.

Corbett J. (1995) *Bad-Mouthing: The language of special needs*, London: Falmer Press.

Corrie, C. (2003) *Becoming Emotionally Intelligent*, Stafford: Network Educational Press.

Cotton, T. (1998) *Thinking About Teaching*, London: Hodder & Stoughton.

Coultas, V. (2007) *Constructive Talking in Challenging Classrooms*, London: Routledge.

Cousins, L., Higgs, M. and Leader, J. (2004) *Making the Most of your Teaching Assistants*, London: PfP.

Cox, S. and Heames, R. (1999) *Managing the Pressures in Teaching*, London: Hodder & Stoughton.

Cowley, S. (2003) *Teaching Clinic*, London: Continuum.

Craft, A. (2005) *Creativity in our Schools: Tensions and Dilemmas*, London: Routledge.

Crosse, K. (2007) *Introducing English as an Additional Language to Young Children*, London: Sage.

Crozier, G. and Reay, D. (2005) *Activating Participation*, Stoke-on-Trent: Trentham.

Cullingford, C. (1997a) 'Assessment, evaluation and the effective school', in Cullingford C. (ed.) *Assessment Versus Evaluation*, London: Cassell.

Cullingford, C. (2002) *The best years of their lives? Pupils' experience of school*, London: Kogan Page.

Cullingford, C. (2007) 'Creativity and pupils' experience of school', *Education 3–13*, 35(2), pp. 133–42.

Cullingford-Agnew, S. (2006) *Becoming a Higher Level Teaching Assistant: Primary SEN*, Exeter: Learning Matters.

Dalton, J. and Fairchild, L. (2004) *The Compassionate Classroom: Lessons that nurture wisdom and empathy*, Chicago, IL: Zephyr Press.

Davies, A. (2007) *Storytelling in the Classroom*, London: Sage.

Day, C. (2004) *A Passion for Teaching*, London: RoutledgeFalmer.

Day, C., Sammons, P., Stobart, G., Kington, A. and Gu, Q. (2007) *Teachers Matter*, Maidenhead: Open University Press.

Dean, G. (1998) *Challenging the More Able Language User*, London: NACE/David Fulton Publications.

Dean, J. (2001) *Organising Learning in the Primary School Classroom*, London: Routledge.

Dean, J. (2001) *The Effective School Governor*, London: RoutledgeFalmer.

Deed, C., Bellhouse, B. and Johnston, G. (2007) *Using Circle Time to Learn about Stories*, London: Sage.

Denton, C. and Postlethwaite, K. (1985) *Able Children: Identifying them in the classroom*, Windsor: NFER-Nelson.

Department for Children, Schools and Families (2006) *Learning and Teaching for Bilingual Children in the Primary Years*, London: DCSF Publications Centre.

Department for Education and Employment (1998) *Health and Safety of Pupils on Educational Visits*, London: DfEE Publications.

Department for Education and Skills (2002a) *Special Educational Needs Code of Practice*, Annesley: DfES Publications.

Department for Education and Skills (2005) *Every Child Matters*, London: DfES Publications Centre.

Department for Education and Skills (2006a) *Primary National Strategy*, London: DfES Publications Centre.

Department for Education and Skills (2006b) *Learning and Teaching for Bilingual Children in the Primary Years*, London: DfES Publications Centre.

Department for Education and Skills (2007) *Social and Emotional Aspects of Learning*, London: DfES Publications Centre.

Desforges, C. (1995) 'Teaching for order and control' in C. Desforges (ed.) *An Introduction to Teaching*, Oxford: Blackwell.

Desforges, C. and Abouchaar, A. (2003) T*he impact of parental involvement, parental support and family education on pupil achievement and adjustment: a literature review*, Research Report 433 for the DfES, London: Queen's Printer copyright. (www.dfes.gov.uk/research/data)

Dickinson, C. (1996) *Effective Learning Activities*, Stafford: Network Educational Press.

Dillon, J.T. (1994) *Using Discussion in Classrooms*, Maidenhead: Open University Press.

Dixie, G. (2007) *Managing Your Classroom*, London: Continuum.

Dockrell, J.E and Shield, B.M. (2006) 'Acoustical barriers in classrooms: the impact of noise on performance in the classroom', *British Educational Research Journal*, 32(3), pp. 509–25.

Doddington, C. and Hilton, M. (2007) *Child-Centred Education*, London: Sage.

Doust, S. and Doust, R. (2001) *Governor's Handbook: A comprehensive guide to the duties and responsibilities of school governors in England and Wales*, London: Advisory Centre for Education.

Drake, J. (2003) *Organising Play in the Early Years*, London: David Fulton.

Dreikurs, R., Grunwald, B.B. and Pepper, F.C. (1998) *Maintaining Sanity in the Classroom*, London: Taylor and Francis.

Drummond, M.J. (2003) *Assessing Children's Learning*, 2nd edn, London: David Fulton.

Drummond, M.J. and Pollard, A. (1998) *Exploring Play in the Primary Classroom*, London: David Fulton.

Duffy, B. (1998) *Supporting Creativity and Imagination in the Early Years*, Maidenhead: Open University Press.

Dweck, C.S. (2000) *Self-Theories: Their Role in Motivation, Personality and Development*, Hove: Psychology Press.

Eaude, T. (2006) *Children's Spiritual, Moral, Social and Cultural Development*, Exeter: Learning Matters.

Epstein, D., Elwood, J., Hey, V. and Maw, J. (1998) *Failing Boys? Issues in Gender and Achievement*, Maidenhead: Open University Press.

Eyre, D. and McClure, L. (eds) (2001) *Curriculum Provision for the Gifted and Talented in the Primary School*, London: David Fulton/NACE.

Eysenck, H. (2000) *Intelligence: A New Look*, Edison, NJ: Transaction Publishers.

Farmery, C. (2004) *Successful Subject Co-ordination*, London: Continuum.

Feinstein, L., Duckworth, K. and Sabates, R. (2008) *Education and the Family*, London: Routledge.

Fisher, J. (2002) *The Foundations of Learning*, Maidenhead: Open University Press.

Fisher, R. (2005) *Teaching Children to Learn*, Cheltenham: Stanley Thornes.

Fitzgerald, D. (2004) *Parent Partnerships in the Early Years*, London: Continuum.

Fox, G. (1998) *A Handbook for Learning Support Assistants*, London: David Fulton.

Francis, B. and Skelton, C. (2005) *Gender and Achievement*, London: Routledge.

Franklin, S. (2006) 'VAKing out learning styles', *Education 3–13*, 34(1), pp. 81–7.

Fried, R. (1995) *The Passionate Teacher: A practical guide*, Boston, MA: Beacon Press.

Galton, M. (2007) *Learning and Teaching in the Primary Classroom*, London: Sage.

Gardner, H. (1983) *Frames of Mind: The theory of multiple intelligences*, New York, NY: Basic Books.

Gardner, H. (1999) *Intelligence Reframed*, New York, NY: Basic Books.

Gardner, J. (2006) 'Children who have English as an additional language', in G. Knowles (ed.) *Supporting Inclusive Practice*, Exeter: Learning Matters.

Garrick, R. (2004) *Outdoor Play in the Early Years*, London: Continuum.

Garnett, S. (2006) *Using Brainpower in the Classroom*, London: Routledge.

Gill, V. (1998) *The Ten Commandments of Good Teaching*, Thousand Oaks, CA: Corwin Press/Sage Publications.

Gipps, C., Mc Callum, B. and Hargreaves, E. (1999) *What Makes a Good Primary School Teacher?* London: RoutledgeFalmer.

Goleman, D. (1995) *Emotional Intelligence*, New York, NY: Bantam.

Goleman, D. (1999) *Working with Emotional Intelligence*, London: Bloomsbury.

Goleman, D. (2005) *Emotional Intelligence*, 2nd edn, New York, NY: Bantam Books.

Grainger, T. (2003) 'Creative teachers and the language arts', *Education 3–13*, 31(1), pp. 43–7.

Grant-Williams, R. (2002) *Voice Power*, New York, NY: AMACOM.

Greenwood, C. (2004) *Understanding the Needs of Parents: Guidelines for effective collaboration with parents of children with SEN*, London: David Fulton.

Griffiths, N. (1998) *A Corner to Learn*, Cheltenham: Stanley Thornes.

Grossman, H. (2003) *Classroom Behaviour Management for Diverse and Inclusive Schools*, Lanham, MD: Rowman and Littlefield.

Hallgarten, J. (2000) *Parents Exist, OK? Issues and visions for parent–school relationships*, London: IPPR.

Hancock, R. and Collins, J. (eds) (2005) *Primary Teaching Assistants*, London: David Fulton.

Hardman, F., Smith, F. and Wall, K. (2003) 'Interactive whole class teaching in the National Literacy Strategy', *Cambridge Journal of Education*, 33(2), pp. 197–215.

Hargreaves, L., Pell, A. and Merry, R. (2003) 'Teacher–pupil interaction and interactive teaching', in Moyles, J., Hargreaves, L., Merry, R., Paterson, F. and Esarte-Sarries, V., *Interactive Teaching in the Primary School*, Maidenhead: Open University Press.

Harlen, W. (2000) *The Teaching of Science in Primary Schools*, 3rd edn, London: David Fulton.

Harnett, P. (2007) *Supporting Children's Learning in the Primary and Early Years*, London: Routledge.

Hart, S. (2000) *Thinking Through Teaching*, London: David Fulton.

Hastings, N. and Wood, K.C. (2002) *Reorganising Primary Classroom Learning*, Maidenhead: Open University Press.

Haydn, T. (2006) *Managing Pupil Behaviour*, London: Routledge.

Hayes, C. (2006) *Stress Relief for Teachers*, London: Routledge.

Hayes, D. (1998) *Effective Verbal Communication*, London: Hodder & Stoughton.

Hayes, D. (2002) 'Prospering on school placement', *Primary Practice*, 32 (Autumn), pp. 32–4.

Hayes, D. (2006) *Inspiring Primary Teaching*, Exeter: Learning Matters.

Hayes, D. (ed.) (2007) *Joyful Teaching and Learning in the Primary School*, Exeter: Learning Matters.

Haynes, J. (2007) 'Thinking together: enjoying dialogue with children', in D. Hayes (ed.) *Joyful Teaching and Learning in the Primary School*, Exeter: Learning Matters.

Hayward, A. (2006) *Making Inclusion Happen*, London: Paul Chapman.

Heeks, P. and Kinwell, M. (1997) *Learning Support for Special Educational Needs*, London: Taylor Graham Publishers.

Hewitt, S. (2007) *Bullying*, London: Franklin Watts.

Heyda, P.A. (2002) *The Primary Teacher's Survival Guide*, Portsmouth, NH: Heinemann.

Hicks, D. (2001) *Citizenship for the Future: A practical classroom guide*, Godalming: World Wildlife Fund.

Holmes, E. (2003) *The Newly Qualified Teacher's Handbook*, London: Kogan Page.

Holmes, E. (2004) *Teacher Wellbeing: Looking after yourself and your career in the Classroom*, London: RoutledgeFalmer.

Houghton, D. and McColgan, M. (1995) *Working With Children*, London: Collins Educational.

Howe, M.J.A. (1990) *Sense and Nonsense About Hothouse Children*, Leicester: BPS Books.

Hughes, M., Wikeley, F. and Nash, T. (1994) *Parents and Their Children's Schools*, London: Blackwell.

Hutchinson, N. and Smith, H. (2003) *Changing Behaviour in the Early Years*, London: David Fulton.

Hymer, B. and Michel, D. (2002) *Gifted and Talented Learners*, London: NACE/David Fulton.

Jacklin, A., Griffiths, V. and Robinson, C. (2006) *Beginning Primary Teaching*, Maidenhead: Open University Press.

Jackson, M. (1987) 'Making sense of school' in Pollard, A. (ed.) *Children and Their Primary Schools: a New Perspective*, Lewes: Falmer Press.

Jackson, M. (1993) *Creative Display and Environment*, London: Hodder & Stoughton.

Jacques, K. (2007) 'Managing challenging behaviour', in K. Jacques and R. Hyland (eds) *Professional Studies: Primary and Early Years (Achieving QTS): Primary and Early Years*, Exeter: Learning Matters.

Jaksec, C.M. (2005) *Difficult Parent*, Thousand Oaks, CA: Corwin Press.

James, F. and Brownsword, K. (1994) *A Positive Approach*, Twickenham: Belair Publications.

Jeffrey, B. and Woods, P. (2003) *The Creative School*, London: RoutledgeFalmer.

Johnston, J. (2002) 'Teaching and learning in the early years', in Johnston, J., Chater, D. and Bell, D. (eds) *Teaching the Primary Curriculum*, Maidenhead: Open University.

Joliffe, W. (2007) *Cooperative Learning in the Classroom*, London: Sage.

Jones, R. and Wyse, D. (2004) *Creativity in the Primary Curriculum*, London: David Fulton.

Kalliala, M. (2004) *Play Culture in the Changing World*, Maidenhead: Open University Press.

Katz, L.G. (1995) *How Can We Strengthen Children's Self-Esteem?* Illinois: ERIC Clearinghouse on Elementary and Early Childhood Education (www.kidsource.com).

Katz, L.G. and Chard, S.C. (2000) *Engaging Children's Minds: The project approach*, 2nd edn, Stamford, CT: Alex Publishers.

Kay, J. (2003) *Teaching Assistants' Handbook*, London: Continuum.

Kelly, P. (2007) 'The joy of Enhancing Children's Learning', in D. Hayes (ed.) *Joyful Teaching and Learning in the Primary School*, Exeter: Learning Matters.

Kendall-Seatter, S. (2005) *Primary Professional Studies*, Exeter: Learning Matters.

Kerry, T. (1998) *Questioning and Explaining in Classrooms*, London: Hodder & Stoughton.

Kewley, G.D. (2001) *Attention Deficit Hyperactivity Disorder*, London: David Fulton.

Kidwell, V. (2004) *Homework*, London: Continuum.

Killick, S. (2006) *Emotional Literacy at the Heart of the School Ethos*, London: Paul Chapman.

Kinder, K., Wakefield, A. and Wilkin, A. (1996) *Talking Back: Pupils' Views on Disaffection*, Slough: NFER.

Kirton, A., Hallam, S., Peffers, J., Robertson, P. and Stobart, G. (2007) 'Revolution, evolution or a Trojan Horse? Piloting assessment for learning in some Scottish primary schools', *British Educational Research Journal*, 33(4), pp. 605–27.

Kohn, A. (2004) *What Does It Mean to be Well Educated?* Boston, MA: Beacon Press.

Koshy, V. (2000) *Mathematics for Primary Teachers*, London: Routledge.

Kovacic, G. (2005) 'Voice education in teacher training', *Journal of Education for Teaching*, 31(2), pp. 87–97.

Knowles, G. (2006) 'Gifted and Talented', in G. Knowles (ed.) *Supporting Inclusive Practice*, Exeter: Learning Matters.

Kreider, H. (2000) *The National Network of Partnership Schools: A model for family-school-community partnerships*, Cambridge, MA: University of Harvard, Harvard Family Research Project.

Kutnick, P. (1994) 'Use and effectiveness of groups in classrooms: towards a pedagogy', in Kutnick, P. and Rogers, C. (ed.) *Groups in Schools*, London: Cassell.

Lawrence, D. (2006) *Enhancing Self-Esteem in the Classroom*, 3rd edn, London: Paul Chapman.

Lawson, S. (1994) *Helping Children Cope With Bullying*, London: Sheldon Press.

Lee, C. (2004) *Preventing Bullying in School*, London: Sage.

Leicester, M. and Johnson, G. (2004) *Stories for Inclusive Schools: Developing young pupils' skills in assembly and in the classroom*, London: RoutledgeFalmer.

Lewis, M. and Ellis, S. (2006) *Phonics*, London: Sage.

Lindon, J. (1997) *Working With Young Children*, 3rd edn, London: Hodder & Stoughton.

Liston, D and Garrison, J. (2004) 'Love revived and examined', in D. Liston and J. Garrison (eds) *Teaching, Learning and Loving*, London: RoutledgeFalmer.

Lloyd, C. and Beard, J. (1995) *Managing Classroom Collaboration*, London: Cassell.

Lloyd, G. (ed.) (2004) *Problem Girls*, London: RoutledgeFalmer.

Loomans, D. and Kolberg, K. (2002) *The Laughing Classroom*, Novato, CA: HJ Kramer Publishers.

Lord, L. and Slinn, K. (2007) *Curriculum Planning and Assessment for the Foundation Stage*, London: Sage.

Lougy, R.A., DeRuvo, S.L. and Rosenthal, D.K. (2007) *Teaching Young Children With ADHD*, Thousand Oaks, CA: Corwin Press.

Lowe, V. (2006) *Stories, Pictures and Reality*, London: Routledge.

MacGilchrist, B. (2003) 'Primary learners of the future', *Education 3–13*, 31(3), pp. 58–65.

MacGrath, M. (2000) *The Art of Peaceful Teaching*, London: David Fulton.

McEwan, E.K. (1998) *How to Deal With Parents Who Are Angry, Troubled, Afraid or Just Plain Crazy*, Thousand Oaks, CA: Corwin Press.

McNamara, S. (1997) 'Children with special educational needs' in Kitson, N. and Merry, R. (eds), *Teaching in the Primary School*, London: Routledge.

McNamara, S. and Moreton, G. (2001) *Changing Behaviour*, London: David Fulton.

McNess, E., Broadfoot, P. and Osborn, M. (2003) 'Is the effective compromising the affective?' *British Educational Research Journal*, 29(2), pp. 243–57.

McPhillimy, B. (1996) *Controlling Your Class*, Chichester: John Wiley.

Makins, V. (1997) *The Invisible Children: Nipping failure in the bud*, London: David Fulton.

Manning-Morton, J. and Thorp, M. (2003) *Times for Play*, Maidenhead: Open University Press.

Manuel, J. and Hughes, J. (2006) 'It has always been my dream: exploring pre service teachers' motivations for choosing teaching', *Teacher Development*, 10(1), pp. 5–24.

Maynard, T. (2001) 'The trainee teacher and the school community of practice', *Cambridge Journal of Education*, 31(1), pp. 39–52.

Medwell, J. (2007) *Successful Teaching Placement*, Exeter: Learning Matters.

Merry, R. and Moyles, J. (2003) 'Scuppering discussion: interaction in theory and practice', in Moyles, J., Hargreaves, L., Merry, R., Paterson, F. and Esarte-Sarries, V., *Interactive Teaching in the Primary School*, Maidenhead: Open University Press.

Mills, J. and Mills, R.W. (1995) *Primary School People: Getting to know your colleagues*, London: Routledge.

Morgan, N. and Saxton, J. (1991) *Teaching Questioning and Learning*, London: Routledge.

Morgan, N. and Saxton, J. (1994) *Asking Better Questions*, Markham, Ontario: Pembroke Publishers.

Morrison, K. (2001) 'Jurgen Habermas', in Palmer, J.A. (ed.) *Fifty Modern Thinkers from Piaget to the Present*, London: RoutledgeFalmer.

Mosley, J. and Grogan, R. (2002) 'Quality Circle Time for Teachers', *Primary Practice*, 32 (Autumn), pp. 4–8.

Mosley, J. and Sonnet, H. (2006) *Helping Children deal with Bullying*, Cambridge: LDA.

Moyles, J., Hargreaves, L., Merry, R., Paterson, F. and Esarte-Sarries, V. (2003) *Interactive Teaching in the Primary School*, Maidenhead: Open University Press.

Murphy, E. and Lewers, R. (2000) *The Hidden Hurt: How to beat bullying in schools*, Thriplow: Wizard Books.

Neill, S. and Caswell, C. (1993) *Body Language for Competent Teachers*, London: Routledge.

Newell, S. and Jeffery, D. (2002) *Behaviour Management in the Classroom: A transactional analysis approach*, London: David Fulton.

Nias, D.J. (1997) 'Would schools improve if teachers cared less?' *Education 3–13*, 25(3), pp. 11–22.

Nias, D.J., Southworth, G.W. and Yeomans, R. (1989) *Staff Relationships in the Primary School: a study of school cultures*, London: Cassell.

Nilsen, B.A. (2004) *Week by Week: Documenting the development of young children*, New York, NY: Thomas Delmar Learning.

O'Flynn, S. and Kennedy, H. (2003) *Get Their Attention*, London: David Fulton.

O'Hara, M. (2004) *Teaching 3–8*, 2nd edn, London: Continuum.

O'Quinn, E.J. and Garrison, J. (2004) 'Creating loving relations in the classroom', in D. Liston and J. Garrison (eds) *Teaching, Learning and Loving*, London: RoutledgeFalmer.

Orr, R. (2003) *My Right to Play*, Maidenhead: Open University Press.

Otterton, M. (2004) *Teaching Techniques*, London: Continuum.

Overall, L. and Sangster, M. (2003) *Primary Teacher's Handbook*, London: Continuum.

Packard, N. and Higgins, S. (2007) *The Really Useful ICT Book*, London: Routledge.

Papworth, M. (2003) *Every Minute Counts*, London: Continuum.

Perkins, D.N. (1992) *Smart Schools*, New York, NY: Free Press.

Pollard, A. and Filer, A. (1996) *The Social World of Children's Learning*, London: Cassell.

Pratt, N. and Berry, J. (2007) 'The joy of mathematics', in D. Hayes (ed.) *Joyful Teaching and Learning in the Primary School*, Exeter: Learning Matters.

Prendiville, F. and Toye, N. (2007) *Speaking and Listening through Drama*, London: Sage.

Pye, J. (1987) *Invisible Children: Who Are the Real Losers at School?* Oxford: Oxford University Press.

Qualifications and Curriculum Authority (2000) *A Language in Common*, Sudbury: QCA Publications.

Qualifications and Curriculum Authority/DfES (2000) *Curriculum Guidance for the Foundation Stage*, Sudbury: QCA Publications.

Quinn, V. (1997) *Critical Thinking in Young Minds*, London: David Fulton.

Ransom, S. (1993) 'From an entitlement to an empowerment curriculum' in Barber, M and Graham, D., *Sense, Nonsense and the National Curriculum*, London: Falmer Press.

Ravet, J. (2007) *Are We Listening?* Stoke-on-Trent: Trentham.

Reid, G. (2007) *Effective Learning Strategies for the Classroom*, London: Sage.

Richards, C. (2006) 'Primary teaching: a personal perspective', in J. Arthur, T. Grainger and D. Wray, *Learning to Teach in the Primary School*, London: Routledge.

Rigby, K. (2001) *Stop the Bullying*, London: Jessica Kingsley Publishing.

Robson, S. (2006) *Developing Thinking and Understanding in Young Children*, London: Routledge.

Roffey, S. (2006) *Circle Time for Emotional Literacy*, London: Paul Chapman.

Roffey, S. and O'Reirdan, T. (2003) *Plans for Better Behaviour in the Primary School*, London: David Fulton.

Rogers, B. (1998) *You Know the Fair Rule*, 2nd edn, London: Pitman Publishing.

Rogers, B. (2006) *Classroom Behaviour: A practical guide to effective teaching, behaviour management and colleague support*, London: Paul Chapman.

Rose, R. (2005) *Becoming a Primary Higher Level Teaching Assistant: Meeting the HTLA standards*, Exeter: Learning Matters.

Salaman, A. and Tutchell, S. (2005) *Planning Educational Visits for the Early Years*, London: Paul Chapman.

Sallis, J. (2007) *Basics for School Governors*, London: Continuum International.

Salo, U. (2002) 'What a teacher! Students write about teachers', BERA Conference, September 2002, Exeter, England.

Sanders, C.E. (2004) 'What is bullying?' in Sanders, C.E. and Phye, G.D., *Bullying: Implications for the classroom*, Amsterdam: Elsevier.

Sarason, S.B. (1999) *Teaching as a Performing Art*, New York, NY: Teachers College Press.

Sclafani, J.D. (2004) *The Educated Parent: Recent trends in raising children*, Westport, CT: Greenwood Press.

Sedgwick, F. (1989) *Here Comes the Assembly Man: A year in the life of a primary school*, Lewes: Falmer Press.

Sedgwick, F. (2007) *So you want to be a School Teacher?* London: Sage.

Sharman, C., Cross, W. and Vennis, D. (2000) *Observing Children: A practical guide*, London: Cassell.

Sharp, S., Thompson, D. and Arora, T. (2002) *Bullying*, London: RoutledgeFalmer.

Silcock, P. and Brundrett, M. (2002) *Achieving Competence, Success and Excellence in Teaching*, London: RoutledgeFalmer.

Simister, C.J. (2007) *How to Teach Thinking and Learning Skills*, London: Sage.

Skelton, C. (2001) *Schooling the Boys: Masculinities and primary education*, Maidenhead: Open University Press.

Smart, J. (1995) *Educational Visits*, Leamington Spa: Campion Communications.

Smethern, L. (2007) 'Retention and intention in teaching careers: will the new generation stay?' *Teachers and Teaching*, 13(5), pp. 465–81.

Smidt, S. (2006) *The Developing Child in the 21st Century*, London: Routledge.

Smith, A. (2007) 'Fit for play?', *Education 3–13*, 35(1), pp. 17–27.

Smith, C. (2006) 'From special needs to inclusive education', in J. Sharp, S. Ward and L. Hankin (eds) *Education Studies: An issues-based approach*, Exeter: Learning Matters.

Smith, J. and Lynch, J. (eds) (2005) *The Primary School Year*, London: RoutledgeFalmer.

Sotto, E. (1994) *When Teaching Becomes Learning*, London: Routledge.

Spear, M., Gould, K. and Lee, B. (2000) *Who Would be a Teacher?* Slough: NFER.

Stacey, M. (1991) *Parents and Teachers Together: Partnership in primary and nursery education*, Maidenhead: Open University Press.

Stallard, P. (2002) *Think Good, Feel Good*, London: John Wiley.

Starbuck, D. (2006) *Creative Teaching: Getting it right*, London: Continuum.

Stern, J. (2003) *Involving Parents*, London: Continuum.

Sternberg, R.J. and Davidson, J.E. (2005) *Conceptions of Giftedness*, Cambridge: Cambridge University Press.

Stierer, B., Devereux, J., Gifford, S., Laycock, E. and Yerbury, J. (1993) *Profiling, Recording and Observing: A resource pack for the Early Years*, London: Routledge.

Street, J. (2004) *Welcome to Friendship*, Bristol: Lucky Duck.

Suschitzky, W. and Chapman, J. (1998) *Valued Children, Informed Teaching*, Maidenhead: Open University Press.

Thody, A. and Bowden, D. (2004) *Teacher's Guide to Self-Management*, London: Continuum.

Thomas, G. and Vaughan, M. (eds) (2004) *Inclusive Education: Readings and Reflections*, Maidenhead: Open University Press.

Tileston, D.W. (2004) *What Every Teacher Should Know About Classroom Management and Discipline*, Thousand Oaks, CA: Corwin Press.

Tizard, B. and Hughes, M. (1984) *Young Children Learning: Talking and thinking at home and at school*, London: Fontana.

Tizard, B., Blatchford, P., Burke, J., Farquhar, C. and Plewis, I. (1988) *Young Children at School in the Inner City*, London: Erlbaum.

Torrance, H. and Pryor, J. (1998) *Investigating Formative Assessment*, Maidenhead: Open University Press.

Trodd, L. and Goodliff, G. (2007) *Achieving EYPS: Success in your Assessment*, Exeter: Learning Matters.

Turner-Bisset, R. (2003) 'On the carpet: changing primary teacher contexts', *Education 3–13*, 31(3), pp. 4–10.

Twiselton, S. (2006) 'Developing your teaching skills', in J. Arthur, T. Grainger and D. Wray (eds) *Learning to Teach in the Primary School*, London: Routledge.

Varma, V.P. (ed.) (1993) *Coping With Unhappy Children*, London: Cassell.

Varnava, G. (2002) *How to Stop Bullying: Towards a non-violent school*, London: David Fulton.

Vincent, C. (2000) *Including Parents? Education, citizenship and parental agency*, Maidenhead: Open University Press.

Vincett, K., Cremin, H. and Thomas, G. (2005) *Teachers and Assistants Working Together*, Maidenhead: Open University Press.

Waite, S. and Rea, T. (2007) 'Enjoying teaching and learning outside the classroom', in D. Hayes (ed.) *Joyful Teaching and Learning in the Primary School*, Exeter: Learning Matters.

Walker, D.F. and Soltis, J.F. (1992) *Curriculum and Aims*, New York, NY: Teachers College Press.

Wallace, W. (2005) *Oranges and Lemons: Life in an Inner-city Primary School*, London: Routledge.

Walsh, J.A. and Sattes, B.D. (2005) *Quality Questioning: Research-based practice to engage every learner*, Charlestown, WV: Edvantia.

Waters, M. (1996) *Managing Your Primary Classroom*, London: Collins.

Watkins, C., Carnell, E. and Lodge, C. (2007) *Effective Learning in Classrooms*, London: Sage.

Watkinson, A. (2003a) *The Essential Guide for Competent Teaching Assistants*, London: David Fulton.

Watkinson, A. (2003b) *The Essential Guide for Experienced Teaching Assistants*, London: David Fulton.

Weatherhead, Y. (2007) *Creative Circle Time for Early Years*, London: Sage.

Weil, Z. (2003) *Above All, Be Kind: Raising a humane child in challenging times*, Gariola Island, British Columbia: New Society Publishers.

Wenham, M. (1995) 'Developing thinking and skills in the arts', in Moyles, J. (ed.) *Beginning Teaching: Beginning Learning*, Maidenhead: Open University Press.

Westwood, P. (2004) *Learning and Learning Difficulties*, London: David Fulton.

Whalley, M. (2007) *Involving Parents in their Children's Learning*, London: Sage.

Willan, J., Parker-Rees, R. and Savage, J. (eds) (2007) *Early Childhood Studies*, 2nd edn, Exeter: Learning Matters.

Williams, J. and Ryan, J. (2000) 'National testing and the improvement of classroom teaching: Can they co-exist?' *British Educational Research Journal*, 26(1), pp. 49–73.

Willick, S. (2006) *Emotional Literacy at the Heart of the School Ethos*, London: Paul Chapman.

Wilson, D.F. (2004) *Supporting Teachers, Supporting Pupils: The emotions of teaching and learning*, London: Kogan Page.

Wise, S. (2000) *Listen to Me! The voices of pupils with emotional and behavioural difficulties*, Bristol: Lucky Duck Publishing.

Wolfendale, S. and Bastiani, J. (eds) (2000) *The Contribution of Parents to School Effectiveness*, London: David Fulton.

Woods, P. (1997) *Restructuring Schools, Reconstructing Teachers: Responding to change in the primary school*, Maidenhead: Open University Press.

Woods, P. and Carlyle, D. (2002) 'Teacher identities under stress: The emotions of separation and renewal', *International Studies in Sociology of Education*, 12(2), pp. 169–89.

Wragg, E.C. (1997) *Assessment and Learning*, London: Routledge.

Wragg, E.C. and Brown, G. (1993) *Explaining*, London: Routledge.

Wray, D. (2006) 'Looking at Learning', in J. Arthur, T. Grainger and D. Wray (eds) *Learning to Teach in the Primary School*, London: Routledge.

Wright, D. (2006) *Classroom Karma*, London: David Fulton.

Wyse, D. (2001) 'Promising yourself to do better? Target-setting and literacy', *Education 3–13*, 29(2), pp. 13–18.

Yelland, N. (ed.) (1998) *Gender in Early Childhood*, London: Routledge.

Zucker, J. and Parker, D. (1999) *A Class Act*, London: Sapphire Publishers.

Index